Economics, Society and Culture

Economics, Society and Culture

GOD, MONEY and THE NEW CAPITALISM

Robert Ghelardi

Delacorte Press/New York

First printing

Library of Congress Cataloging in Publication Data

Ghelardi, Robert, 1937-
Economics, society, and culture.

Includes bibliographical references.
1. Economics.   2. United States—Social conditions—1960-
3. United States—Civilization—1970-
I. Title.
HB71.G5   330   76-3512
ISBN 0-440-02341-6

1913951

*For my mother,
and all my other supportive relatives.*

CONTENTS

FOREWORD

The aim of this book is to lay out a new theory of economics that may perhaps deserve to be considered that replacement for Keynes which the "experts" are universally seeking. But it will be some time before we can get to it, because beneath the economic crisis, and causing it, is a massive cultural problem that is being roundly ignored, and which we must discuss first. For the mistakes of Keynes, and those of Marx also, are rooted essentially in historical, or rather cultural, pressures that prompted Keynes to regard economics as not only an autonomous science with its own distinctive methodology, but as an encapsulated science of what I will be calling a "totalist" system, and prompted Marx to regard economics as not only a science with crucial *intrinsic* links to other disciplines and areas of life, but also as methodologically indistinguishable from philosophy —Marxist philosophy. Both erred equally, but in opposite directions. The integrated theory that appears here, perhaps not as brilliant as those of Marx and Keynes, nevertheless aspires to transcend both by including both in a new synthesis.

Yet many of the ideas advanced in this study may be so unfashionable that by the time the new economic theory "proper" is laid out, passions may have become so inflamed that the theory will not be received on its merits, but rather in accordance with the reader's response to the cultural analysis that leads up to it. Fortunately for those readers who might be seriously disinclined to entertain the cultural analysis, the economic theory, in accordance with the legitimate requirements of economic science as even Keynes conceived it, can stand by itself, and those who wish to judge it strictly on its merits may be best advised to skip the first two chapters until they have done so. But it would not seem to make complete sense to ignore them indefinitely, since they are intended to suggest a whole new dimension in economic theory that might permit us to abandon at last the limited "specialist" points of view we have long been professing to try to escape. Outside of Marx, this is, as far as I know, the first integrated theory of economics, society and culture.

The book is divided into three parts. The main theory ends with the first part. The second part, about which more tentative feelings are experienced at this end, explores what appear to be the political implications or possibilities of this new theory about economics and society. The first chapter in this part is a somewhat cursory probe of the deficiencies in the recent American liberal political movement. Rather than resorting here to tedious conceptualization, I have instead relied on a tartness that I believe does the job on the whole fairly well, although perhaps with occasional injustices. (I think that liberal ideology is flawed, but I doubt that more than an influential few who still subscribe to it harbor any ill will. When the readers see "liberal" in this book—as he will almost *ad nauseam*—he should understand "liberal ideology.") The second chapter in Part Two focuses on the specific problem of Vietnam, which revealed the deficiencies in the views of both the left and the right with respect to the State. The third chapter formulates the American political problem in light of the earlier cultural analysis.

The third part is little more than a mopping-up operation, although it contains one of my favorite essays. This chapter, on literature, also is, as the somewhat defensive tones of its first paragraphs reveal, rather tentative, but I think most readers would agree that it deserved to be attempted. I also could not resist trying my hand at a problem whose eventual resolution will have incalculable implications: defining the nature of Sociology. If it only serves to indicate that, even in the West, Economics and Sociology are inseparably linked, this chapter will be justified.

R. G.

Part
ONE

Society and Culture

"Modern" Western society is the product of a transition from a society religiously constituted under a myth of hierarchical order to a liberal (or Communist) society economically constituted under a myth of autonomy.

Once we have sorted out the meaning of that opening statement, we will have a basis for understanding the situation, or predicament, we are in today. First of all, then, let us consider the meaning of the word "constituted." What "constitutes" a society? This term was coined in the present context by Peter Drucker in his classic work *The Future of Industrial Man* to refer to society's organizing principle, that sphere of social activity the culture appoints as the dramatic focus or principle of coordination for all its other spheres. The constitutive spheres for the West since the Middle Ages have been, in chronological order, religion (or theology), art, politics, and (today) economics; the next probably will be sociology. It is important to note that a constitutive sphere is not imposed on society, for to say that it is appointed by the culture means that society spontaneously adopts it. An organizer, or socially constitutive sphere, comes so to dominate even the most powerful minds during the period of its ascendancy that they come to see it as the crux of all social "problems" and the source of all real "solutions." For its cultural primacy gives it the appearance of "ontological" primacy as well. And once an organizer gets itself established, it tends to forge for itself an emblem to serve as a dramatic focus for social life at the point of deepest spontaneous social unity, where the lion must be induced to lie down with the lamb. In the Middle Ages this emblem was the cathedral, in the Renaissance it was the theater, then for a brief while perhaps it was the salon or tavern, after that the Parliament or Court, and then finally the market. The next candidate—note the increasing impersonality of the constitutive spheres—appears to be the computer. What causes the constitutive spheres, or organizing principles, to change? The answer is suggested in the phrase above, "point of deepest spontaneous social unity." The cause of the shift is the appearance of conflict within the constitutive sphere itself, which eventually makes the sphere itself a cause of conflict rather than of social coordination. In order to understand this process, we must first consider the nature and function of "culture."

What is "culture"? A rummage through the definitions provided by modern anthropology usually turns up two general meanings. One will advert to something called "high" culture, or "literary" culture—which, roughly, means the consciously philosophical or aesthetic preoccupations of an intellectual elite. The other points to "popular" culture—the "mores," habits, and unreflective quotidian activity and crafts of a whole society. Seldom is there more than a hint that these are elements of the same basic process, that "high" culture is little more than a higher concentration of what occurs in "popular" culture. A global appreciation of what culture is suggests that culture is a principle of dynamic social equilibrium, its object to integrate and coordinate all human latencies in the social order where human "nature" must find its realization. In its cognitive aspects, culture is always a shared meaning system, and, precisely because it is shared, it always gives rise to a moral order. Yet the meaning system is not only, nor even basically, "rational," for it is both affective and rational at the same time.

West—as Dunne shows—has been constructed against the background of either a "mediation" or a "non-mediation" of God into society, God has been the implicit principle of even the Western myths. For example, the mythic "autonomy" of modern times is essentially negative, reflecting the "alienation" *from* society that is a result of the abolition of the mediation of God *into* society.)

Dunne's success in precipitating out from Western history the serial social myths seems almost miraculous, for philosophy had almost inextricably confused the myths with the culture. The basic social problems of meaning and death become linked in philosophy when a culture begins to deteriorate, because the philosopher begins to ask first and primarily of his own philosophy that question every reflective person at some time asks himself in the face of his own death: "If I must some day die, what must I do to satisfy my desire to live?" And philosophy then becomes, under the urgencies of the mythmaking impulse, mainly an answer to this question, to which other problems soon become subsidiary. But when a myth, because of its inevitable incompleteness, loses its credibility, so also do the philosophies that too enthusiastically embraced it, and soon philosophers themselves grow skeptical of philosophy's possibilities. We will eventually have to discuss in this chapter the major philosophic problem of contemporary Western society, but are lucky to be able to begin our historical considerations with an age when the distinct functions of myth and culture were not yet confused in the cumulative baggage of later philosophical systems. We can use that age as an illustration of the generalizations sketched above, and then continue with our chronological survey to confirm how our own basic problems began during that time.

For that age, the watershed not only of what we call Western "civilization" or "culture" or "society," but of most of its problems as well, is in a sense the archetypal age of Western culture, though not many today (especially among the intellectuals) regard it as in any way admirable or seminal. Yet it alone can suggest the nature of the only remedy for our problems that can preserve Western cultural achievements. That early age to which we allude is now called the "Middle Ages."

The word "medieval" is an epithet of derision in our "enlightened" age. Not only confirmed rationalists like Bertrand Russell, but even one as suspicious of mere rationalism as Lewis Mumford, must strain to find anything to praise in medieval life or thought. In his enormously erudite works on the Enlightenment, Peter Gay seems to swallow all its prejudices, as if scholars like Etienne Gilson had written nothing deserving of much attention. Were not the Middle Ages "superstitious"? Were they not priest-ridden and ridiculously "narrow"? Does not our social order, smoothly organized around the economic system, leave them as far behind in contentment as in time? Wrong question. There is no reason to overlook the deficiencies of an age when invasions by real savages were still almost fresh in memory, but applying our enlightened standards to such an age, whose own accomplishments remain unique, is an exercise in hypocrisy. And extolling in comparison the wonders of our high-speed lives, often lonely thruways to nowhere, merely induces a nostalgia for the slower and infinitely richer pageant of medieval life. Medieval society had nowhere to go but up, toward our social order, but medieval culture had nowhere to go but down, and did—toward our "cultural" order or, rather, lack of same. It ill becomes our enlightened age, when no aspect of art or culture has not been declared "dead" by some notable votary—symphonic music by Leonard Bernstein, for example, and even the whole liberal arts tradition itself—to mock with such smug complacency the period when the modern university, the parliament, and the basic dualism between sacred and secular areas of life, not only first appeared, but (except, one hopes, for the last) appeared in almost their definitive forms, and all forms of art were germinating a spectacular efflorescence. Of course, the "individual" perhaps was not sufficiently protected by the communal cohesiveness of his guild or class from certain fateful grounded on a supposedly universal "act-of-existence" even perceptible only to one supremely receptive to wholeness (his argument, not mine). He used an analogical method to reach this ground because he thought it could be reached directly only in a rare moment of concentrated philosophical intuition. The method purported to show that everything shares, each in its own intensity, in a universal act-of-existence by which we perceive things in their unique individualities, but only because "reflexively" present in them in analogical intensities is the fullness of "Existence" itself. This method and doctrine infuse Aquinas's work with a sort of polymorphous quality. He conducted his analogical thought with a rigor and logic that put off all but his most intrepid readers, but it seems to have exceeded mere rationality, and depended on a spontaneous, direct and sensuous experience of natural and social reality with all their modulated intensities. His act of philosophizing at least was organic, required his whole personality; many later thinkers, notably Descartes, who was all brain, seem to have excluded many aspects of their personalities. Perhaps it was just that their personalities were so conflicted. A conflicted culture produces conflicted personalities, who only with the greatest trouble, and then not by purely rational means, can solve by way of thought the conflicts causing their thought in the first place, conflicts that are all but impenetrable without a source of dynamic wholeness distinct from society itself.

Turning to literature, we come upon Chaucer, and the same "polymorphous" quality found in Dante and Aquinas. The full conception of the *Canterbury Tales* is implicit in each story, becoming fully clear only in all of them together. Yet each part is so perfectly autonomous, so unique and self-contained, that by itself it could be regarded as an entire creative universe implicitly equivalent to the whole canons of later writers with no less "raw" talent. An organic and wholly unmonolithic unity pervades an immense richness and variety, in a fusion of sensual fullness in verse and language with an intellectual brilliance in organization and perspective matched only by Dante himself, for even Shake-speare did not achieve it, and it never again appeared.

That unique quality radiates even from the political life of the medieval age. Again, we cannot overlook the residual feudal hierarchical order, as it was powerfully reinforced in ideology by the incorporation of the hierarchical vision into myth, but demo-cratic movements became extremely powerful all over medieval Europe, and the reason was perhaps a key difference between that age and ours: Medieval society did not regard itself as basically a political (or economic) unit, and so could countenance funda-mental change on these levels. As Christopher Dawson, the fore-most modern scholar of the medieval period, has demonstrated in his many books, medieval politics were suffused by a common spiritual ideal, more or less adequately embodied for a while (as the late Karl Barth also observed with no little admiration[3]) by an Empire whose federative structure allowed each part of Europe to lead its separate life while sharing in the common life of a single cultural community. As Dawson says, this was not basically a political order of the modern variety, for the very political units regarded themselves as subject mainly to the common spiritual and moral standard. The basic belief behind medieval politics was that "society is not a political unit, but a community made up of a complex variety of social organisms, each possessing an autono-mous life and its own free institutions." The French historian Sorel described how catastrophic the disintegration of this community was for Western culture. Fanatical secular ambitions and merely parochial loyalties were unleashed, so that by the time of the Renaissance *raison d'état*—understood as the total freedom of the national state from any moral requirements whatever—had come to seem so "natural" that even thinkers as searching as Pascal came to believe in it as strongly as Machiavelli. Recent dogma is that the nations could not have developed except at the expense of this wider cultural community, but the price in blood and treasure (described by Sorel) that they paid to bring down their own

Christian neighbors staggers the understanding, and causes one to wonder that any even survived until the incredibly competitive Louis XIV finally doomed his own monarchy with his wars. This contrast between the requirements of Christian faith and the murderous rivalries between Their Most Christian Majesties, with the complicity if not the connivance of religion, needs some explanation, and it goes back to the other side of the medieval coin, the weaknesses in the medieval myth. But in closing this part of the discussion we might remember that the medieval period managed, at least for a while, to subordinate politics to a moral standard and a cultural community that provided terms and grounds for real solutions, not perpetual makeshifts, and when this community was disrupted and politics took over the balancing function in society from religion and art, the only limit on power, and its only recourse, became (as Maria Theresa discovered) power. If any period can contest Freud's belief that all history is but one general neurosis, it has to be the Middle Ages, and a balanced appreciation of that time gives us reason to view the later history of the West as something like the psychological development of the child, who also begins blissfully as "polymorphously perverse," but must go on painfully to develop his powers, rebelling against his tutors, until, like our age, he comes to a dynamic reintegration and the beginnings of real maturity.

Yet if all but the most bigoted among us are involuntarily charmed by something sweet and unlimitedly whole in medieval life, for which our minds can suppress a nostalgic regret only by invoking the terrors of toothache, we also know that medieval life also failed, else it would not have so completely disappeared. This failure has been made really comprehensible for the first time by Dunne. Most of us would still intone the tired saw that the cause of failure was the excessive influence of religion, but in the way this is usually meant it is nonsense. Religion was only a proximate, not the ultimate, cause of the medieval failure. The far more indirect and implicit way that our culture permits us to share in a knowledge that medievals held instinctively (and which now must be laboriously demonstrated to the poor liberal)—that is, that the ultimate questions about the meaning of life and death are also the basic *social* questions on whose answers even the structures of society depend—is no great advantage for us, yet we do share in it. But medievals, who otherwise had neither superior virtue nor even a superior sense of social order, were never tempted to think that a political, economic, or sociological "system," or even art, provides a sufficient basis for social unity and order. This is why saints like Francis, Thomas, Catherine, could also be great social leaders, and why medieval life incarnated—in marked contrast to the modern liberal order, which regards religion as a purely "private" affair—the late John Courtney Murray's commonsensical observation that religion is the most public of all public matters. There was nothing wrong with religion's playing a major, even decisive, *cultural* role; this is a quite "natural" situation. The troubles arise when religion begins to help in maintaining social order, for religion *has no necessary connection* with social order. It was the appearance of such a connection in the Middle Ages that caused the medieval failure. For even though it offers a cultural meaning system, religion *need* not even endorse the social order's efforts to maintain itself, much less directly support its structures—although religion certainly has at least a negative interest in preventing social structures hostile to its own tenets. Thus, any society, whatever its religion(s), tends also to relish any available social myth capable of infusing with value the effort to maintain it in the face of death's inevitability. Two societies with substantially the same religion but different social myths will be substantially dissimilar societies. (On the subject of social myth the reader is again referred to Dunne, for one of the most rewarding reading experiences he is likely ever to enjoy.)

How did religion acquire a connection with social order? Actually, this is not very remarkable, in view of the different functions of myth and religion. Myth, which deals primarily with the problem posed for society by death, is concerned mainly with *this* world, the land of the living. But religion is concerned not only with this world, but also with the "next," the land of the dead. Now, since the ultimate public reality in this world considered in itself is power, and myth is concerned only with this world, myth must fix on power to get itself implemented, while subjectively justifying to each "individual" this recourse to power by its apparent ability to neutralize his own personal death. But all justifiable coercive power is located in the State. Thus, every myth almost invariably must assimilate the State. At the same time, though, a myth is often unable to establish itself on the level of meaning without drawing also on religion, not so much for religion's "real" content as for its metaphysical framework, which myth then adapts to its more limited purposes. Only by the utmost vigilance and purity of motive can religion be kept from being sucked into the vortex of power politics, and perhaps cannot be, except at the price of opposition to the established order, when a myth is abroad, if myth, as man's attempt to satisfy his own desire for life, is, as Dunne seems to suspect, ultimately futile.

The fault, then, with the Middle Ages lay not, as is often popularly supposed, in religion, but in the inadequacy of the medieval social myth. This myth conceived of the world as a divinely endorsed hierarchical order with a fixed hierarchy of social roles, in filling one of which any person could achieve vicarious social immortality. Thus, maintaining society seemed worthwhile. But this myth contradicted itself in proposing as an answer to death, under the aegis of the Christian God, a strictly secular sort of immortality. Nevertheless, because it fastened on the Christian God for its legitimation, the myth had to allow religion to go about its cultural business, and the culture integrated itself before the weaknesses in the myth really took hold. The culture's carnal and spiritual latencies were brought into cooperation; the integration resulted in the three-dimensional glow. But before long the weaknesses in the myth began to victimize the integration by identifying God with the status quo. The Church, in fact, was the first to be troubled by the myth's implications, but, unable to work out a solution, put its trust in the secular power the myth assigned to it.

That the Church itself first became a power structure in the Middle Ages is the real key to later history. The late Roman Empire's total embrace had limited the Church's autonomy, and soon the invading barbarians appeared, arriving in wave upon wave for century after century, ravaging Western society and being assimilated by the Church's "civilizing" mission. During all this time, the Church's institutional organization remained tenuous and open-ended. But when the invasions finally ceased, religion and the Church alone (as an institution) pervaded the whole social order. Consolidating its hold, the Church soon found itself disputed by kings and emperors with often overweening ambitions of their own. Since both Church and State sincerely shared the religious view of life current at the time, no cultural problem was yet raised. But then the Empire, in conformity with the hierarchical myth, began insisting that its concrete social and political order was identical with Christianity as such. In reaction, the Pope claimed the right to "invest" the Emperor (*symbolic* primacy for himself) in order to reestablish a correct ordering of values, for this deepening conflict was not so much over power as such as over the correct ordering of values. Yet if the Pope could withhold the crown, he would have temporal power, so the Emperor claimed the responsibility for "protecting" even Church institutions. Had the Church rejected the hierarchical myth it could have solved its problems, for the legitimacy of the State would have been thrown into question, but the Church did not realize this. Instead, a seductive paradigm from the psychological background St. Augustine had bequeathed a thousand years earlier reemerged and took hold once again. Augustine had constructed a social myth that divided the human race into two "cities"—the City of God and the City of Man. This myth had been his response to the earthly "city's" attempts to divinize itself, as when it called its emperors gods;

Augustine never suspected that it might do anything else. But by separating the earthly city from the heavenly city, he had left the former unable to justify constructive efforts. The medieval social myth was essentially an attempt to solve this problem. Medieval churchmen did not regard their conflict with the secular power as a struggle between the godly and the ungodly, yet the hierarchical myth by which the Middle Ages tried to close the gap between the earthly and the heavenly cities—each alike recognizing the permanent divine order in the social and natural worlds—suggested that either the State or the Church must be on top. Dante said (see Dunne) that the Church was man's guide to his heavenly fulfillment, the Empire his guide to earthly completion, but when the problem of establishing a correct ordering of values in actual *practice* arose, the question of final earthly primacy within terms of the myth became inescapable. In order to underline the Pope's claim to at least symbolic primacy, and lacking a better myth, the Church unconsciously reverted to the two-cities myth, and moved in the fateful direction not long ago lamented by Thomas Merton, who said that since the Middle Ages the answer of the Church to the amoral politics of secular society has been to operate, as Dostoyevsky charged in his legend of the Grand Inquisitor, an alternative but equally oppressive power apparatus second to none in thoroughness. The Church developed its own power structure to oppose the State's, in a failure to realize institutionally the clear injunctions of the Gospels that later led to disasters like opposition to the Magna Carta and to almost every other advance. Its inability to solve the problem posed by the hierarchical myth led the Church to confound the distinction between sacral and secular functions, until then so beautifully fertile for the cultural life of the age, and the healthy inner tension between sacral and secular became a merely political antagonism between Church and State.

The medieval social myth, in trying to bring the heavenly and earthly cities into harmony, permitted religion to perform its cultural function, but still remained only a partial solution for the problem Augustine had bequeathed. Its solution to the social problem posed by death was to fit the person into a rigid, putatively immortal hierarchical order by virtue of which he could achieve vicarious immortality through his social efforts. But this attempt to immortalize social structures rather resembled the Classical era's attempt to divinize them, and the Church soon began viewing its role as socially conservative. This is why, when the time for decision arrived, it saw no contradiction in developing its own structure of power. But no power structure—at the very least only a "better" social myth—could have served it, and it was Luther who came up with a new myth—a god-of-the-dead who had so little power in or concern for the secular world that He would turn it over lock, stock, and barrel to the State.

The god of a myth, if it has one, will tend to be the distorted reflection of the god of a religion, because of myth's specialized function. Thus, the "Christian" God of medieval *society* was a mythic god-of-the-living, and so medieval culture was regarded as bound to the status quo, for everything under a god-of-the-living-only is sacred, including the status quo, and this god will have a direct stake in the established order. But nothing is sacred under a god only of the dead, and Luther transformed the medieval mythic god-of-the-living into a god-of-the-dead-only. And this was the god on whom the later modern myth of "autonomy," in which modern man "transcends" death by a willingness to welcome and embrace it (like the Lutheran Christ), was modeled. So the modern God remains a mythic god only of the dead, and society remains in effect cut off from any culture, because a god-of-the-dead not only has little power in the secular world, he also has little interest in it, and abandons each person to "alienation" toward his own death, leaving him entirely self-dependent for his own meaning in time. Each person subsists in an atomized condition for which an atomized social order will not seem (at least, theoretically) problematic, for the very vacuum of community appears as cultural "normalcy."

Like every social myth, the medieval myth had three primary dimensions: spiritual, philosophical, and political. The spiritual content of the medieval myth was provided by the Christian God, the philosophical content by the doctrine of hierarchical social order, and the political dimension by the model of the medieval Empire. Now, though Dunne himself does not remark on this, every myth has, and must have, a political dimension because myth relies, and must rely, on power for its implementation in the social order its purpose is to preserve. Myth must assimilate the State because all legitimate power is concentrated there. *It is thus that the State itself gains the appearance of normalcy and legitimacy.* Any "legitimacy" the State gains is mythic in nature, and no more ascribable to "reason" than religion is. *In fact, the acceptance of both religion and the State are basically matters of "faith"*; that is why, normally, people prefer not to choose and simply accept both. Yet the *inevitability* of the State's existence is not in itself a legitimation. And the State, always concerned primarily with its own power—its "authority," if you will—is always in tension with its own host culture, if any. Culture and power are not intrinsically inseparable; they only appear to be. What gives power and the State their aura of legitimacy is not culture, but myth. A clever reader may now begin to discern the dimensions of the pickle we are in; for the original, and correct, concern of the early liberal tradition was to defend the culture from the medieval State, but now it is "defending" the State against any culture.

Because we are primarily concerned in this section with culture, we cannot devote much more attention to the intrinsically important subject of myth, which Dunne has treated so magnificently in his epochal book, without which we simply cannot understand much of Western history. (For example, the Bourbon passion for "glory" simply has no explanation other than Dunne's perception that it was a substitution of impersonal social status for the more personal "victory" over death achieved in the medieval myth.) Let us simply and briefly review the series of myths that Dunne deciphered, and then go back to our main purpose, which is to explain the periodic shifts of the culture's "constitutive" spheres.

The medieval myth, ostensibly an answer to death, began to lose its hold when it failed to cope with the Black Death. A gap seemed to open between the putative immortality of one's public person, as defined by one's role, and the ever more oppressive mortality of one's private person (and Dunne regards this gap as the basic inspiration of Shakespearean tragedy). At first, the (Bourbon-type) solution was to overemphasize the public role in compensation. Hobbes made this obsolete when he transferred the mythic "divine right" supposedly wielded by kings directly to the "body politic" (the State) itself, so that the same belief once directed ultimately toward God by way of the King would now be directed toward human authority itself. For Hobbes, all human authority was reducible to the (formerly divine) power of life and death wielded by the State. Locke, drawing also on Calvin, modified Hobbes only to say that the State possessed only the "rightful" power of life and death; thus Locke left some room for rebellion. The "rightful" use of the power of life and death, according to Locke, was to protect property. But for Rousseau, as for Hobbes, the State retained power not only over the individual's property, but also over his person and life, and Rousseau made Hobbes's "mortal God," the State, immortal: "the general will is indestructible." The next major step, to make the general will not just infallible and indestructible, but also irresistible, was taken by Hegel. Instead of, like Calvin, despairing utterly of the individual's own ability to vanquish death, and making God's power over it one's own by faith, one should, Hegel counseled, despair of *any* deliverance from death, thus making its inevitability one's own will and its sovereignty one's own autonomy. Thus was born the myth of autonomy, whose two modern forms derive from Locke and Rousseau; one envisages only a right *to* life (Locke—for whom life was just another form of property!), the other a right *over* life (Rousseau, Hegel, etc.). Marx agreed with Hegel, that the "people" have a right (on which modern totalitarianism has arisen) *over* life, but asserted, against Hegel (and doubling back to a position parallel to Locke's), that this right has been usurped by the State, whose power over life and death, therefore, is reducible not in its "rightful" use but only in its actual historical use to the protection of property. Thus, man's alienation to the power of property (rather than to the Hobbesian State power of life and death, which the people will take back) could make the people's new will to autonomy an historical force leading to a classless society. However, the "people's" will to power has instead, in both the French and the Russian Revolutions, led only to terrorism. Locke's "inalienable rights" are a claim to autonomy, and an answer to death in that they can never be taken away, *even though one die*. Yet in both the Lockean and the Rousseauistic forms, the alienation that is excluded is that produced by absolute monarchy, and both forms simply transfer the unlimited power of life and death to the "people," and simply pose the basic problem of the power of life and death all over again.

Dunne shows how the modern social myth of autonomy has been ramified into the three dimensions every myth exhibits. On the spiritual level, the myth of autonomy solves the problem of death by a complete (and paradoxical) acceptance of it, so that one becomes "free" (and autonomous) with respect to death by incorporating its inevitability into one's own will. Philosophically, the myth holds that the ideals of reason are neither limited by nor oriented toward transcendental ideals (Beauty, Truth, Good, etc.) so that man's reason is its own measure. Kant successfully criticized the spiritual and philosophical dimensions of the myth of autonomy, but did so before the French Revolution expressed its political dimension, of which he remained unaware, so the myth continued on in its political extension in Europe until Hegel sneaked the other dimensions back in by embodying the "absolute" (i.e., autonomous) spirit in a political incarnation, the State. Locke's more benign expression of the political dimension, because he envisaged it as based on a right to property, perhaps required an economics-constituted society for its matrix.

Let us return to our main subject, the shifting of society's organizing principle. But the importance of myth in this respect should now be apparent, since it is myth, which provides our answer to death, that hides from us the importance of culture. But this could hardly have happened had not culture been encouraging the confusion. The cause of this lay in what had happened to religion. Of course, religion did not play a significant role only in the Middle Ages, because religion normally plays a crucial role and still does in a hidden way. Religion's role in the Middle Ages was unique only in that it was then that religion finally suffused and integrated the social order. The great Johan Huizinga wrote that: "If one should want to specify in what age Western Christian civilization took its definitive form, its configuration, one would have to decide on the Twelfth Century. The Twelfth Century was a creative and formative age without equal."[4] Dawson described St. Francis as the first saint in whose life sheer holiness and sheer human genius were so fused that no aspect of his adult life is reducible to one or the other (whereas the personality of the earlier, no less saintly, Ambrose was only an unfused amalgam of Roman administrator and Christian apostle). Similar integrations appeared in Dante and Aquinas: Thomas was the first, and perhaps last, philosopher in whom Christian revelation so perfectly fused with reason that each remained fully free while wholly reinforcing the other, while in Dante's art the Christian faith achieved for the first, and perhaps last, time an expression in which natural and supernatural elements are perfectly reinforced without absorbing each other. Personal and cultural integrations appear at their best only together. The reason why these men could appear and become social leaders was that through them, in them, the Christian faith finally suffused and integrated the culture; and nothing has ever integrated any culture except religion. And probably as a result, something that greatly puzzled C.S. Lewis occurred.

Lewis's masterful study of medieval literature, *The Allegory of Love*, includes a discussion of sex and culture. He said that the new passionate-love theme (which was entirely unknown in the Classical era) of the Courtly-Love literature that swept medieval Europe was, compared to Renaissance literature, like a ground swell beneath a mere surface ripple, for Courtly Love immediately caused a whole new understanding of love in the West. Elementary changes like this in human sentiment are quite rare—"there are three or four on record," said Lewis—but he could not explain why it had happened. Considering all possible explanations, such as Byzantine and Arabic notions, Ovid's love poetry, and the structures of the feudal order, he found that even combined they could not "explain" Courtly Love. The Classical era's conception of love had comprised only two possibilities, a sort of domestic comfort and a merry sensuality, but recoiled from any more consuming attachment as a great misfortune (as in Horace's poem "*Quis multa gracilis te puer in rosa . . .*"). The poets Catullus and Propertius exhibited their own infatuations as mere curiosities. But neither did Christianity any more than Classical culture seem to require or lead to anything like Romantic Love. Indeed, early Christianity saw in sex an experience laced, however innocently the person might approach it, with objective evil, and if Aquinas overcame this suspicion even in the facc of Augustine's testimony, he still saw in sex a threat to reason's control of life. Lewis could not see how, in this context, Christianity could be called any true "cause" of passionate love.

But if Christianity was no direct cause of passionate love, the appearance of passionate love just when the culture was achieving its own full integration seems hardly coincidental: As Erich Auerbach has written of Dante, the poetic power that bloomed so lushly sprang from roots mostly unconscious and involuntary. Similarly, all of a religion's cultural effects can hardly be consciously intended, especially if the religion's own understanding of itself is permeated by unintegratable alien influences, as Christianity was by world-denying platonic and oriental ("Manichean") attitudes in Augustine's writings. That is, the appearance of passionate love resulted not only from all the influences Lewis mentioned, but also, and basically, from the integration of the culture. This long-incubating cultural integration percolated up from below the range of reason and imparted a cultural momentum that immediately overflowed in the cultural order in an entirely new feeling and attitude toward sex. Any deep transformation of culture would inevitably bring changes in the consciousness and expression of the erotic, one of any culture's major ingredients. But if the integration of the culture by the faith was the cause of the new feeling, why did this feeling soon oppose itself to "official" Christianity? Because the Church was transforming *itself* into a power structure.

Everyone should recognize what the term "power structure" means in this context. That institution is a power structure in which power becomes the main consideration whenever it appears as an issue. It may normally be hidden or latent, but when it is sensed to be implicated or challenged, all other considerations virtually evaporate or become camouflage for the main consideration. In this sense, the Church has been a power structure since the Middle Ages, the power in question being that of the hierarchy, which clothes its claims in rhetoric about "authority." But religious authority is not only distinct from, but basically alien to, all forms of secular power, or control over people. The secular order's whole problem with the tenaciously clinging Church has been to drive it back little by little from its claims on essentially secular power, at this time limited almost entirely to claims over its own members, but seen as ready to reassert themselves elsewhere when the time becomes ripe again. The Church itself accomplished the secular order's aims by making a fool of itself whenever it relied on secular power to enforce Church values.

A drive toward power upsets the balance of both personality *and* culture. Succumbing to the lure of power, the Church became a form of life-denial, Marx's "opiate of the people." This made it an enemy in principle of Courtly Love. To assimilate the new feeling fully the culture would have had to sustain the intensity that produced it, but the culture became conflicted in the struggle over power, and the subordination of cultural life to power brought a suppression of erotic energies. Thus the early ambivalence in the new passionate-love literature. Moving south after its birth in Provence, Courtly Love inspired the Italian *Dolce Stil Nuova* (sweet new style) and Dante's almost perfect poetic integration of cultural and psychic forces. But the opposition of the Church prevented full assimilation of the new feeling, and the fusion Dante expressed in poetic symbols never got an opportunity to work itself out into concrete social forms. So the new feeling, although in itself neutral, as Lewis showed, adopted an anti-Christian tone as it spread rapidly northward, and became almost an alternative religion. It transformed the culture's understanding of love as it swept through Europe, but the culture broke up on the erotic conflict.

The consequences the Church brought down on itself and the culture for this failure must be incalculable. As an example, the inner equality of the sexes, if not the actual primacy of women, expressed in Dante remained little more than a poet's fancy. The social systems became more neurotically masculine and aggressive, and women remained mere functionaries. Development in the social relationships between the sexes ceased, and sexual morality itself became subordinated to economic considerations, for the Church was expected, as a culture-legitimating power structure, to endorse not only society's "religious" orientation but also the social structures seemingly supporting it. (This had another epochal consequence. For the new mercantile classes were developing new social forms far more dynamic than the feudal ones that had served an earlier age so well. But the contributions of the merchants—whose Corporatism, with its guilds and general social orientation, remains to this day the most integral economic order the West has ever produced—were actually resented. The disowned merchants therefore became a potentially revolutionary class, and finally triumphed by default when the old order canceled itself out centuries later.) The ideological conservatism mandated rigid tabus in sexual morality: Sexual pleasure remained only an excuse for procreation; a sexual union, even when most arbitrarily imposed, was considered indissoluble; and sexual roles became rigidly prescribed. (Yet these short circuits may have seemed less intolerable then than now since the culture remained still so emotionally rich and full that, if these failings were even suspected, they could be dismissed as almost negligible.)

Many of the Church's great personalities seem to have sensed the basic problem, because they became increasingly concerned with freeing their own followers from institutional constraints. For the followers of St. Benedict, the sixth-century founder of the Western monasticism that remained the sole vessel of ancient culture for hundreds of years, the regulations of monastic life must have seemed an almost providential release from the confusion and chaos of a distintegrating society. But the medieval problem was quite different, and founders like Sts. Dominic and Francis became anxious to prevent regimentation, and later founders went much further. But the Church's new concern for its power remained an obstacle to social vitality that just the ever-reforming religious orders could not displace. It fell to the "secular order" to push for solutions to the erotic impasse, and it did so in a series of at first covert rebellions the Church found difficult to meet. First there was the discreetly anti-Christian Courtly-Love theme, then came the monk Rabelais, and in the Renaissance there appeared the humanists Ronsard and Botticelli. None of these renounced his faith, because their rebellions were erotic, not theological. But as the rebellions became more overt—as the institutional Church's grip on society was loosened—they also became more and more mechanical as a result of the alienation of the integrating principle from the culture's center. The frankly sensual eroticism of the courts of Louis XIV and XV, of Voltaire, Rousseau and even

Madame du Barry, did express a certain vestigial vitality, but were highly deficient in other respects, and this was even more true of Wagner, who later returned to old Germanic myths for a vehicle, and of Rilke and Nietzsche, who formulated new erotic doctrines in reaction to what they regarded as Christianity's repressed, slave mentality. In our time, "black humor" in literature and Picasso's symptomatic "eroticism" have suggested a tortured sexuality void of content or real vitality. The erotic rebellions have begun to seem like automatic reflexes of animals, or even robots.

The erotic problem seems sharply defined in the life of that poet often and justly called the second greatest of the Renaissance. As a poet of love whose fame surpassed even that of his own king, Ronsard remains a rebuke to us, whose attitudes toward any poet of love who might get himself past our various cultural censors and "liberationists" might be best expressed by the IRS. His culture's "order of priorities," now almost completely turned on its head, and its enthusiasm for life and love are unimaginable to an age devoted to GNP. Squandering his life on the seven women who consecutively inspired his verse, Ronsard became so aware of their inner power and mystery, which fill his song, that he almost (but not quite) overlooked their carnal charms as well. The fresh experience in his poetry was, though, more than a little alarming to the clerics, whose formal standards of sexual conduct could not easily be reconciled with Ronsard's way of life. But he never repudiated his ancestral faith, and toward the end of his life even reaffirmed it against the gathering secularist ideologies that offered sanction for his conduct. It was as if he saw some inner link between his pursuit of love and his neglected religion, and as if the sacrifice of every other consideration for the pursuit of the unexplored promise in Romantic Love had been not merely justified, but made urgent by a Church that had made the pursuit of wholeness by way of religion so difficult. Melancholy overcame Ronsard in later years; it probably was inevitable that his pursuit of love would put him in conflict with the clerical power which had never faced, and as yet had no intention of facing, the questions posed by the erotic.

This brief summary is not irrelevant, for the erotic dimension is crucial for any culture. When the erotic dimension is well integrated with the spiritual, the culture is vigorous and healthy; when they split, the culture becomes schizoid. What we may be witnessing today is the final separation of sex from any culture whatever, its disintegration into a wholly atomized activity. For instead of trying any longer to resolve the separation, society today tries to avoid it by becoming a depersonalized, impersonal machine. No one even sees the need anymore for coordinating his (her) sexual practices with society's requirements, for society, become a machine, has no specifically human requirements at all. As Diana Trilling has acutely observed, the sexual radicalism of the 1960s was an escape into sex from social conflicts and problems, and was socially regressive compared even with D. H. Lawrence's sexual radicalism. This does not amount to a repudiation of women's rights, only of the idea that women can be "liberated" at the expense of men. The essence of sex is communication, of one's *self*, the sacrifice and submission of one's ego to another's needs in the service of a common ideal. What can be objected to about Western sexual standards is their imposition by force basically in the service of property and established power. People should be permitted to follow their own lights, and if they choose not to follow the light the choice is punishment enough. But the need to link sex and sexual morality to some matrix of shared meaning is humanly inescapable. For it seems that sex and technology are the plastic media in which a culture expands. The moral quality of sex depends on its integration into the culture for which it provides the dynamic and plastic medium. This does not mean that sex is morally "neutral," only that any intrinsic and static "ideal" moral content it might have could not be known *as such*, for the very perception of an *a priori* morality in sex would appear as a cultural construct itself. (We can say that sex is oriented to communication because we can deduce this from the nature of culture.) Even if there *be* an *a priori* morality in sex, it could not be achieved apart from a culture. But since human sex is dynamically oriented toward communication, which is impossible outside a matrix of shared meaning, this notion of sex is not equivalent to "situation ethics," for what specifies the morality of a sexual act is not an "individual's" convenient perceptions about it at any moment, but a truly shared system of meaning.

Neither does all this imply that distinctions between the sexes have no "ontological" basis, only that few if any concrete social bonds appear to be necessarily implied in them; yet the lack of *a priori* specification is not a *positive* good but a "potentiality" that needs to be fulfilled. Freud was only half wrong when, typically focusing on material rather than formal differences, he said that "biology is destiny." "Morphology is destiny" might have been closer to the truth. For is it not presumptuous to suppose that the morphological forms of the male and female bodies have no ultimate significance for male and female "destiny," as if the form were merely an accident of haphazard biological evolution? Taking a leaf from the Enlightenment's book, we could say that anyone who can believe that the organisms known to modern biology could have evolved purely by "chance" can believe anything. In other words, female or male "nature" is not just a cultural construct, but is rooted in something ontological (though it is difficult to separate the one from the other). But the ontological rootedness of gender does not predetermine how masculine and feminine will be expressed. And a notion of an "eternal feminine" is not in the least incompatible with full affirmation of women's complete social and legal equality; the law is concerned with persons, not sex roles.

But sex can be approached from two different directions: from the direction of society, which is concerned with roles, and from the direction of culture, which is concerned with meanings. Meanings focus on gender. Some members of one sex can perform better than members of the other roles now assigned to that other sex, so there appears no reason why roles must be rigidly prescribed. But this does not evacuate of significance the distinction between genders. That some people in whom sex and gender do not coincide cannot feel comfortable trying to act out one gender in a body of the opposite sex suggests that either sex or gender must be absolute, that one "should" conform to the other. But no one any longer changes gender in order to accommodate sex; rather, one changes one's sex in order to make it coincide with one's gender. So it must be gender that is absolute. It also seems that social roles are at least approximately or generally appropriate to designate gender today, for no one would desire a body of the opposite sex who did not think that having it would ease rather than complicate the social problem, too—that is, that the roles prescribed for each sex are more appropriate than inappropriate to the corresponding gender, or at least more appropriate than would be the roles prescribed for the other sex. (On the other hand, a man whose gender was masculine but who still wanted to fill "female" roles would simply seek to change the social designation of sex roles. And of course some men of female gender also attempt to change the social designation of sex roles because for one reason or another changing their sex would be inconvenient.) But though gender "should" be reflected in sex, and may in a general way determine cultural role (the meanings "masculinity" and "femininity" embody in a culture), it need not rigidly prescribe social role, one's function. The real problem is cultural role: if what one's gender means need not mechanically determine what one does, still culture must specify what to be a man or woman means, for femininity and masculinity must be achieved, they are not inherited. Without a concrete ideal, men and women will be unable to communicate *as* men and women; they will become simply two forms of the same basic biological machine, their sexuality mere "epiphenomena." Turning women into men will not solve this problem.

The present-day insistence on sexual "equality" tends to be "male-chauvinist" itself, for that in which all are proposed to be equal is a highly articulated male-dominant pattern. As women, seeking "equality," try to adapt to role constructs infused with expectations of "masculine" behavior, they abandon the "feminine" just as it has already been abandoned by men, yet men will hardly abandon with grace their often meaningless jobs to women, Keynesian theory having been teaching men for forty years that apart from their function in the system-machine they have no value either. The claim that society (not law) can be "neutral" with respect to sex is to say that it is "neutral" with respect to morality, both claims representing an attempt to evacuate society of meaning and to deny that the problem of meaning has any social relevance, when actually this problem is basic for society, too. The big, wide social-world participation which women covet so much today consists merely of an abstract "system" indifferent if not inimical to *anyone's* real fruition. If women are finding entrance into it any easier it may be not only because men are developing consciences, but also because men no longer regard their positions as worth defending. Meanwhile, the machine society seems to be reducing even women to machines; Erica Jong's novel *Fear of Flying* portrays a "heroine" who, in search of what she calls the "zipless fuck," aspires (?) to a depersonalization as mechanical as that of the Nazi society she professes to loath. Yet this is a moral judgment not so much on that heroine as on the culture whose schizoid split the novel reflects so well. With respect to sex, there has been a gradual loosening of prohibitive and restrictive social sanctions since the Middle Ages, along with an evaporation of the culture the sanctions ostensibly were, and the liberation presumably is, supposed to serve. But severe confinement and extreme liberation avail nothing in themselves; what is all-important is the cultural order, the spontaneously and freely shared common meaning system.

The highly structured Courtly-Love theme was the well-inte-

grated culture's symbolic expression of erotic forces well integrated
with spiritual strivings, but finding expression in an unhealthy sub-
limation.[5] Religion's integrating power had given the culture
psychic richness and structure, but the medieval bent for allegorical
and symbolic thought,[6] in combination with the medieval myth,
encouraged viewing the social structure itself as the cause of the
cultural harmony, so the integrated and dynamic culture adopted
a static social ideal that society's legitimating institution thought
was in its own institutional interests—all this just when the beginnings of a more dynamic social order were appearing with the
now disowned merchants. The Church had only set itself up for
the Reformation, the religious wars, and the cultural eclipse of
religion.

The paradigm of Luther's life contains all the ingredients of a
drama that would be replayed time and again on different stages.
First, troubles appear in the social order because of conflicts in
the culture. Then, if the conflicts cannot be resolved, an attempt
is made to push them away from center stage, and some not yet
conflicted sphere of culture is endowed with social primacy. But
the conflicts then push their way back into the new "socially constitutive" sphere, polarizing it between radical individualism and
authoritarian or abstract order. Then the cycle begins again. And
since radical individualism is not a sufficient principle of social
order, it, too, gradually surrenders to abstract order, only by a
more circuitous route.

In *Young Man Luther* Erik Erikson argues that the Roman
Church had become totalitarian, and the local nobles were eager
to support any rebellion against the fading Empire holding them
in thrall.[7] Meanwhile, the Renaissance was imparting a new ego-
strength and displacing the "negative identity" built on guilt foisted
by the power-centered Church. And though seemingly oblivious
of Renaissance humanism, Luther, by emphasizing the crucial role
of personal conscience, provided the indispensable support for
Renaissance anthropocentrism, and drove into the forefront of con-

sciousness what the humanists dared take only as far as art, scholarship, science and literature. Historical science now recognizes a far stronger religious impulse in the Renaissance than its admirers have usually admitted; its multitudinous madonnas were not just exhibitions of man's own skill and glory. This, together with Luther's crucial contribution to Renaissance humanism, suggests that the Renaissance might have produced a new integration. But alas! The Renaissance never became a true religious "event," which is probably why Luther ignored it, even while dealing with the crucial issue on which its lasting vitality depended. The necessary connections were never made. Why? For two reasons. The integration of the culture, which had made Luther's own intense individuality possible, had been shattered by the Church's defection from its true social mission. As a result, first, the institutional Church was no longer able or inclined to put itself, as the early-medieval papacy had, at the head of the forces of reform, thereby preparing the way for the later flowering—thus the Church was not receptive to Luther's protest; and second, the culture, having become conflicted itself by the Church's defection, was both shying away from the sphere where the conflict was arising, and failing to provide the psychic nourishment that a qualified reformer would have needed to take the Church on without destroying himself. As a result, Luther's talents, made to call the Church to account, were absorbed instead in his agonized preoccupation with his own perpetual anxiety and dread, which appeared in his theology. In a divided culture, the fires that drive a personality as divided as Luther's can become (as we see so often today) tragically sacrificial. Luther could not, without the institutional help of the Church and the psychological support of a healthy culture, reform the Church, but only attack it, and he remained as oblivious of the wider culture, which his theology simply ceded to the State, as it remained of him. Yet the Renaissance, without Luther, could not deal with the crucial theological level on which the Church power impeding the Renaissance was justifying itself. The Church was a key to the "crisis," but only Luther and the Renaissance supporting each other could reform it, and they could get together only over what they had in common—the Church. So only Pyrrhic victories were possible. Luther remained so blind to the social origins and consequences of his own thoughts and acts that he fell to viewing his every solution to every problem caused by his own conflicts as direct interventions by God. This burden was too heavy; the violent fanatical attacks on clerical culture by which he discharged his tensions became, with uncanny rapidity, a supine surrender to merely secular power, for opposing which he had no more energy. His personality's conflict with itself and with the already conflicted culture may have brought about his first explicit awareness of the crucial importance of truly personal conscience, but he could establish this breakthrough only by isolating the conscience from its cultural matrix, and so he could never solve his own disconnectedness. The new centrality of conscience, like the evolution of standards of sexual conduct, remained ambiguous because it reflected a new "alienation" resulting from the disintegration of the old cultural meaning system. Even Luther's realization that the believer meets his God above all in the passion of life could not imply a merely "private" experience, for this passion, since its causes are largely social, is also social as well. Just as the power structure needed to ground itself again in true personal interiority, the new vertiginous primacy of conscience urgently needed to be balanced by an appreciation of its social origins and nature. But Luther's advance to that emphasis was blocked by his inner split, which drove him instead to the retrograde surrender to secular power, and the radical individualism in his incomplete but otherwise marvelous perception could only, and did, atomize the culture. The conscience to which he gave the central role remained at the core of the main Western social tradition, but largely to abet the culture's fragmentation.

The impact of Luther's theology illustrates the effects of mingling myth with religion. The mythic content in this theology was

with our souls. For our quest for autonomy, which constitutes a repudiation of the alienation produced by the failure of the old hierarchical order successfully to mediate God, is essentially negative. Yet the old hierarchical order is now entirely gone, and we desperately need a new culture able to accommodate and enculturate our egos. This may be difficult to achieve, because, as much and as essentially as they may have depended upon God, the myths that have appeared since the Middle Ages have actively encouraged as well as reflected a growing failure to mediate God into the social order—which is why the ego is now so much alone. There is something in myth that seeks not only to compensate, but even to replace what it ostensibly seeks to serve.

Luther's failure made a Calvin inevitable. It may be possible in theory, but it is not possible in practice, to deny the need for community. Luther's schizophrenic surrender of social life to secular power could not go long uncorrected. In order to save a religious social-meaning system, Calvin combined Luther's theological individualism with a rigid theocratic social orthodoxy that strived to *replace* secular power, for, lacking an institutional Church in which the necessary communal bonds might be located, Calvin had to locate them in the secular order itself, and he tied religion as tightly to the social order as it had been under the medieval myth. The dilemmas the Middle Ages and Luther failed to resolve became a permanent confusion between sacral and secular functions.

Calvin's spiritual empire dominated the Protestant West until its formidable grip was loosened by its own inner fragmentation, for Calvinism was more irritant than solution for the cultural split. Needing a principle of social order, and lacking a concrete but apolitical cultural organ like the early Church, it located its communal bonds in secular society by way of newly aggressive and abstract systems that its catalyzing rationalistic and masculine dynamisms were exalting over the more receptive, synthesizing, or feminine, dynamisms in which a healthy culture takes root. Of course, Catholicism, which had also become a power structure, gravitated toward abstract forms of order, especially in the decrees of the Council of Trent, but at least its theology, if no longer its practice, still left generous room for the feminine. Calvinism, resurrecting the Old Testament father-figure Jehovah in a savage new mood, forgot about the mother. Yet its ordering impulse, able to gain the initial advantage in each cultural split, was soon socially betrayed by its own absoluteness, provoking a return of the repressed, either in an explosion or in a more integral fashion on some level of culture not yet systematized. Each time, though, the culture tried again for unity in a new socially constitutive sphere, that too would become split between radical individualism (resorting to abstract system for social order) and mere abstract social order imposed directly by the State, both principles finding homes in a different political bloc. The progressive destruction of the integral culture this serial fission caused gave impersonal historical "forces" their sway and wrecked the possibility of full human fruition.

Luther was the first major victim and example of a destructive dialectic that possessed the West for good, as each indispensable advance had to be purchased at the cost of again denaturing the culture. Without Luther, the situation may have further deteriorated, but his own inner division reappeared in his solutions. So religion's cultural function was aborted in the war between Protestants sponsoring conscience and Catholics sponsoring "cultural" order, and the enervating battle caused a shift of the culture's creative energies into the nearest alternative, art, which the Renaissance was exalting and trying to retrieve from the negativistic ecclesiastical order. But the Renaissance could not afford to recognize the centrality of the issues Luther agonized over, and Luther could not understand even the religious importance of the cultural dimension, to which his consciousness never rose, and so the Renaissance, as its own later internally conflicted art suggests, remained as conflicted as Luther. Thus occurred the first of the periodic shifts of society's constitutive sphere, and this shifting process came to be unique to Western culture. For, due to the nature of the earlier cultural integration, society could, by establishing temporary organizers, exploit the culture's dynamic harmony and evade the full consequences of the integrator's alienation.

This sketch would seem to suggest that Western cultural history has a certain simple and basic unity. Every society faces multitudinous challenges—educational, social, economic, political, military, religious, aesthetic, and so forth. But not only will few, if any, societies do all things well, but each will have to decide which activity is most important, *or* shows the best promise as a coordinator that might, if not enlist all social activity in something like a common purpose, at least hold it all together. And as daily life throws up its sequences of little crises needing some order of priorities, it will tend to be the social organizer that wins out when it is involved.

Perhaps the basic force in all this is the human "psyche's" need for dynamic wholeness; in order to organize even itself the human spirit needs some principle of focus and some goal to aspire to, and it is the deepest aspiration that all in society can hold in common without tearing the social order apart that will tend to be the organizer. The history of the West since the Middle Ages, then, appears as a perpetual search for new social organizers, as old ones, having become conflicted, choke and die. It may be instructive to trace this process and consider its meaning.

The Classical aesthetic ideal, reappearing in the fifteenth century in Boccaccio, made a fuller return in Grotius, Erasmus and Montaigne. The aesthetic focus these men, and others like Leonardo, Cellini, and Bacon, gave to their personalities allowed them to shift proteanly among various occupations. This sudden and widespread new appeal of the Classical ideal, though, only attended but did not cause a Renaissance "rediscovery" of Man, in which the Enlightenment later believed the Renaissance had far surpassed the "dark ages" of alleged medieval superstition. For even the Greeks had not wholly surpassed the Middle Ages in their understanding of Man. Erich Auerbach's famous book *Mimesis* unintentionally suggests another ingredient in the epochal Renaissance shift.[8] The Greeks, he showed, had achieved a remarkable balance, but it was only two-dimensional. They never penetrated as far into human destiny or human personality as did the "Old Testament" writers, so their unique harmony remained on the surface. Even the Greek temple's noble, timeless balance in exterior proportions framed an interior that was anticlimactic and vacuous, whereas the comparatively confused façade of the Gothic cathedral encompasses a glowing interior suggestive of another world. The balance of Greek culture was an outer balance all of whose almost equally developed elements (an exception proving a rule) were held in delicate equilibrium by the personal focus of the Greek cultural community. Still, the city-states succumbed to internecine rivalries, and Greek culture finally disappeared. In contrast, the later medieval order tapped the interiority of its members, integrated it into a culture, and thereby survived a pattern of no less savage rivalries all over Europe and especially in Italy. This new Western order could be highly plastic in its external forms, and its inner dynamism, as it worked outward, kept even the surface in perpetual turmoil.

The Greek synthesis had been psychologically two-dimensional and unapologetically erotic; the Greeks wrestled as passionately—if no more successfully—as any later period with the mysteries of human life, and the Greek artistic achievement was formidable. All these qualities were precisely suited to attract the admiration and emulation of the Renaissance which, in seeking a principle of order for society that would avoid the troubles (belatedly and unwillingly demonstrated by Galileo) the cultural deeps were now brewing in Europe, was turning to art as a cultural substitute for religion. The anxiety of Erasmus and others to show a continuity between the Classical Greeks and the Greek Christian fathers even suggests that Christians also recognized the Greeks as a standard, for if the Classical Greek perceptions of personality and destiny had been two-dimensional, so too now were official "Christian" perceptions about culture, and at least the Greeks had not evaded the erotic.

The new aesthetic consciousness of society found the source of social creativity in human personality alone, and at first simply assumed that the social "field" it would work in would be congenial and unproblematic. Shakespeare's social world was an organism with its own fluid and self-regulating harmony that effortlessly embraced Nature and rejected evil as an organism rejects poison. And the home for both man and nature was art, so Italian nobles like Lorenzo "the Magnificent" wanted most of all to be able to write poetry (and there was an explosion of poetry). But when, after the savagery of the religious wars had crested, people turned in dismay to making life at best a work of art, they could not afford to admit that cultural life thus might lose touch with its integrating principle, or that even life itself now might be shut out—for, as the Renaissance understood better than the Middle Ages, art demands its own autonomy and self-completion. Kenneth Clark later found the sculptured portraits on the cathedral at Chartres to have surpassed in their intrinsic nobility those of any later period because the Middle Ages, by integrating human personality into a true culture, had made the full flowering of personality even possible. Now the Renaissance was squeezing into its heroic molds the powerful cultural currents the Middle Ages had released, and signals of a fundamental dislocation began appearing from the deeper strata of personality and culture. *Hamlet* and the restless figures precariously balanced on Michelangelo's Medici tombs suggest powerful forces stalled and confounded by inner imbalances. (This view of the Renaissance might seem subversive only because our own seemingly puny and meager efforts to secure *our* inner significance seem dwarfed by Renaissance giantism. But this was probably a secret compensation for Renaissance insecurity. Any sentimentalism that resents criticism of the Renaissance would be just another threat to our ever regaining any hold on our human dignity.)

The great scholar Basil Willey once made an observation that suggests the proximate cause of all these troubles. Throughout the Renaissance, and until after Milton, the heroic epic was universally regarded as the greatest work open to man, because it ennobles and edifies him.[9] The crude, casual moralism in this notion suggests a severe depreciation of the erotic, while maddeningly mocking our incapacity to produce poetry of *any* scope at all. The Milton-like effort to encourage with moralistic exhortation and to celebrate spiritual strivings without reconciling and integrating them (as Dante did) with seemingly unheroic subterranean erotic drives was futile and self-defeating and resulted in a new split in aesthetics like that in religion, dividing the learned neoclassical rationalists with their merely abstract notions about "Nature" from the more spontaneous creative personalities. Now, in this interesting situation we can see how the inner division in Western culture, resulting ultimately from the Church's transformation into a power structure, was ramifying into social life. It is true that there is some danger of self-hypnosis in applying facile categories to the protean expressions of the aesthetic impulse, but it seems safe to say that the closest approach culture afforded to really spontaneous art became the Baroque (allied to neoclassicism). The culture's inner split had shattered the integration by which even the erotic had to find expression, and the neoclassical idea of what was "pagan" (erotic) simply coexisted, in the Baroque, with the piously Christian in an imperfect amalgam (as in Rubens). Yet the Baroque remained much nearer to a healthy spontaneity than the purely neoclassical, in which abstraction overwhelmed art in all but a few supremely creative artists like Racine. Of course, a few artists, notably Rembrandt, exceeded even the official Baroque in pure spontaneity, but on the whole the intellectual and spiritual dimensions of the culture were separating from the emotional and carnal, and art could not reunite them. The great figures of this age hang suspended in an inchoate inner division that gives them no small concern, but that later critics, grateful for so much emotional richness, would see as mere "complexity."

The early emotional power of the Renaissance eventually gave way to the brilliant but rigid intellectuality of the neoclassical period, when the human spirit finally lost touch with its carnal roots and flew off into a dazzling but superficial pyrotechnical display of "pure reason." Only Pascal, concerned to heal his own inner division, penetrated these pretensions, for most of his contemporaries feared (not unadvisedly) that to acknowledge any weaknesses in themselves would only gratify their enemy, the Church. So the Enlightenment grew ever more bloodless and abstract, and, even more than it claimed the medieval Church had been, dogmatic. Meanwhile, the ferocious religious wars had killed first religious unity and then also the neoclassical humanist compromise, which Erasmus and others had hoped would patch Europe back together. So the cultural sway of art abruptly ended, and politics became the new cultural focus. (Perhaps not without a transitional *social*-aesthetic focus, as the older aesthetic consciousness narrowed, under a realization that society itself was problematic after all, to a concern for social qualities like cultivation, taste and wit, and especially social "charm," which would give a patina of superficial elegance to the coming brutalities of political centralization.)

Richelieu's Machiavellian brand of *realpolitik* and his passion for the glory of France announced the new ascendancy of politics in European culture, and the political concerns of Dryden's and Pope's satires soon reflected it in England. Richelieu, forced to choose between the supposed interests of the Church at the expense of "Catholic" France, and the interests of France and the Protestant states at the expense of the Catholic Habsburgs, the Pope and the Church, chose—France. Even François I and Henry IV of France had earlier delighted Protestant Europe with their power politics aimed at their coreligionist Habsburg rivals in

Europe, but Richelieu was the first to conclude that religion no longer could be the foundation of the State's unity; instead, the State itself must be its own *raison d'être*. He compromised with the dissident French Protestant Fronde and absorbed it into the nation's official life in order to pursue French hegemony in Europe, and he could succeed in this only with the help also of the Protestant states. It is difficult now to imagine how cynical this conscious policy would have appeared to his contemporaries; it simply posited the *State's* material interests as *society's* only legitimate unifier. The State not only ceased viewing the "defense" of institutional religion as its legitimating role (which never was legitimate), but also gave up any further hypocritical pretense of putting any values whatever before its own power. The tragic reversal was not in the ending of the pretense, but in the State's new *license* no longer even to pretend that the culture (not just Church power) could any longer call it to account. Religion became a "private" matter, subject to a State that now regarded itself as even the main cultural force. Compelling Catholic and Protestant to live together merely for the sake of France's glory was an implicit demand that the sacral organs of culture regard themselves as subject to the secular; it was a mere caricature of the correct policy of strictly distinguishing between sacral and secular *functions* so that Catholics and Protestants might feel less temptation to identify their supposed theological positions, often poorly perceived, with secular and material differences, usually intensely perceived. That way, the spiritual could keep its *cultural* primacy. But this primacy is exactly what the State as such has no desire to see. Purportedly in order to defuse the religious conflict, the motivations for which had been more secular than spiritual in nature anyway, the State banished religion from public influence, and later found this rationalized by successive social myths preserving and compounding the confusion of sacral and secular functions. The new developments left Church power over its own members intact, but made Church power itself an arm of the State (whereas the medieval

State for a while had been almost an arm of the Church). This further crippled the culture and unleashed the State, as the establishment of politics as society's new organizer relegated the old desire for spiritual and cultural unity to not only political but also social insignificance.

It may be prudent to pause here to reflect on what we are seeing. Though personally concerned only with establishing French hegemony in Europe, Richelieu did this in such a way as to create an implicit need for what later would come to be labeled a "balance of power," the inevitable expedient if some one State was not to swallow Europe up completely. This political balance was established in Vienna after the Napoleonic Wars, and, in turn, was only the outrider of the present "balance of terror," which had only to wait until weaponry had become sufficiently "sophisticated." Now, the only alternative to such a balance, except for outright totalitarianism, is a balance of culture such as briefly prevailed in medieval Europe. The liberal, though no more inclined to face up to this choice than is the "average" man to face up to that between religion and myth, also prefers to hang in the middle. But the position is untenable. Sooner or later, we have to choose between viewing the State either as a necessary evil (as the American Founders regarded it) or as the central social reality, and liberals have opted by default for the State. Thus, though today's liberals be personally as virtuous as you please, they also rely on force as completely as any terrorist they condemn, with the difference that their force defends the secularist-liberal status quo.

Lest this scare the reader half to death, though, let it be understood that it does not amount to an invitation to religion to elbow everyone else out and take over. Rather, it is simply a statement that society's true cohesion lies on the level of meaning, where force has no place. Everyone is entitled to contribute to a meaning system or to attack the one that prevails, as long as he does so in the proper way—by argument. But those who subscribe to a meaning system are also entitled to live it in a *public* (not civic—

"civic" implies force) way, in a structured community conforming to an explicit moral code. It is what all groups can agree on that constitutes a cultural meaning system for society. This may not seem to amount to very much, but the fact is that most "cultural" groups tend to agree very closely on their most fundamental doctrines; their differences seem to stand out mainly because of the repeated confusion of meaning and power, for power tends to divide. What is here advocated is a combination of the cultural strengths of the medieval period with the civic and social strengths of the modern.

It may seem unimaginable to the liberal, but a society with a perfectly harmonious culture would not need to appoint any restrictive constitutive sphere for itself. For all social institutions would come to reflect their cultural meaning and body it forth. The constitutive sphere represents, in effect, a compromise, or *modus vivendi,* between the culture and the State. The State's arrangements of power are vindicated by myth, but myth, at least for purposes of culture, is only "negatively effective" as a principle of social organization—all it can do is to keep death at bay. This is where ideology comes in. It rationalizes the constitutive sphere for purposes of social organization, acting as a derivative meaning system giving effect to the culture as far as possible while accommodating the State's arrangements of power. The more *culturally* important the constitutive sphere happens to be, the stronger the hand it gives the culture vis-à-vis the State; and, of course, the less important, culturally, the constitutive sphere is, the weaker the support it gives the culture against the State. So it is conceivable that the final organizer, sociology, might be appointed not by the culture but by the State itself.

The new political consciousness of culture saw (witness Chesterfield) social creativity in *impersonal* intelligence and will, as expressed in the struggle for national power. As an organizer for society, politics was much less flexible than religion or art, because though politics takes all human possibilities into account, it can achieve little more *as* a social organizer than a fatalistic exploitation of the status quo. Religion or art might hope to shape or mold, but politics could hope only to contain. So it began to become necessary to replace the old inner cultural order with a new external control. Soon yet another cultural split appeared in the political order: On one side were the doctrinaire secularist states like Frederick's Prussia, cultural heirs of Richelieu, that found their final expression in the French Revolution; on the other side were the so-called Christian (because they still gave religion some room) or moderate states, especially England, whose crowning achievement was the American Constitution forged by British-trained lawyers. The Americans leaned not on doctrinaire formulas but on the empirical experience of British common law, while the French Revolution capped the doctrinaire secularist political tradition by falling victim to a lust for abstract order. The American Constitution was infinitely more successful than the French constitutions after Napoleon because it emerged from the mainstream of the basic Western social tradition, and did not have to restructure an entire collapsed social order, as becomes almost inescapable after a spell of cultural absolutism has robbed a society of organic cohesion. England just escaped this threat under Cromwell, who taught the monarchy to make timely compromises that later saved it. And America is being subjected to a similar test now.

The successive splits in the theological, aesthetic, and political "socially constitutive" spheres were caused by the original split in the culture when the institutional agent of the cultural integration converted itself into a power structure. This caused a polarization of the inner cultural order between carnal and spiritual, emotional and intellectual latencies, which now began to work in mutual opposition. This inner polarization in turn infected each successive constitutive sphere, and appeared in the social order in the form of social splits between order and spontaneity, between abstract (and inevitably authoritarian) order on one side, and radical individualism on the other. (But, as noted earlier, radical individualism gradually comes to depend on abstract order, too.) When the culture can no longer integrate, society must choose one or the other as a structural principle. The Protestant side of the religious split, for example, opted for radical individualism, the Catholic side sponsored "cultural" order. But the individualism atomized Protestant society. Calvin tried to resolve the atomization by theologically consecrating the State, while neoclassical rationalism tried to resolve it by way of aesthetics, just as the Catholic Baroque, though more culturally integral in nature, also tried to replace religion with art as the social unifier.

Thus, at least two, and possibly three, basic "forces" can be detected as causes of Western "cultural" change. (The term "cultural change" is used here to refer to changes that hinge on meaning, which are always the most crucial. Technological change does not cause, though it can precipitate, "cultural" change. Technology is a cause of change only in the negative sense that it disrupts physical patterns, but it cannot create a new society in the real sense of the word.) One cause of change is the inevitable inadequacy of serial myths validating arrangements of power. Another cause, and largely a consequence of the recourse to myth, is the deterioration of culture, and the consequent need for serial, and increasingly superficial, socially constitutive spheres through which culture might continue to influence society's organization. In these respects, the Middle Ages and the late-modern period were both watershed periods, because their myths were well matched to the ideologies organizing their constitutive spheres, and reverse mirror images of each other with respect to the relative importance they attached to economics and religion. In the medieval period, the social myth gratifyingly tended to reinforce the social primacy the institutional Church also enjoyed ideologically as the crucial organ in the socially constitutive sphere of culture. This double reinforcement the Church enjoyed in the medieval period, economics, which the medieval period had all but ignored, enjoys in the modern. For in the modern period economics became central both to the myth of autonomy (by giving the myth social expression in a total system) and to the ideology dominating the socially constitutive sphere— i.e., to Capitalism or Communism, as the case might be. So we can identify economics as the third basic factor in our cultural evolution, with the reservation that this prominence of economics is largely artificial, resulting from the repression the economic order suffered in the medieval period in the interests of myth, and from the later cultural deterioration that in turn "unleashed" economics upon the culture. (As will be seen shortly, "philosophical change" is included in change due to shifts in ideology and myth. Not that philosophy *should* not, perhaps, be an independent social force in its own right, nor that it sometimes almost is. One could wish that philosophy were stronger, to act as a check on myth and ideology as well as a guide to religion, but the opposite appears to be true: Only those philosophical arguments that conform to or establish a myth or ideology are ever accepted as "reasonable." Ideas may have consequences, but only those ideas that basically reflect the current defense against death are allowed to have consequences. Only a very narrow range of ideas, if indeed any real ideas at all, are tolerated as respectable or acceptable.)

The interaction between myth and ideology aside, in one sense, the entire basic history of the West can be described (à la Marx) as the rise of the mercantile classes to ideological and "existential" ascendancy—to, as it were, practical and ideological self-sufficiency. For in reaction to the aristocracy's and the Church's claim to be expressions of irreplaceable intrinsic values (but actually these claims were made to serve a drive for power) the merchants developed a philosophy of utility with which to dispel the aura of exclusive legitimacy the old elites emanated. So when Church power largely collapsed in the Reformation, and feudal power collapsed in the Revolution, the utilitarian philosophy was waiting to take their place, soon to be reinforced by an extension of Montesquieu's and others' interest in politics to practical action in general. And when the results of the Revolution then (in Europe, at least) discredited political ideology, economics was all that remained. Thus were laid the foundations of Capitalist society.

The philosophes of the late Enlightenment had been forced to recognize the self-delusion in the early Enlightenment's olympian ideals of rationality, and had begun hatching plans for more concrete social changes. But their seemingly salutary new respect for material reality—not excluding their own flesh—remained far less than an "objective" readjustment of the old dynamic cultural balance since, early and late, the Enlightenment, in its hostility to the Church, remained unwilling to retrace the steps that had led from the earlier integration—which indeed the philosophes were almost incapable of appreciating. Instead, their apparent rediscovery of the material and carnal only reflected a complete loss of faith in the spiritual and immaterial. So the two poles of the culture's real creativity—the person and the culture as a whole—were now being ignored.

All this gives us another glimpse of the basic "forward" dialectic of Western culture. The continuing capacity for truly creative innovation on successive organizing levels was transmitted by the original cultural synthesis, but each partial advance further victimized the cultural patrimony, so that every solution of one problem created at least two more. The philosophes' concentration on the material world flowed more from an anxious and ideological need to dominate and keep it under control than from any true concern for it. (Ideology is only a temporary, expedient surrogate for a true cultural integration of life forces.) Since both sides of each split in the culture only carried forward the weaknesses incubated earlier, even the Americans failed to escape the temptation of ideology, which found expression among them as Deism and caused an ideological resolution of the so-called conflict between Church and State, the problem of coordinating its sacral and secular dimensions that any culture faces.

A split appeared in the political-cultural order when the revolutionaries in France sacked the conservative monarchy and turned on the more moderate states whose impertinence in continuing in existence affronted the revolutionaries' new certitudes. But Napoleon only shook out the old cultural detritus and accelerated the centralization that produced the modern State. The results of the Revolution had discredited political (practical) absolutism, if not the more intellectual variety (which soon reappeared in Marx). The Napoleonic Wars between "Christian" Europe and "godless" Revolution then demonstrated the futility of using political ideology as social organizer, and extended the questioning to the possibility (if not the wisdom) of organizing society around politics at all. So the culture deposed politics and elevated economics, replacing the struggle for power as society's focus with the competition for markets, and, all spiritual creeds now discredited, society resigned itself to the fat materialist complacency Balzac and Marx began to satirize (they both saw the new quasi-religious or fetishist significance of money). The Romantics inherited cultural leadership from the philosophes, but rejected the rationalist god, the intellect, and simply left for the economists society's more pressing problems and the preparation of the new organizer, as the Romantics themselves fled in despair to "Nature" after it became evident that society somehow had become cut off from the Nature of which the Enlightenment had regarded itself as the final exemplar. (Dunne believes that this Nature was conceived "reflexively" as the background for a society beginning to seem "artificial" because its credibility in mediating God to the "individual" had failed.) But in their attempt to regain Nature, the Romantics abandoned society completely to the denaturing rationalization that had caused their flight and would in the next century all but do Nature completely in. And as the organizing focus passed into economics, once-proud states were reduced to competing for mere markets and territory, and the white man, become imperialistic by national and cultural policy, took up his burden of educating the colored races in the

realities of European culture. Meanwhile, the Church, surprised by
an opportunity to recoup all its losses after the Revolution's disasters, exploited the occasion, in a testament more to its sincerity
than to its wisdom, to proclaim only its chronic attachment to the
monarchies, so the finally victorious mercantile classes saw no
alternative but to reject the values sponsored by the Church and
to enshrine their own utilitarianism—which also contradicted itself,
by refusing to recognize any intrinsic values but the right to property.[10]

Politics lost its cultural hold in Europe only after Hegel died,
and in America probably not until the Civil War; for a severe
trauma seems to be required to shake society out of its current
illusions and—alas!—usually into new ones. Colbert's economics
had served the State, but now the State had to be content to serve
economics. And soon the Communists resurrected the old cultural
schizophrenia, both by insisting on the communal nature of economics in contradiction of the individualist conception, and by
importing the absolutistic ordering impulse directly into the economic sphere. Improving on Hegel, who, predictably in the era of
politics, had seen the State as the locus of community, Engels discovered the community of the State to be only an illusion,
"abstract," a "fetter." Only economic communism could restore a
true unity.[11] It was "self-evident" to Marx and Engels that the
economic explanation is crucial for any social reality: "Upon the
different forms of property . . . rises an entire superstructure of
distinct and peculiarly framed sentiments, illusions, modes of
thought and views of life."[12] This revelation infused all of Marx's
work, too, with the same vestigial élan that characterized the
exuberances of the robber barons:

Thus the Tories in England long imagined that they were
enthusiastic about monarchy, the Church and the beauties of
the old English Constitution, until the day of danger wrung

from them the confession that they were enthusiastic only about ground rent.[13]

Here Marx put a finger on a crucial change. The one thing the nineteenth-century Tories would not tolerate was an invasion of their property rights. But as Saint-Simon's famous chronicle shows, the French nobles of the *ancien régime* would have tolerated anything but an invasion of their political position. De Tocqueville's ruminations on the spectacular vices of a displaced nobility show that these men care more for the exercise of power than for money, which to them is only useful. But if an age of politics makes power the real coin of the realm, in an age of economics even the *ancien régime* must have either transformed itself into an economic elite or disappeared. Marx's insight was no accident. Economics indeed was now the bone of contention, partly because the deeper cultural levels had become too systematized to allow much room for fundamental change, partly because there was no more energy for continuing the old cultural disputes, and partly because both the deterioration of the culture and society's increasing material complexity were making a systematic economics necessary. But if the Marxist revolution succeeded mainly in carrying the illusions behind the French Revolution—especially the lust for order—into economics, even the Capitalists themselves also carried the unresolved cultural conflicts into the new order, and they, too, made economics king. Both sides basically agreed in their economic view of life, which in effect, but on the Capitalist side only implicitly, subordinated all culture to economics and contradicted the inner value structure of the Western tradition. The Capitalist side was preserved from even further corruption only by the example of the American political achievement, which preserved spontaneous participation and tried to establish a reasonable separation of cultural functions, although it partly failed and achieved only an ideological separation.

At last the Western nations staggered for no good reason into World War I, from the effects of which, Barbara Tuchman suggests, we have never really recovered. The first major war with no ideological cause, it revealed how far the culture had deteriorated. Some now look back with nostalgia to the century after the Congress of Vienna as the most "peaceful" in Western history, but it was a peace of inner exhaustion, over which the balance of power constructed in Vienna after the Napoleonic Wars could endure, like latticework over a chasm, only until the weakest link crumbled. It may have been superior to that "peace" of the grave we have known, but it saw life as without passion and containing nothing worth living or dying for.

The distinguishing creative principle of Western culture has been its concern for uncoerced and spontaneous personal participation in a common cultural unity. This concern at first was common to the entire culture, in which a rich diversity and balance of cultural institutions within a political order well aware of its own limits was supported by an unconscious (but all the more powerful for that) integration of erotic and spiritual capacities, of personal and communal spontaneity and order. But the inner split in late-medieval culture condemned Western life to a long quest for reintegration that led through a series of organizers that tried but failed to reconcile the twin needs for spontaneity and order, which then found separate homes in new cultural splits (in theology, between Protestants and Catholics; in art, between the Baroque and the neoclassical; in politics, between doctrinaire secularist absolutism and "Christian" constitutionalism; and in economics, between Communism and Capitalism) in each of which the side sponsoring order resorted to a rigid, absolutist rationale (in Catholicism, for example, this appeared with the Council of Trent), while the side that kept faith with personal freedom and initiative transmitted the main Western social tradition. But free initiative was not *exclusive* to the main tradition: In the early stages, the common cultural unity still outweighed all differences, while in the later stages the main tradition tended to radiate to other receptive areas. The main concrete Western social tradition persisted by avoiding the swamps of (conservative) theocratic social regimentation (as in Habsburg Spain), on one side, and of (radical) secularist absolutism (as in Revolutionary France) on the other, but the main tradition was gradually constricted by its confinement to areas where the indispensable commitment to personal initiative persisted through all periods. Thus, England was its primary vessel during the era of politics and, by developing the practices and principles that went into the American political achievement, while also incubating Capitalism, played the role between politics and economics that America may be called upon to play between economics and a coming sociological order. For only America has sufficiently developed the possibilities of Capitalism in the West to incubate a higher (or lower, depending on the direction it takes) type of social organization. But the main tradition has perhaps reached a final impasse in the new secularist absolutism of liberal America, while a retarding cultural "drag," expressing and causing a collapse of the medieval synthesis, has produced an inner schizophrenia so cumulatively devastating to the emotional vitality of Western society that its effects seem to have ranged from the extinction of poetic drama, long lamented by critics, to the apparent drying up of Western music. From Vivaldi through Bach, Handel, Mozart, Beethoven, Brahms, Schubert, Berlioz, Wagner, Tchaikovsky, and into our day, for whatever it is worth, we can detect an almost linear improvement in technique, but an equally persistent decline of emotional purity and power. If not Bernstein, who will compose great music today? But he has produced only *West Side Story* and *Mass*.[14]

The West's evolution since the Middle Ages appears, then, as a transition from a highly integrated culture beginning to work (through the early liberal tradition) on an institutionally rigid and hierarchical social order—supported from one direction by presumed economic necessity, and from the other by a social myth contradicting the cultural dynamics emerging with the merchants—to a sociologically (i.e., physically) flexible but now economics-constituted social order no longer nourished by any culture at all but, at best, only by a waning myth. Religion's social centrality was the secret of medieval cultural health, its social insignificance the reason for the modern cultural malaise. Yet religion was largely the cause of its own troubles. Today we experience the result as a radical cultural schizophrenia. Subjectively, the split feels like a social incompatibility between our carnal and spiritual latencies. When the secular order's attempts to allow fuller expression to the carnal-erotic were defeated by the rationalism and scientism it threw into the growing vacuum it created by its virtual denial of the "spiritual," seemingly monopolized by the Church, and the repeated rebellions against erotic suppression became more and more "fixated" on genital sex, secular society simply dispensed with "spiritual" sex and almost spitefully turned itself into a machine. Socially, we experience the cultural split as an inability to reconcile "object" and "subject" in social practice and thought. (At best, we try to sustain the "subject" by insulating him from society.) Yet it was the artificiality of the Church's own notion of the "spiritual" that caused the exile of religion's integrating principle. As a result, society could not reconcile the paradoxical twin needs for spontaneity and order (which seem parallel to Freud's pleasure and reality principles), and the culture was cannibalized in the growing antagonism between them. It was this separation between emotional and spiritual capacities, between "sensibility" and intellect, that created the lamentable series of cultural splits in the social organizers, and the periodic shifts of the focus of organization to ever more superficial levels, each (already doomed) new organizer riding in on the despair of that being abandoned for its (inevitable) failure to overcome the split between order and life. Each shift was attended by a new organization of social life, but the successive organizers offered "official" scope to less and less of human capacity, until finally society simply became a machine. The cultural order gradually yielded to regimenting abstract "systems" as society shunted aside those capacities not finding formal expression within the current organizer and regarded them in the inevitable crunch as mere dispensable embellishments to its current version of "real" life, which invariably turned out to be a fool's paradise. By and by, even the embellishments came to seem annoying impedimenta to the "solution" of "real" problems.

We have arrived at a new model of Western culture, and find ourselves in some respects closer to Communist theorists like Georg Lukács than to recent liberals. But we feel constrained to defend Liberalism against Lukács's dialectical materialism, however noble or impressive the heights of philosophical consistency to which he raised it. The target of Lukács's critique—perhaps even more brilliant than that of Marx—was what he analyzed as Capitalist society's inability to reconcile object and subject in thought, and its attempt to erect a total "system" going its way independently of man and subjecting him to its requirements. Because this objection is philosophical in nature, the liberal West is at once both fascinated by Lukács and disposed nevertheless to brush aside his objections as after all "theoretical" and irrelevant: Having all but abandoned the attempt to reconcile object and subject in thought, and having no philosophical resources with which to confront the problem, the West hopes this is a "nonproblem" rather than the key to the social order. But Lukács's objection is as valid as his analysis of the denaturing of modern Western philosophy is accurate. He sees the explanation for the decay of philosophy, however, in the West's economic infrastructure. And indeed, we must partly agree. The sociological and economic foundations of society have powerful influence on philosophy, in that people are disposed to recognize only those truths that seem to support their own material interests—as, for example, the hierarchical society recognized hierarchical metaphysical values and the liberal utilitarian society finds much to admire in philosophical positivism. But this does not mean that, necessarily, philosophical doctrines are mere epiphenomena.

They also have a truth content, even if this *is* always perceived only by men with material interests. There is a certain imperishable truth in the hierarchical metaphysic, just as there is lasting value in Peircean pragmatism. Our debt to Marxism for exposing the influence of power even in philosophical thought is great, but we need not conclude that such thought is either dispensable, epiphenomenal, or incapable of achieving real truth. We must also take exception to the Marxist version of the evolution of economic classes. For this evolution is not the basis of history, but rather the residual dead weight that history drags along, as the creative cultural forces try somehow to exert themselves in spite of history's inertial mass. For example, the class structure of medieval society was inherited from the feudalism of the early Germanic "pagan" tribes. This structure had no intrinsic connection with Christianity, the catalyzing ingredient of the medieval integration, but was, so to speak, the material the cultural process was given to work with. But the cultural process was frustrated by the medieval social myth which happened to be modeled on the feudal social structure. No social myth is primarily concerned with justifying any class, and it is only because all classes are only too eager to subscribe to a social structure embodying a myth that can exorcise the specter of death that any one class can gain an advantage from it. Not the feudal structure itself, but its incorporation into a myth, caused the culture to break up in a struggle for power. But no myth can simply be extrapolated from class structure, and if it was myth that sabotaged the cultural process Marx's analysis is inadequate.

We can now construct an alternative model of the decline of Western philosophy. Of course, this is not (fortunately) an essay in philosophy, and cannot deal with the question on its intrinsic merits. But then, philosophical questions seldom are decided on their merits even by philosophers themselves. For example, among those many fully persuaded of the strictly philosophical merits of the Thomist metaphysic there seem to be an inordinate number of Catholics, while philosophical positivism appears to be somewhat overrepresented at places like M.I.T. This is reminiscent of the fact that most Catholics are born Catholic, just as most Jews are born Jews. Does this suggest that Catholicism and Judaism are largely irrational? Not at all. What it suggests is that the true appeal of a religion is not basically rational or, rather that the true appeal of a religion cannot be understood if it is not first *experienced*. For the appropriation of truth is not only an intellectual, but also an affective, and even volitional, matter. A similar situation appears to obtain in philosophy: That philosophy appears most reasonable that best fills other needs as well. Or, in short, philosophical systems often respond as much to the urgencies of myth as to the requirements of "reason" (whatever they might be). Thus, in one way, the evolution of philosophy appears to reflect the rise and fall of social myths. When a social myth becomes well established, philosophy appears to be vigorous and waxing, as in the Middle Ages, but when the myth begins to fail, philosophy too seems to lose confidence in its own constructive and system-building powers, which seem to collapse, as in the fourteenth-century Ockhamist school. When a new myth becomes established, a corresponding philosophy arises that is critical of the old philosophy on grounds that the latter would have regarded as secondary or beside the point; the new philosophy confidently asserts new principles and systems that an even later philosophy will dismiss out of hand as obviously flawed, as the late Enlightenment dismissed the early-Enlightenment Idealists. The most recent dominant "school," called "logical positivism" (the later linguistic analysis appears hardly to be a real philosophy at all), recognizes no verifiable truths, and is this not because the society in which it appeared was dominated by a (now waning) myth of absolute autonomy and alienation? But this myth was congenial to us, because it "solved" the overwhelming problem of death while simultaneously neutralizing spiritually for us the inner conflict in our culture. That is, this inner conflict became a foil, by absolute opposition to which we defined our own personalities. When the old mythic God departed from the social world, we became alienated toward our own death, and rather than, as before, under the medieval myth, cooperating absolutely with the established order so as to overcome our death, we now "overcome" it be affirming our existence *in the face of* the social world from which we have become alienated.

But if nonrational factors are so important even in philosophy, it is (even discounting the modern myth of autonomy) no wonder that modern society is so reluctant to acknowledge the philosophical problem as crucial, for it vaguely knows itself to be without both the "nonphilosophical" resources to solve it, or the cultural resources to apply the solution. For as Lukács perceived, philosophy in the West has long been in decline, increasingly unable to reconcile object and subject in thought. But what Lukács in turn fails to perceive is that the "philosophical" resolution, which is usually powerfully influenced by myth or religion or both, is not only seldom strictly philosophical, but never merely a reflection of economics. Our criticism of Western philosophy, partly echoing Lukács's, can be registered as a not strictly philosophical, but a phenomenological, observation: It is true, and greatly to be applauded, that philosophy has achieved a growing technical expertise and sophistication, but all this has worked on a constantly shrinking metaphysical content, and if philosophy has any substantial contribution to make it is on the level of metaphysics. Notwithstanding the notion that metaphysics has any "place" only where empirical science has not yet arrived (this positivist notion is itself metaphysical), there is a crucial sphere in philosophy where metaphysics is and should be undisputed ruler. We are not faulting philosophy's critical tools, but the progressive diminution of its constructive power. This observation may not be philosophically conclusive, but as part of a catalogue of similar failures in all spheres of culture, it is powerfully suggestive. However we might value that persisting but contracting core of metaphysical affirmations in Western philosophy (which are not equivalent to cosmological principles about the physical universe), its relentless shrinkage could be attributed to something other than the march of "reason." From Descartes on, each major philosopher finds a "flaw" in the system of his predecessor while recognizing in that system new possibilities for development, and constructs around his own original insight a whole new system. But while each sheds valuable new light on all that preceded him, these thinkers so relentlessly jettisoned affirmations essential to the preceding systems that finally, in the positivist school, no commitments at all remained, and philosophy seemed paralyzed, the domain of mere technicians. No doubt the philosophical systems did contain inner deficiencies and difficulties, and incompletions (and such systems probably always will), but the constant shrinkage into systems metaphysically ever narrower and more reluctant to affirm anything at all could be interpreted, on a phenomenological level, as evidence not of the advance of reason—especially when the end result is paralysis—but of inner exhaustion. (Incidentally, it may be useful to note that system is as useful in philosophy, which is concerned with understanding, as it is dangerous in social organization, which is concerned with control.) As long as this apparent exhaustion persists, it will be difficult to answer Lukács's criticisms.

Lukács was correct when he said that the decline of philosophy, especially in the growing inability to reconcile object and subject in thought, is both the sign and the cause of the crucial Western failure. He was correct when he said that the philosophical problem is indeed a crucial problem for any society, and liberal society, if determined not to face it, can only go down the path to the disaster he predicted for it. But we cannot admit the total and exclusive validity of Lukács's dialectical-materialist model of philosophical evolution. The inner split in the culture did give economic "forces" exaggerated influence in Western cultural history, and there *was* a sort of dialectic of material forces clashing like blind armies in the night. But the inner logic controlling the clash was not that of a Hegelian, rationalist, immanent, cunning "force" in history, but a logic of culture. Material forces clashed so harshly because the ultimate cultural control had partly—but not entirely—broken down; even the device of making economics society's organizing sphere was a *cultural* expedient. The culture still compelled the material factors at least to respond, and remained the ultimate reason for new social alignments, even though it has never since the Middle Ages been able to get the material forces entirely under control. The real dialectic was between a persisting but gradually fragmenting cultural order and strictly material social forces pushing for chaotic autonomy. Yet even the vitality of the economic classes depended finally on the culture.

We should honor Lukács's magnificent and lucid demonstration that the philosophical problem is a crux of our social malaise, and pay homage to his noble search for consistency and comprehensive intelligibility, a search in which he is now being followed, perforce, by us. We must even acknowledge the powerful heuristic value of his dialectical-materialist model, and recognize its partial validity. But finally we are forced to admit that its remaining deficiencies must lead to just that subordination of dialectical materialism to power that Lukács's whole effort was aimed at preventing, and an analogue of which he correctly saw developing in Western economic "systems." Withal, we might hope, like Lukács, that our model for explaining the decline of Western philosophy (which to the liberal is little more now than an ornament, as "interesting" as but in the crunch no more profitable than a Chinese puzzle box) provides a crucial key to our social and cultural problems.

Yet, as we saw above, a mere philosophic resolution of the cultural malaise is apparently insufficient as well as impossible, because the cultural integration must come before or separately from the philosophic. For not only would philosophy alone not give us the tools to implement a resolution; we could not even arrive at a general philosophic consensus unless the resolution were first achieved. Though a philosophical integration might be indispensable in preserving a cultural integration, it could not bestow it. One reason, of course, is that though some people might find unity with

others in a philosophical meeting of minds, philosophical differences
are notoriously difficult to compose (perhaps precisely because
they usually are not wholly "philosophical"); even Classical Greece
came to no philosophical consensus. And perhaps it is because the
whole truth is so difficult to encompass in any philosophical school.
But most important of all is that between society and the "objective" truth there intrudes the overwhelming practical problem of
death, for which there are only two possible solutions, and philosophy alone is not one of them. They are religion and myth, either
of which philosophy can serve, and has served, well, but as *social*
phenomena they are more powerful and active than philosophy.
Thus, as a practical matter, the possibility of a free society seems
to depend on religion's freedom to go about its cultural business.
Religion's claims, though, do not arise simply from its incidental
ability to solve the social problem of death; religion also has an
intrinsic right, now unrecognized, to perform sacral functions even
for society as such.

Earlier, the latter-day liberal devotion to the State was briefly
attacked, and it was asserted that the State is never intrinsically
legitimate, especially when it is disputing *culture's* social primacy
because religion maintains culture. In preparation for the integrated
theory of economics, let us consider how culture maintains its hold
on the social order. This exercise will have the additional advantage of helping to explain why liberals became so attached to the
State.

Every society, says Alvin W. Gouldner, has two principles of
stability: economic gratification and moral legitimacy. A society
reliant on myth will try to maintain the precarious linkage between
these by an exercise of power. Basically, all social myths in the
West since the Middle Ages produced either hierarchical or radically egalitarian societies, and each type of society has tended,
whether by accident or by nature (probably the latter), to favor
one principle of stability over the other. But to favor one principle
over the other snaps the link. Actually, it is no mere "linkage" that

is needed, but coordination. The hierarchical order, enforcing the old feudal economic order for whatever gratification it might give, and content with that, in fact ignored gratification as a stabilizing principle in favor of moral legitimacy. In reaction egalitarian liberal society fastened instead on economic gratification, all but abandoning moral legitimacy in service of its own myth of "autonomy," in which the moral dimension of *social* life all but disappeared from view. Liberal society declared that there was no public morality, that all moralities were private, and that society itself was simply "neutral" with respect to values—i.e., amoral. All that saved early liberal society from moral bankruptcy was its divinely naive identification of moral legitimacy *with* economic gratification—an identification accomplished by the establishment of "property rights" as society's morally legitimating principles. This preserved a subjectively legitimating moral order that society at large spontaneously acknowledged. But having resorted to property rights for morally legitimating principles, liberal society could not then ignore them and retain any moral legitimacy, a dilemma it had set itself up for when it defined property rights in such a way as to replace the culture with a totalist system (of economics) as social integrator.

What do the terms "totalist system" and "social integrator" mean? First of all, the word "system" has two quite distinct meanings, which, as applied to society, have radically different implications. On the one hand, "system" can indicate a whole whose parts gain meaning and function only by virtue of their inclusion in that whole; this we could call a primary, total, or absolute system. But the same word can also denote what Gouldner calls merely "a group whose interchanges restrict their functional autonomy," a whole whose component elements are partly or even largely independent of each other and of the *systemic* whole; this is a secondary, or "partial," system. Now, since a total system must give its *own* functional autonomy priority over that of its human participants, whom it would reduce to functionaries with no real autonomy of their own, no total system can be imposed on or assumed in the social order. As a *social* phenomenon, a total system is totalitarian. But a secondary system could make its primary concern the actual enhancement of the autonomy of the parts composing it. Thus, only a secondary system is permissible in the social order. And it clearly was in this sense that liberal Capitalism was first recommended by the theorists and received by the public: Capitalism would free the "individual" from old feudal-type dependencies and allow his personal initiative far greater scope. But from the beginning the theorists also claimed, self-contradictorily, that the economic order must be self-contained, virtually autonomous of other social spheres, and wholly unlimited by any wider culture, to which the theorists claimed neutrality—nay, "scientific" indifference. Why did they contradict themselves so? Partly because they were trying to establish economics as the socially constitutive sphere —but this hardly required going to such lengths. More important, the theorists, acting under the aegis of the new myth of autonomy, which was actually an alternative for culture, were trying to *replace* the culture with a totalist system as the social integrator.

Though culture itself is always integrated on the level of meaning, society can be integrated either culturally (on the level of meaning) or materially, on the level of material function. As we will consider later on, Liberalism came to odds with religion over the latter's recourse to power. In order, then, to banish religious power, Liberalism sought to displace culture, which depends on religion, as the social integrator. The only alternative was to integrate society on the level of function—by a totalist system. This project seemed innocuous, even "natural," because in egalitarian liberal society all individuals became functionally interchangeable, and so long as persons could change their functions the integration of society on the level of function would not seem particularly oppressive. That is, though society might become impersonal and mechanical, this did not seem to mean that the "individual" must necessarily do so, too. Rather, the very impersonality of this new society would seem to promise a new autonomy for the individual on the level of meaning: He could subscribe to any meaning he chose, or even none, without society needing to care one way or the other.

But, as the sociologist Anton Zijderveld recently—and accurately—observed, when meaning is rejected as social integrator, all social institutions become autonomous on the level of meaning and henceforth serve only themselves. Their integration thereafter merely on the level of material function must be enforced by the State. Thus, the State becomes the fundamental and crucial social and "cultural" institution. Meanwhile, as the integrated meaning system that formerly fused society evaporates, the individual withdraws allegiance from society and retreats into his private existence, trying to become autonomous of the system: He becomes *subjectively* autonomous as the institutions become *objectively* autonomous. In this schizoid social situation, the individual experiences a pervasive social control ("alienation") but a great degree of private autonomy ("freedom"). When meaning is forced out as social integrator, morality is phased out as social category, and society no longer even rises to a moral level, aspiring to only the functional integration characteristic of the machine. As a result, all moral questions devolve upon the individual as *socially* "epiphenomenal," but, as a result, his "rights" only appear to become more important. For these rights are only residual, being left over from what the bureaucracies have not yet claimed but eventually will. A preoccupation with freedom grows in direct proportion to the alienation from society *as such*; real freedom, though, is always subjectively experienced as a function of meaning: It is existentially real only when absent as a problem (when social structures seem to reflect an accepted meaning system) and is existentially absent when it is real as a problem (when the individual becomes alienated from social institutions).

The institutions do not become collectively monolithic—all that they have in common is the subhuman totalist system that functionally integrates them (and whose detritus they clean up). As institutions, they are pluralistic, each reflecting its own meaning system. So the multiple roles the individual must play become almost interchangeable, and, recognizing their lack of meaning integration, he experiences a distance growing between him and society: alienation. Nor has he any emotional identification with institutions either: The bureaucracies are *rationally* organized. And difficult to attack: The dominant groups in the various segments tend to overlap, but never coalesce, so their power remains diffuse and unfocused. And since most people tend to exercise at least some power in the segments of their own "professional" concern (although everyone is largely dominated by the powers in the other segments), no class consciousness, and no revolution, are any longer possible. In fact, so long as the individual is allowed *some* privacy, is not compelled to identify completely with one institution or purpose, control and coercion can become quite severe without provoking revolt. Social control is now so strong and pervasive in our pluralistic society "precisely because of the privatization of the modern individual." But if the individual is permitted even a tiny sphere of privacy, a totalitarian order can arrive almost unchallenged.[15]

In medieval society, as Drucker has observed, property had been a function of status. In liberal society, status became a function of property (even labor, for example, was made a mere commodity so as to be manipulable in terms of property). This reversal was accomplished by Locke, who declared that a thing becomes a man's property when he commingles his labor with it. The trouble here was not that Locke went too far, but that, if he was going to go this way, he did not go far enough. For this definition views social property rights as a matter only of atomized "individuals," but no "individual" has any real human reality apart from others: A man commingles his labor both with the thing he produces and with the labor of others whom he joins in production. But Locke was deliberately creating a radically individualist and atomized—a *mercantile*—economic and social order in response to the cultural tensions of his times. He was aiding in *replacing* the conflicted culture (which was the locus of community) with a wholly rationalized and "self-balancing" totalist system as social integrator. Now, it was the great illusion of Locke's period that the supposed cosmic "clock" (itself an illusion, dispersed by Einstein) could be replicated in the social order, in a self-balancing economic system-machine (acting as a balancer for society in place of a culture). Yet no social system can in fact be self-balancing, but will always draw—healthily and overtly if it is a secondary, or partial, system, but unhealthily and covertly if it is a total system—on an underlying culture for its real life At least the earlier system had been content to mind its own economic business, professing complete indifference to "lesser" matters, but eventually, the economic problems caused by the original *static* total system of mercantile society forced Keynes, in creating a new *dynamic* total system, to unleash the totalism of the system directly upon the lingering culture. But Keynes's hand was all but forced by the transformation of mercantile society into an *industrial* society whose communal aspects became central even to economics, but no longer achieved any theoretical recognition. As a systemic "remedy" for the persisting atomization, and in order to rebalance the "system" once again, Keynes had to forge a new collectivism centered in government. Thus, the old improperly formulated property rights, swamped by new forces they could not control, were swept aside and could no longer legitimate the Capitalist order, while the theoretically unacknowledged communal dynamisms in economics slipped all traces of social moral control and acquired an autonomous and disruptive life of their own. As Drucker has observed, the economy split into two parts: the "real" economy of concrete industrial structures and organization, and the economy of symbols (now largely outdated) with which we futilely try to understand and organize it. The power in the "real" economy is neither controlled nor limited by any morally legitimating principles, has neither moral purpose nor moral legitimacy. Social-Keynesian liberals hope to "remedy" this deficiency by sweeping aside the individual owner's lingering legal right (seldom exercised) to control his industrial property and giving control to the government. But this, as Drucker also shows, is just another formula for a totalitarian order, since this centralization would give the State social as well as political power. (The legal owner's continuing appropriation of the financial "return" from industrial property would not in the least embarrass the State's control of property, as Nazism in fact showed.)

To see fully why a union of political and social power must be avoided at all costs, the reader should consult Drucker. For the purposes of this study, it is enough to emphasize that it is because these two "powers" arise from opposite, even antagonistic, principles, and can unite only when one is destroyed. Political power arises from the legitimate threat or use of force, while social "power," which is more like *moral* force, arises from the moral authority enjoyed by a social elite freely recognized by society at large as guardian of a culture's moral order. (From the point of view of the State, which is consecrated by myth, the one great drawback of ideology is that it gives a window, however narrow, on society to culture. This window preserves the tension between political and social power, a social reflection of the "spiritual" tension between myth and religion.) These two "powers," then, reflect a dualism between, and social coexistence of, State and culture. (And since liberal society is—as Garry Wills has argued —primarily concerned about institutions and structures, the dualism between State and culture becomes in liberal society a dualism between "Church" and State. Which is not to suggest that social elites are "religious"; they are composed out of the "socially constitutive" sphere of culture, but religion plays an important role in determining this sphere.)

Political and social power normally coexist in uneasy alliance, but social power seldom, if ever, needs to resort to force and combines with political power only when the latter (as in the eighteenth-century "Enlightened Despotisms") takes its place. The State will rationalize its new social power by a charade of moral legitimacy, while becoming in fact a totalitarian monolith. But when government tries to usurp the social functions proper to a social elite it causes a crisis of its own moral legitimacy and must either manufacture a new "official" morality to justify its social power or adopt a program of universal psychiatric adjustment, so as to dispense with morality altogether. It will claim to be only filling a vacuum left by the "failure" of the elites, but will not acknowledge its own role in dispersing them.

The social elite in Capitalist society was the business elite composed mostly of large-scale entrepreneurs. We can quibble about its merits, but the point is that society recognized its guardianship of a moral order based on property rights, established as the principles of social legitimacy when the culture appointed economics as "socially constitutive." It is true that economics then *seemed* to be constitutive not because of mere cultural considerations but by the very laws of nature itself; this is at least partly true of all social organizers. That is why the very gratification of needs, with which economics apparently by definition dealt, could seem to *constitute* moral legitimacy. There was nothing especially objectionable in all this. The problem is that the totalist "self-balancing" system became a *replacement* for the culture, so that the proviso for property rights became for many less a positive moral injunction than simply a negative rubric for keeping the early Mercantilist State (still controlled by old medieval *power* elites) out of the "autonomous" emerging system whose new social centrality was being used to bring the old power elites down.

When Capitalism began to exclude the culture from which the moral order arose on which the very justification of property rights had been constructed, the links between the "system" and moral legitimacy began to disappear, and property rights were, because of the inadequate way they had been formulated, swept away along with the social elite assigned to guard them. The way was then clear for the State both to attempt to balance the system and to usurp social power in order to do so. No longer was the State merely protecting property rights (its main social function); it was ultimately controlling property itself.

To many liberals this no longer presented any moral problem, because they had acquired for themselves the power of the old power elites they had evicted. When, with the repudiation of culture, property rights became not just vulnerable, but even difficult to comprehend, the liberals began to exploit the dimly remembered communal dimension in economics to justify the State's latter-day grab for control of industrial property, ostensibly in order to "protect" the individual. Yet only with respect to or by benefit of culture, where force has little if any place, has property any workable communal dimension; with respect to the State, property should be well-posted with "no trespassing" signs. (The State's only concern with property is to protect the rights to it.) If and when economics should cease to be socially constitutive, the formal difference between gratification and legitimacy will reappear, but if no culture survives, moral legitimacy and property rights will have to disappear too.

In fact, both moral legitimacy and property rights appear to be disappearing already. Our present economy is described as a massive, organizational, pressure-group economy, from which the "individual" has disappeared as a detectable force, as numberless organized special-interest groups compete for preferential benefits and protection by government. This pressure-group economy breeds inflation (by replacing productivity with influence as the source of rewards) and skews the way income is distributed, the organized groups gaining the greatest rewards. And that all this is accomplished mainly through the political, and not the economic, process leads many to think that even economics is really a political function. Such notions prepare the way for a totalitarian order, yet any remedy for problems like these must curb the power of the special-interest groups and remove their corrupting influence on government.

A good illustration of the nature of the problem is found in the growing difficulty of resolving apparently conflicting rights. For example, many communities are now trying to check their growth by preventing people from settling in them. This policy threatens the citizen's right to live where he wants. Because the more local the level at which the restrictions are drawn, the narrower the interests they serve, it has been suggested that the central government should acquire a land-use authority imposable on the states. Yet it is by no means clear that the citizens' interests will be served in this way, for the government will acquire still more power over the citizens' lives. In reality, part of this problem is definitely cultural; the chaotic nature of the growth this century has seen was due largely to the breakdown of cultural controls over economics and the unleashing of merely financial exploitation: Capitalist growth has tended to be culturally parasitic. A reviving culture could by itself resolve many of the problems, composing the differences between "interests" in the service of shared ideals. It is precisely the business of a culture to mediate between conflicting claims of a collectivity and the individual, to make the one the place where the other finds its fulfillment. Once a culture achieves a balance in society, the State can help creatively to give it concrete form, but the State cannot by itself perform the balancing function without becoming totalitarian.

Modern Liberalism has rested on the fundamental proposition that everyone should pursue his own meaning. But no meaning is anything but social. The devaluation of social meaning only cleared the way for Capitalism's chaotic and parasitic growth, for which the State is now being advanced as the solution. But the State can only further imperil any rights or autonomy the "individual" still effectively retains. The State may, of course, choose to "respect" certain individual rights, but no counterbalancing power will be able to compel it to respect rights it chooses (for the most urgent reasons, of course) not to recognize. The provision for the individual person's right to pursue his own meaning is only a prohibition—certainly in itself a consummation long devoutly wished—on external force. But how in fact *does* an "individual" pursue and appropriate meaning? In communion with others. Yet the structures that were supposedly protecting the individual's "rights" became power structures themselves and now propose to protect the "individual" by effectively eliminating his personality. Its systematic atomization that made Capitalism a totalist system ruthlessly subordinating every cultural question and every participant to its own reification. Thus, modern Liberalism may be only a halfway house on a circuitous route to totalitarian "order."

The expression in the social order of Western cultural ideals, original Liberalism—in Magna Carta and the medieval communal and constitutional movement—had held freedom as its first concern. (As Drucker remarks, real Christianity must—and perhaps only Christianity will or can—make freedom a central concern, for only it holds that no man is perfect, thus no one has any intrinsic right to rule, but that all must seek perfection, thus everyone must be free.) But the churches' resort to power in the religious wars radicalized the Enlightenment rationalists and separated Liberalism from its sources. Thus appeared in the seventeenth century, as the rationalists secularized the cultural ideals, what would remain the basic inspiration of Western society for the next two hundred years —the liberal *ideology*, a confluence of the medieval tradition of political liberties with the Enlightenment's new secularized version of the Christian ideal of spiritual freedom—and from the beginning of this period Liberalism became ambivalent, divided between its religious origins and its newer rationalist orientation. In the age of politics, Liberalism would become primarily a political movement, as in the age of economics primarily economic. Its political period featured a struggle of the State with the "Church," which by then had long been a power structure easily amenable to classification as a political entity almost competitive with the State. But the espousal of Liberalism's own values by a Church *power* structure did not help the Church—only compromised Liberalism's old religious orientation. So the rationalist liberals identified instead with the State, and concocted their "Enlightened Despotisms," which soon were sweeping all before them, until the *socially* counter-revolutionary American political revolution against this absolutist liberalism rolled back the tide. Rationalist Liberalism then almost discredited itself by sponsoring the Jacobin and Marxist revolutions, but the healthier form of religious Liberalism had also lost its rooting in any integral culture and could no longer re-create any society's organic cohesion once wrecked; it could have creative effect only in places where the commitment to personal freedoms persisted through all periods. When the rationalist total system became socially aggressive under the Keynesian theory and the State finally acquired the balancing function from culture in economics-constituted Western society, the rationalist side eventually won even in the main tradition the victory denied it earlier by the American Revolution, and today, "liberal" and "conservative" signify merely degrees of support for State interventions in the individualist and rationalist economic total system.

When the Enlightenment turned against it, religion adopted reactionary social ideals, hoping to stop the clock. Thus, the Catholic Church in the nineteenth century reaffirmed its support of the moribund monarchies that knew they would need "religion" to validate the old status quo and their own return to power. As a result, the anticlerical rationalism of the late Enlightenment began crystallizing in the early nineteenth century into a new *programmatic* political and economic Liberalism and socialism, of which the first forms were forged by the French liberals who opposed Napoleon and by Gladstone,[16] and the Enlightenment "intellectual" hostility to religion as "superstition" from the era of the liberal ideology crystallized into a more tangible "separation of Church and State." The rationalists' justified grievance against the Church's pointless power politics had confirmed the liberals in the Enlightenment mistake of writing religion off as a creative cultural force, and just as the Protestants had long ago appropriated Augustine's apocalyptic biblical imagery of "two cities" and used it to send the Catholics off to join the forces of Antichrist, the liberals now dispatched the Protestants to join the Catholics and transformed the ancient polarity so that liberals represented social good, and aristocrats and churches social evil.

Liberalism's matricidal attitude toward its own sources is the reason for much that otherwise would be inexplicable: the disdain for philosophy and exclusive reliance on "pragmatic" adjustments and improvisations; the reliance on the State as the basic social and cultural institution; Liberalism's alienation from the masses it pretends to serve, and most especially from the "conservative" elements who are classically liberal in their beliefs about economics but cling to their religious identities; and the ten thousand liberal professors waiting in the wings behind their prophets Galbraith and Skinner for the call to power, after which they can inflict their nostrums on a distracted and demoralized public.

Liberals can regard the social order today as basically satisfactory (does it not deliver social influence and most often also political power to them?) and virtually identical with the culture only because hardly any culture any longer remains. Even the evaporation of many art forms as living traditions causes no real alarm as a symptom of cultural collapse, for the very evaporation of the culture only lends plausibility to the identification of the social and cultural orders. And though the only coherent oracles that artists seem to deliver anymore appear to be savage repudiations of the society over which atomizing Liberalism presides, the very compartmentalization of the ("structuralist") liberal world makes art merely the atomized "individual's" own self-assertion, the artist's anguish merely a sign of his noble reluctance to conform, his oracles another excuse for extending liberal control so as to "solve" the social "problems" that presumably cause all the *angst*. Liberalism's strategy for retaining power is (1) to maintain the totalist (physical) economic system in place of the sadly deteriorated culture, while (2) justifying the dominance of the State over the culture and hopefully of the liberal over the State by the need to "balance" the economy, and (3) confining religion to a marginal social role by means of a doctrine of "absolute separation" applied in any area the liberal State finds convenient. The political polarity between "Church" and "State," a mere caricature of the correct distinction between sacral and secular functions, accomplishes the eclipse of cultural groups catalyzed by religion and their eventual replacement by the encroaching "system." Meanwhile, the liberal suspicion of religion leaves the people prey to the exploitative religiosity of the likes of Richard Nixon and inspires them to resist any proposed changes because they sense (usually correctly) that these changes will lead ever further from all the values the liberals profess. The liberals are beginning to claim now that the old market mechanism (interesting word, "mechanism") has become inadequate as a social equilibrator, and that the real focus of balance now is the State. But the hypothetical social function of the market "mechanism" always was a fiction, and the focus of equilibrium never was in the market (which at best coordinated only the economic order) but in the culture Capitalist society exploited, and the new "social Keynesianism" down the road, which hopes to correct the imbalances caused by the old liberal view, can only be totalitarian in principle and entirely wreck any culture that survives. But by then even Liberalism will have disappeared down the maw of its own creations.

Liberals must permit religion to go about its business. This does not entail turning the social order back to religious fanaticism. Instead, the true primary groups must be allowed to create a true culture that could protect the atomized "individual" from the tyranny of totalist systems. This need becomes ever more urgent as the accumulations of computerized data by impersonal State and other organizations increase: Atomized "individuals" have no more defense against these faceless monoliths than Cro-Magnon man had against the dinosaur. Man cannot survive except in the group, and that it is regarded as a mere encumbrance only shows how little the modern liberal understands that his own fulfillment depends on mutuality with others in trust and love rather than on the exploitation of "material interests" in the human jungle he has conjured up.

It is true, of course, that religion has often been party to terrible injustices. But the fanaticisms that have become attached to religion have usually done so only after secular interests seeking to energize their own causes have adopted disputed theological points in order to exploit the confusion of motives among the conventionally pious. It is for this reason that a distinction between sacral and secular functions has been urgently needed ever since the Middle Ages. Even the churches have not made this distinction well. But we need no distinction that sees "sacral" as meaning "private," "secular" as meaning "public," and "public" as equivalent to "civic," distinctions that consign religion to the closet. Some sacral functions are, or should be, extremely public, impinging on activities the State may happen to be conducting, threatening what the liberals call "entanglement"—i.e., the State's even putative cultural primacy. In order to fight the fires of religious tyranny, the liberals have fanned the flames of State ambitions. But every State is rooted in force, however rightly it may seek to wrap itself in principle, and no State can always afford to be more virtuous than its most unscrupulous rival, because for the State as such no consideration comes before its own survival. In itself, the State is nothing but a cause of corruption, and compromises made merely for the sake of possessing it, it might be added, are more likely to be corrupting than redeeming. (This is what Robert Payne, Hitler's biographer, meant when he wrote: "To enjoy power is to be damned. . . . It is a law of nature that a man in power will use it to his own advantage." This law applies no less to liberal "public servants" than to Hitler.) Any positive value that accrues to a State arises from its role as the visible sign of the least common denominator of a nation's *prior* unity; only insofar as people are already united does the State acquire its borrowed majesty, which it well knows how to exploit. The State cannot unite, but can only make uniform, and has no intrinsic moral or cultural value at all.

This emphasis on groups would not now pose as great a threat to public order, "individual rights," or the smooth functioning of the social machine as the liberals might imagine. The group is valuable not for its coercive aspects (which can be meliorated by civil society's protection of individual rights), but for the opportunities it affords for direct interpersonal relations, for the defining of the self holistically in terms of the global needs and gratifications of an integral social unit, rather than of the vastly specialized bureaucracies which by their very fragmentation of human social reality succeed in eliminating the personal as such from social contemplation. The secularized bureaucracies would be acceptable were they not essentially the servants of a totalist social system for which the personal as such is a positive threat. The emphasis on groups would replace this structure of denatured abstractions dominating society as the person's primary reference with a true human community with rights prior to the abstract "society" of mere bureaucracies trying to reduce man to a machine. The real problem is that not many real groups any longer exist. The abstract society has succeeded in splintering and atomizing any groups and reducing their members to dehumanized functionaries of a subhuman system. We recognize the group in order to save it from extinction along with the true wholeness of human personality itself. We are not "unleashing" the groups on the "individual"— rather, by also preserving the provisions for civil rights, we strip the groups of their coercive power over nonmembers and even members who do not wish to conform to all the group's standards. We are only acknowledging the group's basic right to exist and its *cultural* primacy over the civic order. Recognizing the group's cultural primacy does not dispense the group, which must live in tension in society with other groups, from trying to find common ground with other groups, as meanwhile civil society provides the structures within which their common life proceeds.

All this is a way of saying that modern industrial society's *structural* and *functional* integration by bureaucracies, replacing a cultural integration by meaning, is neither necessary nor desirable. The resort to mere functional integration resulted from the growing cultural pluralism of modern society, which in turn resulted from the imposition of cultural meaning by way of force—or, rather, from the rebellion against such force. But still, the integration of society on the level of meaning, not mere function, that is, the integration of society by the fusion of its objective and subjective dimensions rather than merely by the exclusion of the subjective, remains the ideal and optimal, the *human* integration. As we saw before, the reason why liberals tried to do away with the group as a social force was that they wanted to relegate the problem of meaning (and the conflicts it caused) to secondary importance. They accomplished this by exalting as the social "bond" the social creativity of material interests. They had to rid themselves of meaning systems as the bond of unity (thereby isolating religion's power structures) in order to legitimize a totalist system in economics. But actually they did not so much do away with meaning systems as take their own meaning wholly for granted, and when *their* ideological meaning system began to disintegrate society was exposed to the imminent danger of total reification. The social value of the group lies in what constitutes it *as* a group: its shared meaning system. This is the fundamental constituent of any *human* society.

Among religions themselves, all this presents a problem mostly for the Catholic Church—and not because Protestantism has no instinct for power, but because the Catholic power structure is the largest obstacle to religious unity and the recognition of religion's proper cultural role. This is not a challenge, though, to the Church's spiritual authority, which has no more intrinsic relation to power than morality has to social order. Any authority the

Church has is spiritual, not secular; the keys Peter received were to the Kingdom of Heaven, not of earth. This authority should be exercised not as power but as service, and on the matters to which it applies—matters of faith, not "discipline," in a community of love whose members have united by choice, not compulsion. Religion's cultural role is to form a true community, but the Catholic Church sees its institutional concern as preserving "the unity of faith." But from what does this unity arise? The focal element in the Catholic Church is the Eucharist, not the Creed. If unity had to be seen as arising from conformity to a verbal formulation of belief it would be totalitarian or impossible: The smallest point of doctrine can be construed in many ways, and language itself keeps changing in a slippery fashion. But the Eucharist is a concrete event, the literal meaning of which is understandable by all, and anyone who can believe in it should have little trouble with the rest. With respect to the Eucharist, the unity of faith is like a result. Certainly a religious community would seem to benefit from some recognized authority able to clarify theological issues and pronounce on them definitively, exerting a centripetal force, but if it sees its role as enforcing conformity it becomes just another secular power and an active principle of exclusion rather than inclusion. There is every reason to seek the whole truth, but just as much reason to acknowledge any part wherever found, and any enduring community has probably found a good deal.

(In fact, that the Eucharist, not the Creed, makes a congregation potentially a seed for a whole new cultural order is what accounts for both the similarities and the differences between the Classical Greek and the medieval cultural integrations. As H.D.F. Kitto has written, the Greek synthesis was achieved by a *personal* community, the *polis*, that passionately resisted its own conversion into a mere abstract organization concerned mostly with power. It is because the Greek synthesis permitted in *public* life the widest possible range of *personal* capacities that the citizen was as absorbed in his now-classical drama as is the American citizen today in football; drama was the only concrete event that could encompass the full range of the Greek's actual public life, whereas for us there is no public life outside the marketplace, except for the periodic convulsions of national elections. [Society perpetually seeks dramatic focus for its life and, if it cannot have actual drama, liturgical or otherwise, settles for something less, even much less.] But if only because it depends on the rarest possible balance and restraint in the political forces acting upon it from without, a cultural synthesis like that of the Greeks must be extremely rare. This synthesis was "horizontal," while the medieval was "vertical." No society could be more repulsively narrow than that of the Germanic tribes among which Western Christianity took root, but what they lacked in breadth they soon gained in depth as the Eucharistic meal brought an integrating intensity that radiated out and generated an integration fully as impressive in its way as the Greek. The desire that moved the Greeks to make social life primarily a personal and not a delegated activity is necessary to any integration, for in any integration the emphasis is on the personal.)

One would not suggest, even if many would like to believe, that those who presided over the institutional Church's transformation into power were knaves or fools. It is not just that a Church, without its own power structures and proclaiming a Gospel in which the seen world is subject to an unseen world, will soon be in hot water with secular interests. Power was not even much regarded as a problem in the medieval Church, because, as Dunne shows, the mediation of God into social life by the "lords spiritual" and the "lords temporal" was so humanly satisfying that the medieval period regarded the possibility of any contradiction in the Church's identification with the established order as almost a negligible consideration. And perhaps until we at least sense why they felt this way we will never solve our own problems, for the abolition of this mediation, of the lords spiritual in the Reformation, and of the lords temporal in the French Revolution, created the structure of modern spiritual anxiety. A better solution for Church and feudal power than trying to get rid of the Church and of all elites —there is nothing wrong with elites or with a Church mediating between a person and God—would have been to strip the Church of power, thus to check the *State* by a new revival of culture. The Church only goaded the State on by becoming itself an obstacle to the cultural process, casting its lot with the aristocracy and making itself a prime enforcer of established class distinctions and power structures, so that while its saints were seeking social integration it was institutionally supporting a stratification based on mere power. So Liberalism stripped the Church not only of its power but also of its cultural function. Dispensing also with elites, it gave the world modern "egalitarian" social utilitarianism, which no longer recognized any *intrinsic* dignity in the person. But in its own new concentration on results, modern Liberalism suffered from what Gouldner calls a "built-in disposition to amoral normlessness" and anomie, all disguised by a lingering theory of natural rights and a vestigial morality unanchored in the social order.

Well, then, if religion recovered its old cultural role, would it not resurrect old conflicts arising from disagreements in perceptions of the ultimate truth? Not if force were recognized as functionally incompatible with the pursuit of truth. And surely it *is* clear now that no worthy purpose is served by using secular power to enforce religious doctrine, which can acquire any real relation to power only through myth, itself an alternative to religion. But it is the pursuit of the *common* truth that gives society whatever harmony it has, and banishing this search from the public consciousness is no corrective to religious power if it merely clears the way for the State. Let the State be forced to concede that the active appropriation of the truth in common is society's principal business; let all groups recognize the urgency of finding shared truths for a common life so that no vacuum is left for the State to fill. But let no group seek to force its vision upon others. The plurality of "ultimate" beliefs in society may seem less than an ideal to any sect, but this should be a spur to the search for deeper common ground. On the other hand, pluralism is only a political ideal, a remedy precisely for intergroup conflict that has no positive *cultural* value at all, and when the State proclaims the priority of its pluralist politics over the cultural process itself, it is only creating a device for keeping conveniently divided the groups that might offer the State some resistance. If groups cannot be free to take up their cultural function, no truly shared public morality that could sustain even an adequate State is possible. Only if the collectivity of the State were regarded as more basic to society than the cultural community would religion have to try to control the State again, or perish. *Is* the life of the State, though, which Hobbes was pleased to call the "mortal god," autonomous or derivative? If derivative, can it possibly be the primary community even for "citizens," rather than merely the arena in which the primary groups interact through the personal consciences of their members? This cultural primacy of groups poses no threat to the State, if care is taken to protect from secularization, and struggles for power, those "ultimate concerns" in which far more ground for real community can be found than in the "material interests" exclusively recognized by the present-day State. Religion, not the State, has primacy in the culture; the citizen, not churches, has primacy in the State. The line between the State and culture is that between sacral and secular *functions*.

Just as this does not mean that groups will have to fight for control of society, neither does it mean that the State will again have to try to impose "moral order." Culture itself constitutes all the "moral order" a society needs, and culture should have no use for force. The law's direct concern with morality is only in imposing the moral principles that constitute the State's own foundations. The crucial problem is to give scope to the cultural process where it is entitled to have it—primarily in the sacral functions with which the State has no legitimate business even when these functions are voluntarily surrendered to it. Nor will all this make second-class citizens out of "unbelievers," who often seem to believe more than believers in the essence of what the latter supposedly believe anyway. The criterion of belief is irrelevant to the notion of citizenship. But denial of religion's cultural function *does* deny first-class citizenship to believers: The State can challenge the Church; the Church has no ground on which to challenge the State. Only insofar as sacral and secular functions are exercised by *institutions* should they be separated, so that the Church exercises only the former and the State the latter and only the latter.

But the Catholic Church, like the liberal order, has a better idea. Of course, as the Pope says, the Church is no democracy. But that is because it is not a *political* structure at all. And so neither is it a Renaissance court. The desire for democracy in the Church is only part of a longing to abolish Church power. And if the Church can model itself on a Renaissance court, it can also model itself on a modern democracy. Why does it not? A peek under the table shows the reason: a little game of footsie is in progress. The Church abandons to the secular order the exploitation of the erotic, while itself exploiting the spiritual abandoned by the secular, and the two powers find convenient common ground in economics: As Peter Berger has shown in *The Sacred Canopy*, even religion in this century has become an economic marketing operation. Who needs democracy?

What is there to choose between liberal Capitalism and Communism? For a while Capitalism may allow some room for "freedom" and initiative in economics, but in its liberal social-utilitarian matrix, which requires men to be "useful" and implicitly denies the social relevance of either immaterial realities or the exigencies of mere philosophy, it is as thoroughly materialistic as Communism, and leads as certainly to a totalitarian order. Communism postulates material factors as ultimate and primary, but this postulation itself is philosophical, and as such leaves as much room for something outside economics as does a Capitalism that sees the spiritual as mere "private" ideals. As Heilbroner wrote, contemplating Capitalism's readiness to oppose at any cost any evil supposedly caused by Communists, and its nearly total indifference to all other varieties of misfortune, Communism is opposed mostly because it demonstrates an economic alternative to Capitalism and therefore seems a threat to the status quo.

Any person who wants to be whole and free anymore has nowhere to turn. He can either surrender to the liberals or become a fugitive, hightailing it to whatever hills the "system" has not yet posted with its own "no trespassing" signs.

But modern society might find a parable in the fate of Carthage, its spiritual ancestor, which also cared for nothing but money. Fate bestowed on that ancient city a rare prize, a great genius whose father swore him at the altar to the Carthaginian cause against Rome. But the commercial Carthaginians were disgruntled by his strange urgencies, and as soon as they thought the immediate dangers past, they cut off the support they had only grudgingly supplied. Hannibal fought on brilliantly for a while beneath the very gates of Rome, but at length succumbed. Then Scipio took his Roman army to Carthage and left not a stone upon a stone. For Hannibal read "man's spiritual nature," or even "religion"; for Rome—well, Rome.

APPENDIX:
WESTERN CULTURE AND WESTERN MUSIC

Some readers may wonder whether Western music really fits into the theory of Western culture elaborated in the first chapter. For one thing, Western music seemed to flower most luxuriantly a good deal later than other types of Western art, and this would seem difficult for the theory to explain, for the flowering would have occurred when other forms of art were, according to the theory, in decline. If culture is a unitary (although not monolithic) thing, as the theory holds, how could this be possible? The explanation suggested here is not incorporated into the body of the theory because there is no way to verify it without technical expertise in music. One must rely on what one hopes is sympathetic understanding. But it may be important that some account of music could be given within the terms of the theory.

Why did Western music reach its apogee so late, compared to other forms of art? Partly, it was because the technical means had to be developed slowly—musical theory and musical instruments, the latter in their full variety and technological refinement. In contrast, theater and poetry could develop on a much simpler technological base. Partly also, perhaps, it was because the desire for great music was not as strong in earlier periods as it later became; the early culture was emotionally rich and polymorphous and gave emotional fulfillment in ways other than music. But as the verbal media became constricted by ideological conflicts, the pressures on music grew, just as its technical resources were providing the means to satisfy the demand. Not that earlier music did not remain in some ways unsurpassed, especially in its emotional purity. But it never achieved the almost cosmological completeness that Mozart and Beethoven achieved with an almost comparable integration. For while artists in other media were projecting a growing inner split, the worlds projected in Mozart's and Beethoven's music remained integrated and whole, even though their lives exhibited a sort of split (that sometimes did appear, as in *Don Giovanni*). This tells us that the human personality still had control of itself, if not of its environment.

In music, as in life, the artist struggles to objectify himself in his medium, which resists him but also offers the opportunity to make himself present to himself as he imposes himself on it. The scope of his opportunity is determined by the technical resources he inherits from his predecessors. Now, there was no possibility of a full personal objectification in music until these resources had been developed sufficiently in the direction of a perfectly formal, or formally perfect, art; until that time, all music would be, even though at times exceedingly personal in particular mannerisms such as we find in any composer's work, generally impersonal by reason of its impersonal conventional structures. All composers would be expressing emotion through a conventionalized form (constantly evolving) to which, however superbly an artist, such as Bach, might manipulate it, the strictly personal or individualized elements would be subordinated or secondary. For example, Bach's most impressive achievements would be expressions not of his personal religious emotion, but of religious emotion as such, emotion that might be common to all, and his greatness lay in expressing this better than anyone else. Composers were still pushing into the *structural* possibilities, pushing, as it were, to make form an adequate vehicle for an entire life experience, and to develop the skills and consciousness by which music could actually be made to express such experience.

The purely formal reached its perfection of range, balance and flexibility in Mozart. There was no further to go in this direction. Mozart's music, it has been said, has the quality of crystal, of a perfect summer's day, the formal and the personal achieving a complete symbiosis. Not until this had been done could a Beethoven be possible. In Beethoven, the formal seems almost to disappear, because our attention shifts to the personal. For form presented itself to Beethoven as a three-dimensional volume. By using or rejecting (or violating) the established formal devices and structures he achieves a double (three-dimensional) perspective suggesting a personal experience within the general experience. Gamboling off in violation of the rules, he achieves not meaninglessness, but a suggestion of the uniqueness of his individuality, and this affirmation is then corroborated by his measuring up after all to the exigencies of the formal rules. Simultaneously departing from one rule and observing another, he achieves a new three-dimensional effect; earlier composers had not so much violated the rules in order to express new emotion as extend them. Before Beethoven the rules had not been well enough developed, the possibility of expressing within them a whole personal life experience enough advanced, to endow departures from them with any cosmic or universalized resonance, or to make such departure an affirmation of individuality as such. For the first time, music presented to Beethoven a receding volume or space which his personality could fill without meeting some limiting boundary. Technical innovation continued after Beethoven, but did not develop *as a whole*. Efforts went to enlarging this or that specific possibility, and the danger was that the personality not able to fill the vertiginous new volume as Beethoven's had would turn away from the whole to fuss with some particular technical possibility or, facing the whole as such, would lose its integration, balance and force in face of it.

Within the new volume, Beethoven seems to have achieved as perfect an integration as Mozart. He repeatedly seemed about to lose his balance but never did. For he never bogged down, like later composers, in *merely* personal emotional quandaries. His major works achieve as complete an objectification of emotion into art as any work by Mozart. All this gives his music a miraculous quality; perhaps more than any other composer he suggests God's own freedom and power, his works generally obeying the rules but departing from them in a perpetually fresh and uncannily personal way. Perhaps not only the high point, but also the turning point, of both Western music and Western culture is Beethoven's Fifth Symphony, the most concentrated musical expression ever conceived. In the first movement we have, as it were, the objective, universal, or common aspect of the tragic emotion; in the next two movements we seem to have the subjective aspect of the emotion, how it impacts on Beethoven's consciousness. The possibility of realizing the subjective in art depends on the possibility of the objective, and in Beethoven for the first time can the two be separated, because for the first time the purely personal and subjective has full, free scope within the medium. Beethoven could not fully have objectified the tragic emotion unless his own personality could have had full release in the music, nor could the impact of the tragedy on him find expression unless he could fully objectify what caused it. The subjective and objective aspects were mutually intrinsic, two aspects of one reality, and could not have emerged separately. But having objectified them separately in art, Beethoven could then resolve them. His act of aesthetic assimilation enables him to transcend the tragedy, and not only survive it but make it the foil of his own self-affirmation. Perhaps it is not entirely fanciful to speculate that, basically, the tragedy was his culture. It was not the loss of his hearing any more than for Ahab it was the loss of his leg. The latter could have been prevented by safer conditions in the whaling industry, the former by a faster development of medical science; in each case the tragedy becomes almost adventitious.

In any case, the Seventh Symphony is, in relation to the Fifth, perhaps the most tangible intimation of our own personal immortality, although perhaps we would have to sense the inner nature of Western culture to feel this. Beethoven not only survives whatever caused the ordeal expressed in the Fifth, but emerges whole and unimpaired, still creating with a freedom and power even he cannot understand (he thinks his Eighth is better than the Seventh). The experience of death, of helpless vulnerability in the Fifth, remains embedded like primeval rock in the second movement of the Seventh, and possibly even becomes the cause of new creative power. Death does not really kill, it does not really win. From now on Beethoven penetrates deeper into his experience, but its configuration never basically changes. The heartbreaking sadness notwithstanding, it retains the most joyful and creative exuberance.

There seems to be only one negative element in Beethoven—he rarely seems to rise above the struggle, and then only briefly. Probably this is what Shaw meant when he wrote that Mozart seemed to dwell on Olympus, but Beethoven, when he got there, became drunk. If there is a flaw in Mozart, it is his apparent complete impersonality, his personality having become fused with his wonderfully flexible form. He seems to invest his music with purely personal content only with great difficulty (except in his last symphonies). Perhaps this is only a way of speaking; it may mean little more than that neither Mozart nor Beethoven possessed self-contradictory musical gifts. But there seems to be something objective here, too; to some degree, music for Mozart was also an escape from life. For Beethoven it was not completely a solution. It is as if they stood on opposite sides of a summit.

Beethoven's Fifth Symphony is the most immediate and convincing affirmation of Western man's superiority over "fate"—whatever aspect (death, culture, misfortune, etc.) this might wear. Because music is the most immediate personal expression, and also the most dependent on technology, the Fifth represents the culture's supreme effort to integrate before the split in the culture finally takes over completely (and brings the liberals in). What the culture repeatedly had done in other ways, it now did in the supremely difficult mode of music. This might even be viewed as the ultimate vindication of the medieval cultural synthesis, in that without this vindication the synthesis could have lost much of its historic significance as a benchmark. But from then on, Western culture could no longer bring object and subject together. Already having been, for hundreds of years, more or less unable to bring them together in thought, it has become unable to do so in the inner reaches of emotion and affectivity. But it did so once, in Beethoven, and Western culture thereby proclaimed its creative power, to which Beethoven's music is testimony that can never die.

After that, it gradually became almost impossible for composers to reconcile or integrate the objective and subjective. They tended to focus on mere moods (Chopin), or, when attempting to be more "cosmic," artificially and self-consciously mixed objective and subjective. On the other hand, a growing technical individualism became content to abolish rules rather than to use them creatively. Music became more idiosyncratic. This need not be a personal judgment on later composers, whose music has its own beauty and is no less intriguing than Beethoven's within its narrower range, especially when compared with our music—which also, in its own way, may be as great as Beethoven's achievement, in that the culture has almost evaporated. But no composers fill, because they cannot, the space that Beethoven filled in music (and Dante filled in poetry). It is not just that they lack the "talent"; the culture will not afford any composer the inner scope to challenge Beethoven's objective achievement, however great any later composer's (Bernstein's?) native "talent" may be. After Beethoven, there are no more Ahabs in music (just as there are no more in literature after Ahab), no one who overcomes "fate." No exception for Wagner; he achieves scope by substituting fantasy for the reality principle, so that tensions are eliminated by eliminating those aspects of the personality not expressed in the fantasy. Reacting, like Nietzsche and Rilke, against the "slave mentality" of pseudo-Christian culture, he succumbs to the Romantic tendency to mistake escapism for wholeness. In any case, he chickened out in the end and ignominiously reverted to a pious Christianism, repudiating earlier themes embodied in *Tristan*. Artists became focused on their personal quandaries, more and more tempted by self-pity, trying to resist it but increasingly constrained by it, driven into a "neutral" middle ground of mechanical innovation expressing at last an unintelligible, if not wholly marginal, emotional mush. No recent composer, with the possible exception of Mahler or Gershwin, enjoys anything like the popularity that Beethoven enjoyed in Vienna. People do not reject modern music only because it is difficult, but because it is so overwhelmingly idiosyncratic, so emotionally homogenous.

Although there is something artificial in a facile distinction between objective and subjective, it gets at something real. "Objectivity" in art is the projection into art of the impact upon oneself of an experience with some more than subjective cause. Only a perfect such projection can also objectify the subjective aspects of the experience without distorting it or causing one to lose one's balance. The two aspects are mutually intrinsic, two aspects of one whole. Where one is overt, the other is always latent; it is not possible, for example, to project the subjective without being objective about it, or to give the objective any meaningful reso-nance without being subjective about it.

Finally, is there a contradiction in suggesting both that there was a persistent decline in the emotional purity and power in Western music, and that this music reaches its apogee in Beethoven? No. The purity and power were at first more a reflection of culture than of any composer's personal life as such. The culture was (com-pared to ours) so well integrated, so harmonious, that these quali-ties suffused the music almost involuntarily. Vivaldi's sweetness and charm were reflections mainly of his culture; music simply did not express personal experience *as personal*. In Beethoven's art it did this for the first time. Whatever direct sense of the culture Beethoven's music projects, however, appears more in the new sense of conflict and strife, the tragic aspect (which had been largely sublimated in Mozart). Beethoven's own personality fully affirms itself in the music *against* a highly problematic and con-flicted culture that soon would make any new such self-affirmations impossible, at least to the same degree.

FOOTNOTES

¹ John S. Dunne, *The City of the Gods* (New York: The Macmillan Com-pany, 1965); see also his *The Way of All the Earth* (New York: The Mac-millan Company, 1972).

² Lewis Mumford, *The Pentagon of Power* (New York: Harcourt, Brace, Jovanovich, 1970).

³ Karl Barth, *Protestant Thought from Rousseau to Ritschl* (New York: Harper, 1959), Chapter 1.

⁴ Johan Huizinga, *Men and Ideas* (New York: Meridian Books, 1959), p. 179.

⁵ Denis de Rougemont, *Love in the Western World* (New York: Harper & Row, 1974).

⁶ Huizinga, *The Waning of the Middle Ages* (London: E. Arnold & Co., 1952).

[7] Erik Erikson, *Young Man Luther* (New York: W. W. Norton & Co., 1958).

[8] Erich Auerbach, *Mimesis* (Garden City, N.Y.: Doubleday Anchor, 1957).

[9] Basil Willey, *The Seventeenth Century Background* (London: Chatto & Windus, 1946).

[10] See "Sociological Positivism," in Alvin W. Gouldner, *The Coming Crisis of Western Sociology* (New York: Avon Books, 1971).

[11] Karl Marx and Friedrich Engels, *The German Ideology* (Moscow, 1964), pp. 91–92.

[12] Marx, "The Eighteenth Brumaire of Louis Napoleon," in *Marx and Engels: Selected Works* (Moscow, 1955), p. 272.

[13] *Ibid.*, p. 273.

[14] See the Appendix on this subject.

[15] See Anton Zijderveld, *The Abstract Society* (New York: Doubleday, 1970; also, Doubleday Anchor, 1971).

[16] See "The Failure of Liberalism," in Christopher Dawson, *Judgment of the Nations* (New York: Sheed & Ward, 1942).

The "Church" and the Liberal State

You have to feel sorry for the liberals. With what they thought were the noblest of motives they rallied to defend the embattled State when they saw a mortal threat forming on its frontiers. Was this a threat to the State, or to liberal control of the State? In any case, loaded with honors, they quite forgot that the impregnable wall they had erected to secure the boundaries of State power would also prevent any maneuver against that wall that was now free to grow from within. Eventually, to oppose that power would mean not only calling in as an ally the barbarian horde on the other side of the wall, but also acknowledging an early miscalculation of where the danger lay.

In fact, the Tartar horde outside has often seemed unnervingly ambiguous. Although its unifying quality is a supposed disposition to value putative "community" over "individual rights," only one element in it has remained stable enough to offer any fixed target for moralizing, and even that now seems to be collapsing: the Catholic Church, whose stability has even earned a certain gratitude, by justifying the liberal strategy. Other churches, though, show disquieting ambivalence, appearing, according to their several inclinations, now on one side of the liberal wall, now on the other.

Sometimes it seems that there is no wall at all, or that it runs right through the middle of the kingdom. We find Protestants on both sides of the wall, because they often tend to be as individualistic as liberals. Jews were not quite as individualistic, but saw good reason to keep all religions on the far side of the liberal wall. Even Communists, in some ways children of Liberalism, often manned the liberal parapets to defend economics' primacy over religion. Only "popery" seemed wholly antagonistic to the structure of the liberal strategy, even though many Catholics endorsed most of Liberalism's more limited aims. And while liberals could contemn Catholicism, they could ignore the war they were losing at home. So now that even the Catholic redoubts seem to be collapsing, liberals search anxiously for signs of life, and sometimes even appear to be grateful that Catholics continue to spar with liberals at what have become the two most important gates in the wall. Still, Catholics perversely continue to insist that it is the liberal State that threatens *them* with extinction, as if *they* were circumscribed by the wall, not the liberals. Liberals are only irritated by the claim that all secular power now rests in the State.

By what right does the State exist? By none. The State does not exist by intrinsic right, but simply by irresistible fact. We casually assume that the State is a "normal" part of human life, but this is true only in the sense that politics are inevitable, but not in the sense that the State's existence is normative—that the State itself is normal. Rather, politics is a fundamentally questionable, even though inevitable, aspect of social life, because it is the sphere where force is brought to bear in human relationships, which "should" be constituted on a basis of mutual trust. Reducing the matter to its simplest terms, culture arises on the human need for mutuality and love, the State on the drive for dominion. The "State" is nothing concrete; its constituent principle is the human heart's desire to control rather than love others. It is to human culture what oil is to water: incompatible.

This is not to suggest that the State is dispensable. It only means that the State is not intrinsically legitimate. Its justification must be conferred by a concrete contingency that calls it forth; no sooner does one man deal with another by force than the necessity of the State arises, that the innocent might be protected. But no sooner, too, does another man acquire even what is called "legitimate" power over others by virtue of the State, than that power tends to become *his* primary objective, and he is tempted to become a manipulator and aggressor, too. The State easily becomes a greater evil than that it was called forth to set right.

The remedy for the intrinsic arbitrariness of the State, its impatience of all restraints, is to compel it to acknowledge its subjection to moral principles embodied in its constitutive charter. Yet this provokes a new problem. It is certain that a State cannot go about its routine business without at least a minimal consensus among its subjects as to its rights and limitations, and as to the social philosophy by which they allow the State to exist and which they oppose to its ever mutinous power. But if this consensus can be presented by the State as a uniformity, and the State can then claim this social philosophy to be also its own, the way is clear for the State to act as spokesman for, and enforcer of, the social philosophy, aggrandizing its own power, as it were, through the back door. Thus, the State will often be found advocating philosophical homogeneity, but this advocacy is aimed not at discovering or preserving the truth, but at smoothing the way for its own power. For this reason there must be ironclad guarantees in the State charter that the State cannot declare the social consensus irrevocably fixed in a particular verbal formulation, nor oppose any person's holding any principles he chooses. What the State can and must oppose are concrete acts violating specific laws emanating from the supposed consensus as expressed in the State charter. A latent conflict between the material exigencies of the State and the imperatives of human conscience remains, but because of the State's nature is irremediable.

The State, as such, never acts for anything but its material interests. It does, of course, recognize moral elements in its evaluation of its situation, but only insofar as these affect its material interests. Most clear-eyed observers have recognized that the State is the greatest of hypocrites in a hypocritical world, trying to dress up its material interests in moral rationale, and to cloak itself in morality in order to achieve a crucial subjective legitimacy with its subjects. And because these subjects can be just as eager for their own material interests (and just as eager to dress the pursuit of them in moral guise), they may be both willing and eager to accept the State's pretensions as sincere. Yet all this does not mean that the State never acts for "idealistic" reasons. The people, precisely in their character as *one* people, can impose moral aims upon the State in spite of the State's intrinsic indifference to them: The people can subordinate even the State to their culture. But the indispensable precondition is a common "moral" consensus. Often, the State's moral aims amount to "enlightened" compromises between immediate material interests and the categorical imperatives of "individual" conscience. An example might be the Marshall Plan, which was pursued, or at least subjectively justified, because it was in the long-term interest first of all of America (which did not want to see Communist States springing up in Europe), not of its beneficiaries. (The Marshall Plan, in fact, may be one of the best genuine examples of "enlightened self-interest," since this famous liberal doctrine probably works best only between States —nexi of power, where any infrequent accommodation of power to moral imperatives is highly to be valued.) But if moral principles are to be imposed on States on anything but an intermittent basis, the culture must remain vital and healthy.

A really basic question, then, is why the individual will favor the State even over his culture. There are two reasons: "concupiscence" and fear. The "individual," as Dostoyevsky wrote, often prefers bread to freedom. He likes his comfort and wants the State to defend it. So he commits himself to the State out of fear of losing both what he has become inordinately attached to

(those goods the possession of which he identifies with life itself)
and the very life he is tempted to cling to no matter what "values"
are violated. Insofar as his "values" become mere clandestine
servants of property and physical survival, rather than interior
responses to "truth," the State appears more valuable to him.

Are all "transcendental" values, then, hollow, and does human
life categorically bring a submission to power? Are all values only
hypocritical rationalizations, and must we at last give up all hypocritical pretense to have any? The answers to these questions will
hinge on our identification of the ultimate good. If this good is to
be found in this life, then there is no value higher than this life, but
if this life is not in itself final, there can be a "higher" value. This
has to mean, though, not only that this life and its goods can be
given up, but that they can be surrendered as the basis of *social*
life to some ultimate principle other than life itself—that some
other ideal can be *normative*, and not just abstractly, as "merely"
an ideal, but as a concrete contingency; that is, life *must* be surrendered under certain conditions. This ultimate ideal need not
mechanically regulate every possible moment, since this life and
its goods are not rendered by it any less desirable, but the ultimate
ideal cannot be allowed to be contradicted by our stronger attachment to life and property. Now, all of this would seem to require
that the "individual" be capable of actually surrendering, or be
willing to surrender, life and property not only when some immediate physical emergency makes the choice unavoidable, however regrettable, but also when no immediate physical crisis is at
hand and the ideal is contradicted in principle by, for example,
some policy of the secular State. How difficult it may be to find
such an ideal is perhaps suggested by the speed with which radicals
make their compromises when apprehended by the State. Their
"cooperation" with what they believe to be a "pig" government
is always rationalized as a strategy for better "helping" the "movement" or "brotherhood" later. There is never any point at which
life and property must be surrendered or put at imminent jeopardy

for the higher ideal, which remains, therefore, merely abstract, just as it is for the liberal whom the radical says has failed.

What could possibly give the individual the necessary determination, resolve, and contempt for the pomp and power of the world? One must confess, at the risk, or rather certainty, of being regarded as a quaint simplist, that one thing that certainly could is the Christian faith. Whether anything else could one does not know. Such a faith, such a wholehearted self-surrender, is what most people need and seek; they settle for security only out of disillusionment or despair. Outside of religion, there is only virtue for its own sake—some form of Shaftesbury's ideal, of which we must be dubious, since it was, as Willey wrote, little more than a device for getting along without Christianity that simply took for granted (as we also do) all the ethical wealth it inherited from the Christian past. Especially since Marx, we must be suspicious of claims, however often repeated, to be acting for "pure" morality for its own sake. Among religions, though, only Christianity seems to exhibit a balanced view of the State: since most Eastern religions tend to deny any autonomous value in the physical world (which, with its States, is for the liberal the only reality), they tend to ignore the State as a moral problem, while Judaism's attitude toward Israel suggests that Judaism envisions no intrinsic conflict between itself and the State (but perhaps only if the State is Jewish).

If, to keep the State in check on the public level, the "individual" has to make a certain contempt for this life and its material goods the ultimate principle of his personal life, such that he will be willing to sacrifice them in service of a higher ideal when that ideal is contradicted, then he has to be willing to base his social life, too, on something other than power, has literally to take some equivalent of the gospel injunctions to forgive his enemies, to turn the other cheek, and not to meet power with power. (Of course, the State can *only* meet power with power; it can do nothing else. We are discussing a principle to keep the State itself as a social power in check.) To the "world," all this is folly, because the "world" sees no higher value than life and the present enjoyment of it (and one of the greatest enjoyments is to wield power). The world cannot understand such a principle until it actually sees it, but this principle is more powerful than any the State can command, because it heaps burning coals on the "enemy's" head and effects mysterious reconciliations. The only true security is to stand naked and defenseless before the world; to find one's life one must "lose" it. (But this must happen on the personal level before it can happen on the public.) This is the ultimate and the only real power. Every other sort beguiles, then betrays, sacrifices everything in the name of which it is pursued. This is the Christian "gamble"—or, rather, the gamble that Christians cannot avoid. Those who will not take it cannot be Christians, and should cease confusing themselves with those who will.

Is power, then, "bad"? "Power" over "Nature"—no!, when used for holistic human ends. "Power" over men? Even this, who knows? Even God has power over men. But God has renounced power in His dealings with men, and appeals to them only through love, and so "should" men. It may not be so much the nature of power that is bad, as the nature of man that makes power bad for him—although what good power might achieve is difficult to see. Categorically, any man who learns to enjoy power has become corrupt. Power over men is at best a relative good, a "negative" good, compared to what it (perhaps) prevents. Power may be inevitable, but it is not a human good.

The early Western State's desire for consensus became an excuse for forcing doctrines upon conscience—the State could make an appearance of virtue out of suppressing dissent. But banishing value questions from public life, as liberals have done, and substituting for earlier meaning systems as social equilibrators physical total systems the State can control, was no solution. The liberals achieved this through their doctrine of "absolute separation" of "Church" and "State," which frames the issue in terms of power—i.e., in the State's terms. Jeffrey Burton Russell has perceptively noted that any distinction between "Church" and "State" would have been useless in the Middle Ages because in any dispute between the secular and sacral powers the majority of bishops was as likely to be found on the secular as on the sacral side. What even Russell may not see is that the distinction is *still* irrelevant, because, though the problem is power, the real issue is secular and sacral *function*. Only by the distinction between functions can the *State* be held in check, and the churches be left free to go about their own business, because this correct distinction also achieves the liberals' legitimate objective of preventing the churches from seeking power and playing the State's game. Today the State usurps even sacral functions while forcing the churches out by accusing them of seeking power when they are found in areas the State covets for itself.

Just as the State in the hierarchical order imposed religious orthodoxy, today it imposes liberal homogeneity. Thus, American liberals smile on religion for others as long as it endorses the liberal status quo, but what they really favor is the civic religion called "Americanism" that gives the processes of political compromise on interests and issues a higher importance than the issues themselves, regarded as "divisive." As the State acquires primacy over culture, all rhetorical values become drained of their real content. The notion of "brotherhood," for example, becomes conveniently abstract and impersonal, no longer requiring any personal sacrifices by those who take so much credit for it (calling themselves "humane and altruistic" while dismissing as "fascist" the middle classes privileged to pay for all the impersonal benevolence—and for liberal careers). Does not a liberal look first to his *own* place in the "system," only then turning to criticize it (superficially) so as to satisfy his "conscience" (become a focus for all sorts of discontents)? Is he not, though, committed first to his own safety and comfort, and only *then* to "social justice," so long as he can control whatever "system" emerges from any adjustments? *He* takes no personal risks that cut to whatever bone remains beneath his fat. He conveniently projects moral challenges onto the "benevolent" government programs the middle classes will pay for. For him, all virtue consists in acknowledging the incrementality of human progress and social liberation. But this becomes an excuse for ridiculing the single eye and the wholehearted self-surrender, which render real religion as suspect as radical politics to the incrementalizing liberal. What liberals admire in radicalism is not its uncompromising wholeheartedness ("fanaticism") but its corrosive skepticism of religious belief. What they accept in religion is its apparent consecration of the status quo. But "structuralist" Liberalism is hostile to the really healthy elements in religion and radical politics alike. Personal concern and engagement have become for "society's" purposes quaint anachronisms, for liberal modern man's whole intention is himself to depend on no one; like Garbo, he wants to be alone. But simply because it *is* abstract, liberal society is atomized, and neither encourages nor even permits real brotherhood, only increasing dependence on impersonal State "benevolence."

This impersonality is "regretted" even by liberals, but regarded as "inevitable," because it arises from the totalist system functionally integrating society as a surrogate for the one-time integration by culture. In addition, it seems vindicated on the theoretical level by the lingering liberal attachment to the Enlightenment notion that the universe is a cosmic clock that human society should imitate by becoming a machine; though the clock metaphor was exploded in science a long time ago by Einstein, its hold on the liberal social "imagination" has, if anything, tightened (how many experts have not lately tried to figure out what has gone wrong with the social "machine"?). Liberals seem incapable of appreciating that the truths of human life and personality have a special quality that the "truths" of science, which satisfy best as pure abstractions, do not share: "Human" truths gain concrete reality for us only as the basis for a common life, because they appeal to, and are assimilated by, not only our intelligence, but also our affectivity and will. The real truths about human life always require a *decision*; they are always two-edged blades. To be appreciated, they must be appropriated. The Enlightenment notwithstanding, truth may, and probably does, have transcendental value, with a primary referent beyond "individual" consciousness alone. As for religion, liberal-type abstraction is its enemy, because a religion that cannot create a culture becomes itself abstract and dead, nipped in the bud and prematurely cut off wherever it might flower into new social forms.

Actually, liberal atomization does not really free the "individual," but only renders him at last completely helpless. For all that can effectively bring people together any longer is their "interests," not their beliefs, and so it is much easier for exploiters to combine for limited objectives (such as profit and power) against the collectivity of individuals than it is for others to combine for whole-istic purposes against the organized exploiters. "Interest groups" tyrannize over atomized "individuals" in a collectivism that is just the other face of the atomization. True cultural groups have two basic functions—one negative, the other positive. Their negative function is to protect the person in his necessary social life from the attacks or claims of special interests serving mainly themselves, even though often (like the State) in the name of all. (A specialized institution can serve only itself if it does not serve common ideals held by all.) Their positive function is to promote humanization through the concrete appropriation of shared meanings and moral ideals.

So one can only suspect that all the artificiality and abstraction must be onerous for even liberals to bear, and in fact there is a deeper, compelling reason for it, not unrelated to those discussed above. This reason is historical experience. As we have already discussed, the Christian religion became the formative principle of Western culture, but also provided much of the metaphysical framework for the medieval myth of hierarchical order. The medieval Church was half conscious of a conflict between its gospel message and the requirements of the myth, but in trying to resist the growing power the myth assigned to the State, the Church became an alternative power apparatus and put itself into conflict with the cultural order it had itself incubated, and over which the new liberal tradition (in turn the culture's creation) watched. The liberal tradition, the culture's organ to give its ideals social effect, was repelled by the Church's recourse to power, and the religious warfare that soon ensued turned the liberal tradition away from religion and caused it to become, during the Enlightenment, on the whole a rationalist movement. Yet a more religious form of Liberalism continued as well within the main Western social tradition.

(It is interesting to note—thanks to Hans Urs von Balthazar for this observation—how the Enlightenment accomplished the dismissal of religion. The early Christian Greek Fathers had sought some way to give Christianity a universal intellectual authority. Their solution was to argue that Christianity was the fulfillment of all other religions, because Christianity completed what in each of them was incomplete. The Enlightenment turned the argument around: Since religion is everywhere found, something could be extracted from all religions—exactly what remained unclear—that could be called "natural religion," with respect to which Christianity was only a variation—indeed, an oddity. Therefore Christianity should look to its own business and cease trying to become universal. Liberalism then applied this idea to society: Which religion might be more correct was no longer an important public issue; presumably all religions had something—God knows what —to recommend them to their votaries. But the normative principle for society now was Reason, and with respect to this the "spiritual"—if it exists, and whether it exists is not socially important—is merely an excrescence. This justified handing the social world over to the rationalist "experts.")

The inner split in the culture caused by the Church's conversion to power infected each successive socially constitutive sphere thrown in to replace religion, and caused similar splits in each in turn. On one side of each split the rationalist, ordering strain would win out; on the other side, where the concern for personal liberty endured, the religious form of Liberalism prevailed. After the theological split, it was always rationalist Liberalism that raised the challenge to the more religiously oriented Liberalism at the core of the main Western social tradition: Rationalism was the galvanizing force behind neo-classicism in art, Enlightened Despotism in the political sphere, and the Communist ideology in economics. However, there remained a great ambivalence within the main tradition itself. For the religious elements in Liberalism were compromised by their association with religious power structures. Thus, the main tradition was heavily pressed by the rationalist strain even from within, and England, no less, almost became an Enlightened Despotism under George III, before the *socially counter*revolutionary American political revolution prevented this by denying George the base of outside power he needed to bring it off.

Though the main social tradition kept faith with individual initiative, and though this was indispensable to maintaining a free society, it did not provide a sufficient principle of social order. Before the Church had become a power structure, society could locate its communal bonds in an apolitical institutional Church, but when this became impossible the rationalist liberals became indispensable even to the main tradition. So there was an uneasy détente in the main tradition, with the religious strain managing to maintain its ascendancy. But as the socially constitutive spheres became increasingly amenable to regimentation, the influence of the rationalist systems grew, and the closer to sociology the West came in its series of organizers, the closer it came to an exclusively material principle of organization. The rationalist strain finally overthrew the religious when the Keynesian total system prevailed in the liberal State. The myth of autonomy, which makes society's atomization and the disappearance of communal bonds seem "normal," and normative, when they are only highly idiosyncratic responses to specific historical and cultural pressures, appears, for the liberals, to have justified the State's arrogation of control of the economic system, and the replacement of culture with an abstract system. The defocalization and diffusion of the liberal power maintained by the exclusion of meaning from the social order should not blind us to the fact that the liberal power "elite" has simply usurped the power of the old hierarchical elite it ritualistically condemns.

Thus, Liberalism no longer defends any culture—the central task that would have made a continuing social tradition so valuable—but instead now "defends" the State's centrality against any culture that might arise from religion. And though we have lately been gratuitously subjected to liberal lamentations over the decline of everything from cooking to construction, this is only the inevitable consequence of a total system, which is embarrassed by any real humanity. There is a great hue and cry about the lack of new leaders, but a total system needs no "leaders," only bloodless functionaries. There is regret that, ironically, even with women's liberation, almost the only movie roles open to women portray prostitutes. But women are just discovering what "equality" with men in a total system means.

It is still more ironic that the basic justification even liberals use for their view of the State is taken from religious scriptures. Let us recall it here by first telling a parable of our own, which goes as follows. Once there was a little impoverished tribe despised by all other nations. But it happened that this little tribe for some reason found favor with God, Who sent a prophet to announce His desire to join it. Hardly able to refuse, it soon began to look around with new pride, and to covet the kingships that had brought glory on other nations. So the tribe asked God for a king. He answered that, having God, it needed no king. But the tribe insisted, so God instructed a prophet to anoint a king for them.

This, of course, is no parable, but part of the Hebrew scriptures

—and a paradigm of our whole problem. It is no exaggeration to say that the basic Western understanding of the relationship between religion and the State rests on a brief remark by another Jew who was well aware of this precedent—Jesus Christ. The story suggests that the Hebrews, having God, did not really need a king—a State. God acquiesced because they insisted on having one, but would seem to have preferred that they not insist. The traditional interpretation of Jesus' remark "give to Caesar what is Caesar's and to God what is God's" is that Jesus here recognized the State's claims. Yet the evidence suggests otherwise, according to one of the most accomplished biblical scholars in America, John L. McKenzie. In this incident, Jesus was well aware of his adversaries' intention to trap him. In offering an alternative between God and Caesar, they wanted Jesus either to choose God, and implicitly criticize the Roman occupation, so that he could be handed over to the Romans for sedition, or implicitly to accept the hated occupation, and discredit himself with the Jews. But Jesus, well instructed in the scriptures, knew how the Jews had acquired their own king. His reply, therefore, meant basically this: "Why are you asking *me* if it is lawful to give tribute to Rome? You Jews have already *accepted* Rome, for you are using the Roman coin. Your question is merely academic, and my opinion irrelevant. I neither endorse nor repudiate the State—Jewish or Roman; I simply recognize it as a fact, as you, indeed, have done. So to Caesar give what (you have already recognized) is Caesar's, and to God what indisputably is God's."

Once the State is accepted, an insoluble tension, perhaps an irresolvable contradiction, arises: The community has a right to create a culture, part of the right to be human; any legitimate State has a duty to protect the "individual." Neither of these mandates can become absolute because the very fact of a State represents a compromise: The community will depend on power as well as on love, and power then needs to be limited. The "individual" has no absolute right to "self-expression," for he is limited not only by the "rights" of other individuals but also by the right of the community to maintain its public environment. But this right of the community is also relative, for a culture cannot grow if people are not free to create it. What seems to be called for is this: The "individual" should be permitted any behavior in public that does not insult the community, but otherwise he can be compelled to keep it private; specific concrete acts can be excluded from the public eye because the community has both a duty and a right to create an acceptable environment. If this right to suppress acts (but not ideas) contradicts the individual's impulses, or even his "convictions," too bad; he does himself no favor by displaying contempt for the culture he needs as much as it needs him. If his freedom of "expression" is impaired, there is no remedy; what makes the State necessary makes such conflicts inevitable.

For, having accepted the State, we have accepted the division between men as virtually irreparable. Thus arises the necessity of private ownership of property, of which the State basically is the protector. But then the State becomes itself a threat to personal liberty, and the very privacy of property becomes the material defense against this. We also need to limit the State by *moral* principles, so that it can be forbidden what is improper to it. We confine the State within moral limits and base it on moral principles not because the State itself is (as the liberals claim) a moral entity, like society (which they say is not), but precisely because the State in itself is merely a recognition of and reflects the amoral "facts." (The early American's basic contempt for the central government was healthier by a long shot than the liberals' cosiness with it.) The State's law protects people and their property not only from other people, but also from the State. The principles on which the legitimacy of a State depends are not intrinsic to it, but must arise out of a philosophic and cultural consensus, for which the State will nevertheless retain animosity, for when restrained by a culture a State will always seek to supplant it, yet cannot without attacking its own moral foundations. Culture and power have always appeared together, but have no *intrinsic* relation. It is just that society also usually has a social myth, which uses power to see itself through. Never in the past has there been a society without a social myth, and we very well may never see one in the future. But power as such is irrelevant to culture, a shared meaning system that gives rise to a freely shared moral order.

Thus, "public morality" arises out of a culture and restrains the State, and the State must "impose" it in order to preserve its own legitimacy, for culture has a higher priority than the State. But if the only morality that the State as such *must* impose is that constituting its own moral foundations, nevertheless, because the State also represents an imposition upon human culture, *people* have a right to form even within the State's own precincts a "civic morality" consisting largely of rules of public order and convenience. The social environment does not belong to the State, whose only positive obligation there is to see that no one is forced to conform *in private* to any morality, in violation of his right to practice his own morality or even lack of same as long as others are not unreasonably inconvenienced. And neither does the social environment belong to everyone who might hope to exploit it for private gain, so the community can prevent individuals, not from expressing their ideas, but from committing acts that violate explicit communal standards. (If proscribed acts are embodied in "art," promotion of such art—not including editorial comment— can be, but need not be, prevented without necessarily any imputation as to its "artistic" merit or any prohibition on private enjoyment of it. If anyone thinks certain acts should be publicly accepted, let him persuade others by the merits of his ideas; this might attract more attention to ideas than they now get in the empire of money.) The law must mediate apparently contradictory claims, but it imposes no specific morality at all, since any person may do as he likes privately; all that the law imposes is the *community's* right to preserve its own environment. Thus we agree in principle at least with the Supreme Court's *conclusion* in this matter, if not with its reasoning. The media's passionate advocacy of "free expression" would seem more compelling if the media's financial stake in it were not so obviously overriding. Media "concern" for ideas, though, seems to be limited to their value as purveyable commodities. (Many publishers are now accepting submissions only from "known sources"; so much for "free expression.") If community standards cost the media some inconvenience, or even, God forbid, some profit, too bad for the media, and too bad for liberal power.

As for the place of politics within a culture, it remains almost as ambiguous as that of the State itself. Thus, Eugene McCarthy's conclusions on this matter seem suspect. McCarthy decided at length that politics are not merely a "negative" or relative good, but a positive good, because even a society of saints would be political. True. But would their politics be an exercise of power? Even saints tolerate power only because they know most men are not saints. Note the familiar paradox: For McCarthy, when he had no prospect of a political career himself, politics was an unqualified evil, but once he had acquired power himself they became an unqualified good, for making human life a little less bad. But why is life so bad, if not because of the pursuit and exercise of power (over men, not necessarily over "Nature")? Power is sterile, always sacrifices as much as it "creates" or "preserves." It is not politics that is evil, but the desire for power, and our unsaintly politics is inextricably mixed up with power and the usually not very well-concealed lust for it, so for us politics can be only a qualified, a "relative," good, compared to what it (perhaps) prevents. If all were saints, politics would be an exercise not mainly of power, but of service—"selfless." Not everyone could have his own way, but no one would want it, either, for its own sake. The common good would actually prevail. That this is precisely what does not prevail now is why politics becomes an exercise of power. And this in turn is why politics cannot itself achieve the common good. Politics still *can* be, perhaps, a high vocation, as McCarthy affirms. But this is *in spite of the State*. Its suffusion by power makes politics a fundamentally questionable activity. Power exercised by any man over another is never an unqualified good, but at best only a relative good, and only, as it were, by default. This is not a new Manicheanism, but simply a minimal recognition of the evil that indisputably (except for liberals) is there. We do not say that politics is intrinsically bad (because, abstractly, politics could be practiced without a State!), but neither is it, as we will ever practice it, an unqualified good. But the State itself often becomes almost an absolute evil. This amounts to a warning: Christians, for example, must participate in the political process, but no one should claim that such engagement is of un-qualified "service" to others. The sooner this sort of nonsense is exposed for what it is, a justification of the desire for power, the better. One who engages in politics is trying to make the best of a relatively bad bargain, is acknowledging a certain hopelessness in the situation by his very resort to power. "Public service" is usually primarily a service of oneself. The best way to serve others, if there is any real hope in the situation, is not in the political process itself. Politics should be viewed as at best ambiguous, a com-promise between contending "interests" in the hope of service of common values (if any) and wholly in spite of the State. For evidence of the truth of all this, just review the way most States come into existence. Not through the "will" of any "people," who normally have nothing to say about it, but, most often, through rapine, violence, brutal enforcement of one will upon another, or defense of one autonomy against a chaotic other. Out of "deals," conquests, etc., arises a perpetually shifting patchwork of States with no intrinsically limiting principles except the range of the force one or another ruling group can manage to impose. Consider, for example, the way the State of Palestine appears to be coming into existence today. The Palestinian Liberation Organization, a terrorist group, has been declared its "legitimate government" *by other Arab States*, even before the State itself has achieved its existence, and the PLO promptly set up a "government in exile." How much did the "Palestinian people" have to say about this? Virtually nothing. Still, this hardly presents a suitable target for liberal moralizing. The main difference between the liberals and the terrorists is that liberal force serves the status quo, remains, for now, a fist gloved in velvet.

But even more ironic than the source of the liberals' rationale for their position is the clear fact that power cannot be retained merely by efforts of will. Though there isn't today, and isn't likely to be, any lack of worshipers at power's shrine, they can neither preserve it nor prevent its departure, for it comes and goes for reasons that cannot be finally deciphered. It is not just that no "people" either prospers or fails simply because it wields or lacks power—except as the lack of power reflects a lack of cultural vitality on which the succubus of power feeds. Rather, power's ministering angels alight and depart for reasons only they know. Often, real power has long since departed before its absence has been detected. An example of this might be the United States Congress. Too bloated to function in anything but the most mechanical way, the times when it responded to the "national interest"—assuming the solons ever knew what this was or even much cared about it collectively—have long since passed. The people themselves are no longer concerned and cannot afford to be: They long ago exchanged their political for their economic citizenship.

Perhaps it doesn't really matter. The rewards of power go not to the people, but to those who administer it (almost every headline teaches us that), and the more power beguiles them the less likely are the people to have any share in it. The liberal State was, perhaps, one of the more benign manifestations of power, but power is power, and whether or not it is exercised by a liberal State is hardly the most crucial factor in the personal fruition of the "average" person. The only agent that could possibly preserve true liberal values much longer would be a revitalized supporting culture, which there seems little reason to believe liberals are any more interested in achieving than they are in becoming canonized saints. The State's *inevitability* may be obvious, but, apart from a fatal "pragmatism" selling itself to whatever status quo, its *necessity* can only be regarded as a "mystery," akin to those mysterious "musts," like wars and scandals, to which the Christian scriptures refer. The State knows, and every day shows it knows, it is *intrinsically* limited by no moral principles whatever, even those comprising its own legal foundations. This will seem shocking nonsense to the enlightened liberal whose social power rests squarely on the primacy of the State, but nevertheless, his so-called community of States is nothing but a savage jungle of States devouring each other "like monsters of the deep." One must recognize the inevitability of the State's existence, and, like the American Founders, deal with this fact as best one can. But to pretend that the State itself is the locus of "community," for the privilege of participating in whose "life" and of subordinating one's rights to whose claims one is supposed to feel grateful, is a cruel hoax. This leap from the attempt to disentangle theological doctrine and State power to the assertion of the cultural primacy of the State is what suggests that the real aim of the benevolent liberal State is not only to defuse religious conflict but to take religion's place.

But liberals do not have any very coherent theory on this matter. Actually, the State's role for them is mostly *ad hoc* and "pragmatic," with no real underlying theoretical vindication, except as provided by myth. For example, Max Lerner's "vision" of what America's ultimate goal should be—to achieve and maintain a world balance of power—turns out to be only more of the same. A relative good this might be, compared to the realistic alternatives. But the real problem, which Lerner would only perpetuate, is the primacy of power. No such "balance" will avail much if all cultures are swallowed up in it. What is needed is a world *culture* to get power back under control. Lerner tries to argue that American power is qualitatively different from that of the ill-fated Roman Empire. But Rome's troubles lay not so much in the nature of its power as in the fact that, first, its myth gave out, and, second, Rome at last became nothing *but* power. The solution for us is not to goad citizens to take responsibility for themselves again, even if they could. People in Protestant society took responsibility for themselves, the Lutherans simply leaving society to the State, the Calvinists trying to disarm the State by appropriating it. In both cases, culture, then the Church, became prisoners of the State. People must take responsibility for themselves *and* for others, in an explicitly communal way, so that as little room as possible remains for the State to fill. The State cannot save us, and neither can the liberals.

Yet people have accepted the liberal slogans on the State, especially the "Church-State" formula that has maintained their atomization by defining "Americanism" as a strictly political affair with no specific moral content. Such formulas were accepted, as a practical matter, for various reasons. Protestants thought America was a Protestant country destined to remain so, and hoped the separation formula therefore would inhibit the Catholics; they never suspected it might eliminate all religion as an effective social force. Catholics accepted the formula because they had little choice in their minority and unprivileged status, because they wanted to be regarded as just as "American" as anyone else, and because they sensed that the formula at least partly got at very real problems caused by *Church* power (until even very recently the hierarchy still claimed the absolute right to impose its truth, saying that "error has no rights"). And indeed, not only is political pluralism a practical good, implicitly recognizing the fact of ideological conflict; even cultural pluralism is a relative good, reflecting the practical difficulty of encompassing the whole truth in any sectarian formula. Nevertheless, the cultural process, the formation of integral meaning systems, is the absolutely fundamental social process, and if political formulas like "Church-State separation" actively hinder it they are positively illegitimate and socially destructive.

Let us go back now and try to unravel the problem of "Church" and State as it developed in the American context. The first of the major gates in the liberal wall is called "State aid to Church-sponsored schools." The liberals' main "defense" here is what they call the "fundamental principle" supporting "absolute separation" (the wall) between "Church and State." But whose fundamental principle is this? It is no conclusion from any long and careful philosophic reflection, nor even embodied in any State document or juridical classic. Roger Williams first used the phrase "wall of separation" while trying to defend religion against the theocratic State. Jefferson later added the ideological intensive "absolute" while inveighing in a *private* letter against the unjustified usurpation of secular power by religion, or the "Church." In both cases the objection was to a usurpation of *secular* power—by the State in one case (imposing religious doctrine) and by the Church in the other (getting its doctrine imposed—*by the State*). So in both cases the State as well as the "Church" exceeds its rightful authority. The "Church" could have no political power at all without the cooperation of the State, and the State could not have absolute power without the cooperation (voluntary or forced) of the "Church." Yet if all secular power is denied the "Church," as indeed it should be, how can the "Church" be protected from the State if the State no longer needs to worry about the Church's political power? There is no way the "Church" can be protected if the issue is, as Jefferson made it to be, mere power, for though of course the "Church" should have no power, if the issue is *merely* power the State must be supreme. What is really implicit in the insistence on a "wall of separation" is that *both* "Church" *and* State are alike *political* institutions, for erecting a wall between them can solve all problems only if these problems constitute simple disputes over power. But that is not what really is at stake at all. It is true that the "Church" previously had often reached illegitimately for political power, and insofar as the "Church" acted like an intrinsically political unit a "wall of separation" would have driven it back. But if this is made merely a question of power, and the State in this respect can have no rival, then a "wall of separation" the *placement* of which has not been specified (because supposedly all that counts is to get the wall erected) can be placed anywhere the *State* sees fit. Thus, the State's usurpation of the culture need have no limit. In reality, the basic issue is *function*: which functions *belong* to the State and which to religion? The correct "separation" is not horizontal, but "vertical." For "Church" and State are not, intrinsically, contending political powers but institutions that deal in fundamentally discrete spheres of culture. Inevitably these spheres will overlap in society's *concrete* activity, in the sense that the same activity sometimes will be serving two functions; this is part of the economy of life and is not remediable by liberal rhetoric. In other words, an "absolute wall of separation" should be erected, if anywhere, not between physical institutions regarded as power blocs but between distinct and separate *functions* insofar as they are assigned to this or that institution. Jefferson uncharacteristically ignored the question of the legitimacy of State power here because, when it came to religion, Jefferson was a mere Deist ideologue.

Jefferson never saw what, in context, his crank phrase actually incorporated in a document of the national State, because most of the other Founders never intended to arrive at the prophetic extremity his Deist prejudice brought him to, at least in his private letters. Most of the Founders were religionists, not Deists, or at least enough of them to insure that no State document refers to, much less mandates, anything like a "wall of separation," which the Constitution itself never mentions. Is this how founders lay down "fundamental principles"? Can their thundering silence here really be construed as a universal affirmation of a "principle" most of them need never have heard of? Should Jefferson's prejudices carry a weight far surpassing that which even the greatest saints can command in Christendom? If the Founders enshrined any "principle" of separation, their failure to comment on its obvious application with respect to their own support of "religious" education would seem odd, unless liberals know better than the Founders what the latter *should* have meant. The Founders were still only groping through this subject, an indication of admirable prudence, but a misfortune nevertheless, in that this cleared the way for a takeover by the doctrinaire liberals.

If Jefferson's private opinions must be regarded as State charters, why is his recommendation that every generation have its own revolution not a "fundamental principle" also? Because another revolution could only tumble the liberals from social power, and probably political power as well, and what is to become a "principle" from Jefferson's writings depends on whose ox it will gore. (So his insistence that personal freedom depends on economic independence of the government also can be ignored and dismissed as a quaint parochialism.) *Both* of Jefferson's private remarks merely illustrate his highly inorganic and rationalist conception of social order, and he was no more infallible in one than in the other.

So any legal support for the "separation" dogma must be found in the "establishment" clause of the Constitution, a document, however, which mentions neither separation nor anything that might be construed as "separation"; it merely states that Congress may make no laws providing for an "establishment of religion." Let us remember that during the Enlightenment hostility to religion was based largely on grounds of "intellect" and Reason; Deism itself was an intellectual, not an economic or social ideology. So it would have been almost instinctive for the Founders to refer to an establishment of "religion" rather than a "church." For most of the Founders probably understood by "religion" not *primarily* its institutional forms, but the doctrines these institutions put forth as exclusive truth—and in those days the question of ultimate truth was still considered important enough to argue over. That is, the Founders were saying that no religious doctrine should be endorsed or enforced by the State. This was wider than and *included* a proscription against establishing a church. But it did not mean that all religions that conformed to civil law should not be tolerated. Nor did it prohibit the State from doing whatever within the State's ordinary course of business might ease the citizen's practice of his own religion. Neither did it, because this would have attacked the State's own philosophical foundations, extend to philosophical principles: The Founders had to support their own doctrine on the State's role by reference to "unalienable rights" that the "Creator" (not society) endows on all men. Perhaps, too, the Founders did not use the word "church" because many sects did not consider themselves churches.

Whatever the Founders meant by "religion," though, what they meant by "establishment," the crucial word, should be difficult to mistake. The clear meaning of this word, as applied to religion, was then, and is *now*, the setting up of one religion (or church) as the official, State religion, as the Anglican Church and religion were "established" in England and the Catholic Church and religion were "established" in Spain. Is there any practical difference between establishment of religion and establishment of a church? No, because no religion could be effectively established without establishment of an institutional structure, adherence to which could be used as a test of conformity and to which the State could address its exclusionary benevolence. But the State's normal and inevitable interchanges with *all* religious groups cannot be called "establishment" in any meaning of the word the Founders would have recognized, and that they did not seek to refine or redefine the obvious meaning of the word is *prima facie* evidence that they neither meant anything more, nor suspected that the word could be construed as meaning anything more—even if it be true (which there is no reason to believe) that, as the liberal courts now see it, they should have meant something more. The Founders probably would have divided along strictly ideological lines over the further question whether the State should be actively friendly to all religions or hold itself aloof from all, but this never became for them a constitutional question. The monotonous insistence that the Constitution somewhere prohibits "unnecessary entanglement" between the State and "religion" conveniently leaves unformulated what is "unnecessary," and the failure to define what activities rightly belong to the State makes "establishment" equivalent to "limit on State jurisdiction," and pushes the "wall" right up against the church's and synagogue's front doors. So as not to permit themselves to become "entangled" with the universal State, religions would for all practical purposes have to go out of business. But there is no warrant in law, history or semantics for believing that anyone else ever meant by "establishment" what the liberals now say it means, or that the Founders themselves even suspected that it could be so construed. Indeed, the early support of religious education, the innumerable official chaplains, swearings on Bibles, etc., not to mention the later adoption of the motto "In God We Trust" (which, of course, we do not), all tend to confirm that early Americans desired as friendly as possible a commerce between government and *all* religions rather than the relentlessly adversary relationship the liberals have imposed. The Founders wanted to prevent the "establishment" of a State religion and church on the British pattern, precisely what had driven so many early settlers to the colonies, so they forbade the State to proselytize for any religion or to support one directly with State power. That the Founders should have gone further is pure ideological speculation, but that the government should not or could not do all in its capacity to ease the citizen's own private practice of his own religion and even his public practice of it, *as long as the State does not discriminate between religions,* the Founders nowhere suggested, except perhaps in Jefferson's private letters, which somehow fail to be conclusive.

The liberals rightly resented the early Western State's invocation of the necessity of philosophical and even religious consensus in order to justify imposing detailed doctrines that actually went beyond the consensus, for a supposed philosophical or religious consensus becomes, *a priori*, spurious when imposed by force. But the State had not been guilty of all this out of any excessive zeal for religious truth—anything but; it was simply trying to disarm the eternally irresolvable antagonism between the material exigencies of the State and the spiritual exigencies of personal conscience, by wrapping itself in the cloak of religious truth. Nevertheless, the early State was more honest than the later State that thinks the problem can be solved by pretending it does not exist, as when it is proposed that a mere prohibition against so-called entanglement between "religion" and a supposedly universally competent State somehow now protects "freedom" of conscience.

Only when the liberal tradition itself crystallized into *concrete* political and economic forms in the nineteenth century did the purely political polarity of "Church and State" that frames the contrast purely in terms of power rather than competence or cultural function finally submerge the correct distinction between *sacral and secular functions*. The liberal formulation became a device not only for limiting the "Church," but also for exalting the State, which now has only to declare its interest in some area of cultural activity (and nothing can prevent its declaring any interest it chooses without some clear distinction between sacral and secular functions) in order summarily to push religion out. For the Church is no match for the State in terms of physical power, the terms on which the liberal insists on framing the contrast (and perhaps the only terms that any longer interest him). So now the State can at any time and any place arbitrarily assert its own primacy and dismiss the sacral as a matter of merely "private" (and hopefully insignificant public) concern. It can afford to tolerate the sacral as long as seems politically convenient, keeping the churches docile meanwhile with tax breaks, and then dispose of all churches when convenient. The means for banishing religion from any area when the time seems ripe is simple and highly characteristic of modern liberalism—it is an economic means. The State begins to use its taxing power, and the citizens have that much less to spend on comparable activities conducted by their churches. This is the most effective possible means in a society organized around its economy. The State tightens its hold on the culture, and the liberals try to control the State.

But only secular functions rightly belong to the State; sacral functions belong to the churches, and distinguishing between functions is a matter for philosophy, not for liberal ideology.

What is education, then—a sacral or a secular function? It is both. The value aspects of education lean toward the sacral, the skill aspects toward the secular. The State's direct concern is with the latter; responsibility for the former lies, as far as the State is concerned, with parents (the State never deals directly with churches as such). But the State now sees its rights in all of education as prior to those of the parents. The State's putative "needs" come first—as if education were primarily or entirely its own responsibility—the parents' needs come last, and the State recognizes no obligation to apportion fairly revenues it forcibly collects for education. Before this century, education was always considered an initiation into a sacred order. We have transcended that. Now liberals say that if the State must conduct a school system (of course it now must) all citizens must share the burden (of course they must) but that the "establishment" clause, as interpreted, of course, by liberals, "forbids" the return to "church-sponsored" schools of any tax revenues thus exacted. Balderdash.

No one could seriously argue that the public schools were not one of the most admirable and effective public enterprises in American society. However, they always harbored one overwhelming weakness: As State institutions, they were incompetent to teach values. As a practical matter, though, they compromised and inculcated "Americanism." Yet a school teaches as effectively by what it omits as by what it includes, and State educational policy, by the simple fact it cannot treat questions of values on the merits, always threatens to degenerate into mere ideology. Moreover, any State usurpation of the right to final decisions on what should be taught or excluded is totalitarian in principle. This is the reason why local control of the schools was once considered important: That way, though the State controlled routine administration, parents, through the local boards, could influence teaching policy, especially in the selection of texts. (So-called local control today amounts to exactly the reverse.) This was at best a compromise, but probably all that could be reasonably expected, since the relationship between a State and its host culture amounts to an implicit antagonism anyway. The State's responsibility, though, is simply to assure each child the *opportunity* for a good education; its function is essentially supportive: to build up the base and to fill any gaps, but not to smother from the top.

But the State's present taxing policy gives the State a *cultural* monopoly, for any group that desires its own schools now must pay twice for this basic right, no matter how high might be the exaction for public schools that could be grossly mismanaged or hostage to some ideological party line. And not only is the financing of schools inequitable; the centralized State bureaucracies continue to usurp decisions on what will be taught. So much for "local control." Yet it is liberal researchers who have concluded, under the pressure of rueful experience, that schools cannot remedy social ills, can really function only in support of a culture. The liberal contradiction seems evident even in the busing controversy. Of course, the ostensible objective—to make the black the social equal of the white—is unexceptionable. But the liberals are only trying to include the blacks in the totalist system in order to subject them to the same colonialization imposed on the white workers, thus robbing the black of his culture and virtually forcing him to become a black white (with all the privileges of membership in the plastic and cardboard white "culture"). To forcibly bus whites out of their own schools threatens the precarious integral cohesion of any lingering white communities with the State's ruthless moralism, the basic staple of any totalitarian regime. No child should be bused unless (1) no local school is available (though one should be), or (2) the parents agree to it and the school to which the child is bused is better than the local alternative.

Whites fear blacks as symbols of poverty and deprivation, from which working-class whites rightly never feel very far themselves. But for liberals, who seldom live in "integrated" communities themselves, to blame white ethnics for this may be the laugh of the century, for liberals have been teaching the ethnics for most of this century to put their beliefs aside in favor of material interests. An excuse for subduing the ethnic communities, this teaching is conveniently forgotten when integration would better secure liberal power. As we will see, the way to make the black the social equal of the white is to give the black the base of economic power indispensable to retaining autonomy and dignity in any society ruled by a State. Then we might see prejudice disappear with astonishing rapidity.

Simply by renouncing any value-creating role, the State cannot evade the inescapable fact that ultimate responsibility for the value aspects of education rests with parents. This is itself a position on values. And if parents object to what is taught or not taught, they have the right, if not the duty, to withdraw their children from the public schools and to set up their own, and the State, since education is not basically its business, would have the obligation to give them a proportional rebate of their tax monies. Yet the protests by West Virginia hillbillies against the secularist world view inculcated in the schools hardly found anything like the echo on the front page of the *New York Times* that the South Boston integration riots did. Hillbilly—or Catholic or Amish—revolts against liberal paternalism do not qualify as "news." But the riots could be presented not as an embarrassing defiance of liberals, but of "authority." (The *Times* saw the crux of the Boston riots in their defiance of authority.) Well, the *Times* regarded the upper class's defiance of the laws on abortion as simply a reason (along with "economic inconvenience") for letting the lower classes have abortions, too. Now, when the *lower* classes defy laws liberals like, suddenly there is a challenge to "authority." Whose? Not the law's, but the liberals'. Maybe this suggests why there *is* a growing contempt for "authority."

The fatal weakness in the Catholic camp, at least, is that Catholics have been asking the government to distribute tax monies to schools legally controlled by an ecclesiastical power it is perfectly evident even Catholic parents have no control over either. Understandably, this sticks in the liberal craw. Parents may have a right to educate their children within broad guidelines the State may lay down for children's protection, but the State should not be asked to cooperate in maintaining the power of an ecclesiastical power group, any more than to contribute to schools that institutionalize any *de facto* violation of civil rights. The State may have no legal right to refuse parents, but it seems to have some sort of moral right to refuse the power group, even though the money would come out of the taxes of those whose children were involved. But if the legal control of Catholic schools passed to parents, the State would have no more justification at all for withholding tax revenues exacted from them, whatever the courts might say, and if the "aid" were not forthcoming the parents would have every reason to plead economic hardship, close their schools, and begin systematically suing the public schools over every objectionable statement made in the public classrooms and texts. This, to the liberals, might smack of blackmail; to religionists it might bring survival. The sincerity of the *New York Times*'s pious admonition that State "aid" must lead to State control can be judged by the paper's total opposition to such aid in *any* case; a State taxing for education but recognizing no obligation to apportion the revenues fairly is going to wind up with a complete monopoly—willy-nilly. Defenders of public-school financing often contend that "religious" schools deprive students of the invaluable discovery of common values with people of different persuasions. But citizens should not be forced to find their civic unity by suppressing all they hold to be fundamental. Better to allow children to go to the schools of their own groups for education in the values of their groups, and to public schools for education in the things in which all citizens share. They might then find common ground in what separates, and these things could achieve the public recognition they deserve. But liberals believe that religion belongs in the closet.

The other cause of conflict between Catholics and liberals hardly needs to be identified, but is much more complex in its implications. It is, of course, the question of abortion. The liberal position here perhaps is adequately summarized in the following way. The attempt to outlaw abortion, it is held, is an intolerable imposition of private morality upon the public and intrusion of private morality into the public sphere. The public sphere is not where such moral judgments should be imposed, for, except in the impersonal proscriptions of law, public life is neutral with respect to moral values. Those who object to abortion have every reason to abstain from it, but those who see the matter differently should not be coerced. Every person has the obligation and right to form his own conscience and to act upon it, and even if he fails to raise to the level of conscience what requires a decision of conscience—even if he acts only out of immediate and selfish convenience—there can be no legal remedy for this regrettable failure, which remains his own responsibility. It is not the law's business to impose "moral" order but to provide rules of civil order and procedure that protect the individual's rights. In addition, several subsidiary arguments can be made against the attempt to outlaw abortion. First, such an attempt unjustly infringes a woman's rights to her own body, forcing her to bear personal inconveniences of major magnitude, simply toward observance of moral standards to which she may not subscribe. It is also unjust to the child brought into the world unwanted, resented, and condemned to an "uneven break" from the start. Finally, it is unjust to society, depriving it of a major tool for control of a dangerously increasing population.

All these arguments are reinforced by more or less suggestive evidence offered by actual Catholic conduct. The lesson has not been lost of the Catholic Church's repeated attempts to settle scientific and philosophical questions by dogmatic pronouncements in which again and again the basic consideration has seemed to be Church power rather than the real merits of the issues (heliocentrism, evolution, political revolution, birth control, etc.), and the opposition to abortion seems suspiciously like another example of Church interference in secular matters—here of law. Official Catholic hostility to abortion also seems rooted in the patriarchical Church's desire to keep women mindful of their subordinate "place," for the Church hardly distinguishes itself by its efforts to alleviate the problems for which abortion is sought as a solution (although the Church may have little material capability to alleviate them itself). And since the Church leads no chorus of protest over other injustices, like war, its intransigence in this matter seems suspect. Finally, the notion of "person" on which the Catholic bases his opposition (calling the fetus a "person") is basically philosophical in nature, in the sense that it cannot be maintained without philosophical tools. And since it would appear to be impossible to achieve philosophical consensus, philosophical and theological principles cannot become translated into civil law.

The first observation that might be made on all this is that we seem to discover here the influence of the modern myth of "autonomy." This myth holds, as we earlier saw, that human reason, because neither oriented toward nor limited by transcendental ideals, is its own measure. But since one man's "reason" can be another's unreason, the only reason that might serve as a principle of social order must be mathematically demonstrable. The myth only appears to give the individual person priority over society as such, a priority that seems to reinforce the healthy aspects of the main Western social tradition, for the person does here enjoy a certain primacy—with respect to his own self: Each person can treat with society in a way by which society with respect to him becomes a mere "neutral" medium through which he directs his own atomized course of self-realization.

But the other side of this coin is the social *as such*, and if society in the myth of autonomy loses some of its former potency in the person's *private* life, it acquires an overwhelming, homogenous power in its own sphere, for the person withdraws his moral judgment from it. The objection that the attempt to prohibit abortion is an intrusion of "private" morality into public life implies not only that obvious distinctions must be made between "personal" and social morality (and even a morality held by a large group remains "private"), but that an absolutist separation must be made between society and any morality at all. For *any* morality is first of all "private." Thus, liberal society is quintessentially amoral: The unquestioned priority for society's putative moral "neutrality" in the event of its apparent contradiction of "private" morality gives this neutrality a higher social value than morality itself. Society no longer is obligated to make concessions to the exigencies of *merely* personal conscience, which itself must abandon any claims to any social relevance at all, except perhaps through the personal acts of the atomized subject. Conscience surrenders its social potency to a "neutrality" that becomes an absolute the conscience cannot frontally challenge. It is not that society actively resists conscience, but that "neutral" society is essentially impersonal and resonates no response to the personhood of the personal subject; this is why the claim that the fetus is a "person" seems beside the point—the notion of personhood is itself irrelevant. The personal becomes, with respect to society as such, a mere "epiphenomenon" systematically subordinated to the impersonally social, to the material parameters of modern structuralism. At the core of this social order is not a moral order arising from a culture, but an abstract "system" in which the personal

aspects of the subject have play only by sufferance and only insofar as they do not disturb the impersonal "system's" smooth
mechanical functioning. The suggestion that this impersonal system monopolizing the social order is merely "neutral" is quite
false, though; the system is instead amoral.

The God of the myth of autonomy remained a god only of the
dead. But this mythic god had no intrinsic relation to the "real"
God of Christianity from Whom it was derived; it was simply a
conception of God that contributed to a solution for death. This
god of the myth of autonomy, having neither function nor desire
for function in the secular world, the land of the living, lost any
direct social relevance, and therefore so also did religion. And
since in the myth of "autonomy" the strictly "cultural" or communal aspects of social life, concerned with the social construction
of meaning, disappear from view and become socially irrelevant,
meaning loses its former socially integrating function and becomes
a "private" matter. And morality, which derives from meaning,
becomes irrelevant, too, replaced, at best, by mere law.

Perhaps all this makes clear how deeply the notion that all
morality is "private" is entrenched. If we could only shake off the
excessively rationalist Enlightenment notion of "Reason" (unori-
ented toward any transcendental ideals) and the seductive power
of the modern myth of autonomy, the real merits of the issues
would become clear at once. Is it really so obvious that religion is
a "private matter"? To say that *God* is a private matter—that just
because some have sought to impose their views on Him, God
Himself becomes socially irrelevant—is grotesque, and ridiculous
on its face. What *is* private is the integrity of conscience, but truth
is fundamentally a social category, and *obviously* whether God
exists or not is fundamental for society itself, although "society" is
a mere abstraction and cannot decide this for itself. The question
must be decided by individuals in the way that such questions are
always decided: communally. So what is "private" about religion?
Obviously a person's religion should determine not only his char-

acter, but his view of society and of life itself. But not just the individual's, even society's own, ultimate coherence arises from meaning, so religion is clearly a *very* important matter even for society itself. Religion is private only with respect to *power*: No one has any right to force his views upon others. But everyone's *real* freedom depends on the *arrival* at shared truths. Society dares not pretend to indifference, and must leave the way open for actual public pursuit of such consensus. But today, even an apparent threat to one person's "rights" becomes the reason for entirely driving religion out (from the schools, for instance). And it is the *State* that drives religion out. It is hard to believe that this is "disinterested," really designed to "save" public tranquility. The State itself should keep out of sacral functions.

Since society itself is basically a system of meaning, meaning as it concretely impacts on us and determines our modes of inter-action, a society not culturally integrated on the level of meaning must be simply incoherent. No harmony is possible if the processes by which people come to agreement are excluded so that no con-flict can arise. And every viable meaning system must be holistic and integral—arise out of a vision of life. The natural locus of such meaning is a group; no viable social-meaning system can ab-stractly arise apart from a group that lives it, for a social-meaning system is appropriated from the institutions that structure social interaction. Society's organic coherence arises not by any applica-tion of abstract principle, however "noble," from above, but out of the structured group. Conversely, a group remains incomplete until it becomes identical with society as such so that it has its own life entirely under its own control. Thus, society remains *subjec-tively* abstract, its meaning system disintegrated, until it becomes identical with a full-*bodied* integral group, and a group remains incomplete until identical with society as such. These tensions are not to be avoided or regretted; they are the way by which we arrive at the deeper truth. It is no less wrong to deliver society over to an abstract, dehumanized "system" so that the cultural process is aborted than to deliver it over to religious power. Any true reform of abstract society will depend on cultural groups; revolution or the overthrow of the "Establishment" will gain nothing unless a cultural group is able to reabsorb within its own culturally integrated life the functions now exercisable only under the constant threat of force. This is a call not for revolution, but for the reestablishment of a *cultural* balance in society. All groups will still live in institutional society, which, whatever its present flaws, is basically a human good. What must be remedied is society's institutional separation from culture. The groups, by seeking mutual accommodations that will make a general culture possible, must be permitted to reabsorb the institutional society and transmute it into an instrument of human culture.

But where does all this leave us with respect to abortion as a *social* problem? It disposes of the contention that society is morally neutral, but not all moral questions are public; in fact, perhaps most are not, and abortion still might be, as liberals contend, a matter strictly for a woman and her physician. Were this so, an abortion would be no one's business but the woman's, even if abortion were wrong; for any person has the right to ride to hell in a handbasket if he chooses. *Is* abortion, then, a private matter after all?

What do we mean when we call a moral issue a "private" matter? Certainly I cannot think myself so singular that a morality good for me might not be good for others as well. Morality can be a *wholly* private matter only for that purely fictive "individual" who is totally atomized, for any personal development rising above the most elementary level becomes inextricably mingled with other lives. Morality is *by definition* social; the correct name for a morality that is wholly private is "amorality." What most mean to suggest in using the term "private morality" is that, because true morality reflects a free interior response, not a mechanical conformity, civil authority may not force us to practice a particular morality *unless* our failure to observe it would undermine public order, the civil rights of others, or the State's own moral foundations. Can abortion be fitted into any of these categories?

It has been suggested (again by John S. Dunne) that the coming age may be impatient of old moral restrictions, since what *can* be done tends to *get* done, and that the resistance to new standards of morality may be merely the lingering resistance of an old order until a new one becomes more securely established. In this sense, to argue for the old morality may well be just an anachronistic defense of the old order. Yet the argument from development and evolution can become facile and hollow, too. And in any case, it would seem that the liberal position on abortion implies the end of the liberal State itself.

If morality is going to count for anything at all, *some* "private" morality must become public, for *all* morality is first of all private. But *what* morality is going to become public? Public life can become morally "neutral" only by becoming *sub*moral. This is not an argument against tolerating a pluralism of moralities, which at least keeps before us the true dimensions of the difficulty of finding a common morality, but actually *finding* it has a higher cultural priority than simply settling for a political pluralism. The nation's founders were perhaps too sanguine in assuming that some truths are "self-evident"; for us, none are. But they realized that any State not based on explicitly shared principles will be based on unprincipled force. By the very exigencies of its own foundations the State must, unless it is to abandon moral rationality altogether, "impose" the philosophical principles that constitute its own moral foundations, although the State does not *arrive* at them but only recognizes them. (The Founders thought this "self-evident" doctrine should command a consensus.) Unless law expresses only "enlightened" self-interest—not, as the Founders naively held, "unalienable rights"—laws against the taking of human life "impose" doctrine *about* human life. But what *is* human life? This is a central doctrinal problem even for the *State*, thus so also is the question of the moral value of the fetus. When the State forbids murder but encourages abortion it goes beyond simply recognizing doctrine to creating it, by defining human life for itself. But this question is philosophical, and the Founders did not explicitly treat it in the State charter, so the State is incompetent to decide *for itself* whether or not the fetus is a person—not because the matter is an issue for "individual" discretion but because it involves a principle too fundamental for the State to attempt to pronounce on: A State that directly pronounced on this would ominously subject the lives of all citizens to its willingness to recognize their right to exist—in light of the Constitution, if of nothing else, an absurdity. Yet to hold that there is no basis for objective morality is an attack on the "unalienable rights" and "self-evident" truths on which the Founders grounded the nation. So neither can the liberal State pretend to "neutrality" on abortion, any more than to its own foundations. The result is that the State can only helplessly hope for a basic consensus, exactly as it must hope for one concerning its own foundations. Until and unless a consensus is reached on such questions the State's own moral foundations are imperiled. The only ways this consensus can be politically expressed is by legislation, or better, by constitutional amendment, from neither of which can there be appeal to the courts, for if the courts exercise a veto they "establish" their own doctrine in place of the Constitution itself, for the issue remains not basically law, but the basic morality (once considered "self-evident") on which the law rises. There can be uncertainty, but not "neutrality," on the moral value of the fetus, as on the philosophical foundations of the State, but if the latter are no longer regarded as true, they no longer morally justify the State. Implicit in the abortion question is the further question whether philosophical principles are still to be regarded as the State's foundations. The Supreme Court has instead established "enlightened self-interest," attacking the State's moral rationality and perhaps even sounding its own death knell. It has not (to its credit) attempted to be "neutral," but still has swept the real issue under the rug and adopted a working definition (which, when it is the State that is adopting it, is the only kind that matters) that now sees life as possibly human only in proportion to its material capability to subsist independently of others. This criterion imperils anyone who grows dependent—all of us, all helplessly dependent on others. Of course, we're all working very hard to fix that. But meanwhile the liability of being merely human can become the pretext for abolishing all moral independence of the State.

When the State *prohibits* abortion, it is not necessarily defining life, but only including in the prohibition against killing it any manifestation of life with a coherent claim to be called human, until such time as the citizens (not the liberals) have concluded that one or another possibility has been improperly included. But they can finally decide this only on philosophical grounds, the grounds on which the very notion of person has been constructed. These grounds should not be shifted lightly, since they are, paradoxically, the only solid check on State power (until now). Any refusal to recognize the need for a correct *common* morality on so basic a question as abortion is a turning away from the requirements of human liberty and moral responsibility, a reckless denial of the spiritual foundations of human dignity on which not only the possibility of true human community or an adequately moral State arises, but the American State actually arose. The premium is on actually finding the adequate public morality, not on the liberals' perpetual hypothetical "search" for it (meanwhile everyone can follow his immediate convenience) that in effect relegates all moral problems to virtual social irrelevance. This is just another aspect of the competitive liberal social "race" in which supposedly everyone begins as equal and seeks his own advantage but is never recognized as definitively arriving. But an erroneous morality could destroy society. If the Founders could not have assumed a basic morality identifiable by all ("self-evident truths") there could have been no Constitution, and though it may now seem a cruel dilemma that if the State permits laws against abortion some people will have a morality "imposed" on them, while if the State forbids such laws it imposes, willy-nilly, a morality itself, this is only an extension of the dilemma out of which the necessity of the State arises. The cruelty, if any, is in reality, not in the State's recognition of it. It is not necessarily true that the State should directly legislate *against* abortion, if the people will not observe such laws, for there is not much point in bringing the law further into contempt. But for the State to *forbid* laws against abortion is an intolerable affront to moral conscience. How could something that the Founders of the State never mentioned be regarded as a "fundamental principle" of it, when what they regarded as the self-evidency of certain truths is dismissed as little more than a linguistic liberty, because if truths are self-evident, they must lead to a public morality? The Supreme Court has not only not argued the philosophical merits (which it cannot), it has usurped a prerogative it does not have; so its decision is morally bankrupt. It cannot be denied that abortion seems to bring certain advantages, which might make it expedient if the philosophical objections could be removed in some way other than ignoring them. But just as Vietnam turned out to be the catastrophe of liberal self-contradiction in foreign policy, abortion may turn out to be such in domestic policy, dividing citizen from citizen again, liberal from religious believer, tearing the fabric of civic life dangerously beyond repair, at least as far as believers are concerned, though they may indeed be few. To forbid laws against abortion in the present state of knowledge is *not* simply to maintain the State's moral neutrality; it is directly to establish *liberal* morality—or, rather, nonmorality—in a yet more fundamental sense than the liberals say that to grant "State aid" would establish religion. The requirements of democracy now run counter to liberal objectives, so the liberals are ready to relieve the citizens of their "awesome" responsibilities and give them to Big Brother—a patronizing that will make even the new ecological concern for "respect for life" just another potential instrument for regimenting now valueless

Man in the name of environmental integrity. But without a real culture, "Nature" will disappear as a constitutive factor in society, too.

As Gouldner notes, we may soon see the concept of "man" crowding God in His grave, or, as Phillip Reiff predicts, the rise of a social order coordinated not internally but by psychoanalysis, adjusting "individuals" into a total system without moral content, in which, as C.S. Lewis foresaw, only two classes will survive— the conditioners and the conditioned: the brave new world of *Playboy*.

The liberal might feel innocently affronted by any suggestion that he, and not the radical, is the one who is carting away the foundations of Western culture, on which both Liberalism itself and the Constitution arose. It may not be his "fault" that he is playing such a role: His resentment of religious power has become linked to a powerful myth of autonomy in which cultural processes grounded in religion disappear from view. But the liberal's subjective innocence renders the consequences no less grave.

For every society is destined or doomed to a search for cultural order, and banishing the questions that prompt the search will only condemn society to sterility and decay. If a supposedly "private" morality sees a practice as murder, this is a charge serious enough to warrant consideration of the charge on its merits. In any case, holders of the morality can hardly avoid opposing the practice, and asking them to hold their peace is to ask them to withdraw from society and live in opposition to it. Our real burden is a social order in which the only language in which we can settle moral questions is power.

It has become fashionable to depict the opponents of abortion as enemies of individual rights, but few rational anti-abortionists have any desire to limit anyone else's freedom; their purpose is to secure their own. The argument is no longer over just the possible personhood of the fetus, although that is basic, but over the importance of the notion of personhood itself. Liberalism professes to defend every person's rights, but few liberals have attempted to show that the fetus is not a person—the only such attempt I have seen was a rather tentative and inconclusive groping by Marya Mannes, who at least had the wits to see where the problems lay, and generously refrained from invective against the so-called hypocrisy of "right-to-life" groups. The importance of this issue grows steadily greater as we come closer to the dangerous biological manipulations on which society intends to embark, but the notion of "personhood," much more than many other such notions, is basically philosophical in nature, and difficult to maintain without philosophical support.

As Garry Wills has pointed out, liberals have just recently told us that philosophy is only a liability in the pursuit of "consensus" —a consensus apparently now without content. But this abandonment of all of Western philosophy as irrelevant arose not from considerations of the real case for philosophy but from considerations of social power: Philosophical considerations, if any longer tolerated in public life, might complicate the resolution of social problems on a purely material basis, the liberal specialty. So when, in the 1960s, a writer in the *New York Times Magazine* declared that "American Philosophy Is Dead," no one thought that American society might be dead, and the *Times*, having published the obituary, went right on assuring everyone that America was basically sound, as if it made no difference whether philosophy were dead or not. At that time, philosophy was a social liability, a nuisance, at best a mere ornament to the individualist cultivation of private accomplishments and enjoyments, but it had no place in public life as such. Of course, all this has now changed. Practically the same philosophers who fifteen years ago were dismissing all moral questions as "emotive" are now contending for the moral leadership of Western society, according to another article in the same magazine. However, without a metaphysic or an epistemology, the new "moral philosophy" can hardly be more than another ideological prop; the old indifference may have been better. In any case, no "pragmatic" ideology will be able to balance the notion of "individual" (the principle of individuation, philosophy tells us, is matter) with the notion of "person" (the principle of personality is spirit). All the essential things persons hold in common arise from their personhood, but all that "individuals" have in common is their individuality—their isolation. The liberal thinks it is sufficient that the "individual" be allowed more and more social "freedoms"; so much for personality. In return, he should have the decency not to intrude on the freedoms of others—including the freedom to abort, to promote and sell lewd materials in the public sphere, and so forth.

Let each rely on his own "enlightened" self-interest its wonders to perform. By some mysterious alchemy, this pragmatism of self-interest confers a warrant for regarding the fetus as a person (or is it an "individual"?) only some time after its fourth month (or is it the eighth?), even though any distinction in which the fetus is regarded as a mere thing one moment and a person the next still remains a medical, and so a logical and moral, absurdity. On what grounds is such a distinction affirmed? On economic grounds, no less, which have suddenly become decisive—no need to debate any philosophical merits: The economic inconvenience of alleged hordes of reluctantly pregnant women (mostly lower class) is conclusive. The upper classes can get abortions any time *they* want, so even if abortion is not "all right" it would be "unjust" (also imprudent—the natives might get restless) not to let the lower classes have them. But then how could this same sort of claim have been dismissed as irrelevant when made by parents who wanted to send their children to nonpublic schools? (After all, the rich have their own schools.) Because there it invaded the *liberal* "principle" of separation. Note pragmatism's marvelously protean ability to arrange moral priorities to fit certain objectives—the first of which, of course, is to exclude all spiritual considerations ("private morality") from public contemplation. We need not prejudge the moral value of the fetus (in fact it does remain somewhat obscure) to recognize the question as crucial for society *as such*.

We can be very grateful if, as Professor Paul Freund of Harvard holds, the liberal interpretation of the establishment clause keeps "explosive religious questions" out of public debate. But few questions of this sort stir even casual public interest today. What Professor Freund apparently means by "religious" (thus subjecting them to the liberal "principle" of separation) are actually *moral* issues, like State "aid" and abortion. Yet moral issues from Socrates's time until now have been *prime* subjects of public debate, and positions on them have been the cornerstones of public and civic life. Even the American Founders appealed to "unalienable rights" conferred on all not by society but by the "Creator" (did they therefore violate this latter-day "principle" of separation?). Professor Freund seems to regret that moral issues continue to be viewed as moral issues, or else that moral issues continue to be publicly viewed at all.

Certainly there is a wondrous passion and strength in the anti-abortion movement, even after media barrages. Usually, mass deaths overwhelm the imagination and provoke nothing but yawns. This issue has broken the pattern because everyone knows that the question of social control, of who will rule, is latent in it. We could wish that people would concern themselves as passionately with the visible as with the unborn, but the possible double standard in no way confirms that the "bigots" and "hypocrites" are wrong on the issue. Liberal power is hardly disinterested here, either. And as for the "economic problem" supposedly justifying abortion, it is only a reflex of the *general* economic problem, and has no significance at all in the determination of abortion's intrinsic morality.

The liberal dreads like the plague any too-passionate commitment to ideas or moral absolutes, not just because this might lead to tyranny, but also because it might threaten liberal social power. Socially, religion, when not a cause of tyranny, is only a cause of division. Yet political pluralism, given primacy over a culture (through a doctrine like "absolute separation"), is as lethal to the culture as theological tyranny is lethal to healthy politics. The liberal thinks that merely his own "mediation" between the "pure" intellectual and the unwashed masses preserves the integrity of both the idea and the political process. But Harold Rosenberg suggests another interpretation.

Rosenberg denies that the "middlebrow's" reputation as a "mediator" is deserved, for the middlebrow is interested in ideas only for their value either as commodities purveyable at a profit (thus, the middlebrow as "communicator" or editor) or as tools of power (the middlebrow as political liberal). The man haunted by "the idea" itself is the middlebrow's enemy. Rosenberg's use of the word "idea" here is deceptive, for what he calls "the idea" becomes debased when put into any verbal formulation subject to translation into politics as an excuse for purges. What Rosenberg means by "the idea" is "the absolute," but he does not want to use that word because it suggests religion. Thus, Rosenberg, middlebrow Liberalism, and religion constitute a triangle of mutual repulsions; modern Liberalism is a reaction to religious power, and Rosenberg in turn reacts against liberal power. But he does not like religion, either, any more than the liberals do, because it makes the Absolute an excuse for purges, whereas the liberals try to *exclude* the Absolute from society. Religion supported the transformation of a hierarchical "metaphysic" into a mere prop for a hierarchical class system—it had done this for considerations of its own social power, with which it had no legitimate concern—and the liberal reacted by attacking not only the class structure but even the notion of a public morality, which had become only a mask for power-grabbing. Though the liberal proclaimed the end of class structure, and of an explicit public morality, as a social advance, all this became just another regression. The liberal cannot acknowledge the moral vacuum as a social liability because the vacuum extends his own social power. Thus, the old "moral consensus," spurious insofar as imposed by religious power, has been replaced by a vacuum, yet the liberal remains content to have no public morality, because it would require some shared meaning system and perhaps public recognition of transcendental ideals that might dispense with his putative "mediating" role, or at least with the power that flows from it. But it is untrue that the *public* pursuit of values and truth cannot be separated from the exercise and pursuit of power. All that is true is that this has never been tried.

A man haunted by "the idea" or the absolute is like Ahab. There are no Ahabs today, especially among the intellectuals, who are prepared to, and regularly do, sacrifice even ultimate convictions—commitment to "the idea"—for the sake of preserving their selves. They see their selves as threatened by "the material weight of society" (an ironic turn, in that *they* gave this material weight preponderance in the first place). Since the self is no longer oriented to or dependent on transcendental ideals, the intellectual can sacrifice even his (wholly individualist) "convictions" in order to prevent further dilution of his self. When he complains that his personality is being crushed by social forces, his middlebrow keepers commiserate, but as long as social power rests in their hands they are ready to see personalities "fall like leaves."

In place of Ahab, says Rosenberg, we get J.B., the "hero" of MacLeish's epic of liberalism—self-pity hiding behind false pity for others. Ahab and Raskolnikov outlawed themselves by their total commitment to "the idea." When Ahab got his leg bitten off, he did not try to blame it on unsafe conditions in the whaling industry. He became a social outlaw, precisely because he refused to *remain* a victim, a refusal manifested in his undeviating pursuit of "the idea." In the fiction of Fitzgerald and Faulkner all this disappears. The hero is now content to break even, haunted not by any absolute, but by the image of a more conventional self that he would be were he not prevented by his "handicap." He becomes only a pseudo-outlaw, self-made by his desire for conformity, become passionate through frustration. His pain in turn gives pleasure to those readers on the inside who see their own desirability confirmed. But Gatsby and Joe Christmas are not real outlaws. Gatsby's predicament can hardly be taken seriously. Yet, like his author, he too must be crushed, by "the material weight of society." The author is actually against his own hero, against man, and in favor of any parochial set of values that excludes the absolute. Social climbing becomes mistaken for a metaphysics of identity. Fitzgerald persecutes Gatsby (whom he likes) in order to demonstrate his solidarity with those who despise him; so Gatsby perishes by a decree of "fate." Instead of attacking the status quo, the author becomes its backbone.

Rosenberg goes on to show why we no longer attack society but are willingly victimized by it, and here too he seems just slightly off the mark. He says it is first of all because social change has destroyed the old romantic situation, the class structure against which romantic revolt was directed. We now find no entrenched classes with real authority, and the prejudices and snobberies of those in charge find no expression as structural attributes of an established order. So any attack today must occur on the level of abstraction, by which the snobs maintain their power: The drama of social reform is dead. Passive surrender to social snobbery yields only a literature of dispossession; the new alienation is mere peevishness and rancor. New kinds of social climbing succeed each other rapidly as individuals, climbing over and under each other, thoroughly confuse the question of status. Liberalism becomes not merely class-destroying, but mind-destroying as well.

But the real contradiction of Liberalism, which Rosenberg does not entirely perceive, is that it only *pretends* to be class-destroying, just as it only *pretends* to respect ideas, which in fact it values only for their contribution to that liberal power identified with morality itself. Liberalism is not really class-destroying because it preserves a mechanism of new class formation, based now not on spuriously imputed values, but only on money. In liberal Capitalist society, almost all labor continues to have what Marx called a "surplus value" (the key to his attack on Capitalism); that is, merely by participating in the economy the worker causes an increase in the money-value of the stream of goods greater than the amount of his own compensation. This difference between "making a living" and "making a contribution to society" is the difference between the labor necessary for mere subsistence and that which in addition also supposedly contributes to the common good. But this surplus is now appropriated not directly by society, but by the owner of capital, with the result that, although the economy, *as* an economy, is dynamic, the social order remains fixated and static. The social value of the worker's surplus is aborted and Capitalist economics becomes socially sterile. The capital owners who appropriate the surplus need not struggle for subsistence and can regard everything they do as "making a contribution," which in fact consists largely in administering their power over the masses and finding ways to assure its continuance. The privileged few become allies of the liberal middlebrows (who have absorbed the intellectuals); the foundation of Capitalist wealth is liberal theory, and the foundation of liberal power is Capitalist wealth.

The liberal vision of cultural history was illustrated recently by an article in the *New York Times* by Fred M. Hechinger, called "Crisis of the Spirit."[1] Hechinger says that labor unionists have transformed themselves from poor men who believed in the "liberal, progressive, humane and altruistic" American traditions as their last hope into affluent people who now appeal to the old values only to defend their own material comfort. "The American people seem to have become largely incapable of rousing themselves out of their debilitating satisfaction." Hechinger attributes this malaise to "the central point" that "there is no longer any single group whose self-interests coincide with the long-term humane national interest," as those of the unionists apparently once did.

Now, what about this breezy linkage of "liberal" with "progressive, humane and altruistic"? The only alternative to Liberalism prior to the New Deal was the fundamentalist, religious and ethnic groups liberals wanted to assimilate, if for no other reason than an "enlightened" and self-interested desire to neutralize any potential threats to their own growing hold on society, for the ethnic groups alone were immense. The liberals were also seized by their brand of altruism, which, including a certain innocence that Wills quotes Graham Greene as warning should wander the world ringing a leper's bell, always seems to coincide with liberal power. That liberals were more concerned about basic values than about this power may be true; however, its truth is self-evident only to liberals: What else, after all, could they appeal to but those values, since the public believed in the values more than it believed in liberals? And the union movement probably represented a majority whose eventual dominance anyway may have depended on no one's altruism.

But if liberals really do still have some true understanding of the "long-term humane national interest," the true self-interest of *every* group in the nation would have to coincide with it. What Hechinger means is that the immediate *material* interests of no single group now appear to coincide with the long-term national interest. Let us overlook that millions of people in this country still live in poverty; apparently their needs for some reason do not conform to the long-range humane national interest. Still, the general *spiritual* crisis becomes nothing more than the putative lack of some one group whose *material* interests would coincide with that "national interest." This is a strange "national interest." Not only, to be achievable, does it require a group whose strictly material interests wholly depend on it (and not just any group, for many present-day poor are summarily excluded), but every other group, also primarily concerned with *its* own material interests, must still recognize the priority of the disadvantaged group's claims. And by its very definition this "national interest" can never be achieved, because it always requires a group with unfilled material needs. In fact, this "philosophy" has no real vision; it is only a mechanism for legitimizing liberal power. The "national interest" results simply from the composition of particular material interests (once done "automatically" by the "system"; in the future to be done more efficiently by liberals themselves), and what constitutes the nation is simply the totality of material interests. Yet Hechinger thinks the unionists are following some principles other than those they learned from liberals, just as other liberals think that businessmen are, too.

The real reason for all these contortions is the same as for the "absolute separation" dogma: It is to deny any relevance in the spiritual dimension of social problems. Rather than the foundation of the social order, as once believed and the nation's founders naively affirmed, the spiritual has no more reality for it than the gases that drift through interstellar space. The spiritual amounts to little more than a private fantasy the sole public value of which is to lend to the liberal order an aura of legitimacy on the crucial subjective level, through the suggestion that the door remains wide open to purely "private" (suddenly the door is closed) ideals.

The liberal will not deny the spiritual per se, because that is still a political trap. Yet he well knows that it could jeopardize his attempts to solve all social problems on purely material criteria. So the spiritual must be avoided at all costs, and some ostensible basis for social unity other than the spiritual values propagated by mere religion becomes indispensable. Enshrining as a precedent the deviousness later imitated by the bureaucrats who conducted the Vietnam War, liberals proposed "enlightened" self-interest as the social unifier. In this phrase, the operative force, self-interest, was made to seem chastened by being yoked, through powerful associations with religious "charity" and Enlightenment intellectual illumination, to the inoperative modifier "enlightened." Now liberals could claim that the true national interest is achieved not by misguided religious idealists but by groups and "individuals" pursuing their own economic and political advantage—trying to take the advantage of others into account, but able in the end to leave the larger whole to the "automatic" adjustments of the "system," which the liberals controlled. People were absolved from any more real responsibility for each other than they were willing to recognize (and this often turned out to be very little) and the economic "system" institutionalizing only material self-interest (considered somehow the new cohesive bond) was separated from the culture centered on persons. Any plausibility in this ideological reversal resulted from the prominent presence in most human problems of a material component, an adequate, even creative, response to which is a pragmatic flexibility; the failure was that it ignored the equally significant spiritual dimension (centered in persons) to which "pragmatism" is simply irrelevant: Pragmatic flexibility is creative only in the service of adequate values, which the liberal seems to take wholly for granted. So he had to regard the "system" as conceptually closed on itself, and had to urge all to find a new common self-interest in their material prosperity. He may have been the only one still concerned about others' problems (or was this only a veiled drive for power?), but his appeal to higher values had the objective, or at least the effect, of blending beneficiary groups into a culture dominated by the abstract, atomized liberal systems whose atomization removed any foundation for resistance on the part of the group toward Liberalism to match Liberalism's own resistance to what made the group a group or community—usually religion.

But the social creativity of the trade unions did *not*, in fact, flow primarily from some adventitious (otherwise, it could only be called "providential," and would liberals like that?) coincidence of the unionists' material interests with the national interest, but from the unionists' strong new reaffirmation of the old cultural ideals of Charity, Justice and Brotherhood, which Liberalism certainly had no intention of denying, but did in fact deny if not primarily concerned about them, since Charity and Justice vanish when no longer valued strictly for themselves. Only their exhorting power had made clear, even to the unionists, that the national interest and the unionists' material interests coincided. And the poor still remain legion today; but the exclusive reliance on self-interest, "enlightened" or otherwise, has all but obliterated the deeper values, driven them out of not only the schools, but society as well. Self-interest can be creative for economic and political purposes only when subordinated to a culture, without which very few can know what actually *is* in their long-term self-interest. As a cultural principle itself, though, "enlightened self-interest" becomes only a temporarily more devious form of self-seeking, and soon becomes even more sinister than the usual varieties when dressed up to look like what it is not—something akin to charity. No longer allowed the older virtues for their own sake, we must depend on this laughably inadequate parody of social cohesion to hold off the beasts of that jungle even the moralizing *Times* now dimly senses our society is becoming. But that the basic values now seem more remote, unreal and inapplicable than ever could to some suggest as much the bankruptcy of Liberalism as the corruption Hechinger sees in the masses.

Thus, for every bomb-throwing, liberty-loving latter-day Patrick Henry who in the 1960s shouted that society was corrupt, the *Times* ran another editorial insisting that things were basically sound and using the rebellions as arguments for more cosmetic changes desired by liberals, the intention being to preserve and extend both the "system" and the control of it by liberals, who regarded themselves as the custodians of the national best interest. The commitment was not to morality as such, but to a moral system that yielded order. The *Times* saw the disruptions by radicals as intrinsically immoral *because* disruptive, but this attitude only goes by a more circuitous route to the goal pursued by— *mirabile dictu*!—that supposed *bête noire* of liberals, Richard Nixon. As the sociologist Alvin W. Gouldner says: "Disorder does not stem from the search for a new order as such, but is a symptom of the failure of the old order: a rising 'disorder' stems from the breakdown of the old order that is compounded by the compulsive effort to resist the new." And: "The overt commitment to social order is a tacit commitment to resist any change that threatens the order of the status quo." (Since "spiritual values" appear to be quiet values, acquisition of which for oneself, as Gouldner notes, does not diminish those held by others and requires no redistribution of power or goods, liberals smile on religion for others so long as it remains socially passive.) The quest for order "speaks on behalf of an imputed common interest shared by the privileged and the disadvantaged alike, and it thereby presents itself as nonpartisan," but it favors those who have more to lose. Real morality has no intrinsic relation to social order. Champions of order may seek to ameliorate the lot of the disadvantaged, but "such counsel is not impartial to the status quo. It is a policy of *prudence on its behalf.*"[2]

The *Times* was correct, though, in criticizing the radicals for attacking the confused society; they should have been going after the kind of liberalism imposed on it. Heaving a great sigh of relief when youth apparently grew more "mature" and resumed settling into the "system," even though no longer going off as enthusiastically as before on "idealistic" wild-goose chases that could have no impact on the "real world" dominated by "enlightened" self-interest, the *Times* failed to detect a new sense of spiritual calamity that was even more disturbing than the earlier ebullience of protest: This was the first generation in American history to experience the fact that "ideals" mean, not nothing, but less than nothing. The consequences will go deep, subverting all that the *Times* professes to hold dear, yet the paper had the naïveté to wonder how Watergate could have occurred, and why the reaction to it was not stronger. But after all, Watergate, in principle, was nothing new; it was just an application to politics of the business way of life. "Material interests" were coming home to roost.

All these arguments do not add up to a "conservative" line. The typical conservative would defend the basic economic and social status quo, even with its exploiters, in order to beat off the liberals. This analysis is more akin to "radicalism." For only in a cultural approach, and there inexorably, do the "conservative" and "radical" positions come together, isolating the liberals who now hold them apart (and benefit by doing so) in the name of a putative "mediating" function that really is only political, but which they have raised to a cultural strategy to divide the culture's resistance to liberal power. The "conservative" at his best tends to champion cultural integrity, while the radical stands radically for the integral wholeness of the person, and these twin principles of Western culture, lately denatured by the rationalist system composed only of "individuals," essentially are one. We may need a vital liberalism, but not necessarily the rationalist variety we have got.

To sum up, the false distinction between "Church" and "State" should be replaced by a distinction between sacral and secular *functions*. This new formula would return to religion its proper cultural role and, by keeping the State out of sacral functions, re-establish culture's primacy over power. This distinction would not return to the churches their old political power; indeed, it was the failure to make the distinction that cleared the way for religious warfare in the past. Nor is this any call to rid ourselves of our hard-won liberal social institutions; rather, it will save them from being swamped by problems they haven't the capacity to deal with. Indeed, the State itself is the greatest threat to these institutions. With this change, meaning might again have a chance to become the social integrator, establishing a cultural balance for a social order whose secular conflicts pluralist politics could compose, while cultural groups sought for common ground and greater unity on the level of culture, restored to its proper prestige. Cultural conflicts would not have to be translated into struggles for secular power, and then maybe, just maybe, some true culture might yet arise in the wasteland that rationalist Liberalism has created. We need the liberals to save us from religion; but we need religion to save us from the liberals.

FOOTNOTES

[1] October 16, 1972, p. 37.
[2] Alvin W. Gouldner, *The Coming Crisis of Western Sociology* (New York: Avon Books, 1971).

Economics and Society

I want to offer now a new theory of economics, which should be the replacement for Keynes's that the "experts" are universally seeking. But they may be more shocked by the source from which it comes than by the theory itself, for I am no more a professional economist than probably you are. History is still full of surprises.

Let me begin by describing what I intend to do here and how I expect to do it. Basically, I will start by presenting in schematic outline the structure of modern Capitalist economics. This outline will reveal two related features: the logical structure of economic science itself, and the "domain assumptions" upon which the science is now built. Such domain assumptions are, roughly, the principles by virtue of which, it is generally believed, a certain science is constituted a science. If these basic domain assumptions happen to be flawed—as I hope to show those presently prevailing are—the entire structure of the science is called into question. But we will not stop there. For the very criteria by which we cast doubt on the old domain assumptions also suggest not only corrections for them, but practical remedies that could give the new insights effect in the economic order. The reason why it takes an "amateur" to arrive at the new domain assumptions is that the "experts," by reason of their long training (which amounts almost to indoctrination), are simply too committed, as "experts," to the old ones to be psychologically capable of getting any perspective on them. Indeed, such assumptions are not adopted for purely "scientific" reasons anyway: The main influences controlling which assumptions will be adopted are cultural in nature. Not the least revolutionary feature of this foray is that it confronts the challenge to give an account of the domain assumptions it substitutes for those now accepted practically on blind faith. This theory, except for Marx, almost uniquely, and therefore almost alone correctly, offers a theory of culture to support and justify the place it gives to economics *within* culture. This is indeed an innovation in economic science. For, at bottom, the whole effort of economic science has been to maintain the pretense that cultural factors have been kept *out* of economic science.

At the time when Capitalist economics was born as an explicit theory, the absolute standard and model for all sciences was Classical Newtonian physics, which reflected a hypothetical cosmic "clock" with a balance of discrete and purely mechanical material forces acting and reacting on each other in a strictly mechanical way. Any "discipline" that aspired to be a science would, it was thought, have to imitate this mechanicalism or fail to measure "up" to the requirements of science. Consequently, it was considered no disservice to "Man," but rather almost a compliment as well as a favor, to postulate him for purposes of economic science as virtually a robot wholly and predictably driven by a consuming desire simply to maximize his profit and consumption. This conception relegated his more "idealistic" needs and impulses to *social* irrelevance, because they would have embarrassed the attempt to conform man to the mechanical "requirements" of science, and at that time economics was already becoming society's constitutive sphere. It was considered beyond question that man's greatest glory was to *be* conformed to the requirements of science, since, as the rationalist Enlightenment had taught, "Reason," which science simply reflected, was the ultimate constitutive principle of the cosmos itself. If the cosmos saw fit to organize itself mechanically, could mere "Man" aspire to more—or less?

Since "Economic Man," therefore, was driven exclusively by the desire to maximize his profit and consumption, it followed that all incomes automatically reappeared either as consumption or as investment in productive capacity by virtue of which the output of consumable goods might be increased. Incomes spent directly on consumption, though, created only salaries for current workers, but incomes that went into savings (i.e, investment) created not only the same amount in salaries, but also new productive capacity by virtue of which *new* workers could be hired. So the key to any recovery from a recession, and to economic growth itself, had to be savings. The mechanical laws of economics were regulated by the rate of interest which, depending on whether it was high or low, allocated incomes toward either savings or consumption. In this conceptual world, money was but a "neutral medium of exchange."

Practically anyone could verify from his own experience why saved money, which became investment and created new productive apparatus, eventually would swell the stream of goods. Without an accumulation of boards and nails, for example, one could not even erect a building, but once it was up one could get in it and produce more than before. It seemed only natural that producers should apply the same logic, cutting wages in order to increase savings and investment. Yet the worker could always find work, if he would only reduce his wage demands to the point where some employer would find it profitable to hire him. There was no involuntary unemployment, because producers would always give in to wage demands at the point where the possibilities for profit made it expedient to do so. Like some mechanical Venus, Classical economics had appeared whole and entire out of the sea.

The mechanicalism seemed softened, even dissipated, by

Keynes, who detected a flaw in the Classical logic. Some producers were raising their prices simply in order to increase their profits, yet, though the higher price level had lowered the real wages of the workers, they were still able to hire new workers at the lower real wage. This could only mean that the new workers had been *involuntarily* unemployed. Wondering how this could happen, Keynes realized that when all employers cut their wages, they also cut into something he called "aggregate demand." One producer might benefit by cutting his wages, but when all producers did it the markets shrank and curtailed production. And if demand, not wage-bargaining (the producer's saving), was the ultimate determinant of economic growth, demand and not savings must be the ultimate determinant of the employment level. So Keynes began to reconstruct the whole body of economic theory.

Classical theory had implied that if workers received wage increases that they did not somehow entirely redirect toward either consumption or savings, production would fall off. Keynes showed that when workers retained large proportions of increases in their incomes, expansion often continued anyway. The continuing expansion had to be fueled by something other than consumption, and the only alternative was investment. But the workers were not saving either, but holding their increases as cash balances. Yet it seemed unlikely that investors would invest at a much faster rate than consumers spent. So Keynes reached for a fortuitous new idea proposed by a colleague, about a "multiplier" effect resulting from normal investment. The idea was that any new investment in equipment produces not just an *equivalent*, but some *multiple*, of itself in terms of employment and consumption: Any money spent on a new machine creates not just the machine but a series of expenditures in making it that total more than the investment and that in turn give employment, as it were, to the machine by creating the markets for its products. So a greater expansion could continue through investment than the increase in consumption among former consumers would by itself generate. What led someone to invest, thus, was no mechanical "force," but simply the *expectation* of profit.

Keynes showed that workers often retain out of current income, because of expectations about future economic conditions, cash balances that for a time become neither investment nor consumption, and in the Classical scheme any such interruption of the flow of money must have caused recession. The only explanation for why, normally, it did not was that new incomes arising as multiples of the new investments generated by expectations of profits were outweighing the withdrawals of cash balances from the money stream. So expectations was the absolutely critical factor, but, since it was so highly subjective, it appeared incompatible with a crudely mechanistic conception of economics. This seeming incompatibility made the experts think that Keynes had overcome the mechanicalism, while, as it turned out, he had only included psychic factors in it.

Keynes completed his basic innovations by applying his reasoning to that central and system-balancing concept in Classical economics, the rate of interest. Supposedly an adjustment between people who needed money for investment and people who could be persuaded by the right rate of interest to postpone spending on consumption in order to invest, this rate, Keynes suggested, is instead itself determined by expectations—again as to the future condition of the economy on the part of speculators who thereby adopt preferences for liquid or unliquid assets. In fact, these expectations are *self-fulfilling prophecies*: the rate of investment rises when the profits expected from investment exceed the rate of interest, but declines when the profits expected from interest exceed the profits expected from investment. And since the multiplier magnifies any investments and soon generates the profits expected from them, you only had to expect investment profits, it seemed, in order to create them!

This suggestion that the very habit of confidence tends to generate the profits in which the confidence is placed implied more than a revolution of economics. If people only need do what they want to do, live exuberantly and without paralyzing fear, and the means to do so will appear, then economics is virtually an illustration of the Gospel injunction that life is more important than the means to it, that no more than the lilies of the field need we worry about how or whether we are to be clothed, and that when we value life over the means to it other things take care of themselves. Of course, our experience today seems to give the lie to this assumption, which was at the heart of the Keynesian theory. For today hardly a single aspect of life is not entirely dominated by its economic aspect. The question arises, then, whether Keynes was wrong in this conclusion and in his theory. The following analysis suggests that he was wrong not so much in this assumption, but in the way he acted upon it, and that his error resulted from his understanding, which he derived from Classical economics, of how economics is to be structured as a science, and of how its social function is to be accomplished.

Keynes reasoned that, since the major systemic accelerator of demand is investment, and investment results simply from the anticipation of strong demand, investors, merely by expecting strong demand, can create it. Yet, though investment *can* by itself create demand, in fact it *will* not until demand first gets the support of government to *inspire* investment. There is a circularity here suggestive of a hall of mirrors, an illusion or conjurer's trick called forth out of thin air. If the system really is "dynamic," why is the State, at bottom, crucial to it, and why can the "system" not inspire the investors by itself?

The key to this problem of demand is that Keynes is looking at it from the wrong perspective: It is not a local problem *within* the system, as he thought, but *of* the very attempt to systematize at all. Since for Keynes the problem was the weakness of demand, and his solution was to stimulate demand in order to strengthen investment so as to multiply demand, investment acquired a strategic priority over demand. Strictly speaking, of course, it was not so much his conscious decision as his discovery of the multiplier that gave investment its strategic priority, even though the *problem* was demand. But with the discovery of the multiplier, systemic demand (or, for practical purposes, labor) was revealed as chronically inadequate systematically to capital (i.e., investment): Investment could multiply demand, but demand could not, without the help of government, create investment. As Keynes saw it, the problem was not so much *why* demand was systematically unequal to investment, as *how* to crank demand up. (As we will see, it was because of certain "cultural" pressures that he *could not* ask in the fullest sense why demand was inadequate; so his best hope was simply to exploit the multiplier in order to get the system moving again.)

Paradoxically, it was Keynes's total reliance on this "new" factor, the investment multiplier, contained *within* the system, that enabled him to overlook the need, the comparably crucial necessity for, a matching dynamic factor for demand *within* the system that could rebalance the system in its new dynamic state. Instead, Keynes went *outside* the system, to government. Yet, as a result, capital's power *within* the system increases, for the system in fact *still remains mechanical*, in order to accommodate the persisting, but now anachronistic, mechanicalism of demand. It was, in fact, only because of this anachronism that any extrinsic factor such as the State was "needed" to rebalance the system otherwise made dynamic by Keynes's discovery of the investment multiplier. And since the theoretical system remained "closed" and self-encapsulated—i.e., a "totalist" or "absolute" system (as explicated later)—the old mechanicalism was communicated to the new, supposedly "dynamic" context—that is, was extended beyond the old limited economic context and imposed on the general society by way of the extrinsic balancer for the economy, the State. The mechanicalism was thereby widened in scope, so that, like a parasite, it could feed for a while on new provender, the culture. But the old Classical imbalance from the old mechanicalism

Keynes supposedly had attacked eventually had to reappear, and it recently did, bringing predictable calls for yet another extension of the mechanicalism, in the form of a latter-day *social* Keynesianism.

The basic problem was somehow to make demand *within* the system adequate to investment or, in other words, to make labor adequate to capital—its *systemic* equal. Any social system, even if it is a "total" system, must, if it is also—like our economic system —less than equivalent to society as such, be balanced from outside itself. But while a "secondary" system can look to culture for its balancing principle, a "total" system, because it is a functional surrogate for culture, must look to the State. Keynes resorted to the State for a stimulant for demand in order to make demand systemically more adequate, more equal, to capital. But this recourse outside the system for a rebalancer, while it relieved the immediate pressure, also widened the scope of the mechanicalism. In effect, government's new "benevolence" was now making the worker dependent not only on capital, but also on the State.

Keynes, like the Classical economists, was *most* concerned about the *system*—in implicit contradiction of his own suggestions about the priority of ends over means. In reality, it is not "investment" that creates demand, but human need, nor is it "investment" that satisfies demand, but human enterprise. Keynes wanted to satisfy human needs in order to preserve the system, by giving needs greater scope as "demand" within it, but his priority should have been the other way and led to other solutions. Since there was no intrinsic limit on investment, which *could* create as much demand as it wanted, but systemic restrictions persisted on the autonomous expression of real needs as demand, government had to be brought in as an extrinsic stimulant to *make* demand systemically more adequate to investment. But it is still the "system" that controls (and limits) the expression of real need, not need that controls the system. If investors decline to give it scope, need can find no expression in the system. Far from having replaced savings (and capital) with demand as the crucial variable, Keynes still left capital to determine, insofar as anything *within* the system still did, both whether human needs would be given any scope within the system, and whether such needs, by achieving systemic expression, would be satisfied. The system as such remained the fiefdom of capital, insofar as it was not also preempted by the State from outside. Of course, government could, by its spending, induce capital to play a benevolent role and to permit, by investing, human needs to find systemic expression. But this was little more than a manipulation of capital, which went along because this was the only way it could exploit its morally arbitrary advantage in the system. But it is not the workers who really come out ahead in all this; they get their needs satisfied only by wholly conforming themselves to the "requirements" of capital. Both the capital owners *and* the workers are being regimented by the "system," but the workers most of all. Certainly the economy is satisfying more needs, but at the cost of the regimentation. The party that comes out entirely ahead here is that wholly extrinsic to the system: the State. The people are reduced by theory to mere functionaries of some abstract "system" that acquires a higher social priority than the people themselves. This "reifying" aspect accounts for much of the sense of unreality and legerdemain in Keynesian theory. Proximate control of the system is retained by the owners of capital, but ultimate control (gradually becoming more proximate itself) passes to the State. Demand is no longer a variable contained within the system; it becomes the instrument the State uses to aggrandize its own power by seeing to the satisfaction of needs. The *State* is the conjurer. The system expands not to free the workers, but to add to the power of the State by withdrawing autonomy from the worker while satisfying his needs.

And what the capital owners really retain is not so much the primary *power*, but the primary economic interest in the system, for the real power begins to shift outside the system to the new extrinsic force—government—that Keynes introduced to restabilize his "dynamic" new system now rendered chronically unbalanced by the further elevation of capital and by the system's separation from any such *intrinsic* stabilizing factor as the old strictly mechanical mold was for the old static system. We are not suggesting that the old static situation was ideal or even acceptable; it, too, constituted in effect a denaturing of a "polymorphous" social reality by the mere abstract "requirements" of a system more and more conformed to mathematics. But the old Classical system was, as a theory at least, "self-balanced" by its strict confinement to the economic sphere—i.e., by the coordination of its variables in practice by the market and in theory by the mechanical static structure. Keynes's new system was no less amenable to mathematics, but no longer confined itself to the economic order as such, and reached out to drag other social institutions in to trail behind government, which it needed as a restabilizing principle and fixed point after it had broken open the old mechanical stasis. The Classical mechanicalism, which reduced men, for the system's purposes, to mere functionaries, was inadequate as a *social* equilibrator, but at least it confined itself to the economic order and was balanced (theoretically, at least) in its stasis. Keynes's new system no longer limited itself to economics, where it had become chronically unbalanced by the addition of the multiplier, for it brought government in ostensibly to act as a rebalancer, but in fact only *extended* the mechanicalism to the social sphere. This did not work out very well; it could not have worked under even the most "enlightened" of governments. Let us trace what happened in Keynesianism in more detail.

Keynes suggested that, in order to stimulate demand, the government could grant tax reductions, freeing private funds for investment, or could buy its own securities in the open market, releasing disposable funds and adjusting the national income by some significant multiple of the change in the rate of investment. Fearful businessmen, however, might still choose *not* to invest. Alternatively, then, the government could step directly in with spending programs, creating jobs and stimulating demand, creating more jobs and demand, and so on. The government deficits this stimulation of demand would create could be financed by bonds, the services on which in turn could be funded by taxation. Such government spending would inconvenience no one, because for every dollar the government spent, someone within the economy would become a dollar richer. This spending, that is, would amount to little more than a debt the community held to itself, yet, by transferring assets and encouraging productive activity, it would create wealth far surpassing what might have been created in the earlier economy without such spending. This process would endlessly create new confidence and new wealth. Like the lead rods in a uranium pile, the deficits would simply influence the rate of activity and wipe out their own "liabilities." Even the tax "burden" for debt service would become negligible, because the tax base from which the deficits were retired would rapidly expand. All these debts could be retired overnight simply by taxing everyone and turning the proceeds back, but this would be superfluous.

Why, then, do we not retire the entire national debt overnight? It is not just because of the inequities of the tax structure, onerous as they may be. Rather, the reason is rooted in the structure of the economic order itself—in capital's primacy within the theoretical system: Should the debt be retired overnight, in the morning the rich would wake up with absolute control.

Let us read a crucial passage in Keynes's *General Theory*, that famous passage in which he tries to explain the logic of his remedies to the average reader. This passage, often quoted as an amusing example of Keynes's style, in fact gives the game away:

> If the Treasury were to fill old bottles with banknotes, bury them at suitable depths in disused coalmines which are then filled up to the surface with town rubbish, and leave it to private enterprise on well-tried principles of *laissez-faire* to dig the notes up again . . . there need be no more unemploy-

ment and, with the help of the repercussions, the real income of the community, and its capital wealth also, would probably become a good deal greater than it actually is. It would, indeed, be more sensible to build houses and the like; but if there are political and practical difficulties in the way of this, the above would be better than nothing. . . .

Ancient Egypt was doubly fortunate, and doubtless owed to this its fabled wealth, in that it possessed *two* activities, namely, pyramid-building as well as the search for the precious metals, the fruits of which, since they could not serve the needs of man by being consumed, did not stale with abundance. The Middle Ages built cathedrals and sang dirges. Two pyramids, two masses for the dead, are twice as good as one; but not so two railways from London to York. Thus we are so sensible, have schooled ourselves to so close a semblance of prudent financiers, taking careful thought before we add to the financial burdens of posterity by building them houses to live in, that we have no such easy escape from the sufferings of unemployment.[1]

Keynes is saying that if money is a "medium of exchange," but people cannot buy goods, money is not really serving its purpose. If the very people to whom government spending might give money to buy goods object to such spending, the government might as well bury new banknotes in the ground and let private enterprise dig them up. That way, with the government having "spent" nothing, the people still would get the money they needed to create markets and increase the community's real wealth. It would, of course, be more sensible to start off by building houses, but if *laissez-faire* ideologues object to house-building, the digging of holes in the ground would be better than nothing.

Notice, though, that *neither* of the alternatives Keynes offers in the passage above is reflected in his own concrete prescriptions. He suggests that the choice is between the government spending directly on consumer goods and the government virtually *giving* away bills it has had printed up. *Either* of these might have been better than the nostrums he actually proposed, which amount to no more than a "compromise": a way of stimulating the system *indirectly*, so that government spending neither directly increases the supply of consumable goods, nor permits the worker to escape the constrictions of the financial system. If the government had spent directly on consumer goods like houses, it would have been socialistic (an evil word in Keynes's day), but at least there need have been no subsequent inflation, because supply would have preceded demand. If the government had, on the other hand, merely printed up money and buried it in the ground, workers who dug it up could have created new systemic demand, and some inflation, but at least the workers would not have been reduced to mere functionaries of an autonomous "system," would not have been directly subjected to the dominant control the system now gave to capital (rather, the opposite would have happened: capital would have had to pay a premium to get labor to work for it), and could have in time forced adoption of arrangements more favorable to them. Instead, Keynes managed to get the disadvantages of both alternatives and the real advantages of neither, for in the Keynesian scheme government spending both creates inflation by stimulating demand before supply, and directly subjects the worker to the autonomous system, without really increasing the overall sense of satisfaction. And the system gradually becomes, as we will see, socialistic anyway.

The Keynesian remedies (as distinguished from the basic Keynesian theory) were a response not so much to the "objective" situation as to the cultural and psychological situation. Keynes's solutions to the "objective" problem had, in order to be taken seriously, to meet two ideological requirements. First, they would have to preserve the "absoluteness," the self-containedness, of the system, so that experts could be satisfied that the solutions met the highest requirements of "science." Second, the solutions could not be "socialistic." Keynes's prescriptions satisfied these requirements. But the requirements actually were self-contradictory: Any "absolute" system (the notion of which will again be discussed shortly) cannot help but exceed any restricted sphere (such as the economic) if its constituent elements (here, people) transcend that sphere. As a consequence, such a system cannot help but become socialistic, in the sense of falling under the government's ultimate and arbitrary control.

Something else demands attention. Keynes poses as one of the rhetorical alternatives the digging of holes in the ground in order to get the banknotes first buried and then dug up. This is a curious complication; why cannot the government simply distribute the bills to all comers and achieve the same result that burying the bills would? The reason is: in order to get *labor* into the picture. This is a signal that Keynes is interested not so much in getting the consumer something to spend, as in finding a *systemic* reason for getting labor back to work. No doubt, if the system was going to function at all, there had to be a "reason" built into it permitting or even causing labor to work. But the basic objective was not to permit the "system" to function for its own sake by forcing the laborer to work by taking away his freedom not to work; rather, it was to remove any systemic impediments that might be preventing the worker from going to work if he wanted to. Keynes means to show that it would be far better for the *system's* purposes to pay the worker to work at a productive job than to reward him merely for digging up banknotes. But the basic purpose of the work in the one case is exactly the same as in the other in Keynes's scheme—to get the *system* moving again—and has no objective relationship to the subjective needs of the worker or to the human purposes of work. In other words, both expedients in Keynes's rhetorical alternatives—this is what he was really communicating —make it the basic purpose of human work itself—whether the building of houses or the digging of holes—merely to create *systemic* purchasing power; neither expedient cares a whit about the intrinsic nature of work itself. Directly subjecting work itself to the "requirements" of a new financial system that supposedly was liberating work from its former vulnerability to Classical systemic rigidity instead merely denatured work of its real human content and significance. Any kind of job could be created now; its intrinsic social content had no relevance. All this could have been done, though, only under the implicit assumption that people work primarily or even only in order to eat. But they do not. Even Keynes said that we should not worry about whether we are going to eat.

Keynes blandly suggests that two pyramids, two masses for the dead, were better than one not, as the benighted ancients thought, because of the *meaning* these activities embodied, but because they almost accidentally created employment. In this more "enlightened" age, we should be able, Keynes thinks, to get the same economic result without resorting to all the gibberish. But he fails to realize that the great economic value in these activities crucially depended on their social meaning, without which, in the face of inevitable death, they might have seemed pointless. Pyramid-building ancient Egypt possessed one of the most stable social myths, and medieval society one of the best integrated cultures, the world has ever seen. But Keynes pretends he need not worry about any meaning problem, half-consciously knowing that the validity of his own schemes will depend on the validity of entirely dismissing the meaning problem from economics—that is, of splitting the "totalist" system completely off from the culture. His "sophisticated" Voltairean wit reflects a modern desacralization that doesn't spare God, man, or nature, but the real joke is that even in the face of his own moralizing Keynes draws out of his examples the precise opposite of what they clearly teach: that when the culture is healthy the economic problem tends to take care of itself. Even Egypt was economically fortunate not so much in having two activities as in having a meaning system that infused both with transcendent value, but such intimations might cast doubt on system-mongering. Keynes would crank up the economy by creating a cultural short-circuit, by this Pyrrhic victory preparing the way for far more difficult dilemmas to slam into society somewhere in the future. What he imitated was not so much Egypt's formula for prosperity, but, by bringing in the State, its formula for becoming a hive. What could make Keynes's hole-digging coherent? Nothing. Except perhaps a renunciation of meaning. His notion that "the above would be better than nothing" is the ultimate key to Keynes's remedies; it rests on the assumption that the system of finance might legitimately have functional priority, creating its own meaning and justification. But this is false.

The experts will object, of course, that though the digging of holes *is* an absurdity, Keynes never intended it to be accepted as anything more. What is wrong, they will ask, with building houses, which Keynes did seriously intend? Nothing. But the crucial point is that unless Keynesian spending can go *directly* into consumer goods by way of productive capacity, it winds up forcing the worker to conform to a financial "system" simply to perpetuate the system. But Keynesian spending cannot go directly into consumer goods, because if the government itself started building (for example) houses, it would be socialistic—what Keynes wanted to prevent. Government spending can stimulate the production of goods only *indirectly*, and before the production appears the spending has created inflation, while the worker has been forced to conform to a system whose rewards are conditioned upon absolute conformity to the established structures of power and wealth.

Perhaps the reader is becoming confused. Does it really matter whether the main purpose of the jobs Keynes created was to sustain the system itself (if this *is* true) or to serve some obscure purposes of "culture"? After all, the system did apparently serve man's purpose to stay alive (though of course Keynes said this was not worth worrying about), and the immediate task for Keynes—

and thank God he filled it!—was to get the unemployed working
again (or was it the system?—oh well!). Keynes did get the people
back to work, and the objection to him seems wholly abstract. It
is difficult to get excited about abstractions. Oh, how true! And
this is precisely why the present "system," itself so abstract that
only mathematicians, and perhaps not even they, fully comprehend it, remains so impervious to criticism. In order, then, to
understand the basic problem, let us contemplate its most naked
form.

What *is* a "system"? In fact, as noted earlier, the word has two
distinct meanings, with radically different implications for a social
order. On one hand, the word can indicate a whole whose parts
gain meaning and function only by virtue of their inclusion in that
whole—a primary, total, or absolute system. But the word can
also denote what the sociologist Alvin W. Gouldner describes as
merely a "group whose interchanges restrict their functional
autonomy," a whole whose parts are partly or even mainly independent of each other and of the whole; this is a secondary, partial
system. To what degree, then, can a "system" be assumed to
operate in, or be imposed on, the social order? The answer is that
any *total* system must, because it gives *its* own functional autonomy
priority over that of its human participants whom it reduces to
functionaries with no real autonomy of their own, become totalitarian. But a secondary or partial system could make its own
primary purpose the actual enhancement of the autonomy of the
parts composing it. So only a secondary system is permissible in
the social order. And it was clearly in this sense that Capitalism
was first endorsed by theorists and accepted by the public: Capitalism would free the "individual" from old feudal-type dependencies and allow his personal initiative far greater scope. But
even from the beginning Capitalist theorists also claimed that the
economic order must be self-contained, virtually autonomous of
other social spheres and wholly unlimited by the wider culture, to
which the theorists claimed neutrality—nay, complete indifference.

Why did the theorists want to view the economic "system" as autonomous and self-contained? Because they wanted to make certain intractable cultural problems seem socially irrelevant. Yet it was these problems that had caused economics itself to become socially constitutive, the only condition under which it could have even aspired to autonomy. Though the problems were now dismissed as no longer relevant, that theorists might present their systematizations as controlled by nothing but the requirements of systematization itself (thus the "positivistic" character of all of modern social science, where economics became the model), in fact the very attempt at systemic abstraction, as it actually developed, was itself a cultural expedient; it constituted an attempt to isolate the cultural problems from the socially constitutive sphere so that they would not in turn attack the new economics-constituted social order they were so instrumental in bringing in! In addition, the theorists were infected by the Enlightenment's doctrine that "Reason" is the constitutive principle of the cosmos. But when this is applied to society, the question arises, *whose* reason? One man's reason is another's folly, so the only reason that could become social order had to be mathematical—deductively demonstrable. This was another reason for making the system absolute. Thus, the new science not only became *scientifically* autonomous, as was its right, but the sponsor of a total, mathematicized system, to which it had no right. And the beliefs that economics should constitute not just an autonomous science, but a *socially* autonomous total system as well (one assumption correct, the other wrong—and Marx simply reversed the mistake) became the prevailing domain assumptions of Capitalist economics. Yet the totalism of the system appeared to be in social fact not a denaturing of economic life, but a positive social advance, because it did seem successful in shoving aside the cultural problems causing the "system's" replacement of culture as the principle of social integration. Any challenges to the ongoing systematization of economics by way of mathematics were dismissed as trivial or academic, not least because they might have shaken the props supporting the power wielded by the experts, the total system's trustees. But those who objected to the systematization could offer no persuasive general solutions for the cultural problems the theorists were using the system to circumvent, so the theorists could think of themselves as dealing with these matters from a "higher" and supposedly superior level of abstraction, which they charged their critics with failing to reach. Confronting charges of insensitivity and dehumanizing abstraction, the experts professed to consider the economy a system only in the secondary sense, from which they said they departed "only" for purposes of theoretical abstraction, which they would never presume to impose on anyone's concrete activity; for, they said, they regarded the system not as closed and mechanical, but as open and dynamic, because it needed to be (at least after Keynes) not absolutely and mechanically, but only generally and statistically, predictable. But they failed to see that the general and statistical predictability to which they aspired became absolute and mechanical in effect when used to modify the behavior it supposedly only predicted, and so these protestations became little more than self-deluding attempts to disarm criticism of what actually was going on in the science of economics long before Keynes. Our culture is still deteriorating because the hopelessly schizoid theory at the heart of our economics forces upon the culture as a "solution" for its conflicts a self-enclosed mathematical system that compels people to regard each other as objects for manipulation by the "experts" and for exploitation by themselves.

Economists are still heroically devoting their lives, their fortunes and their sacred honors to the improvement of this economic "system" they think is the cause of our "prosperity," and if few among them really expected any theoretical breakthroughs soon, still, the mathematical disquisitions—so abstruse that even their authors can hardly understand them, and few others care to—that continue to infest the technical journals presumably inch closer and closer to some as yet unimaginable new synthesis that will raise the science of economics to even more rarefied heights of mathematical precision. But this so-called system the experts regard as incontrovertible fact, perhaps the single such fact in the entire science, the basic premise behind all calculations, is nothing but a mirage, and the fervently awaited messiah of economics actually appeared a long time ago, in the fifties, but was crucified by these orthodox priests in the temples of academe, presumably because such a *simplistic* impostor could never produce anything good. But there seems to be little point in clinging to the old platitudes and bromides now, when the very walls of the temple are cracking and threatening collapse, as the impostor predicted before being so rudely dispatched.

If economics is to be a science it must be systematic, but this does not mean it must construct an absolute system. Economics is itself a "function" of a culture, and its systematization of economic life remains valid only while it remains a sort of epiphany in economics of a cultural dynamism. When a system of economics tries to become functionally independent of the culture and arrogates to itself the culture's social functions, it becomes parasitic. As long as a rationalization of economics works harmoniously with an underlying cultural dynamic which it contents itself with serving and expressing, it grows increasingly valuable. But when it tries to separate itself from the cultural matrix and asserts its systemic independence it cannibalizes the culture. This Gordian knot has exercised theorists for centuries, but a social system's inability to be wholly self-contained does not wreck any possibility of theorizing; it only warns against permitting any system to give its own systemic considerations priority over the needs it supposedly serves. The culture must have priority, and one way to ensure that it does is to remember that the most important of the basic categories and concepts in any social science have implications that extend well beyond the boundaries of that science itself. Any social science is functionally independent as a *science*, but the behavior it studies does not conform to the requirements of any absolute system, and must not be nudged to do so. Neither are definitions within that science, if limited by considerations of some absolute "system," adequate to the realities they try to encompass.

When the government launches a spending program, and creates new jobs, consumer demand rises. As a result, prices rise before production can accelerate to meet the new demand. Soon, though, companies begin to expand their capacity in order to satisfy that new demand. (They can finance the expansion either out of accumulated capital from profits, or at outside sources of credit.) According to Keynes's rationale, this expansion of capacity will cause a series of expenditures that will stimulate demand even more. Thus, the government spending multiplies the economy's real wealth at a rate exponential to the government spending itself, and the larger subsequent tax base makes the government deficit for spending almost painless to retire. In fact, the government could expand the economy almost indefinitely simply by continuing its spending, were it not for the limits on the workers' capacity to work, and for the inflation resulting from the perpetual appearance of purchasing power before the capacity to meet it. Thus, it would seem to be more prudent to hold expansion to a moderate rate, so that steps might be taken, mostly through monetary policy, to keep the inflation acceptably low.

But all this is illusion. In the Classical economy, investment and demand theoretically were in static balance. The discovery of the investment multiplier exposed this "balance" as a mirage, for in fact any amount invested caused a multiple of itself in demand. Conversely, any decline in investment caused a multiple of itself in a decline of demand. Two new factors had appeared to make the theoretical economy "dynamic": the "multiplier," discovered by Keynes's colleague, and expectations, which Keynes himself discovered. But Keynes erred in trying to exploit the "new" multiplier simply by manipulating expectations to hold the economy in balance. He was the first to recognize that psychological (i.e., human) considerations had any relevance in economics at all, but still, the *basic* imbalance was in the "objective" situation, not simply the psychological, which Keynes tried to use to rebalance the objective itself. The imbalance arose from the excessive systemic weight the multiplier gave to investment, or capital, on which demand, or labor, now even more helplessly depended in the new context, because investment was now released from restraints that earlier theory had imposed. Demand had no way to exert an *internal* balancing weight on investment without government's help. Missing, in other words, was a dynamic multiplier acting directly on investment through demand to balance the multiplier acting on demand through investment. Or, to restate the problem, human needs could not find adequate expression as systemic demand without recourse outside the "system" for an artificial (governmental) stimulus that manipulated the newly discovered psychological dimension in economics, but left unchanged the inner structure because of which demand remained *systemically* inadequate. The human needs were there, but could find no expression in the system without government interventions, which, however, really solved nothing, because they left the basic imbalance in the new dynamic situation untouched. After a little initial credulity, even the investors grew skeptical.

When the government creates demand with its spending programs company profits rise along with prices, until the inflation can diffuse throughout the economy, and the producers begin paying higher prices for what they buy. Since the relatively few owners of capital have long since satisfied their own needs, most of their profits reappear as some form of reinvestment, which may again multiply demand. Now, if the new productive capacity can fill all the cumulative new demand, investment in further new capacity may cease, and the government will have to spend again to prevent contraction. But if demand still exceeds capacity, inflation transfers of real wealth to company owners may continue. The key determinant of whether the inflation will continue is whether investors precede new demand with new investments in capacity, as Keynes hoped and assumed they would, or instead wait until the new demand has actually appeared.

If perfect competition prevailed, it might be too risky for investors not to anticipate with new investment an expected new demand. For some time, though, the big question has seemed to be whether there is any competition left at all. So it seems more probable that investors instead will prudently wait. As long as government is providing the initial stimulus for demand, investors do *not* have to respond to mere expectations of demand, as Keynes thought. In fact, Keynesianism may actually curtail the role Keynes ascribed to expectations, since investors indeed may be better off if they respond only to demand they can see, holding or investing elsewhere than in productive capacity any remaining capital; the cumulative inflation caused by government spending might progressively neutralize the markets *their* spending is then supposed to create, and cost investors their investments, while an actually existing demand that exceeds the current capacity at least causes higher prices and consequent inflation-transfers of real wealth to owners without necessarily any diminishment of profits that might follow later. The Keynesian system is structured in such a way that it: (1) always causes inflation, and, thus, (2) gives owners every reason to make the inflation work for, rather than against, themselves by letting capacity lag behind demand until *government* yields to pressures to stimulate demand first. Why should owners reinvest in new productive capacity first when they can more safely invest elsewhere (overseas? in taxfree municipals?) until government stimulates demand? So long as demand precedes investment, inflation-transfers of real wealth to owners continue.

Thus, an expansion of capacity by way of Keynesian spending might be accomplished only at the cost of continuing inflation, at the workers' expense, for the owners sink *their* surplus money into investments (not necessarily productive capacity) whose value rides up on the compounding inflation, while the profits from which reinvestments come do not reflect only productivity, but also capital's positional financial advantages in the "system": not only do the owners receive a disproportionate share of any benefits of productivity because of their control of the means of production, but also their share of the money supply increases with corporate expansion because their appropriation of windfall profits is the very *cause* of the inflation, on which their reinvested profits then can ride up. The systemic hegemony of the rich improves with every new "generation" of demand.

It might be that even though owners appropriate most of the gains of productivity, the basic systemic imbalance between capital (or investment) and demand (or labor?) would not appreciably worsen *if* no inflation transfers occurred as well—that is, if demand did not appear ahead of productive capacity. But government spending causes inflation transfers that result in greater concentrations of real purchasing power in the companies and owners (and companies therefore experience a lack of markets). "Moderate" profits are necessary to fund investment in order to meet an increase in demand. But if excessive amounts are directed toward reinvestment, because those who receive profits have no remaining needs, the systemic balance between investment and demand is further upset. Profits are "moderate" that reflect mainly gains in productivity.

So we can draw two conclusions: First, the more you try to stimulate demand without *first* increasing the capacity to satisfy it, the more economic power shifts to the companies and their owners —i.e., profits should reflect actual productivity, not just, as in the Keynesian system, positional financial advantages within the system; second, profits from capital should go as much as possible to people with unsatisfied needs, so that any inflation-transfers still resulting from demand will ultimately go back to those paying the higher prices. If corporate profits could be transmitted to those with unsatisfied needs, any wealth-transfers would simply pass back as dividends to active consumers and sustain rising demand as long as the multiplier would. When active consumers thus got access to corporate profits, government spending would become superfluous, and, with demand assured and inflation systemically neutralized, expansion could precede demand. And the more any expansion can. *begin* with investment in capacity, the better, because this kind of expansion brings not inflation but deflation (more supply before demand).

What we see, then, is that, *as the system stands now*, any demand that must begin with government spending is too much demand. Not that the resulting investment is abstractly "wrong," but the "system" is now structured to give the rich a positional advantage for which others pay. The "solution" would be to give consumers an equivalent advantage, so that inflation-transfers would cease, and cease to unbalance the economy. In other words, the solution is to make the workers *owners*, thereby to create a multiplier of demand (dividends) *independent* of immediate investment and by means of which investment (capital) and demand (labor) could achieve an *internal* systemic as well as dynamic balance.

There would be one other obvious way to make profits more nearly reflect productivity. That would be to limit companies to only so much profit as actually reflects productivity, and then either to siphon off the remainder by an excess-profits tax or to seize it and redistribute it to workers. But this bundle of expedients has disadvantages just as obvious: First, the only power that could do all this would be government, and its power might increase as much as that of the companies declined; second, the estimate as to how much profit actually reflected productivity could be largely, if not entirely, arbitrary; and third, all this would tend to stifle industrial initiative, since any profits deemed "excessive" would be subject to expropriation. Nevertheless, these nostrums would, in a sense, attack the basic systemic problem that Keynesian remedies ignored. This problem is that capital owners are *so* wealthy already that they have no real need (their real needs have long since been met) for the new return from their capital, and simply re-invest it. As a result, the money becoming available for reinvestment overbalances the money available as *effective* demand, and this imbalance worsens with every new inflation-transfer. True, every new investment creates demand, but every new demand creates a new inflation-transfer to the rich, whose new wealth, wisely invested, rides up on the inflation. Thus, *real* purchasing power (as inflation mounts) tends to concentrate among those who "need" it least. This does, of course, tend to neutralize the inflation, by neutralizing the very expansion for which the inflation was considered an acceptable price. But meanwhile the new buying power tends to get concentrated, and locked up, in the companies themselves rather than continuing to be disseminated among potential consumers, and the only way to get it back out of the companies is by way of a new government spending program creating demand to absorb investments. So the cycle must begin all over again.

The Keynesian remedies were aimed at getting the "system" moving again, so the inflation resulting from the lag between the increase in demand and the actual appearance of greater production was dismissed as merely a bothersome technical annoyance—an inevitable, if puzzling, quasi-moral "price" that "reality" exacted as monitory punishment for a new economic prosperity everyone might otherwise painlessly enjoy (who says Keynes got rid of Puritanism?). But in fact this "technical" complication was a crucial structural flaw that invalidated Keynes's remedies. To repeat, two conditions must be filled before an industrial expansion can become benign: First, the *initial* demand should come directly from investment (rather than by an artificial cranking up of demand *before* the capacity to fill it exists), so that no inflation will precede supply; second, corporate profits should go to those people who will cause expansion *thereafter* to continue (if they need it) by way of demand, rather than directly by way of reinvestment. That is, the Keynesian remedies should be reversed:

What should cause a systemic expansion should be not the "system's" need for new demand (this puts the system before the people), but the persistence of unfilled human needs, as systemically indicated by a potential demand. The adequacy of output should be discovered by the *falling off* of systemic demand. Now, demand can never be *allowed* to fall off. Investors will not invest unless they "know" that markets will appear, and the only tangible assurance of markets is a government spending program. Inflation tends to neutralize such expansions, for the concentration of real purchasing power in the companies renders the consumers unable to sustain demand adequate to the amount available for reinvestment, just when inflation persisting from earlier demand begins to threaten the exchange value of owners' money capital. As a result, pressure on government to start a new spending program mounts from both consumers with unsatisfied needs and investors with immobilized capital threatened by inflation. Yet every stimulation further increases capital's systemic and social dominance. Or, rather, the system is a self-aggrandizing monster. If earnings from capital "automatically" passed to those with unsatisfied needs, pressures on capital might relax, and the economy could settle into dynamic equilibrium.

What Keynesian remedies produce is a replication in the new dynamic context of the *same problem* that exercised Keynes in the old static context. For no matter how great any economic booms become, the *systemic* insufficiency of demand grows even faster and again unbalances the whole "system." Government spending does increase demand, but this new demand causes inflation before an expansion to meet the demand can occur. Yet once the expansion begins, the capital available to meet it quickly grows. With the initial inflation now permeating the economy, the investors search desperately for shelters from inflation for their gains, before the inflation can weaken not just their markets, but also the exchange value of their capital: They want to get all their capital into a position to ride up on the inflation—if not as productive equipment, then as land or municipals.

However they invest their capital, though, it increases its domination of the physical and social environment of the workers. These investments are no longer controlled even by basically rational economic considerations, much less by integrally human ones; the controlling force in society has become artificially financial. Meanwhile, any satisfactions the worker might once have taken free from his environment he now must *buy*, so that if he is merely to stay even *his* income must continually increase. At the end of the cycle begun by government spending (but there is no end to the cycles) the owner's wealth, based on his ownership of productive *capacity*, has multiplied, while the worker's real income (and to some degree the owner's also), if adjusted not only for inflation, but for changes in cultural milieu—that is, for money's ability to humanly *satisfy*—may have increased not at all, and his ultimate control of his social and economic fortunes has declined.

Many besides Robert Heilbroner have noticed that the ownership of capital seems to have been concentrating among a relatively few in recent years, even though the absolute numbers of share owners is increasing. Several years ago, in the sixties, about 2.3% of the adult population owned 80% of the capital stock, and another 6% owned almost all the rest. But by 1973, 1.6% of the people owned 82.4% of the capital stock.[2] There are two obvious and immediate reasons why this could be happening. One is the nature of a dynamic economy. Not because of any special acumen on the part of owners or managers, but simply because of the economy's own dynamic, the financing for most corporate expansions of productive capacity is "self-liquidating"—i.e., it requires on the owners' part the expenditure of not one further cent of their own cash. Whether the expansion is financed out of accumulated profits or from bank loans, it can be paid off out of profits that eventually far exceed the amount of the loans. This phenomenon is well known to experts on finance. Thus, merely by virtue of their *current* ownership, capital owners acquire, in effect, in any expansion of capacity a permanent, increased lien on all future production, with no increase in the risks they take! And what, in fact, *are* these risks? Consider. A successful corporation (one that simply stays in the black) generally takes in more money than it is liable for to creditors. (The difference, each year before taxes, is called "gross profits.") A company takes in money in two ways: as investment, and as payment for goods and services it sells. The "payment" income is usually (though not necessarily) just above the costs of doing business, but at least this much is true: The *average* corporation turns any quantity of invested dollars into a greater quantity over any period of time. But only generally, not invariably in every single instance, for every corporation is exposed to a potential risk higher than the average risk among all corporations, and no corporation can really decipher its own prospects with entire certainty. So though adversity and uncertainty may encourage economic as well as moral virtue, they are also the major inhibitors on investment, for even a successful corporation that has captured enough of a market to reduce its average risk to a very tolerable level is still subject to them. Nevertheless, since an unbalanced economy like ours must contract if it ceases to expand, unless most companies somehow invest (which ones should remains always unclear) there will be recession or depression. Thus a contradiction: The more readily a company responds to the absolute necessity of investing, the more it exposes itself to a catastrophic reversal. But Keynes's point was that the *general* risk in investing, throughout the economy, could be made virtually negligible, if not negative, compared to the risk in *not* investing, for if government spending stimulated demand generally, the heat would come off most companies—inflation notwithstanding; should the government guarantee the markets, producers could insure their own profits by raising prices. Thus (although it is still more profitable, before investing, to wait, if possible, for the government to spend first), government's guarantee of markets makes it generally somewhat *less* risky to invest than not to invest at all. In fact, the now-established system of corporate finance can be described as a species of welfare for the rich, since the owners need not lay out any of their own cash, actually reduce their risks by investing, and still wind up with greater wealth, and more control, than they had before. Since the worker ultimately pays for it, a government spending program becomes far more a windfall for the rich than for the workers and consumers, who benefit initially, but then increasingly lose as they are reduced to dependency as inferior "partners" to capital owners whose proportional control expands as the workers' gains disappear in the continuing inflation.

The other, more obvious, reason why the concentration of capital ownership is increasing results from the way government spending is financed. When government (including local, state, and federal) sells its bonds to finance deficits, it contracts obligations to repay interest and principal to the holders of the bonds. Service on debt has grown to be the third largest public expense after "defense" and education. But who buys the bonds? Not your average person—but the rich, mostly banks. (At the time when combined federal and state debt was $363 billion, the upper 3% of all wealth-holders held most of it, and the upper 10% virtually all. Of the $466 billion then outstanding in corporate debts for capital formation, all was financed so that the upper 10% owned it. The interest on the $460 billion in personal debt, representing the gap between personal income and the supply producers wanted to sell, only served to widen the gap.) So the third largest public expense consists of the transfer of wealth from the less well-off to the rich. Of course, the tax structures force mainly the workers to pay off the interest debt, which, carrying almost no risk, is not so much a mere "neutral" economic tool as it is welfare again for the rich.

Eventually, it becomes (at least for the short run) almost more profitable, if not easier, not to work than to work. The established methods of corporate finance and of bond financing are powerful, almost automatic, "forces" that reverse the sincere efforts to spread wealth more widely by means such as profit sharing. These "forces," of the nature of a dynamic economy, are not susceptible to superficial correctives. They have become malignant because the Keynesian stimulants for demand give one segment of the economy an insurmountable *dynamic* advantage over the other segment. Paradoxically, the more demand is stimulated by government, the more is the worker enslaved to capital.

But do not the poor also get richer? Even after taxes for debt service, are they not better off, and has not the economic base grown? Perhaps. But by no means are these conclusions obvious. As we will soon consider, the increased spending power may well represent nothing more than a trade-off against a deteriorating culture. For another thing, the increase in money income also tends to put everyone in higher tax brackets. This increases the marginal profitability of not working. The Keynesian total system's elevation of the financial means to the status of ultimate economic ends in themselves (to which the true holistic human ends become functionally subordinate) in effect splits the economy (and society) into two unequal "halves"—the owners, and the workers—with the weaker "half" comprising by far the most people. The system becomes, as any totalist system must, colonialist. For in any totalist system there must be, and eventually can only be, two classes: those who control the "system" and those whom it controls. Until recently, the split remained merely economic, but it becomes more universal and social as well as the middle classes disappear.

Keynes exalted the liberal "systemic" aspect of the economy far over its lingering cultural aspects, which, with their Puritan cast, Keynes affected to despise. His system represented simply a further trade-off of culture for economic affluence—or, in other words, a sacrifice of moral legitimacy, which is one principle of social stability, in favor of the other, economic gratification. This is the proximate cause of most of the confusion of our day. Until Keynes, property rights, appointed by the culture, had functioned as Capitalist society's principles of legitimacy. But two liberal influences combined to undermine their normative authority. One was the liberal teaching, derived from the eighteenth-century English Enlightenment, that social good arises from the individual pursuit and the systematic composition of particular, merely material interests. If the "system" could "automatically" produce the common good, what need remained for moral principles rooted in the system to achieve it? The "system" could derive its "legitimacy" negatively, by allowing the individual to practice his own morality, or none, in private, while the public sphere became submoral. Of course, the exclusive recognition of gratification as a social stabilizer was partly a compensation for its earlier neglect, as well as a strategy for dispersing the old feudal elites. But in practicing, perhaps too robustly, what the liberal preached, the businessman, whose social influence was based on his guardianship of the old principles of social legitimacy, fell into a trap. Until recently, liberals have dismissed all moral issues as "merely emotive." This dismissal could not become too explicit because the culture not only had provided the moral order and appointed the businessman to watch over it, but also had appointed economics itself as society's constitutive sphere, and the liberals' own influence was rooted basically in their putative expertise in economics. So the rejection was accomplished indirectly instead, by denaturing economic science of its specifically *human* dimension, thus making it a science simply of material goods, and thus rendering the moral dimension functionally irrelevant in the constitutive sphere, where self-interest was unleashed, regulated only by the "Invisible Hand" of the market, supposedly now adjusting all interests to approximate the common good. When all this, however, did not entirely work out, the liberals blamed the businessman, whom the liberal system itself, built exclusively on self-interest, had cut off from any limiting or guiding principles such as Locke's "property rights" had once provided.

Now the liberals want a more visible—a liberal!—hand to regulate the "system," precisely as a remedy for the lack (which they caused) of any systemic check on or balance for self-interest. They advocate a governmental takeover of more and more functions that once were, with respect to the State, strictly "private" in nature, as the State becomes increasingly important in the social integration by function, which must depend ultimately on force. Yet it goes conveniently unnoticed that the new "containment" of the businessman aggrandizes the power mostly of the State, which, not the businessman, acquires the "rights" and autonomy that capital owners and managers give up. The "people" have virtually no control over the bureaucracies, by means of *their* control of which the liberals can now control the State (in the name, of course, of "the people").

It seems that no one suspected all this more than Keynes himself—except von Hayek, whose book, which was nothing if not a total repudiation and rejection of all that Keynesianism stands for, Keynes himself praised effusively. The reason why Keynes, far from disputing with von Hayek, had nothing but praise for his book, probably was that Keynes always suspected his own scheme (the best he was able to devise, and not lacking in supreme originality in many particulars for which it will always be regarded as a milestone in economic thought) to be, for some reason he could not quite fathom in theory, ultimately unsound and perversely destructive of what he wanted to defend.

Liberals now also want a centralized government policy on land use, and credit rationing, since big institutional borrowers, having readiest access to money markets, can get all the credit they want while other economically deserving units financially starve. Now, one would not argue that the crunches for which the liberals are offering "solutions" are not very real. But their basic cause was the atomization liberals created in the economic order when they imposed their total-system on it, and this atomization has now produced its own other face, the present gathering collectivism. Unfortunately, insofar as the laudable early-Capitalist desire, indeed passion, to keep the State *out* of the economic sphere was merely part of the revolt against absolute monarchy, and its supporting myth, rather than a sign of any true desire for personal freedom, the new modern myth of "autonomy" has simply replaced the old one and substituted its own limitations instead. Only this new myth can explain why the new economic system's "totalism," that reduced society to a machine, could have been so enthusiastically welcomed as a social "advance": The mythic autonomy had dissolved all cultural bonds, and these, to a totalist system, are only an encumbrance anyway. So the fate of the business elite was sealed, and the liberal pseudo-elite began assuming not the old elite's guardianship of any true moral order (seemingly now rendered dispensable), but control of the bureaucracies, with which they squeezed the old elite out. The market became the balancer for society as well as for the economy, and the totalist system began to integrate society on the level of mere function, in place of the former cultural integration on the level of meaning. Yet the market could function well as an economic equilibrator only so long as it did *not* have to balance society as well; the liberals finally had to substitute, for the market, the bureaucracies that had appeared in order to resolve the tensions that making the market the *social* balancer had caused. A merely secondary system in the economic sphere at least could have given the culture continuing indirect influence on the system, and partly relieved the tensions caused in making economics socially constitutive. The market could balance the economy on the level of function only as long as the culture could integrate society on the level of meaning, but the culture could no longer integrate society when the *socially* constitutive sphere was claimed by a totalist system.

The whole vindication of the early-Capitalist economy was that, as a *self*-balancing, autonomous, and socially constitutive area for freedom, it preserved a free society. Yet if the Federal Reserve, for example, becomes able unilaterally to determine a set of social priorities for rationing credit, the government will be taking over the very balancing function it was early Capitalism's whole aim to keep out of the State's control: The very problems the systemic totalism caused become the excuse for extending it. In our economics-constituted society, where supposedly the "system" functions automatically to ensure both individual freedom *and* the common good, any fundamental interference in the market "mechanism" implies a social revolution, but in this case it is imposed from above by those in political power, and remains manipulable to serve their interests, though it is perpetrated, of course, in the name of all. There is seldom any lack of compelling reasons for abolishing freedom, and liberals have never been slow to reject those that might threaten their own control, but an excuse that might increase liberal power seems very persuasive. So now they want "rationally selective" controls on credit, rather than the accidentally selective controls of the present market, for of course the "rationality" will be basically liberal in nature. The new "rationality," the new moralism, will, of course, be administered by new bureaucracies. Some, though, might prefer the old accidental selectivity, unjust as it may be, for at least it remains obvious for what it is.

Meanwhile, the chances of becoming economically independent, a truly free entrepreneur, become ever smaller as economic power continues to concentrate, big corporations divide up markets, and government bureaucracies harass all businesses, including corporations, which, of course, often passionately seek "regulation." But as a replacement for culture (and religion), the merely economic total-system has long since served its liberal purpose, and the liberal does not really much like the "selfish" businessman anymore, with whom he must share social power, and who, stripped by the liberals of his moral role, now seems to be interested only in money, while the liberal has (thanks to the businessman) enough money and is more intent on power. Even more irritating to the liberal, the businessman, in order to perform his economic function, needs a generous measure of freedom, but such freedom (which, in the Keynesian welfare State, even the businessman does not entirely want) puts unpleasant limits on the great and noble ambitions the liberal entertains for society, so the liberal would like to relieve the businessman of it. However much the earnest and relentlessly moral liberal may "aesthetically" admire real spontaneity, he is by very nature suspicious of it as basically frivolous and subversive. Just as the essence of liberal "religion" is the rationalization of belief, the essence of liberal social "philosophy" is the wholesale rationalization of society. He needs to rationalize everything, and as more aspects of social life come within the reach of his systematizations, he resents any spontaneity much more than he loudly tolerates it (for now) in socially "marginal" "private" spheres the State does not yet seek to control, as he demonstrates his open-mindedness and freedom from "dogmatism" (or substantive beliefs with any social implications). But even more fearful of than fascinated by real spontaneity, or evidence of real life, the liberal aims, so as to "solve" social and moral problems, to impose on all of society a good gray "rational" uniformity (his), in the name of justice and environmental integrity.

It is easy to guess how liberal Keynesians will react to the foregoing description of their economic system. They will say that investors need not wait for profits in order to respond to new demand that government deficit spending creates, for they can immediately borrow from banks new money created by the government's sale of bonds to finance the deficit spending. Of course, if the "public" (i.e., private banks) buy these bonds directly, there will be *less* money available for private investment, and because of the increasing competition for money, interest rates will soar, causing more inflation and dampening any expansion. (Government now claims 80% of the capital market, industry only 20%.) If a real expansion of industrial capacity is to occur, therefore, the Federal Reserve must instead buy the bonds itself. What happens then is very interesting.

There are three basic ways to increase the supply of money, and the Federal Reserve is basic to all of them. The first way is to increase the credit that the "Fed" can allow to commercial banks, and this, too, can be done in three ways: by having the Fed make "open market" purchases of government securities; by having the Fed change its "discount rate" (its charge for loans) or other controls on loans so that commercial banks can borrow more from the Fed; or by increasing "float," the time it takes banks to collect balances on checks they have cashed. The second basic way to increase the supply of money is to increase the Treasury's stock of gold, and the third way is simply to increase the supply of Treasury currency outstanding (this way is favored by "monetarists").

As Keynesians well know, to have the Fed buy government securities is the quickest, and most easily manipulable, way to exploit the basic principle behind all these ways of affecting the money supply. This principle lies in the unique quality of any money held by the Federal Reserve. Except to buy government securities, the Fed does not spend money. Its money is simply a "reserve" made up of deposits by commercial banks, whose own loans may not exceed these deposits by more than a stipulated multiple. For example, if the "reserve requirement" is 20%, the total of loans a commercial bank makes may not exceed by more than five times what that bank has on "reserve" at the Fed, and, conversely, the bank must hold in "reserve" at the Fed one dollar for every five dollars it lends. A corollary, though, is that for every dollar the bank acquires in reserves it can actually "create" five new dollars in loans. That is, for every additional dollar that the Federal Reserve acquires (except as a direct result of increasing the reserve requirement itself), the *general* money supply increases by several dollars (i.e., by an amount equal to the proportion of commercial-bank cash to commercial-bank "reserves." At present, the effective ratio of loanable new money to new reserves holds at about 2½ to 1. The whole process of money creation is examined in more detail later in this chapter.)

When the Fed purchases, say, a $1 government security, there is an increase of $1 in commercial-bank reserves, because, though the Fed pays for the security with a check drawn on the Fed, the Fed, with its banking system, is the only place the seller can deposit the check, and so the Fed gets the $1 right back as a deposit. By buying the security, the Fed has simply acquired $1 more in reserves. If its reserve requirement is 20%, the $1 new deposit can "reserve" $5 in new loans by the commercial banks. (If it wanted to reverse this process, the Fed would sell the security back to the government.) This is how the Keynesians get money to the banks to fuel investment. No doubt, since the new money appears before new goods, it creates some inflation, but this is considered an acceptable price for the transfer of wealth to the relatively poor by means of the programs the government deficit spending finances, and the poor then will create demand.

Strangely, the critics of Keynesianism have largely ignored the greatest flaw in this logic. The government security becomes, in effect, part of the money supply, simply because the Fed accepts it as equivalent to money for "reserving" loans. Yet, when created, the security represents neither gold, as a Treasury gold certificate would, nor *present* productive capacity, but only the State's coercive power. For the State has to retire this security, with the interest on it, from the money supply, and must extract the money from the citizens. Furthermore, though it is true that the original increase in the money supply when the Fed purchased the security enabled new productive capacity to come into existence, when the government buys the security back, or pays it off, as much money is "canceled out" as the security had originally reserved, and the means to buy what the new productive capacity could produce disappears with the disappearing money. Thus, the State must continue to spend to keep the new productive capacity producing, as meanwhile the initial inflation has leached out money's buying power. In order to prevent recession, the State must spend more and more, and it becomes a larger and larger presence in the economy, which begins to revolve around the centralized State.

Keynesianism is essentially an attempt to accelerate what the "monetarists" say the economy could eventually do better by itself anyway. The monetarists hold that the way to expand the economy is to print new money so that people will get more money to spend, and to do so at a steady rate so that people will know what to expect. The problem the monetarists see in Keynesian "fiscal" manipulations is that these almost invariably exceed or fall short of the exact amount of stimulation or restraint the economy needs, so that general confidence is ruined by inflation or by erratic swings in policy. Both sides are right and wrong in opposite ways. By relying simply on mechanical increases in printed money, the monetarists would only preserve an already inequitable distribution of economic wealth, since the rich would still gain most; moreover, this is to try to regulate what is dynamic by what is merely mechanical. Limiting the money supply to conform to mechanical theory dooms the social order to the lingering mechanicalism of the economic order. What makes the stabilization of the economy through the money supply so difficult is the uncontrollability of money's velocity—i.e., people's willingness actually to spend it. If people have no confidence they will simply hold on to any new money instead of spending it. But if confidence later suddenly rises, the increased velocity of money could send prices soaring at precisely the wrong moment. The only solution would be to make the system more rigid. On the other hand, when Keynesians affect demand and the money supply by manipulatively expanding or contracting government debt, they make the opposite mistake: They separate the creation of money from any intrinsic structural control—as though a ball swung on a string by a boy should suddenly begin to swing the boy—and the economy begins to cannibalize society. Both approaches reproduce a different aspect of the collapse of 1929: monetarism the rigidity, Keynesianism the speculative frenzy. And because it seldom permits contractions—the dynamics of the economy having become politicized when the State acquired control of it, and too many jobs having come to depend directly upon government spending—Keynesian economics relentlessly encourages inflation.

It is true that the State does not hold the personal wealth it expropriates from citizens; the money the State exacts from them through taxation is acquired by other citizens as payment for government purchases (although it is true that much of the spending goes to the rich). But real money (as we will later see) always moves or it ceases to be money. The real problem is function: Who or what *causes* the money to move? If it is the State, the State acquires a crucial power over citizens' lives, which begin to depend directly on the State. The Keynesian State forces no one to *do* anything (yet), other than to cough up taxes. But everyone is becoming helpless without the State nevertheless. This is the classic power of Big Brother. Those who regard the State as normal and normative might find nothing objectionable here or contrary to their own "faith." But nothing like this was even remotely foreseen or intended by the Founding Fathers.

In reality, that production will be increased partly because of the government's financial manipulations is only an indication of the rigidity of the system, in which such manipulations remain the only way to get production started. Most economists agree that the only true foundation of an economy and a money supply is productive capacity, although some commodity like gold is usually, for convenience, substituted instead. When the Fed, though, increases the money supply by making government's deficit-financing paper (the bonds) in effect "discountable" at the Fed, it not only does not replace gold with productive capacity, but substitutes the State for gold: That State coercive power the early Capitalists passionately wanted to exclude becomes the very foundation of the economic order.

Actually, this whole chapter is basically a critique of the consequences of this shift. Once the problem is correctly stated, the best remedy becomes clear. That remedy would be to make "discountable" at the Federal Reserve a *private* security based not on future production to be stimulated by speculative financial manipulations, but on actual and present productive power immediately purchased from the proceeds of the security itself. This productive capacity would appear along with or even before new demand. How this might in fact be done is the real burden of this chapter.

The questionableness of the basic financial manipulations by the government is what accounts for the strange hallucinatory quality in the rest of the Keynesian operations. The compounding inflation, caused on the one hand by the government when, before any new productive capacity has appeared, it spends the money it has received for its securities, and on the other by the Fed, when it causes more money to appear before supply—this inflation represents merely a trade-off of economic activity for price stability. The wheels of the Keynesian "system" begin to spin, but the real problems are only postponed. Also, deficit spending almost never goes directly into consumable goods, although it often goes into what many consider desirable services. Aimed only indirectly at stimulating production, it causes, as we saw earlier, inflation-transfers of real wealth to owners in the initial surge of government-stimulated demand. Since basically the owner is helped more than the worker, the latter eventually realizes that to work pays him less and less. And since a huge portion of government spending represents simply "transfer payments" back to the relatively poor, in the form of benefits, pensions, etc., the worker learns that the more he can depend on more or less automatic government transfers of wealth to him, the less he needs (or even should) work. This does not, though, mean that he can cease altogether to work, for as "capital" gains more and more control of the physical and social environment, the pressures exerted on the worker to find and hold a job, if only for its fringe benefits, become irresistible. The worker comes to depend on the government, the State's power grows. But as mere considerations of finance deprive the worker of any real social or cultural function, the greater grows the temptation—no, the necessity—to fake the work and to use any creative energy to secure greater benefits. So many jobs having become bureaucratized, there isn't all that much objective work to do anyway. Thus, though the owners' advantages in the old static system might have been unfair, Keynesianism is no solution. It simply subjects owner and worker alike to the State, and the transfer payments it relies on to flatten business cycles are merely exactions on the more productive members of the economy in favor of the less productive.

Insofar as any "real" expansion at all results from Keynesian spending, it arises not from investments financed at banks (unless the financing is drawn from earlier bank surpluses) but from hidden windfall profits owners acquire at the workers' expense. And this expansion remains "real" only until the initial inflation diffuses throughout the economy—until then, purchasing power, simply transferred to the owners, *is* going into productive capacity, and the relative deterioration in the worker's position is hidden in the economic expansion purchased at the expense of the culture. But because, fatally, the worker is not really encouraged to work harder, but less, the government's transfers back to the "poor" do not offset the inflation-transfers to the rich. The "negligible" inflation-transfers to the rich enable the rich to sustain investment, the complex maneuvers do suggest an "open" and dynamic system, and insofar as the "system" is dynamic it is more "creative"—of wealth. But the maneuvers are deceptive: The system is not really open, but still closed, so that the new dynamism renders even more ferocious the social and cultural parasitism of the old economics. What we see here is still a closed circle, a "totalist" system cannibalizing society in order to perpetuate *itself*. That is usually what we are seeing whenever holistic human values are subordinated by "experts" to the "requirements" of some abstract system.

The Keynesians can show no way out. It may be possible to stimulate employment, or to dampen inflation, or even more or less to do both at once, but only at the cost of enforcing a bland new stasis, holding the social order in a vise of immobility while all spice, all fire, all human values, and finally even the basic intelligibility of the social order as well, are sacrificed for the economic "stability" that is supposed to serve human life. And even to achieve this the State will have to maintain constant deficits.

Thus, though more people than before may have greater purchasing power after the Keynesian spending, the apparent improvement may be illusory; people's incomes have risen, but their whole social and cultural situation also has changed. The "system" has acted as a philosopher's stone to transmute the culture into a sort of economic "prosperity" that raises more problems than it puts to rest. Even the perplexed worker seems to resent the Faustian bargain made in his name, and mostly at his expense. Many workers have indicated that if they had the choice their ancestors had a hundred years ago they would be even more eager to flee to some distant "natural" frontier. A recent private survey showed that more than half of the American people would rather live in a "rural" environment than where they live now, in spite of the long-term migration to the city.[3] But no chance: The economy has already absorbed all the land, so people must take whatever work is offered where it is offered. A recent government survey showed that almost one out of every two people in the work force—a "staggering" proportion—now regrets his choice of occupation. But any benefits that are to accrue to a *worker* from Keynesian policies must accrue by virtue of his labor. Perhaps workers do not fully realize that *all* work is becoming uniformly gray as considerations of finance rather than of cultural function increasingly dominate it. As the Communists put it, the Capitalist worker, selling his labor like just another commodity, equal in value to other commodities, is becoming alienated from himself because of this subjection of his own personal expression to the requirements of some abstract "system" of finance, as meanwhile the capital owner becomes increasingly richer merely by virtue of his earlier owner-ship of the means of production.

The social prophets were once unanimous on the obsolescence of mere labor and the imminence of universal leisure, but they have recently become prudently quiet. For most "leisure" is still reserved for humiliated "beneficiaries" of welfare, who cannot find work even if they want it: As yet another documented study has shown, as much as 60%—60%!—of the American people remain underemployed, in the sense that their jobs do not deliver enough money to maintain these people above the minimum the government deems necessary for reasonable *subsistence*![4] The search for work continues and intensifies, even though most people sense that much of the "work" now done is ultimately not very productive. This astonishing statistic suggests that either govern-ment spending has not much helped the worker, or his predica-ment before the spending must have been truly frightful. Is that the impression we get, though, from what we know of nineteenth-century life? As Peter Drucker has pointed out, unemployment was never a problem in any recession before the Great Depression, and afterwards was the problem that improved last "if it improved at all." For whatever apparently small even economic advantages the worker gained through Keynesianism, he now finds himself not only locked into a "system" from which he cannot hope to escape, but an inferior "partner" in that system, his destiny increasingly slipping from rather than being consolidated under his own con-trol. And meanwhile his cultural function, subordinated now to his mere systemic function of creating demand, evaporates; as one writer has convincingly argued, at least a third of all present-day jobs are economically unjustifiable by even minimal standards of productivity, while Professor Andrew Hacker, who grinds no axes, argued (in what Heilbroner called the best single chapter he had ever read on the subject of the American economy) that even most white-collar jobs serve no real purpose (except, of course, to create demand).[5] What all this suggests is that the Keynesian operations mainly stuff with more deadwood an econ- omy already dangerously overstuffed with unproductive and resent- ful deadwood, and any who cannot be stuffed in must live by redis- tributionist handouts that (under the circumstances, mercifully) need other armies of otherwise unproductive bureaucratic dead- wood to administer them. And those fortunate enough to find these meaningless jobs must seek ever higher wages just to maintain themselves in decency. For if, in a "natural" environment like the American frontier in the last century, it took very little money, and at Walden Pond even less effort, to live with some dignity just above subsistence, when the environment and culture become dominated by an economy the picture changes drastically. Increas- ingly, satisfactions must be *bought*. And it is precisely the most basic human satisfactions—those associated with "Nature" and culture—that become the most expensive as the economy absorbs the environment, and the least necessary that become the easiest to get. If the "system" itself is out of balance, the environment will become a bombed-out wasteland abandoned to concrete, glass, plastic, and (in our individualist "system") mutual exploitation. If people do not—contrary to modern wisdom—live by bread alone, it is more than possible, it may be probable, that the grad- ual rise in incomes has not nearly matched the psychic burden placed on them, and in a holistic sense there may have been a further decline; we may be, culturally, worse off than before Keynes. And the savage irony is that we might have had, had we wanted it, even more wealth than we have now, with far fewer un- pleasant consequences, had the experts been willing to listen to a proposal made almost twenty years ago. But since it contradicted all their self-serving platitudes and banal certainties, though they never could show any flaw in it they ignored it.

Let us stop here to recall that the mainstream of Western economic theory has entertained two lines of thought on Keynesian theory. The Keynesian and "neo-Keynesian" schools pretty much accepted Keynes's basic logic. The monetarist school resisted it, refusing to overlook certain remaining inconsistencies or difficulties that the others thought practical necessity counseled to overlook. But even as Keynesianism took hold, the gap between the "haves" and "have-nots" widened; the rich seemed to grow richer at the expense of the poor, who grew poorer, and economics still seemed to be hanging in the limbo of a situation as unjust as it was para- doxical and absurd: Everyone agreed there was the technical capacity to produce virtually everything anyone could need or even imagine himself needing, but economics still had not found a way to get goods to people who really needed them. So even revolutionary schemes that would end economic and political free- dom became tempting to mainstream economists and the general public, and soon the monetarists, who had become vocal in the 1960s, fell silent after their ideas suffered defeat as merely politi- cally inexpedient. But this was enough to stifle the monetarists, and even convert a few, even though the neo-Keynesians had hardly solved the real problems any better than they thought the monetarists could. The hope for theoretical breakthroughs was not in vain, but the man who proposed a simple solution to the prob- lems Keynes had left—it reconciles the Keynesian with the mone- tary schools, reveals some new merit even in the commonsense approach of Classical economics, and even might resolve the differences between Capitalism and Communism, insofar as these differences are rooted in economics—was not accorded even the dignity of rebuttal.

But it would not be enough for our purposes to show that his proposal would work. For the real question is not *whether* it would work—obviously it would—but *why* it would work, and that, strangely, is something that no one has really explained. This key to our economic crisis which has been lying around in broad view for twenty years remains unappreciated because the theory that would reveal it for the sensational remedy it is has not yet ap- peared. Let us try to deal with this problem now.

The domain assumption that economics could constitute a total system achieved expression in various ways. First of all, a *total* system must be entirely material in nature, so that nothing about it might escape measurement and coordination with other variables. Thus, an economics treated as a total system must exclude an entire dimension as basic to the science as its material component, but having the unfortunate property of being the formal link between economics and the wider culture, so that those economists who suspect its importance yield to the fear that alluding to it might invite ridicule from other "experts," even though this dimension is almost platitudinously obvious. But that it might have little immediate relevance for the limited practical purposes of this or that expert hardly diminishes its explosive potential in the economy as a whole. This dimension pervades the science as the basic dynamizing ingredient of what the science studies, and seems platitudinous and banal only because we remain only partly conscious of it, just as we remain only partly aware of the horizon encompassing particular objects at which we gaze. But its significance grows (1) in economic categories in proportion as these are fundamental to the science, and (2) in any branch of economic theory in proportion as the branch's scope approximates that of the whole science. Today, several mere branches are far better developed than the central coordinating theory for economics as a whole, which, under the dominant Keynesian theory, still remains partly undeveloped and confused—a situation mathematical economists are trying to fix by developing not the central coordinating theory itself, but mathematical and statistical systems that might render development of the central theory all but irrelevant, except as a base for new statistical "laws." So the present basic "system" is viewed as basically definitive, at least for general coordinating purposes, even though many more "problems" remain that the statisticians are expected to clear up.

Perhaps the reason why this dimension to which we are referring is never taken seriously is not so much that it might cause economics' self-transcendence into social theory and threaten both the system's putative self-containment and the economists' prestige, because the experts could simply become social "experts" and acquire even more clout. Rather, it is because this dimension might be altogether too useful toward purposes "society" (i.e., the intellectuals) believes no longer can or even should be pursued that it is repressed and obscured by jargon recognizing only the immediately utilitarian aspect of economic practice. What, for example, does the word "financeable" mean? That a loan can be more than retired out of the proceeds from the projects the loan pays for. Here is something on its face very nearly miraculous—a process that turns out to be greater than the sum of its parts. But "financeable" refers to the advantages an investor derives from the process, while no concept really covers the phenomenon as it is in itself. The purpose of economic jargon is to describe quite curious realities from the utilitarian point of view of those who hold the dominant "interest" in them, so that the integral whole is never faced. The economic jargon tends to benefit the owner of capital, who owns the dominant interest in economic procedures.

Now, what is that dimension that is excluded? Consider the definition of economics. We read that economics is a science of the production and distribution of goods. This suggests that as a science of material goods economics can and may be primarily mathematical in nature. But this does not follow. For economics is not a science of just any goods. Is it not, after all, a *social* science? The goods that bees produce, for example, are not included in the definition until man gets involved. Economics is not a science primarily of material goods but of how *men* produce them, and this modification is anything but modest. It is the human aspect, not the material aspect as such, that is the specifying part of the science's definition. Economics is the study of the production and distribution of goods (the material aspect) by man (the formal aspect, specifying the range of the subject matter). But this formal aspect is eclipsed in the focus on mere goods amenable to quantification. Yet this is what the experts—*as* experts—wanted: to deal with economics as a purely mathematical science or "specialty," so that they need not bother themselves about annoying "subjective" questions of, for example, human values.

A brief digression here might illuminate this matter. We recall that economics sprang into existence implicitly whole and complete as practically a branch of celestial mechanics. Its development was at first regarded as proceeding relentlessly, mostly by way of deduction, as a sort of filling-in of the framework definitively established by Smith in one initial stroke. It seemed almost incontrovertible that this mechanical system applied to the social world almost exactly as Classical Newtonian physics, the absolute standard for all science, applied to the physical world. For, as physics revealed, the entire universe was a self-sustaining mechanical "system" functioning like a glorified clock. Keynes's theories in economics and Einstein's in physics jolted these suppositions, Einstein proposing that matter, because it is also energy, and Keynes that investment, because it depends on expectations, could not behave in a purely mechanical way. Yet whatever happened to the mechanicalism in physics, in economics it was simply "raised" to a new psychological level.

This is why economics is now regarded as a science far better grounded than sociology. Economics could continue on in its rut because it could argue that its final concern was not, after all, with mere expectations, but with the actual production and distribution of goods, which were gratifyingly more measurable, and conformable to mechanical mathematical systematizing, than even the strangely nebulous movements and transformations of so abstract, if not ethereal, a concept as "energy." So expectations could be merely absorbed in the system-mongering, rather than becoming a means of breaking the science open to let specifically human considerations in. Because manufactured goods are so concrete, the constant presence in economics of something perhaps even more elusive and problematic than the energy of physics—i.e., human energies—could be overlooked. They were folded into the continuing mechanicalism and forced to conform to the requirements of measurement. Thus, although wages, the rewards for expenditures of energies, were measured in terms of goods the wages could buy, goods themselves were measured only in terms of other goods. As this was the only way to measure precisely—and precise measurement was considered the key to progress—economists refused to see that, since goods could not be measured also in terms of the energies that went into their production, attempts to measure them in these terms would result in a perpetual reductionalism whereby men became for the "system's" purposes mere objects like those they produced. Economics' apparent superiority to sociology as a science was merely the result of denaturing in economic theory the realities it sought to analyze, of thereby apparently conforming them to a continuing mechanicalism, and of hailing this as a triumph of science, which in a way it may well have been. But sociology's seemingly chaotic condition may be less dire in comparison than it seems, because sociology at least recognizes (for now) its problems, and its much wider scope eventually may offer economics a way out of its own impasse. Economics and sociology are both at once social (the critical ingredient even in economics is people, not the goods they produce) and statistical sciences.

The advantage early economics had over early sociology was that economics could start with an established paradigm, the triad of land, labor, and capital, in terms of which the mechanical theoretical "system" could be developed, for even people could be rationalized in terms of them, and, more important, nudged to conform to the paradigm in fact. The society not only was receptive to this effort, but encouraged it as a way of neutralizing its cultural tensions. The hidden philosophical commitments necessary to sustain the effort to mechanicalize were in the air as part of the cultural ambience, so Classical economics could pretend to be treating only of economic activity, as if all else really were left to each person's own discretion. But Capitalist economics could not have worked at all except as the whole implicit social philosophy it really was. That it worked shows that the whole society conspired in the effort. Economics could ostensibly dispense with philosophical questions because its own philosophic supports commanded a general consensus, or at least general acquiescence, however grudging in some quarters, in the absence of anything better. These philosophic supports remained vulnerable to more than superficial inspection, and precisely because sociology now appeared on the scene as a lightning rod for suppressed desires and resentments, a sort of social devil's advocate, its interests and situation seemed diametrically opposite to those of economics. Sociology began as a sort of grab bag of crackpot philosophies (from the Establishment's point of view) with only the most tenuous relation to the concrete social order. It was, though, at least reasonably explicit about its philosophic assumptions, took them quite seriously, and attempted to defend them, while economics was pretending not only that it had none, but that they were irrelevant anyway. The problem for economics has been to recognize its basic inhumanity; for sociology, to find a way to root itself in the concrete social order as well as in abstract theory —to find an adequate methodology as well as an adequate theory.

What the economists have ignored is that, since economics deals with the tangible products of human enterprise, economics is a study of human energies. Yet how might this insight be applied in the science of economics? The expert regards as platitudinous the idea that economics studies the production and distribution of goods *by man*, and would suggest that this "insight" contributes little to the solution of real problems. But what concept holds the modern science of economics together, and coordinates the various branches of theory and practice? Money. This is the most basic concept of economics, but its definitions notoriously remain both circular and the most persistently perplexing conceptual enigma in the science. And because, again, these definitions are entirely limited to the material aspect of what they try to define. Thus, the definitions of money strike anyone with any curiosity about this powerful incentive, builder and destroyer of empires, as the most anticlimactic disappointment in the entire literature of economics. A beginner gets an appropriate introduction to the "dismal science" by reading that money is but a "medium of exchange" or, more ridiculously, "the sum of demand deposits and cash in circulation." Writers apologize but, having nothing better to offer and probably dimly sensing here a real Achilles' heel, quickly move on.

We seem to know more about money's curious properties than about its real nature. It is, for example, the only item in economics that appears as both asset and liability in the same respect on a balance sheet. It is also curious that economists seem to be evenly divided over whether to include time deposits in money's definition, since time deposits remain longer in the bank and while there seem dormant, and money's properties seem to fade as its activity diminishes. If money has no immediate physical function, or signifies some other commodity (e.g., silver or gold) that also usually is physically unfunctional, why does it lose its properties when it ceases to move? It is because when money moves people are doing something with it that its value evaporates when it ceases to move. The current definitions of money do not so much as hint that human energies are intrinsic to money's real nature, but while a barter economy is based on the *products* of human energies, a money economy substitutes for such products the *energies themselves* as the basis of exchange. That is, a supply of money is a symbolic pool of human energies, and this aspect is an intrinsic, not accidental, part of money's real nature. Whatever can evoke energies can be the initial base of a money system, and in some societies it has only the value attributed to it by magic. But money becomes functional only when the energies it represents actually are pooled—that is, only in organized society. Thus, we arrive at a new definition for money: Money is a symbol of human energies, and a money pool is a symbolic pool of potentially organized (social) energies. Money is a claim on the energies of the other people in an economy.

This definition points to the properly "social" (i.e., human) dimension of the science of economics, and in the next few pages we must trace this dimension through the basic operations of economics. It may, of course, seem obvious, but can be dismissed as platitudinous only so long as its appearances in discrete instances are dismissed as unrelated, and this is how we must evaluate them when the definition of the basic concept (money) for the whole science of economics excludes the social dimension. But when included in the definition of money, this dimension soon begins to reveal its revolutionary implications.

An owner of money who has no immediate need for the energies (or products of such energies) his money can claim can transfer his claim to another whose need of these energies encourages him to agree to pay back later with "interest." One of the bank's most important functions is to mediate this relationship. But the bank does much more, and its creation of money seemingly out of thin air gives the bank an almost magical aura. Suppose that several men contribute gold to a pool for lending at a profit. They have become a bank. But to anyone who requests a loan the bank gives, not gold, but a written promise that gold will be delivered on demand, and the bank's reputation can make the promise (or "note") as good as the gold itself. The note thereby becomes money. Most of those with a claim on the gold will not exercise it, because they need not gold but the energies it can summon, so the bank can promise far more in gold than it actually has, until the amount of gold actually being claimed begins to approximate the gold on hand or coming in (for the bank will itself pay interest on new deposited gold). But since the bank will charge more in interest on its own loans than it will pay on deposits, and all borrowers will pay money interest even if they claim no gold, the bank's profits will expand at about the same rate as its lending volume.

And abstractly, the claims on gold can infinitely exceed the gold the bank has on hand, because the bank must have on hand only as much gold as actually is being claimed. If it could persuade all borrowers to leave "their" gold in its vaults, it could multiply its notes indefinitely on a small quantity of gold and still receive corresponding volumes of interest. In reality, though, when this multiplication of money exceeds some limit of the borrowers' ability to repay with *real* interest, inflation will neutralize further expansions of credit, for borrowing and lending are responsibly done only so long as the actual economic productivity of loans exceeds the inconvenience of interest charges. Everyone wants more money, but if more money is circulated than can find productive uses the money becomes debased, people revert to gold, and the banks collapse.

Behind all these promises, claims, and exchanges are two basic facts. First, the base metal (e.g., gold) has no intrinsic relation to the productive role of the banking system. This base is more like excuse than cause. It merely assures that should the organized interaction the bank catalyzes collapse, the first participants reverting back to their former relative isolation will at least have something that supposedly remains valuable (the gold) while all the others will be back where they began, and only mutual confidence prevents such a collapse. (And if mutual confidence, not money, holds a system together, and this confidence derives ultimately from a culture, nothing can prevent a collapse of confidence if the culture collapses.) Second, the bank's creativity appears not in any multiplication of loans and money, dazzling as all this may appear on paper—for the multiplication is *only* on paper—but in *interest*, which has always been the most fascinating and puzzling aspect of money and banking. Interest appears from nowhere. The banks created the loans, but where did the interest come from? All monies except the interest are fully traceable. In a demonetized the interest could economy, take the form of gold or other treasure, but in a monetized economy the interest payments must come from outside the total of all banks' reserves and loans. We cannot say that interest payments come out of loans from other banks, because, since *all* cash in circulation comes ultimately from bank loans, interest payments then would be coming out of principal, and the number of bank loans would have to balloon relentlessly just to stay ahead of multiplying interest charges; besides, if banks simply gave new loans just to cover interest charges, the interest on such loans would infinitely approach a finite limit. All this suggests not so much the irrationality of the banking system as the fact that it is not closed on itself, not an absolute system. It is basically a symbolic reality, and this hints what interest really represents.

A bank does more than mediate energy exchanges. From the many small deposited sums it creates a pool geometrically exceeding the sum of the original parts by the amount of the interest it is progressively generating. Viewing this pool as a symbolic pool of energy exchanges, we can identify the interest as a monetized increment of energy that borrowers contribute to the pool in exchange for the support of the social energies the money they have borrowed represents. We do not have, or need, any exact quantification of specific amounts of energies represented by specific amounts of money (assuming that energies are quantifiable); interest is only a *relative* measure of the amount of new energies attracted into the system by the bank's mediating activity. As the new money represented on the books by interest circulates, it intensifies energy exchanges in the "system." The whole secret of the bank's creativity is that a given amount of money can support a greater volume of energy exchanges in its hands than in those of discrete depositors, since the large and rapid turnover of money (and energies) the bank's loans sustain causes the participants to pool their energies in an economic order. But the statement that interest can represent an increment of energy contributed to the money pool can be immediately modified. For the *common* activity of participants in an economic order might produce a greater tangible economic result than the separate participants could cumulatively produce in isolation. If so, this extra tangible result could itself be the real foundation of interest payments— indeed, might often exceed the interest payments in money (exchange) value. If an increment from group production *is* a real source and support of interest, the interest borrowers pay to banks perhaps in the end is no real burden at all, because the extra production resulting from the pooling of energies might even surpass in exchange value what the banks charge in interest. What is expressed as "profits"—the excess of what cooperating people in an economy (at least those with proprietary rights over the means of production) receive above what they put in or could be achieved by working alone—can well surpass the interest charges banks receive for risking and mediating the common activity. So it need not even be true that interest on a loan wholly represents *more* energy contributed to a pool of energies, if the barter value of borrowed money increases, because of the pooling of energies it causes, at a rate approaching the rate of interest charged. The material productivity of a dynamic economy might well (discounting inflation) increase at rate higher than that represented by the interest charge. The actual ratio might be quite fluid and variable, perhaps depending on social and other conditions beyond anyone's immediate control, but people working together work less than people working by themselves, but still produce more than they otherwise could.

All this would for the first time give an explanation of why money and credit are the only items in economics both asset and liability in the same respect. A bank *must* work with any money it holds because money ceases to be dynamic, that is, ceases to be money, when it ceases to pool energies. The value of money a bank squirreled away would evaporate, and the bank would pay back in real value less than it had received. Active money increases exponentially in value and stagnant money deteriorates exponentially toward the rock-bottom barter value of the original base (e.g., gold). But who would guess that money has no "neutral" or equilibrium point from the still-current Classical definition of money as a mere neutral "medium of exchange"?

A business that fails to return a profit soon disappears, so the average business makes a profit, and business incomes in general exceed expenditures. But the excess of the average business's money income over its expenditures cannot ultimately arise merely from other *business* spending, if businesses as a whole spend less than they earn. All *consumer* spending, though, derives from business income—from business profit or expenditure—and is a neutral factor in the excess of business income over expenditure. A greater velocity of money might permit a greater gap between income and expenditure, but the only real explanation for the ultimate source of the excess of business income over expenditure is the interest charges made by banks. For each dollar of such interest supports several dollars in new loans to new or growing businesses, and these loans, which usually become investment, then cause, as Keynes showed, not arithmetic but geometrical increases in business spending, which eventually appears as profits in other companies' books. The source of the money expressed as new profits is bank interest, but the source of bank interest is the incremental physical productivity of the business system.

If the banks catalyze money's energy-pooling function, but the economy's growth depends no less on the corporation than on the bank, what is the corporation's relationship to energies? Easy. The bank only *pools* energies (its concrete activity amounts to little more than a series of entries in a series of financial books), but the corporation actually organizes them for production. The bank and the corporation are the twin pillars of Capitalist economics because they are complementary aspects of the same basic reality, human energies. Without the corporation the bank's pooling of energies would be almost an exercise in futility, but the attempt to organize energies directly without some provision for spontaneous participation such as the bank represents would be totalitarian in principle.

Now, the energies money pools are potentially deployable in many ways, so the actual deployment of money (and energies) acquires a large direct social significance. The best assurance for a sense of responsibility in deployment is to assign a personal risk to the deployer-investor. Nevertheless, as society's primary producer and primary organizer of its economic energies, the corporation is much *more* than individuals' personal property. Though it is not uncommon to depict the relationship between private ownership and public good as antagonistic, actually they arise out of each other: The corporation's *social* role is already intrinsic in its nature as private property. Since this may seem a confusing paradox, perhaps the best way to suggest what it means is by drawing an analogy with the banks.

When the Federal Reserve, for example, reduces its reserve requirement from, say, 16% to 15%, the amount of money each member bank can lend for each dollar it has in frozen reserves increases to $6⅔. Suppose that for some random bank we will call Bank A this reduction of reserves required by the Fed frees $1 million from required reserves to become working cash assets. The bank could immediately use this new sum as cash reserves for additional loans, and *could* make an immediate new loan to a depositor-borrower in any amount up to $6⅔ million, and additional loans to others of the balance. But if these borrowers cumulatively withdrew a total of more than $1 million, the remaining $5⅔ million in new loans suddenly would be underreserved. Since a borrower normally will use his loan as quickly as possible, because he pays more interest on the loan than it pays to him as a deposit, Bank A probably would lend only about $1 million and simply pass this sum on to whatever bank(s) in which its new depositor-borrower(s) place(s) it. (Of course, if a borrower leaves his loan in Bank A, the bank can use it as leverage for more loans, but must be prepared to acquire, if the borrower then withdraws it, a sum sufficient to cover the reserve requirements on the subsequent loans.) Bank A will continue to receive interest payments on its $1 million loan, as well as gradual returns of the principal; meanwhile, the banks receiving the $1 million as deposits can make total loans of only $850,000, because they must collectively retain $150,000 to satisfy the new reserve requirement, since they have obligations to their new *depositors*, whereas Bank A received the $1 million not directly from a depositor but from the Federal Reserve, a bank for the member banks' impounded funds. In effect, then, a gradually diminishing cash reserve passes from one bank to another until the reserve is gone. And new money exceeding the old reserve by 6⅔ times appears.

The result is that all of the banks share in the common advantages of the larger money pool (which all the banks are enlarging through their reciprocal action at a faster rate than they could collectively but with wholly separate clientele). Yet none of the banks is responsible for the entire money pool, not even the Federal Reserve. Each bank is responsible for only that portion within its own control. Each has only a limited liability that does not approximate to the advantages it gains from its peculiar "reflexive" participation in the entire money pool. In fact, it is this advantage, which the Capitalists have never really discovered, that makes the Capitalist superior to the Communist economic order (and it remains undiscovered because it is incompatible with the ambition to establish a total system such as the Communist system indeed is). The bank, like the corporation's owners, is given a limited liability in order to encourage risk-taking, for the bank, like the corporation, is as much an instrument of society as it is a personal property. But the corporation's social function, like the bank's, is "reflexive"—exercised through the persons of the owners rather than directly by, for instance, State institutions, which are far from necessarily society's true representatives. The genius of Capitalist economics, which is almost systematically being violated in practice, is that its dynamism arises primarily out of the personhood of its participants rather than out of the imposing but sterile monolithity of abstract organization.

In order to free investors to act, jurists defined the corporation as a "legal person" with an autonomous legal existence greater than the sum of its proprietary parts, and the jurists were correct, for the corporation's activity is no more reducible to that of its mere owners than the money pool is reducible to mere claims on silver and gold. However logical it might have seemed by known theories to hold the owners responsible for the company's acts, the jurists understood that the corporation is a direct instrument of society too, even though *through* the persons of its owners. But after limiting the individual owner's liability because of the corporation's social function, the law also rightly limited his control of the money he invests, because he does not necessarily best know how to apply it to actual production, and society has as great an interest in the company's economic success as the owner has. But because the owner bears the initial risks (society's assurance for a sense of responsibility in the deployment of its energies) he claims the profits. The legal formulation that the stockholder owns the company but not its assets in effect gives him a claim on its earnings but no control of the funds he invests, and the more control he surrenders the more, paradoxically, he becomes an owner. (Though he may not control his money, he can and should control the management.) Ownership (equity) securities carry a claim to profits, while debt securities reserve to their holders more control over the invested funds.

Management has control of the funds the common stockholder invests, and its surprisingly independent control of the assets, with no claim on the results, simply indicates that it works as much for society as for the owners. It may even issue debt securities for funds over which it will have less control, but such securities are cheaper, because they have no claim on earnings such as common stock has (but can acquire such a claim by consent of the owners of common). So a successful corporation can finance itself either by issuing "preferred" stock paying lower dividends (that do not increase with earnings) than the common, or by selling long-term bonds. Control over the funds from low-ownership securities immediately begins to return to the investor, but meanwhile the company is able to overbalance—by means of the money's productive potential, which, because it depends on the coordination of human efforts in a common project, *only the corporation can release*— the claim bondholders acquire on static company assets (which constitutes the control the bondholder retains over his funds.) This simple device is the whole secret of the Capitalist economy, and in fact the hinge into a new economic era. The same amount of money is more valuable to a company, in terms of barter, than to a creditor alone because the corporation can release the money's productive potential and the creditor by himself cannot. By issuing and redeeming debt securities, such as bonds, the corporation can harness energies more efficiently than the investors otherwise could, and ends by paying, in absolute terms, less than nothing for the money it borrows, because the profit potential of the goods produced with the borrowed money exceeds the principal and interest combined. This ability to accelerate to higher *stable* levels its own internal dynamism by means of debt financing at only relatively small initial cost to itself is the corporation's distinctive feature. At these higher productive levels it is able to amortize quickly, from the very profits resulting, the original loan and then to receive a continuous return for itself from the investment the loan financed. That is, the intense concentration of productive energies in the corporation brings it to a "critical point" where the productive capacity of these energies exceeds the current barter value of the money that brings them together, the costs of doing business. Something resembling a nuclear chain reaction begins; the corporation is a sort of social *breeder* reactor.

If the observations above have a putative commonsensical quality to them, in that everyone knows that human energies, not mere money, are responsible for corporate productivity, why do the experts insist on speaking of the "productivity of capital," as if "capital," not human beings, did the producing? Is it to save the rewards of economic production for the owners of capital, even though workers, not mere money, make capital productive? Though an owner is entitled to some return from his capital as a reward for his risk, this reward should bear *some* proportion to his actual risk, which often is less than the worker bears. Still, there is no real contradiction between the claims of workers and those of capital's owners! The real cause of the owners' preponderance in the "system" is the very attempt to create a total and absolute system at all.

How can we say that loans to a company carry little real risk, and carry any risk at all only because the nature of the corporation is not yet understood, even by the experts? Well, as we have seen, banks depend on business profits to sustain interest charges—not only for reserves to support new loans and new expansion, but also for vindication, as it were, of loans already made. So most companies *must* make a profit if the system is not to collapse, and, at least as things now stand, this means they must grow. So the average risk in capital investment is really almost negligible compared to the risk in *not investing*, and in certain circumstances could actually be negative, although of course every company should not always invest. It is this, so to speak, "reverse risk" that inspired Keynes's proposals, but it somehow still fails to impress his beneficiaries who propagandize for the rights and "burdens" of capital. Nevertheless—a key point—those who own capital stock run little more risk when their companies invest borrowed money than the rest of us run by getting out of bed in the morning. Just as, though one company might improve its profits by cutting wages, when all companies do this the markets shrink, so one company might protect itself by omitting to invest, but when all companies so "protect" themselves, again (as Keynes showed) the markets shrink. Companies' situations are never static, and companies must invest not only to gratify the cupidity of their owners, which is the usual excuse for corporate policy, but also to prevent the more negative consequences of not investing.

What we find here, in fact, is, looked at closely, a compound contradiction, a contradiction that deceptively appears to give the neo-Keynesian professors some excuse for indulging their now exuberant relish of power. On the one hand, capital owners have a highly unfair advantage over nonowners with respect to the profits the nonowning workers largely create but the owners largely enjoy, an advantage excused on grounds of a risk that is no greater than the risk in *not* risking. However, the owners do face an intolerable contradiction of their own that appears to vindicate their exclusive claim on the profits anyway: If the company does not invest it increases the danger of recession and unemployment, but if it does invest the markets may still not become strong enough to vindicate the investment. For the professors, all this becomes a challenge to their skill in "tuning" the economy via government spending, as if the contradictions thus could be resolved. They hope, by gratifying at once the capital owners by creating markets, and the worker by giving him a job, to vindicate their own relish of power. Yet their repeated blunders obscure from these virtuosi what is both their judgment and their exoneration: that *any* policies they might pursue would eventually fail. For the real solution to the contradictions they propose to remedy by injecting government into the equation is evident in the way the equation is drawn above: As long as workers have no access to the corporate profits their efforts largely create, they will be unable to sustain markets sufficient to absorb potential investments. Yet there is a way they could get such access without infringing the rights of present owners. Thus, the contradictions now being repressed can be brought out and resolved. For should workers gain direct access to corporate profits, the artificial opposition between worker and owner would evaporate (the company would grow so fast in filling all needs that the present owners' wealth would multiply, too), together with the artificial weakness of demand.

To restate the problem: The corporate dynamism cannot be understood without the idea that money represents pooled *energies*.

And since the money from which capital arises has the character of a social trust over the human and personal energies such money delivers to its holders, what makes "capital" productive at all is the efforts of those whom it brings together. Thus, the proprietary right, based on a putative "special risk" actually no greater than that the rest of us sustain by continuing to breathe, owners of capital have to its earnings needs to be reformulated. Certainly money is privately owned, but what is owned in money has a profoundly social nature. The reason why markets are chronically precarious and weak enough to call for the Keynesian remedies is precisely that even though the energies of people it brings together make capital productive at all, the returns from capital go almost entirely to its present owners. But to say that the way to build markets is to cut in the worker, who bears most of the real burdens of capital, on the benefits of ownership raises no contradiction of the proprietary rights of ownership; this seeming contradiction is no more real than that apparently posed by the present precarious strength of the markets that results from excluding the worker from ownership. A better understanding of money will help us to see that these suggestions actually *strengthen* the owner's proprietary rights and interests!

Let us recall even more precisely how Keynes succeeded and failed, and then consider what would have been the correct long-term remedies for the problems he faced. Keynes's creative insight was into money's real *function*—not only to balance the various abstractions (land, labor, capital, investment, consumption, etc.) of the *theoretical* system, but to coordinate the activity of real people (which, not mere goods, is the real material subject of the science). This shift of perspective allowed him to introduce his new discovery, expectations, as the key variable. But Keynes never thought of challenging what he considered a basic *in*variable: the Classical bedrock notion that money coordinates and balances the "system" as a merely mechanical, physical "medium of exchange." This notion *excludes* the human dimension from the center of the science. Here is the basic contradiction in Keynesianism, and it derives directly from Classical economics. The exclusion "permitted" the "individual" to ignore the "system" as a whole, automatically composing everyone's material interests with everyone else's, and to concern himself simply with maximizing his own profits and consumption while the experts watched over the whole. The system itself never rose, or descended, to a specifically human level. Though this atomized economy of theory may more or less have reflected the real economy, the atomization still left businessmen uncertain whether later markets would vindicate decisions to invest now, while the consumer always saw excellent reason to fear that his real income might soon decline. The bank operated as a pooling device on the production side, but no such device aided the consumer. So, even though not to act would debase money's real value, not to act remained almost as prudent as acting, since every decision to act remained a pure act of faith that often was not vindicated. And when one did act, money's intrinsic dynamism only widened the disproportion between the volume of goods that could be produced and the consumers' ability actually to buy them. Initially, government spending somewhat eased this situation by providing a pooling device sending money on its necessary circulation, and building up the industrial base.

But, in effect, Keynes had moved the human dimension of economics ("expectations") toward the center of the science only to subject it, too, directly to the Classical mechanicalism, which Keynes thereby made an *active* social force. This mechanicalism would persist as long as the human dimension was excluded from the definition of the economy's coordinating concept—money. Thus Keynes tried to dissolve the atomization simply by reinforcing the totalism of the system—that is, by creating a new short-circuit. Since the reason why consumers could not sustain markets on their own would have called all system-mongering into doubt, he simply introduced government into the equation so that it could virtually compel money to go on its pooling rounds. But without an insight into money's real *nature*, which might have revealed *why* the disproportion between productive potential and purchasing power had been growing, the discovery of expectations could only add a new economic variable, expectations, without really transforming the mechanical economy at all. The new variable, with its new manipulator, government, did create a more dynamic context, but shifting the focus of the old mechanical framework onto expectations only made the mechanicalism *psychic*, an imposition of the mechanicalism directly upon the culture. Without any understanding of money's real nature, Keynes could not transcend the old mechanical mercantile economy, only make it more aggressive and culturally lethal.

Because of his still-Classical notion of money's nature, Keynes, like the Classical economists he supposedly was correcting, still assumed that the economic order must be an absolute system and locked his followers into the same emulation. And since this system's basic structural concepts seemed already well understood, he saw no need directly to apply any insight on money's function to the rest of these concepts; he simply contented himself with reshuffling them in order to include expectations among them, re-stabilizing things again by bringing government in. He never did seek the cause of the chronic weakness in demand, but simply looked for a way to crank demand up. So his theoretical world, like modern culture itself, remained interiorly split; he compulsively cites the importance of animal spirits in economic life and of a correct order and priority of values in society, but he tries to view economics as a self-contained system cut off from both animal spirits from "below" and cultural forces from above, able to solve social problems itself by its own smooth mechanicalism. The pages of the *General Theory* reek of anxiety and self-congratulation. But the cultural tensions of his age made his ultimate failure appear to be a total success, so Keynes could not resolve the conflicts and fell back on his basically makeshift solution to the problem of demand—a solution which, because it failed to change the Classical understanding of economic categories, had to "solve" the problem of demand by reinforcing the totalism of what until then had mercifully remained a "system" mainly in theory.

Since Keynes's concern was to create demand, not to find out why it was weak, he cared little, in seducing the investor to invest, how demand was created or what kind. Merely manipulating the investor's psychology, he left the inner structure of the real situation basically unchanged, except for this new manipulation. His suggestion that investment would stimulate *multiple* outlays, creating new demand and jobs, was accurate, but extended the manipulation to the worker-consumer, to whom Keynes was concerned to give a job mainly in order to resolve the *systemic* problem of demand. All this placed the financial "system" above the human needs to be satisfied by the creation of new jobs, and the bedrock importance of work as man's major means of creative self-definition became for the first time subordinated directly to financial and "systemic" considerations; the financial means to the end acquired precedence over the end itself. To the new economics it little mattered what kind of job the worker had, if it created the necessary demand. So the worker was soon using his creative energy, which any total system must view as a threat, mainly to make his job, which he despised, *seem* more important than he knew it really was. His needs bound him irrevocably into a financial system dominated by capital, his life and fortunes dependent on the owners of capital, to whom the social and physical environment was handed over. What Keynes had said was unnecessary and repulsive became inevitable: Any person who wanted his needs filled had to conform himself to a "system" dominated by capital and without any purpose but its own aggrandizement; he had to repress his own animal spirits or at best express them through consumption. For the only animal spirits really released were those of the owners of capital, but since their release depended on the enslavement of workers to mere considerations of finance—what Keynes *said* he deplored—the denaturing of the culture this would bring sooner or later would cause the enslavement of the owners, too. In the meantime, the worker could afford really to take to heart nothing but considerations of money.

By tightening the hold of the systematization, Keynes had hoped to solve problems caused by the very attempt to systematize, but achieved only a Pyrrhic victory that contradicted what he was trying to prove—that systems are servants, not masters. Because he did not think or choose to question the earlier Classical categories, he had to seek his solutions merely in the way they were coordinated, but there was no real solution in that direction, so he had to conjure up, within the superstructure he was rightly recasting, a wholly *extrinsic financial excuse for acting* that only further got in the way of the spontaneity he intended to release, because it put the "system" as an independent absolute *between* the person and his own economic activity. The system no longer merely coordinated people's economic activity but determined it, and became itself the controlling and dominating consideration in place of the full human reality it supposedly was to serve. Keynes had postulated the financial system as the *cause* of economic activity, rather than as what it is—merely the expression.

Postulating finance as the systemic cause of economic activity gave those controlling the system of finance control also of the economy and even of society. The way to retrieve this situation, though, is not to advance the State as the individual's champion against the system, which would only aggrandize the State's power over the system *and* the individual. Rather, we should dissolve the artificial antagonism between "individual" and corporation resulting from giving priority to the system's need (specifically, the corporations' needs for markets) over the integral person's need for meaning as well as security. The individual should acquire a proprietary stake in the economy of a kind that makes the corporation's needs and his identical. But this stake should be nonsocialistic, so that a more virulent State power does not simply replace the economic power of the present oligarchical elites.

Let us note in passing that the current atomization of Capitalist economics is making certain large systemic problems, like the energy crisis, greater than they need be. This crisis arises among that 6% of the world's population that already uses about 40% of the world's power. But in his atomized state, the individual needs more and more material gratifications as surrogates for the cultural order that a total system excludes as a basis for social stability, for the culture's deterioration makes the individual so neurotically anxious to increase his functional independence of others that he duplicates for himself, as real public life all but vanishes, all the functions and gratifications he once would have been content to share with others in a richer cultural order. It is the limitlessness of this substitution process, except in the robot-consumer's inability to cram any more consumption into his day, that gives the system its ability and mandate to expand. For this socioeconomic order substitutes the pursuit of material goods for everything, which the culture it professes to admire, Classical Greece, gladly did without.

This is what happens when any "system" acquires priority over culture. Our earlier discussion of money concluded that money signifies a constant (i.e., human energies) present in all economic activity. In fact, because it does pervade *all* social activity we can systematize our social life through economics to an appreciable degree. But there are limits beyond which a specialized systematization of economics should not push, for economics is only one in a whole series, or hierarchy, of social manifolds—art, politics, etc.—which human energies also dynamize and which intersect and co-incide in each person's and society's quotidian life. It is true that all these manifolds will have an economic aspect, but only in economic matters will the economic dimension be primary, and even there it is not exclusive. So any attempt to systematize economics must necessarily be guided by one or the other of two exclusive strategies: Either all human activity will be reduced to functions of economics, and economics reduced to a function of a self-contained mathematical system; or economic systematizing will not only reflect but further release an inner cultural dynamic structuring all the social manifolds by a coherent and all-embracing *meaning* system. In this second alternative, we would not seek to impose our abstractions upon human energies, but try to make the "system" serve the purposes of human culture. But the abstract absoluteness of a total system turns what are equivocal into univocal events and drains them of their human content.

In terms of Keynesian theory, this means closing on itself a system that should be open and "polymorphous." It means trying to tie what is simply a higher abstraction—the "system" of finance —of what is already abstract economic theory back into the theoretical base as if the higher abstraction were not only part of the base but itself the base of the base, rather than a mere epiphenomenon.

Who can object to Keynes's sincere concern for "the man who has been long unemployed"? But sacrificing more of the culture to the exigencies of "system" perhaps was not the best way to help: The fat slave in a system drained of human content might one day even regret his earlier penurious freedom. Keynes temporarily "solved" the economic problem by aggravating the cultural problem; this man who is regarded by some as the Shakespeare of economics was more like its Lewis Carroll. For the process of "transcending" the crude mechanicalism of Classical economics by including psychic factors in it has no inner limit, and the new *social* Keynesianism appearing down the road prepares the way for Skinnerism. People now must serve the insatiable, self-aggrandizing "system" directly rather than indirectly, and "human needs" become the "system's" excuse for tightening its own hold. This "higher" mechanicalism is both psychological and cultural—could not be one without the other. With this "system" supposedly functioning as a principle of social cohesion, no attention has to be paid to the persisting cultural problem that encouraged its appearance in the first place. But the problem of demand, the ostensible reason for all the reductionism, still has not been really solved! More than enough human needs remain, and the material capability for filling them is not lacking, but still the needs and the productive apparatus cannot seem to get together. There are also more than enough unfilled psychic needs, even among the rich, but no culture remains to satisfy them, either.

What is the route out of our present economic troubles? Consider: What is the meaning of "capital" our new understanding of money suggests? Economists refer by this word to either money available for investment, or the productive apparatus the money buys. This curious ambiguity in a systematic science is a clue. After all, the first sense of the word denotes entirely liquid assets, the second sense entirely unliquid assets, while many assets are not called "capital" at all. What do "capital" assets have in common, and why are some assets "capital" while others are not? Of course: Capital represents human energies. Money represents a concentration of human social energies, and capital represents an extra concentration of money. Capital *equipment*, though, *embodies* an indeterminate fund of physical and intellectual energies crystallized, as it were, out of the technological and theoretical expertise of a culture. The function of this capital is to substitute human mastery for mere toil. Whereas *money* capital, like all money, is nothing really concrete, but a pool of potential, as yet unrealized, social energies, equipment capital embodies actual and concrete—realized—energies. And such capital arises out of *labor* as the economic expression of a culture's integrated intellectual and craft activity. "Labor" represents human energies in an individualized and atomized form; "capital" is nothing else than the social aspect of labor *in common*. Thus, in a poorly integrated economy, labor is the key to demand and production, but in a highly integrated economy, the key is capital. These considerations dissolve the lingering Classical absolute distinction between labor and capital that betrayed Keynes. They also reveal that labor's claim to ownership of capital is irresistible, because labor is intrinsic, not extrinsic, to the very finance on which the exclusionary proprietary claims are now based.

In Adam Smith's day, every factory, worker, and shop was far more functionally independent than their counterparts are today, and the machines were more primitive. So the key to aggregate purchasing and productive power was labor. Land was also especially valuable—in England because it was so scarce, and in America because it was so nearly inexhaustible and so rich in resources, giving settlers coming to America a long-term purchasing power that became gradually deceptive, because land and labor became overshadowed by an increasing dynamic other factor: capital. The federal government climaxed the land grab with wholesale giveaways (the exclusion of blacks from which perhaps goes farther than anything else to explain their almost hopeless economic, and social, plight in our times). An economy whose structural units remain largely autonomous depends on accretions of discrete units of land and labor to sustain demand and production. But the importance of capital as an integrator of material resources and human energies—of land and labor—grew by quantum leaps as the frontier closed, and it soon surpassed that of both land and labor combined. Yet as capital became by far the dominant factor in production and purchasing power, its benefits fell largely to its relatively few owners, who could direct toward consumption only a fraction of the purchasing power it bestowed. So a growing gap appeared between productive potential and effective demand. The reason was capital's increasing potency. But here came Keynes proposing to encourage labor when all the other prophets were beginning to agree that labor soon would be almost obsolete. In Keynes's mind, that capital had become incredibly productive in no way suggested that a new look should be taken at capital; it was sufficient that labor should work harder in order to make itself more adequate to capital and thereby preserve the old mechanical balance in the new dynamic context. No more futile or destructive an idea was ever proposed by the most incendiary anarchist.

In short, the solution for the problems Keynes bequeathed is to make every person in the economy an owner of capital. As Robert Heilbroner has written, Capitalism's major failure, and the major cause of its continuing social sterility, is the continuing and even increasing concentration of the ownership of capital. The real trouble with Capitalist economics is not that it is Capitalist, but that it is not Capitalist enough for enough people. For if as many people who now "own" mere labor became owners of capital, the economy's short-circuits would dissolve. Dividend distributions creating purchasing power from accumulated capital now locked up in the corporations would build enormous new markets among those with unsatisfied needs, while routing price increases back as dividends to the very ones paying the higher prices. Could all this be done? Could the vast majority become owners of capital without a forcible redistribution of present wealth, or violating the rights of property? Is the creation of enormous new demand without an equivalent inflation feasible? The answer to all these questions, amazingly, is "yes." A humble financial lawyer discovered a simple but unspeakably profound way by which all these things could be accomplished. And our whole new understanding of economics now permits us to understand *why* his plan would work.

The author of the plan is Louis O. Kelso.[6] He reminds us that skeptics once predicted epidemic defaults when the American government after World War II enabled the Federal Housing Authority (FHA) to guarantee loans banks made to veterans for housing. But defaults remained negligible, and the housing industry boomed. Kelso proposes that we simply extend the FHA principle to the entire economy. Let some new agency guarantee similar sorts of loans, but no longer for purchases of *static* objects like houses, but for purchases of *capital stock*. For example, let the employees of a company form a trust, with themselves as its beneficiaries, and approach a bank or other credit source for a loan in order to purchase *new* stock of any corporation that needs financing. The trust would pledge as security either the stock it intends to buy, the guarantees by the agency, or both, and then turn the proceeds from the bank loan directly over to the corporation. The latter would issue new capital stock to the trust and apply the loan to its own production. As it received dividend distributions, the trust could, because of provisions of tax law, amortize the loan within a period Kelso has convincingly estimated at about seven years. The employees then would own the stock, although they had never paid a cent for it, and they could claim subsequent distributions.

Now, all this may seem familiar; after all, do not many corporations cheaply donate stock to employees out of pretax earnings? True, but their present methods *draw on reserves* and restrict their ability to expand. Assigning income to reserves reduces tax liability, and markets simply do not seem strong enough to justify capital investments such earnings might otherwise become. If, though, rather than invading its reserves, the company reinvested any amount it wanted and issued new capital stock to an employee trust in the exact amount of the investment, the company would have spent none of its own money, but could still expand, while the workers' new ownership of stock would enable them to create new markets. The real financing would have come from a bank via the employee trust's borrowing to pay for the stock, and the company, without laying out a nickel of its own money, could expand *and* simultaneously create the markets to justify the expansion. And if every company did this the investments would infallibly be justified, for the only remaining limit on corporate expansion would no longer be artificial financial restraints but the unwillingness— rather than the present *inability* (largely among the lower classes) —of consumers to consume any more. And every company, even those that now cannot afford to donate stock to their employees, could do this, because the real financing would come not out of reserves but from a credit source.

Note the benefits that seem to accrue miraculously to everyone as a result of this simple operation. Suddenly, corporate financing power for investment doubles! Why? Because *investment financing* now begins to come out of *pre-tax earnings*, in its new character as, in effect, *distributions to a trust with special tax status*. As a result, financing such indirect loans to corporations becomes twice as safe for banks as direct loans to corporations, because direct loans must be repaid out of profits *after* the federal income tax has reduced them by half! Thus, Kelso's method would improve many companies' ability to attract financing by 100%. No financial expert will fail to recognize the salvific implications of this fact for hundreds of economically worthy companies during times of squeezes on liquidity, like now. During these squeezes, usually during times of high inflation, a "normal" investment, no matter how badly a company may need it, would invite further inflation. But, unlike any other financing method, Kelso's method would not. And why? Because there is no lag between the increase in production and the creation of new market power; if anything, the new production comes first, dampening the inflation! This has suggested to Kelso an even more intriguing possibility. As many economists now believe, the real foundation of any economy and money supply is not any commodity like gold, which has only symbolic value, but actual productive capacity, which the commodity symbolizes. Thus, ideally, it is actual productive capacity, not gold, that should ground the money supply. But as things stand, there is now no direct *institutionalized* link between the money supply and productive capacity; the link is accidental, almost adventitious, and so we anachronistically rely on gold. But Kelso's plan for the first time permits us to establish institutionally a *direct* connection. During liquidity squeezes, when banks have no cash for financing even Kelso-type loans, the financing paper itself could be turned into money by being made discountable at the Federal Reserve. No inflationary effect would be felt because of this, because every cent of this new money would be based directly on new productive capacity; no indeterminate time, during which inflationary pressures could mount, would intervene before such new capacity would appear. What instead would appear would be the first rationally organized money supply in history: a money supply based directly on productive capacity.

Any conglomerate that used the "Chinese money" financing methods during the fifties and sixties well knows that judiciously exploiting debt capacity is far cheaper and more efficient *for a corporation* than spending its own cash. It costs a corporation, in absolute terms, less than nothing for the money it borrows (if it uses the money for investment), whereas using its own money reduces its liquidity and makes it rigid. It is this principle of the incremental fertility of *group* effort, on which the corporation's economic superiority is based, that also would make government deficits better for an economy than recession, *if* the deficits did not also aggravate structural imbalances in the economy that Kelso's very plan is admirably tailored to correct. Kelso's plan does for corporate finance what Keynes's theory seemed to do for government spending, and corrects Keynesian theory by giving the relatively poor something of their *own* to spend without invoking the paternalism of government handouts and makework.

Recent markets have held relatively firm during an inflation so virulent that government itself almost dares not spend, and even tightens the supply of money in order to shut expansion off, just when people, continuing to spend, demonstrate not only a collapse of confidence—they do not believe the inflation can be stopped, so they spend before their money can evaporate—but also that the present levels of gratification have become virtually imperative since the evaporation of any culture that might have provided fulfillment in alternative ways. Yet more and more satisfies less and less. The economy has finally run smack into the impasse for which Keynes set it up. The government not only cannot afford unemployment; it cannot afford expansion either. It is trapped. Yet markets remain strong only among the dwindling middle class, because the lower classes are being devastated by inflation, and even the middle classes doggedly sustain the inflationary markets (by demanding higher wages) only because in the absolute sense they too are falling farther behind. This is a moral problem, but not in the masses; it is a moral problem in the controlling theory. And no use counseling the government to be "hard-nosed"; it cannot win either way.

What the State needs desperately is a way of *expanding* consumption while *dampening* inflation. Now, the Keynesian stimulants are all inflationary. But if the return from present capital were going to people with unsatisfied needs, these people would not need higher *wages* in order to sustain consumption, for they would begin to receive the return from capital. At present, though, virtually no portion of any price increases are routed back as dividends to people with unsatisfied needs, so price increases sustain the inflation; routed back as dividends to those who paid the higher prices, the increases would socially cancel themselves out. If more people had direct access to the dynamic investment stream, which is the most prolific source of *purchasing* power too, the disproportion between the dynamism of capital and that of labor (and consumption), growing because of Keynes's remedies for it, would begin to reverse. The worker, who *makes* capital productive, can now depend only on his labor (and wage) for his income; it is the owner of capital who appropriates both the productive excess the worker's labor creates, and the price increases the worker must pay for out of his wage. But if the workers gained access to capital investment, *in the same cost-free way that current owners have it—by virtue of the self-liquidating quality of investment finance*—that is, if workers became owners, they could expand the markets, reduce further any "risk" in capital investment, and yet cause not *inflation*, but *deflation*, because Kelso's plan brings forth productive capacity *before* it brings forth the markets this capacity will serve! Even current owners would benefit, because current capital would increase in value faster because the markets would rest on a substantial foundation: productive capacity, not government financial hocus-pocus. Owners have the choice between retaining exclusive control (which they never exercise anyway) and seeing their capital appreciate at a slower rate as the culture collapses, or sharing control and seeing their capital appreciate faster as the culture revives.

(Some writers, of course, claim that the present inflation is not primarily a "demand-push" inflation. We can disregard their inability to explain where cost-pulls sufficient to account for the present inflation, which was well under way before oil prices rose, are originating, because the point is not really crucial. The basic point is that wherever the inflation may be originating, demand can never be allowed to slack off enough to counteract it. Thus, the Keynesian economy has a built-in bias toward inflation: As Nobel Prize winner Friederich von Hayek puts it, this economy is structurally built directly upon inflation, "solving" unemployment by creating jobs dependent for their continuation upon inflation, and making the price of halting accelerating inflation ever more unacceptable levels of unemployment. Von Hayek does not make clear exactly what jobs depend directly upon inflation—actually, it appears that no one knows for sure exactly where the inflation is coming from: It is too subtle and diffuse, and certainly demand continues to be stronger than anyone once believed it could be during such an inflation—but in any case the economy has no intrinsic deflationary "mechanism" to offset its inflationary pressures. The ultimate or precise cause of the inflation is not as important as the fact that there is no reliable systemic counterweight to it.)

As Heilbroner has observed, a company is a relentless dynamo of capital formation and accumulation. The role of investment capital is to expand the productive nexus to produce greater volumes of goods and services—and greater profits. But these profits accrue only to owners, even though the workers' energies, the productive nexus, produce them. Only those inserted into the investment process can profit by the relentless expansion of the corporate dynamism; the positions of all others remain *relatively* static—which means that in a dynamic economy they become increasingly subordinate. The crucial fact for *both* Kelso's plan *and* the current methods of corporate finance is that the corporate dynamism pays off *by itself* loans made for expanding it, without further expenditure by owners of one nickel of their own cash. But Kelso's plan cuts the worker in on this benefit, while the current methods reserve it to the owners. As far as the production process is concerned, it does not matter at all who the designated beneficiary of the bank loan is, as long as the proceeds go toward production; the process of production itself, not the beneficiary, will pay the loan off. That is, most corporate financing is self-liquidating. In terms of the economy as a whole, though, who the beneficiary happens to be becomes absolutely crucial, and confining this privilege to current owners, even though *workers* make capital productive, not only is actually another form of welfare supported by the working classes. this time for the rich, and not only increasingly concentrates the ownership of capital—a process now identified as the cause of Capitalism's social sterility—but also increasingly unbalances the economy. Since even the immediate benefits to the corporation—never mind the longer-range economic benefits—in the Kelso alternative are so great that the corporation itself profits as much as the new owners of capital, there is every reason even for present owners why present non-owners should become the beneficiaries of bank loans for investment. It cannot be too strongly urged that Kelso's plan is the true consummation of the Keynesian theory, and the only corrective for the disastrous consequences of Keynes's prescriptions.

It has been said that the Modern Age was based upon the split between labor and capital, which extended into politics, where one party stood with labor, the other with capital. If Kelso's simple innovation, then, dissolves the tension between labor and capital, does it not spell the end of the Modern Age? Only after certain "obvious" metaphysical "truths," that provide the basic supports for an era—for example, the idea that society is a neutral medium through which the individual directs his own atomized course of self-realization—only after these have begun to seem questionable can simple adjustments like Kelso's that contradict these ideas begin to seem feasible. This is what has happened with Kelso, who has built better than even he knew.

Without laying out a nickel of its own money a corporation today can gather in clear, continuing and substantial profit from a capital investment financed at a source of credit. (In the jargon of the trade, the capital investment is "financeable.") This is what makes a successful corporation prolific enough to multiply the money it receives from credit sources not only into a profit for the creditors, but also into an almost indefinitely continuing profit for itself—all by merely accelerating (through workers' efforts) its own routine dynamism. When the employees gain access to this credit device through the Kelso trust, they become able to generate a second income at no expense by the very same method that the corporation at no expense generates increased earnings. The workers' purchasing power would dramatically rise, at the same time that the pressure for wages would relax, and repetitions of the procedure would soon make the workers as comfortable, and independent, as current owners now are. Kelso has estimated that his plan would require at the outside thirty years, if consistently applied, to make every person in America a millionaire by today's standards. Though the plan could create demand far more effectively than Keynesian policies, it would also, within a short time, allow the economy to settle into a stable or equilibrium condition, for no political urgencies would mandate full employment simply for the sake of employment or demand, and the hysterical insistence on growth for its own sake could mercifully disappear.

But would not Kelso's plan, it will be asked, still generate inflation even more savage than that now caused by deficits? No. Remember, deficit spending does not go directly into useful goods and services, so it drives up prices as it creates wages (in effect, reducing the wages of those already working in order to create wages for those not yet working, while drastically eroding—through the systemic totalism—everyone's cultural situation and only slightly improving their economic condition, temporarily). But Kelso's plan immediately matches any new purchasing power with new productive capacity, so it would not inflate prices. Well, then, would not this plan dilute the equity of existing shareholders? Only in a limited sense. The *money* value of this equity actually would increase, because the corporation would both sell the new stock to the new owners at current fair market value, and finance new capital through *pre-tax* rather than after-tax income. Furthermore, if the proceeds from the corporation's sale of new stock did indeed go toward purchases of depreciable property, the corporation would, simply through tax savings, recover over the life of these assets more than the total of their cost. So the old equity would increase in money value; what would decline would be only its proportional share of ownership. But any objection to this sort of shift in a society organized around its economy would be an objection to democracy itself. Finally, then, what if the corporation did not prosper after a capital investment funded according to Kelso's plan? What if the corporation failed to deliver dividends large enough to amortize the loan? But the corporation is no more likely to fail by using this method than by using any other; in fact, it would be less likely to fail, because of the method's intrinsic superiority. If an agency like the FHA were guaranteeing such loans everywhere, the only burden would be an immense boom from the purchasing power Kelso's plans would create among those who needed it. A Kelso-type capital investment would much more surely than Keynesian deficits destroy any possibility of general failure.

Kelso's simple innovation has almost unfathomable implications. For example, it is well known to scholars that Marx basically tried to replace the exchange determination of labor's value with a labor determination—that is, tried to substitute a labor theory of value for the Capitalist exchange theory, which held that a product was worth not any "intrinsic" value of the labor put into it, but rather whatever price the product could command on the market. This dispute was not over a mere technicality, but over two radically different attitudes toward culture, and it is to be feared that on this point Marx, no less, was on the side of the angels. For it makes a world of difference whether the quality of a man's labor is to be evaluated by its effects (the exchange theory) or whether the quality of the effects are seen to depend on that of the labor (the labor theory). Under the exchange theory, man's subordination to the products of his own labor makes a real culture impossible; under the labor theory, though, some "intrinsic" standard by which to evaluate the labor which is then used to evaluate the goods becomes indispensable. Thus, the viability of any labor determination of value will depend ultimately on a shared (cultural) *meaning* system, whereas an exchange theory of value can, and will, revert to a wholly mathematicized total system, because its crucial components are not men but quantifiable material goods. Basically, the Capitalist system, in its character as an attempt to replace a deteriorating culture with a totalist physical system as a principle of social order, *had* to rely in economics on an exchange theory of value. In Capitalist society, as Marx saw, a man's value was measured by the market worth of what he produced, and any *intrinsic* value in his work became, for the "system's" purposes (and this system organized society), functionally irrelevant.

Kelso's innovation changes all that. When everyone owns capital, no one will be forced to work merely in order to survive. This does not mean that no one will work, only that the weighting of the influences on choices will be reversed. Goods will continue to be worth their exchange value, *but not labor*, so no goods will be made simply because they can make a profit, for labor will cease to be merely another commodity virtually equivalent to goods. People no longer will work only for money, and the goods getting produced will be those with high *personal* investment. Mass-produced goods will not disappear, but, as *categories*, may be outnumbered by high-labor-quality goods, and the relatively few who still produce en masse will be paid in proportion to the relative unpleasantness, not meniality, of their labor. The labor and exchange values of goods will tend to converge—either toward a rock-bottom valuelessness or toward a new exaltation of man through his labor, depending on the direction the culture takes. If the quality or intensity of labor comes to be the primary determinant of the level of compensation, those who actually do productive work (however defined) should come to earn as much as those who now thrive on merely "managing" (usually poorly) other people's money. Previously, the unstable static economy had been condemned to perpetual cycles of growth and stagnation, until Keynesianism flattened the cycles by aggravating the imbalance between capital and labor; now, an economy would appear in dynamic, but stable, balance, achieved not by a Marx-like assault on Capitalism, but by, at last, a release of Capitalism's dynamic and creative inner principle. As the culture became again the source of economic balance it always secretly was anyway, people could all choose to be millionaires or could direct their aspirations in other directions: The culture would determine the volume of the production of goods. If no culture survives, an authoritarian State will have to provide a balance by means of power and repression, for only a sense of *concretely* shared community can inspire people to carry their fair share of the load against their more selfish or misguided inclinations or illusions. But the totalitarian possibility becomes more imminent anyway so long as the economy remains totalist and unbalanced.

The economy will not collapse if some people cease to "work." People will still need meaning as much as (if not more than) goods, and it will have to reflect their own efforts. That some cease to "work" in what we call "economic" activities will no more mean their activity will have no economic dimension than the engagement of so many now directly in "economics" means these people actually contribute to production. Allowing the economic motive primacy even in noneconomic pursuits has prostituted our culture to economics. The situation will be reversed when economics resumes its service of a culture, but this does not mean that our economics will become weaker. Nor will money's exchange value be diluted when everyone owns stock and fewer "work": The value of money will still be determined by the proportion between goods produced and the money supply. But people, not some abstract "requirement" of a subhuman total system, will decide how much to produce. If no one works, money will be worth very little. But how many among those who hold jobs now do truly productive work?

These questions all lead to one of the most important points in this book—but one of the routine brilliant points in another book that is a milestone of social and economic thought in this century: Peter Drucker's *The Future of Industrial Man*.[7] (Drucker's book would be as valuable for background on this chapter as Dunne's book—on myth—was for the first, for Drucker's argument is a masterful "phenomenological" or historical demonstration of what this chapter has tried to prove more by way of abstract theory.) Did Keynesian theory itself "solve" the problem of unemployment? According to Drucker, it did not. Unemployment, in fact, had never been a problem in any depression before 1930, and thereafter was the problem that improved last—"if it improved at all." That Keynesians could still claim after publication of Drucker's book that their social order was "fundamentally sound" and that they had "solved" the problem of unemployment would suggest that control and not social service is what fascinates them. Why did Keynesianism fail? Because economic security *by itself* can be only "negatively effective," and people during the Depression needed *social status* and *function*—precisely what Keynesianism denied them—as much as economic security, which Keynesianism substituted instead. That the grave danger in this never has been countered goes without saying, but that no attempt has been made to counter it may be as damning of certain people's sincerity as it is potentially mortal to a free society.

One does not doubt that Keynesian liberals could "solve" the *economic* problem of inflation. If inflation again became, as it well might, the major problem, one might do worse than to follow Professor Galbraith's prescriptions: (1) restrict the supply of money; (2) raise taxes—which, though, Galbraith would make a wedge for imposing social policy; (3) impose wage and price controls; (4) search out new sources of commodities, shortages of which might be raising prices, and (5) allow no doubt of one's intention to attack inflation in every possible way. But thereby not the basic "systemic" causes of the inflation, only its manifestations, would have been attacked, and what could lead anyone to think that the inflation would not revive as soon as controls were lifted —if they ever were, since experience shows that measures once applied create new problems and expectations of their own and soon come to seem indispensable. Galbraith, having responsibilities only to advise, has nothing but sneers for the free market, which he says in his book *The New Industrial State* a new technological elite should replace. Yet essentially the free market constituted this economics-constituted society as free. And Galbraith's is far from a lonely croak from the swamp: Daniel Bell regards control by a technological elite as inevitable, and even that ultraliberal Heilbroner cultivates a melancholy resignation to the disappearance of human freedom. What is threatening our freedom, though, is not "reality," but the theory with which such men seek to control it. It is true, as Galbraith says, that the market has become sadly compromised by interference in it by powerful unions and corporations, but these acquired their clout from the ascendancy that Keynes gave capital over labor, and that caused the moral checks upon capital to disappear and union power to take their place. But also eliminated with this power in the liberals' elimination of the market would be our freedoms.

Nor does one doubt that the liberals could "solve" the *economic* problem of unemployment, by creating, as they now advocate, public-service jobs funded by the State. One does not doubt even that Keynesians might reduce inflation and unemployment simultaneously! What one does deny is that they could do so in any way that does not consist basically in accelerating the ruinous conversion of the culture into a total system that sacrifices all human values on the altar of survival, and thereby destroys everything the anticipated "prosperity" (or, rather, by this time, "sufficiency") would be putatively expected to serve. Actually, the real problem is not the conflict between labor and capital—an artificial conflict if there ever was one, but one that the liberals themselves have artificially extended in order to get religion out of the way. The real problem now is the growing conflict the liberals will only further aggravate with their vaunted "remedies" for the artificial conflict the liberals themselves have perpetuated. This new conflict is that between the productive sector of the economy—capital *and* "labor"—and the unproductive sectors, made up of the welfare constituencies, the bureaucracies and academic establishment whose mere power is squarely based on these constituencies, and perhaps the media. The liberal "solutions" for both inflation and unemployment alike call for new government bureaucracies whose only certain accomplishment will be to aggrandize the liberals against the "conservatives"—meaning all those who resent the gargantuan growth of Big Brother—oops, government.

The problems cannot be solved simply by a *social* Keynesianism replacing economics with sociology as the socially constitutive sphere, for the foundations of freedom disappear when the economic sphere becomes authoritarianly regulated. One would follow the liberal prescriptions only because one's freedom retains little value when the economic "problem" effectively prevents one from much exercising of it. But no one should delude himself with hopes that the liberal remedies could rescue our economics without sacrificing everything else. If we wanted to preserve our freedoms as well, we should make the immediate implementation of Kelso's plans our highest (by far) priority. They are responsibly expansionist, and at worst only mildly deflationary, and could be balanced by Galbraithian measures to hold the economy at equilibrium while inflation is drained out of it and its basic structures are fundamentally transformed. This would protect other nations from recession here.

The current liberal strategy for harmonizing interest-group greed and "guiding" the economy to serve broad social needs, rather than interest-group greed, is, first, to set up an incomes policy, and, second, to search for more "effective" ways of planning social development—all, of course, to be administered by the State. But what is wrong with the present total system is its lack of an intrinsic moral dimension, which has been removed by liberals in favor of self-interest (so much for you, religion) as the system's integrating principle. They cannot now expiate this denaturing by acquiring State power with which to impose "moral" order themselves, even while castigating others who try to impose "moral" order in noneconomic spheres. What has happened, of course, is that the self-interest the liberals unleashed has turned out to be decidedly "unenlightened," since where the common good really lay became quite ambiguous in the vacuum of explicit public standards defining it, while one's immediate material interests remained temptingly plain. The moral, the communal, dimension became in Keynesian economics a mere collectivism of competing interest-group pressures, because the economy still remained structurally atomized. Delivering "moral" control now to the bloated government will succeed only in throwing the baby of freedom out after the bath of greed. For how, then, will the *government* be checked? All the prattle about the "inevitability" of a "mixed" economy conveniently overlooks the need for an intrinsic social check on State power; neither economic theory, which once denied the State any major role, nor a true social elite acting as a watchdog over shared values and as precisely a check on State power, will any longer provide it. And, after all, a "mixed" economy remains "mixed" right till the moment when all private initiative and freedom disappear from it altogether.

Heilbroner has distinguished four phases in the history of American Capitalism, each phase characterized by the role government plays in it. Thus, in the first phase, the government's role was merely to act as one stimulus among many others in the consumer sector of the economy. In the second phase, which began with trust-busting, the government intervened directly to regulate markets, so as to protect certain segments from abuses threatening to destroy them, and also to protect these segments from competition from within and without. In the next phase, beginning in the New Deal, the government actively started to "balance" the economy itself. And in the final phase, now appearing with wage and price controls, the government begins to *replace* the market, causing (as Milton Friedman unsportingly observed) a threat to freedom. The force Heilbroner sees behind these shifts is technology. But there was another: the suppression of the communal dimension in economics that might have acted as an *intrinsic* balancer. The power of the trusts resulted from the preponderance of capital, whose weight Keynesianism then only increased. The economy was from the beginning (and still is) atomized, and the only remedy the State can apply is a new collectivism. What happened was that the market was made *society's* (as well as the economy's) balancing principle *in place* of culture, and this burden was too heavy for the market to bear. If it was to play this role, if all of society was to be balanced by the market out of the restricted economic sphere, the latter would have to become a total, closed system. But all that the market could balance were the material aspects of the economy; and because only a culture could balance the other, human aspects, economists simply defined economics as a purely "material" science. Nevertheless, the market could be only the economy's proximate balancer and material, while only a culture could be an ultimate and formal principle of equilibrium, for any truly human purposes.

Because the economy has no cultural dimension, it has no intrinsic moral controls or content. Thus, all those huge organizations can throw their weight around because they have slipped the restraints society's morally legitimating principles—Capitalist property rights—once imposed. The unions, in turn, were merely responses of arbitrary power (in which workers have no real voice, either) to the arbitrary power corporate management thus (somewhat unwillingly) acquired. But to insinuate government now as the "arbitrator" between the various pressure groups unbalancing the market will make the situation not better, but worse, for the interest groups at least more or less checked each other (even though together they crushed the individual), but none of them, nor all of them combined, could check the government. And just because government gains direct control over the interest groups will not mean that the people will regain control of the government: As Andrew Hacker has said, the people have already exchanged their political for their economic citizenship, and a second-class economic citizenship at that. The very arbitrariness of any such new governmental control, with the numberless practical decisions it will require, will force upon society a technological "elite" to decide what is "best" for everyone else. But this pseudo-elite will be restrained by no social-moral limits, nor will its power arise from any widely recognized guardianship of any moral order, except insofar as the State concocts and imposes one.

To prattle about the need "to find more efficient and democratic" ways to plan social development contributes nothing but confusion and hypocrisy so long as the ordinary citizen remains a second-class member of the economy. The root problem could be stated another way, in terms of the "structuralist" bias that blinds liberalism to the mutually supportive roles of person and culture. If all problems are structural, so long as the structures are right the content of social life matters little. Yet structures have no life if they do not reflect and express real content. Liberalism tries to expiate its structuralist bias by defending "individual rights" too, but these do nothing to alleviate the "individual's" *systemic* atomization, which worsens. This atomization can be overcome only through the sharing of common moral principles by virtue of a shared culture. And, conversely, the economy can regain its own moral legitimacy only if control returns to the individual, and government can best help by enabling him to get it, not by trying to exercise "moral" control itself. Now, the proximate (or structural) reason why moral control has disappeared from the economy is that the small few who now actually own industrial property can no longer personally oversee it; the only remedy for this is to make everyone in the economy an owner, so that the State is removed as the economy's functional balancer. When the "individual," through ownership, regains control of the economy he sustains but now controls him, the State will not be "needed" to balance it, for the economy's short-circuits will disappear. Inflation, too, will cease to be a structural problem inviting government intervention, for the workers, owning the means of production and no longer much needing the unions, will be able to deal directly with this problem themselves. They will also become able to devote some attention to *self*-government and thus to break the grip the interest groups now have on the government. In fact, the interest groups themselves might disappear, at least as arbitrary power blocs, when no longer needed to mediate the "individual's" stake in the economy, which would then extend to the economy as a whole.

Now, it is true that Heilbroner already has eloquently argued that economics should be open to social objectives and become an instrument of moral and social purpose. But whose? He seems to ignore the very real possibility, becoming more real every day, that economics might become the instrument of the "moral" purpose of merely a new power elite. Kelso's plan assures that it will be the people and their culture that will provide any "moral" purpose. For Kelso's plan is a structural principle for a truly industrial social order that retains a place for moral legitimacy, too. Though owner-workers would retain ultimate control, management could retain the proximate control it needs, and that is all it really desires, for management rightly feels uncomfortable trying to exercise the social role proper to ownership, as it attempts to do now only under pressure from the moralizing liberals who want to take and use this dimension as a weapon against industry. Thus, Kelso's plan, and only Kelso's plan, would close the gap between the "two" economies and make possible what Drucker has called indispensable to community life: local control of industry, in place of the relentless centralization now giving the State ever more power.

Kelso has been writing about his plans for over fifteen years, although lately he seems to have been giving up in frustration. His first book, written in collaboration with Mortimer Adler, appeared in 1957 (this collaboration is a tribute both to the cogency of Kelso's idea and to Adler's almost unique open-mindedness), and several other books have appeared in more recent years. Yet very few people, even "experts," have ever heard of them. Certainly no one has demonstrated any technical flaw in the plans Kelso has meticulously worked out—which may be why there are occasional rumblings in the American press of reported adoptions of the plans in countries where the needs of living people apparently rank almost before considerations of academic orthodoxy. But the plans have never been seriously entertained here. Why?

There seem to be three main reasons. First, though Keynesians certainly (until very recently) have been unreceptive to and intolerant of any challenges, Kelso has multiplied his plans' difficulties by the almost perverse opaqueness of his writing style and the confusion in his theoretical "explanations" of the plans. He shows no more taste or talent for abstract speculation than do most of his practical business peers, so that his forced explanations of *why* his plans would work become as irritating as they are confusing. For example, he claims that there are two "factors" in the production process—the human (labor) and the nonhuman (capital and land). But defining capital as nonhuman—as if, for example, the hard-earned money of depositors that banks use as investment capital really were "nonhuman"—only *detracts* from the direct claims to capital ownership that Kelso wants to establish for labor. Not only are labor and capital more closely linked than Kelso, like the Keynesians, realizes; this link is the ultimate vindication of his proposals.

(But his distinction between what he calls the visible and the invisible structures of the economy is far more persuasive—he seems to have adopted it from Drucker. It is on this ground that Keynesianism is most vulnerable. The visible structure is the "real" economy, in creating which Americans have always brilliantly excelled. But the invisible structure—the web of financing arrangements internally coordinating the concrete or "real" economy—unfortunately remains at a "preindustrial" level of development. For on this level, more conceptual than concrete, both conditioning and reflecting our understanding of the economy as a whole, "pragmatic" Americans have displayed an utter lack of originality. Hardly a single new American idea has appeared here in the last hundred years, and so, as businessmen and professors have been complaining, not only have we no theory to unlock the productive capacity of the economy; the structures we do have are being undermined by their own inner contradictions. It is the primitive nature of the financial arrangements, Kelso shows, that is blocking our advance. Less than 0.5% of all corporate financing is now achieved through sales of equity, so the concentration of the ownership of capital continues apace. Since corporations finance all capital formation internally, the new capital belongs to the old owners, who, however, have neither spent nor risked a red cent to gain it, but cannot spend even the return they get on their present capital. Whether because institutional investors gobble up the relatively few securities available, or whatever, the "average" person is an ever more unlikely owner of capital. In a society virtually organized around its economy, this is an exact parallel of feudalism: The serfs on the feudal manors could earn only a continuously precarious subsistence, while the lords who owned the land, the crucial factor in feudal economics, could exact an annual tribute without themselves lifting a finger. The present "invisible" structure of the economy enforces an exactly analogous subordination in what should be a fully dynamic economy. Because today the crucial factor is not land, nor labor, but capital.)

The second reason for the poor reception accorded Kelso's plans is perhaps more important, since, after all, real ideas are rare enough in economics that the scores of well-paid economists congesting university faculties had ample opportunity to decipher the potential in Kelso's plans, had they been as interested in pursuing ideas as they are in protecting their own prestige, not to mention their power. But Kelso's plans just looked too simple to provide any remedy for the "problems" they themselves have been making precisely no progress in solving. There is a type of mind oppressively ubiquitous today that, dismissing all received values with contempt while rooting itself in the most preposterous confidence in its own "objectivity," flourishes on reducing the obvious to unintelligibility, and on finding for every "problem" a solution twice as complex, which experience reveals to be thrice as complicated again, by reason of a contingence on certain assumptions and circumstances that the *cognoscenti* had never suspected. So long as it remains inconceivable that the very attempts to systematize are themselves causing the "problems," the more complicated, and unintelligible, the system becomes, the more complicated must appear any "solutions" in order to be credible. And any lingering nostalgia for a simple solution is routed by a final consideration: The complications more and more require direct ministrations by the "experts," while the simple yet comprehensive solution might put them out of their jobs. No need, then, to look any further for the reason why upstart Kelso has been treated like the bastard at the family reunion. Yet many societies have survived quite well and happily without the services of a full range of "experts," and, indeed, precisely on the strength of their freedom from any compulsion to reduce everything to "reason," to self-conscious rationalization of every aspect of the social order toward "management" of every "variable." Far from being a sign of weakness, an astonishing and most unwonted simplicity could be instead a powerful suggestion that a solution might be at last a real one. It should be no cause for wonder that, in fact, all economic problems could basically be resolved in one stroke, if that consists, as Kelso's plan unwittingly does, in breaking the closed circle of the total system and restoring the ultimate balancing function to culture; this is the only sort of solution that could possibly work. This step would not alone, of course, immediately banish all economic problems; but it would render them simultaneously remediable. At least the economic problem itself would become simple, although whether economics ceases to be a problem at all would depend, as always, on the culture, if any survives.

The last obstacle in the way of Kelso's plan is the typical, stubborn American resistance to any suggestion that *anyone* should get "something for nothing," although, God knows, the American people are going to be forced to abandon this prejudice, no matter which way they turn, and probably, under the pressure of the Keynesian-type transfer payments, are about ready to surrender it now. Yet this resistance has held firm even when the prospective beneficiaries might have been the great mass of the people themselves. As Garry Wills points out in *Nixon Agonistes*, it arises out of the heart of the Puritan ethic, which Keynes's celebrated assault on the Puritan savings compulsion apparently hardly budged. (Perhaps *Keynes's* basic notions on economics were closer to those of the Puritans than we now understand.) The belief still lingers, encouraged by the atomization of Capitalist economics, that an atomized society in which supposedly everyone looks out for himself is somehow morally superior. So if employees start getting rich, it is inconceivable that somebody somewhere is not losing. Even the experts hardly understand that economics is no mechanical tit-for-tat but a basically communal enterprise, and that precisely what distinguishes a dynamic economy is that all its participants should get "something for nothing"—just as the owner of capital now profits immensely from every effort made by the owner of mere labor, and the bank draws interest out of its lending of funds it does not even own. The great irony in the individualist prejudice is that those whose ancestors most profited from the windfall land give-aways in the last century are most opposed to anything like it now, even for themselves. Yet America has been a "growth" environment in this century mainly because in the last century anyone could acquire free or nearly free land almost anywhere he turned.

Why should those land distributions even be called "giveaways"? Did not the land in fact belong to the people (including its original inhabitants)? Certainly it did not belong to the State. The State has no rights superior to those of the people it supposedly serves. Even by liberals, whose reliance on the State is exaggerated, the "give-aways" of land are rightly considered to have been healthy and just. Yet land played in those days almost the same role capital plays today; it was the "horizon" that bounded the cultural community, the crucial physical factor controlling its destiny. If we can agree that the distribution of *land* was right and creative then, the distribution of capital would be no less so today, especially since capital even more than land is a social trust as well as a private possession. And although capital would be owned in common (even as it is today, but among a small circle), it nevertheless would be privately *owned*, and secure from government's arbitrary power.

Under the Keynesian theory, the State's power over property is not really offset by any healthy expansion of the economic base, because Keynesian operations, as we noted, increase the dependence of the poor on the rich. And not only are the social fruits of Capitalist production appropriated, as Communists claim, largely by capital's owners, but as Keynesian operations further subject culture itself to the dictates of a merely abstract, autonomous system of finance they reduce the rest of human life to its impersonality; they "reify" the person and make him for social purposes a mere object or thing.

Kelso's plan, though, breaks the precarious wage slavery that has virtually reduced the citizen to even a political cipher. Kelso makes the worker a capital owner without either diluting present equity, encouraging inflation, or invading the rights of property. He makes leisure a reality, not a rhetorical ideal, and stops the ceaseless formation of boondoggle jobs that is making the country into a virtual totalitarian work-state secretly resurrecting that motto of the Nazi concentration camps: *"Arbeit macht frei"*—work makes you free. His proposals could make capital owners out of helpless groups humiliated by "needist" handouts supervised by bureaucrats who themselves make no real productive contribution other than to justify government spending programs. And so forth, ad infinitum.

We have been uncovering here the communal dimension of economic life, which Classical theory ignored. It is still ignored. Economics is not the sum of atomized, self-aggrandizing activity of isolated "individuals," but the materially productive activity of a culture. The communal dimension, which finds its economic expression, but not its *cause*, in finance, is itself the cause of the economy's seemingly magical productivity. And debt, which integrates a person or company more deeply into the system of finance, thereby integrates him or it more deeply into the communal effort. But an individual must pay off his debts by himself, whereas a company can retire debts *directly* from the dynamic incremental productivity that arises from group cooperation. Thus, only a company gets the maximum support of the communal dimension at no real cost, and this gives it an immense and unfair advantage. But it does make sense for a company to finance itself through debt, and this is why Kelso's plan is sensible as well as just. It is only because companies cling to their old Classical conceptions about economics that even now, forty years after Keynes, they often fear debt as mortally as businessmen once feared government deficits, and find Kelso incomprehensible. True, a businessman must act day by day as if organizing the components of his business were all, and the communal dimension did not exist, because it does not exist until he acts. But no one realizes better than an accountant that a merely arithmetic rationalization of even a single business is impossible. Any accounting method proceeds by artificial exclusions of alternative intelligible relationships that in some other method could be construed as significant, but to recognize all of them at once would produce chaos. The accountant only tries to conceptualize a business in a way to integrate it with the wider financial system where the communal dimension dominates. He mediates between the fluid borders of two seemingly incompatible infinities almost impossible to distinguish from each other in practice—the particular and the communal.

It would be a great aid to appreciation of Kelso's plans to view them in the light of the Communist critique, which has been well aware of the Capitalist distortions of economics, and has exposed them remorselessly. This critique developed from an involuted metaphysical tradition with which an American reader (whose genius—like Kelso's—lies almost wholly in practical matters) may feel doubly uncomfortable, but the difficulties may be more apparent than real to those more interested in economics than in philosophy. We obviously cannot do entire justice to the Communist critique in the short space devoted to it here, but we might appreciate its focus. We could take as a reference point the theoretical book by Georg Lukács, which received much attention upon its recent publication in the West as both a capsule summary of Marxism and a theoretical advance.

Lukács grounds his objection to Capitalism in what he calls its "reification" of the human person. Briefly, this word denotes the subjection of the person to the requirements of an abstract logical system that ignores the real content of the activities it denatures by trying to systematize them.[8] Lukács sees this Capitalist flaw as part of a larger philosophical inability to reconcile object and subject (person) in thought. Since he regards philosophical activity as a reflection of the inner cultural (to him equivalent to the economic) condition of society, the philosophical impasse reflects Capitalist culture's inner condition.[9] Capitalism tries to evade the cultural causes of this short-circuit, Lukács claims, by making economics wholly autonomous and independent. Thus, the "formal abstraction of [its] laws transform [*sic*] economics into a closed partial system."[10] As economics reifies the personal subject in economics, it becomes incapable of incorporating the person into a system that does justice to his real existence in flesh and blood. Lukács says that economics can be a science only when economic relations are treated as relations between whole people, only when the inner needs of people determine the structures of economics, rather than the other way round as in Capitalist economics. Economics must be a science of the human totality, of the entire culture.

Lukács claims that the attempt to subject people to an abstract system of finance denatures their economic life, and converts the means into an end. The effort to rationalize human labor as a mere commodity "declares war on the organic manufacture of whole products based on the traditional amalgam of empirical experiences of work: rationalization is unthinkable without specialization."[11] That is, Capitalism subjects the workers to the personally fragmenting requirements of the machine. "*Subjectively*—where the market economy has been fully developed—a man's activity becomes estranged from himself; it turns into a commodity which, subject to the non-human objectivity of the natural laws of society, must go its own way independently of man just like any human article."[12] Labor becomes a commodity for sale, *equal in quality* to other commodities. Soon even the finished article itself ceases to be the object of the work process as it is integrated into a larger, even more abstract system of finance.

All systematic reflections or observations are implicitly or explicitly conditioned by a philosophy, and Lukács achieves and interprets his within a framework of Hegelian metaphysics that must be unacceptable, when comprehensible, to most non-Communist readers. But even though his observations may be constructed to reflect his metaphysics, they are systematic and penetrating, and touch on many points the West seems reluctant to consider. He demonstrates that almost any truly philosophical perspective is better than none at all. His reliance on a neo-Hegelian dialectic subjects his interpretation of "facts" to the philosophical problem of reconciling subject and object in thought, so that he arrives at his conclusions about economics from the "wrong" direction, from our point of view, but on this problem, which to him is both the cause and the reflection of the West's major social and economic imbalances, the West has virtually nothing to say. If the Communist East appears to us philosophically to be on the wrong track, the West appears to the true philosophers in the East as philosophically bankrupt and unable even to understand, much less to refute, the Communist critique. If Kelso's plan is workable, and it is, it shows that Lukács objections are valid, even in our terms: The Capitalist "system" *has* dehumanized the person with its atomizing individualism and has tried to replace the community with an abstract system of finance. That it necessarily did this, or that the system cannot be improved to fit the requirements of an industrial and free society, can be disputed, but hardly that Capitalism has made its societies slaves to its system of finance. It is for this reason that all the truly primary occupations—teacher, social worker, journalist, farmer, laborer—have become functionally subordinated to secondary, even parasitic middlemen, such as the financiers and stockbrokers, so that teachers, for example, in protective reaction, are becoming themselves primarily economic unionists with only a bureaucratic "professional" commitment to the truth. The primary occupations can retain any residual control over their own destinies only by becoming economic blocs themselves. Thus is society delivered over to the iron tyranny of the dollar.

To sum up, now: We can solve our economic problems in either of two ways. One way is to tighten the hold of the systematization and to consolidate in the government control of the system that once was made socially autonomous so as to keep government out. In this direction, an ever greater control of society itself by the government will be necessary, and will leave less and less room for any culture autonomous of political power. Man himself will be reduced, in the name of economics and of his own survival, to a machine. The other way is to dissolve the systemic totalism, reopen the economy to culture, and permit the culture to balance the economy once again. Every worker would become an owner, and the system's short-circuits, which called the government in, but which the government failed to resolve, would at last disappear. Government's social power would be rolled back and new popularly accepted elites could arise to keep it in check. Only this second alternative could preserve a free society.[13]

FOOTNOTES

[1] John Maynard Keynes, *The General Theory of Employment, Interest, and Money* (New York: Harcourt, Brace and World, Harbinger Books edition, 1964), pp. 129–131.

[2] These figures, taken from magazine articles, were the most extreme I could find. There seems, however, to be some confusion or disagreement on the degree of the concentration of capital ownership. Both Louis O. Kelso and Robert Heilbroner cite studies by Robert Lampman as proof of a high concentration. Heilbroner says that, whereas the top 1% of adults owned 61.5% of all capital stock in 1922, this had grown to 76% in 1953. Kelso

says that the top 1.6% owned 82% of all corporate stock in 1953, virtually all state and local bonds, and 10–33% of all personal property. But Peter Drucker gives a different picture, asserting that at the end of 1969 the top 20% of the population owned or controlled but 35% of "the equity in American business," while the middle group comprising 70% of the population owned or controlled half of the "financial assets" of American business (much of this through intermediaries, like pension funds, which owned 35–40% of American equity capital). The one-seventh (14%) of the population that then owned shares directly, owned about two-thirds of the share capital of American industry, says Drucker (see his article in *The Public Interest*, Fall, 1970). But Drucker's figures seem to contradict themselves: how can the "top 20%" of the population "own or control" only 35% of all equity, when but 14% "directly own" *two-thirds* of all share capital? Gabriel Kolko vigorously disputes Drucker's figures, saying that every reliable study of stock distribution indicates a high concentration. He cites the "Temporary National Economic Committee's" conclusion that 4% of all common-stock owners held 64.9% of all such shares, and that 4.5% of all preferred-stock owners held 54.8%, and also studies by J. Keith Butters indicating that 2% of all stockholders owned 65–71% of all marketable shares held by individuals (these figures being understated because they did not include fiduciaries controlled by these individuals for purposes of tax avoidance). A study from the Brookings Institution concluded that 2% owned only 58%, that another 31% owned 32%, and that the remaining 67% owned only 10%. But Kolko argues that the figures on ownership do not reflect actual control, for the investment companies through which many small-scale owners hold stock are too limited by law to get control of companies, while pension funds, whose trustees most often are banks, do not vote their pension holdings and almost never oppose existing managerial control. These funds seldom buy stock in their own companies, and their assets are likely to decline anyway as insured workers retire. Thus, these devices, far from promoting democratic control, leave corporate power even more securely concentrated in a ruling elite. And as Heilbroner observes, control is as important for society as the financial return on capital is in economics. In any case, he says, there has certainly been a regular drift of income toward the upper end of the income spectrum, and this sort of thing was a basic cause of the Depression.

Richard Parker recently documented that drift in a study called "The Myth of the Middle Class," on which William Moyers commented favorably. Parker holds that, whereas in 1958 1.5% of the American people owned 30.2% of all privately held wealth and received 24% of that year's total national income, an analysis of Census Bureau data shows that in 1968 the top 10% were receiving more money income than the lowest 50%. In 1969, one-fifth of the population owned no liquid assets, and 50% owned less than $500. Since then, the gap between the rich's share of the wealth and the shares of all others (including the "middle class") has steadily widened; in other words, the "middle class" itself is disappearing.

[3] *Time*, December 25, 1972, pp. 12–13.

[4] W. Spring, B. Harrison, & T. Vietorisz, "Crisis of the Underemployed," the *New York Times Magazine*, November 5, 1972, p. 42.

⁵ Andrew Hacker, *The End of the American Era* (New York: Atheneum, 1971).

⁶ Louis O. Kelso and Patricia Hetter, *How To Turn Eighty Million Workers Into Capitalists On Borrowed Money* (New York: Random House, 1967); a rewritten version of essentially the same volume appeared in paperback under the title *Two-Factor Theory: The Economics of Reality* (New York: Vintage Books).

⁷ Peter F. Drucker, *The Future of Industrial Man* (New York: The John Day Company, 1942). See especially Chapters 1 through 4.

⁸ Georg Lukács, *History and Class Consciousness* (Cambridge, M.I.T. Press, 1971), p. 128.

⁹ *Ibid.*, p. 105.

¹⁰ *Ibid.*, p. 88.

¹¹ *Ibid.*, p. 87.

¹² *Ibid.*

¹³ One further matter might be discussed: Were the monetarists wrong? The answer is: no more than the Keynesians. The monetarists simply drew the logical conclusions from the mechanistic notion of economics: They are logically right if money is definable simply as "a medium of exchange"—the basic axiom of the mechanistic economic universe. Keynesianism recognized dynamic features in the economic order, but self-contradictorily still held to the mechanistic notion of economics. Though the monetarists at least declined to contradict themselves, their theory remained but a logical structure with no "real" analogue. As McLuhan has pointed out, they ignore the speculative element introduced into the interval between one year's gross production and the next year's, for all that matters to monetary theory is the actual production of this year compared to that of last year. But the transmission of information at electric speeds releases a speculative activity that has anticipated, bought, sold and resold the expected increment long before it appears, and the very expectations partly determine the continuing increment itself. That is, the merely mechanical terminals of the economic process have, in spite of monetary theory, yielded their crucial roles to the intervals separating the terminals; indeed, the significance of the intervals balloons far beyond that of the mechanics themselves. As stock values slide up and down, they change the value of money itself, and monetary policy, plodding along behind, can catch up only by throwing the economy into depression. Monetary policy is simply too crude an instrument for balancing a dynamic economy.

Galbraith correctly calls monetary policy a "small, perverse, and unpredictable lever." The engine of the economy is far too powerful for monetary policy to control. Monetary policy only removes the means (money) by which economic "forces" express themselves. It can dampen activity, curtail the expression, without curing causes. It mistakes symptoms for causes, responding to crisis by trying to wall it up and deprive it of voice. It is upside down. At least Keynesians recognize that the real "forces" in the economy are in the largest sense "social," and that monetary policy is only one tool useful for coordinating forces that have made themselves apparent. Monetary policy is like consciousness and reason: They integrate human life, but are not alone sufficient—in fact, alone they denature and destroy.

The real powers come out of the shadow side. Yet, just as, without reason, psychic forces produce chaos, so with monetary policy; it is important, but insufficient alone.

The flaw in McLuhan's analysis is that he does not recognize as pathological the expressions he describes of the speculative motive. Even in a dynamic economy, the actual processes of production, and the human needs they serve, have functional as well as theoretical primacy. We can solve the puzzle by realizing that, though neither monetary nor fiscal policy are unimportant, even both of them together would be no more sufficient than would be one of them alone. The transfer payments of fiscal policy, besides accelerating or decelerating the economy by releasing or inhibiting selected factors, alter the economy's structure, and thus (even more important) the economy's *social* role: The foundation of the monetarist objection to fiscal policy is that fiscal policy, while trying to rescue victims of the system's unbalance, interferes with free-market forces the liberals themselves first established, and alters the economy's social role and basic structure. Monetary policy, in contrast, sustains or changes only the *general* rate of activity, without direct structural changes. Basically, this is a dispute between Classical and latter-day Keynesian liberals. What the monetarists overlook is that monetary policy, by itself, can only perpetuate the imbalance prebuilt into the "system," that Keynes at least tried to resolve. The early Capitalist economy had been assigned the social-integrating role so that both monarchist absolutism (the State, in early Capitalist society) and religion might become socially more marginal (for the State and religion were the pillars of the old feudal elite's power). But replacing culture with the "system" as social integrator unbalanced the economy from the very start, and Keynes tried to introduce balance by bringing the State back in, and the liberals now not only accepted, but welcomed, the State, because it was now in their hands, the feudal elite having been long since emasculated by the total system. Both the original exclusion of the State and its later rehabilitation in economics were aimed at "freeing" the "individual"—in the one case, from the hierarchical and feudal order, and in the other case from the atomization the total system substituted for that order produced. Yet when the culture was dismissed, the new dynamic Keynesian economy could rest on and encourage only a new collectivism. Neither monetary nor fiscal policy, nor both together, can suffice if the economy remains structurally unbalanced as a result of the way economics is conceived as a science. Rather than "solving" social problems, though perhaps temporarily easing certain economic problems, advancing the economy as a solution for social problems only forces upon a more organic society the economy's own intrinsic and socially destructive imbalance; for whereas monetary policy can only perpetuate the imbalance, fiscal stimulants exacerbate it.

Thus, just as, though they made basic mistakes in opposite directions about the nature of economic science, yet the theories of Keynes and Marx lead to "totalist" systems—Keynes's encroaching upon society from the level of economics, while Marx's is imposed upon economics in the name of social theory and social "justice"—so the Keynesians and the monetarists, liberals all, alike and equally fail, for all view economics as a totalist system divorced from culture. The difference between them is that the monetarists still regard the economy as a socially autonomous and self-contained system of *economics*, whereas the Keynesians want to extend the system to the social order itself so as to "resolve" persisting social imbalances.

The only real alternative to any of the above, incipient despotisms merely more or less advanced, is to view economics as but one aspect of culture. Should the economy achieve a correct cultural balance, monetary and fiscal policy, though they might become much more flexible, would, because become also much less crucial, probably, paradoxically, be less employed, for the social engineers' interest surely will shift to other—more crucial—areas: Like the poor, the rationalists are always with us.

Part
TWO

American Politics
and American Culture

In an editorial on Monday, November 18, 1974, the *New York Times* deplored the steady decline in the percentage of eligible voters who actually appeared at the polls, and urged further reforms, beyond those already implemented, to bring the voters back: Democratic reforms having failed, the only solution was to make more reforms. Yet the *Times* was arguing on Monday for exactly what on Sunday in its own pages had been shown to be bankrupt, for in its magazine section it had printed an article by Irving Kristol that showed that no amount of democratic reforms in other spheres had restored or even showed any promise of being able to restore moral legitimacy to crucial institutions in these other spheres. So much for the application of reason to society's affairs. The problem is, as Garry Wills has often pointed out, that modern rationalist Liberalism, an ideology of structures, has nothing left to offer if structural or procedural reforms do not avail. Liberals prefer to concentrate on procedures because these seem more manageable than arguments over substantive issues, or—God help them!—"truth." Yet, actually, questions of procedure can be quite as complicated, and as vulnerable to "subjective" biases, as metaphysics itself. Besides, the procedures in a system of "common law" derive not from abstract principles but from custom and usage, so their main consensual support arises from a shared way of life. If common and shared life is rejected on principle, or confined merely to procedures, the latter lose their inner life and power to elicit consent and tend to become abstract. The claim that, since, intrinsically, many procedures are compromises somebody's "principles" may be attacked by them, cuts two ways: The seemingly noble-minded putative concern for procedures can itself mask a devious defense of ideological fixed ideas. The more sophisticated tend to have a certain advantage in disputes about "procedures," and can acclaim as triumphs of "democracy" any procedures that advance their own cause, while discovering abuses of procedure in any that do not. For example, Nixon was crucified for intimidating the left-wing press, but no one bothered to resent the Kennedy Administration's intimidation of the right (or its financing a smear of Goldwater very similar to Laurence Rockefeller's financing a smear of Goldberg). Again, liberals saw nothing wrong with the Supreme Court decision on abortion, which completely ignored the basic question, whether the fetus is a "person," but a doctor's conviction for letting a living fetus die was denounced as a "violation of procedures," although the jurors had only faced up to questions the Supreme Court had ducked. Posing as the champions of desecrated "due process," liberals make up the rules as they go.

It may be helpful to have here, for purposes of orientation, another capsule summary of the thesis this book sets forth. The liberal form of domination is difficult to fight because it is not concrete, but abstract. Those who assiduously search for the "ruling class" are mostly barking up the wrong tree. It is true that Capitalist society has created a privileged "class" in the sense of an economic plutocracy, consisting mostly of those who appropriate the economic return from capital, but, unlike a true class, this amorphous group wields no homogenous power with coherent goals. Instead, there is more like a vacuum of real "social" power, waiting for usurpers to fill it. Any power that still attaches to capital is exercised somewhat grudgingly by corporate managements that have little real use for their unsolicited new "social" responsibility. The real "ruling class" is the liberal intelligentsia, which is not based directly upon money but upon its self-appointed guardianship of the norms of "rationality." This elite snipes constantly at those whose lingering influence was based on stewardship of common moral principles. No common moral order derived from a culture any longer holds society together, but a subhuman mathematized "system" does. The influence of the elite tending the system-machine rests upon neither money nor morals, but upon its putative "mediating" role between "pure theory" and "praxis." (See Friederich von Hayek's *Individualism and Economic Order* for an illuminating discussion of the dangers of social "abstraction.")

Though bitter about the squalid ugliness of our environment, the shoddy workmanship that goes into so many products, and so forth, liberals nevertheless will heap scorn upon the head of any poor soul who so far forgets himself as to invoke a lingering public morality to check all this. As von Hayek writes, anything that exceeds the capacity of one "individual" mind to create—and this applies with special force to any issue with a moral dimension—they regard with utmost suspicion. In fact, abortion, atomized sex, and the rationalist-liberal State are all closely linked. Liberals, who are not generally much concerned about the moral quality of the "individual's" atomized "private" life, must regard sex, for example, as a purely "private" matter not only without any publicly definable moral content, but without any need for it: "Moral" content is specified simply by subjective intentions and "sincerity." Certainly, therefore, a person's "private" sex life should not conceivably reflect upon the relevance, much less the sincerity, of that person's noble social "ideals": Since society is impersonal and remote, private matters and social are simply discontinuous. Which is all right, at least in the sense that morality is not imposable by force. Yet how can a man be faithful to his "ideals," which he does not see, if he cannot even be faithful to his wife, whom he sees every day? And the derogation of communal standards that is implied in the frequently aired liberal impatience with those still surviving appears to deny to social life a dimension without which it simply ceases to be human. In effect, the "individual" is granted an anomic autonomy in his "private" existence so that the system-machine can usurp the social sphere.

This censure does not extend to Capitalist economics per se; Adam Smith achieved in economics approximately what the American Founders achieved in the political sphere. Yet, like them, Smith too was unconsciously infected with the Enlightenment rationalism of his time. The contamination appeared in the attempt to make the economic sphere not only "socially constitutive," but also self-contained and self-encapsulated—a "total" system. Should we want to pinpoint exactly where this occurred, we would probably find that it was in the bland assumption that men actually would produce an economic "equilibrium" condition (necessary to systematize totally) *either* by not only all drawing the same conclusions from the empirical "data," but also continuing to converge in their estimations of the significance of any changes in the "data," *or* by diverging in their estimations in such a way that their separate plannings for the future would all perfectly match anyway. It is really quite remarkable how universally such basic assumptions, even when on their face most improbable, will be held, if assuming them is necessary to the retention of other supposedly "self-evident" notions.

Yet strictly on its merits as an economic order, rather than as a wholesale solution for culture (the "equilibrium" condition was in fact a surrogate for culture), early Capitalism was more than effective, preserving freedom for men as they are and not as someone thinks they "should" be, and allowing each man to follow *his* own lights and to pursue what *he* thought desirable. Each man was responsible only for what came within his limited power to affect, and not in some vague moralistic way for the unintelligible whole. In order that a man exercise his freedom, the scope of his *personal* spheres of positive responsibility must be determined as a result of his own activities and planning, but the determination of *spheres* of positive responsibility in general must be the endowment from a common moral order distinguishing between spheres and providing unwritten rules for typical situations. These general rules and principles both carve out the spheres within which all initiative remains with the individual, and prevent clashes between conflicting aims while themselves prescribing no fixed goals. A rationalist order, on the other hand, eventually must give a central authority power to prescribe both aims and means, and in every particular instance.

This Capitalist order, then, represented an effective provision for the pursuit of self-interest in a "global" sense, and not necessarily in the sense of selfish material aggrandizement. It did, of course, encourage the "individual" to pursue economic gratification, and in this was a desperately needed corrective for the earlier oblivion to the importance of such gratification to society's tranquility. But, originally, it also aspired to let the "individual" decide, and take responsibility for, within a common moral order, what the situation he personally was in concretely required. Then the rationalists split off the pursuit of material interests from any moral or cultural dimension by replacing the culture with their totalist system as society's integrator on the level of mere function, and so Capitalism gradually became hostage to the very rationalism Smith wanted to exclude, just as did American politics, even though the American Founders, disciples of Locke and Burke, were also supremely suspicious of rationalist nostrums. The American Revolution was, after all, in Burke's words, "not a revolution made, but a revolution [by enlightened rationalists] prevented."

When staking out a claim for their centralized State, liberals characteristically use a pincers movement. Replacing the correct distinction between sacral and secular functions with a false distinction between "Church and State," they claim an area for the State on grounds that some "individual's" supposed rights are being violated. (The search for martyrs is a favorite pastime of the liberal press, as currently exhibited in the attempt to glorify Roman Catholic objectors to Church "discipline" against abortion. Unfortunately, the "victims" so far have refused to submit to secular canonization.) No need to worry that the State might violate the rights of an entire group: In atomized liberal society, the group, which has no rights, is the heavy, and "individual rights" become a mechanism for legitimizing liberal power grabs (thus, to try to unionize is "good," but actually to be a union is "bad"). A good illustration of the pincers movement is the financial squeeze put on parochial schools, driving them into bankruptcy. But the squeeze extends beyond formally sacral institutions: Since religion is the principle of culture, all real cultural functions are now coveted by liberals for the State. Two recent examples are the push for busing to effect desegregation, discussed earlier, and the novel liberal doctrine of "tax expenditures."

The doctrine of "tax expenditures" gaining favor among liberal "experts" reflects the justified resentment of the ability of many citizens and institutions unfairly to escape taxation by exploiting legal exemptions. The doctrine holds that the "unpaid" taxes represent, in effect, public subsidies, or expenditures. Implicit in this doctrine is the notion that the State has simply not fully exerted some general right to tax. But this is false. The State does not have the right, but only the power, to tax. Or, at least in America, it acquires a sort of "right" to only such taxes as Congress enables it to collect. Thus, exemptions are not abridgments or abatements of the State's right to collect, but denials to the State of any right to collect at all in certain circumstances: The right to tax has been specifically limited. Just because the tax legislated by Congress on certain income is called an "income" tax, the State has not acquired the "right" to tax income the Congress has specifically exempted. It is not the State that makes a concession when it "fails" to collect a tax on exempted income; rather, the State's "right" to tax at all is a concession by the people, through Congress. The doctrine of "tax expenditures" reflects a typical pattern: The State is granted, for convenience, a certain concession, but the anomalies the concession raises then become excuses for turning the entire area over to the State. The result, in this case, is that all organizations granted exemptions by Congress in recognition of an important social function suddenly become hostages of the State. It is up to Congress, not the State, to decide which exemptions are really "loopholes" and to close them in the same way it "created" them. This general principle is only slightly modifiable for the notion of deductions from otherwise legally taxable income for purposes the Congress recognizes as socially important. This is where most real abuses occur. Yet what the abuses invariably show is not that the State is providing unfair hidden subsidies (although sometimes this may be the case, the *State* has no real ability to discriminate between "fair" and "unfair"), but how difficult, if not impossible, it is for the State *ever* to be equitable when wielding its massive power.

Another example would be the continuing talk about credit rationing and wage and price controls, which have been discussed elsewhere.

Liberals will never get caught arguing over substantive issues (*is* the fetus a "person"?), about questions of (God help them) "truth," which for them have no *social* relevance ("what is truth?"). Yet the denial of the direct social relevance of questions of truth leads finally to the corruption of procedures, which soon lose coherence and moral legitimacy (preparing the way for the world's Nixons). It is not that procedures are not important, indispensable, vital, but that they are not alone sufficient. What kind of truth society as such holds determines what procedures *can* prevail. The question of truth is a *public* matter, the most basic such matter. Provisions for the pursuit of and arrival at a social consensus on them—which requires more than groups believing what they want in private —are indispensable. For liberals, society's unifying bond is found only in material self-interest, supposedly creative of itself, since the sum or product of all self-interests supposedly so closely approximates the common good, that, seasoned with just a dash of liberal "enlightenment," they actually produce it—an optimistic eighteenth-century rationalist notion, described by Basil Willey as virtually a compromise between the old Christianity and a new paganism, that has lately begun to seem more dubious. Even liberal "ideals" have never been permitted to stand, if they could, on their own authority: Their real function was subjectively to legitimize the economic prosperity and liberal rule, an inversion of priorities that caused, though, certain problems of face—if the system somehow fails, its failures cannot be blamed on the system without raising embarrassing questions about it (or about its sponsors), nor even on the "charismatic" figures professing the "system's" ideals, whom the system needs to distract attention from its own impersonality. The failures, therefore, must be dismissed as "merely" personal, but on the part of only secondary figures, our equivalent of Communism's "wreckers." Several writers have concluded that America's willingness to spend unlimited funds to fight any "challenge" attributed to Communism, and its indifference to far greater injustices or sufferings in which Communism seems to play no direct role, only show that what America most fears is a demonstration of an economic alternative to its own arrangements. If so, in a sense the Vietnam War was ultimately a failure of the system. Yet no matter how universal the supposed moral failures of mere secondary figures in the waging of that war might have been, they added up to no indictment of the system, as liberals see it. For example, Halberstam finally attributes their mistakes to some obscure "fate." But it certainly helps if some illiberal figure can come along to shoulder some (or all) of the blame. In this sense, Nixon was a godsend for liberals. Schlesinger blamed the constitutional crisis on Nixon's moral turpitude, although it was liberals who had answered John Courtney Murray's charge, that they considered power intrinsically evil, with the new doctrine that instead power beatifies, and no one who has not enjoyed it can presume to criticize it (so much, said Wills, for democracy).

Until Nixon came along, the attempt to blame the system's failures on the obscure moral failings of secondary personages had not been going very well. For normally "individuals" had been expected *not* to raise moral, philosophical, religious, or other irrelevant ("private") objections to the system's smooth, mechanical social functioning. If this new, and still unexpected, though limited (for the "individual" is still expected to discover his scruples only *after* the fact, *after* the system's failure, so that he can take the blame for it), function of the "individual" could be expected to lead to deeper probings of the personal dimensions in public life, nevertheless, it still seems that the crucial influence on the lives of liberal heroes are wholly "social" in nature. Thus, James MacGregor Burns says that Roosevelt had a conflicted personality because he lived between an old and a new world. But who does not? The causes, if any, for the system's failures, if any, are individuals, but the causes of personal failures are social. Disappearing down the infinitely receding but self-enclosed perspective of the hall of mirrors of liberal history, the liberal escapes all real accountability. He cannot criticize the system as such: It is both the foundation of his power and the means of his escape from his own personality. (As Wills has also written, most benefactors of humanity are only looking for some excuse to get out of the house, and of none is this more true than of our liberal benefactors.) The liberal obsession with structures is an escape from the basically personal nature of healthy politics, that finds expression now in pathological imitations, a fascination with "charisma" and the histrionics of political "leadership."

This systematic (no pun) liberal impersonality (even amidst the toils of campaigning for "individual rights," which modern liberals have partly substituted for the earlier rationalists' more ambitious "Rights of Man") results not only, though, from the nature of rationalist-liberal social philosophy. Its secret catalyst is the proximity of the State, which is crucial to liberal social programs. Now, though it may be folly to deny the necessity, or at least the inevitability, of the State's existence, this inevitability does not of itself dictate what our attitude toward the State should be. The State's inevitability would not, for example, legitimate an exuberant relish of State power, as some perhaps have innocently come to believe. Rather, the State's power always appeals in us to something decidedly unhealthy, and the closer to this power we get, the more our vision becomes distorted. It is essential that, if we must assume State power, we remain uncorrupted by it, but how is this possible, if we do not regard State power as an evil? Everything depends on what our guiding principle will be. We can practice politics in either of two ways, making our politics either an expression of the culture, in spite of the State, or an expression of the State, in spite of the culture: We can practice politics either as an art of collaboration, or as an art of manipulation. Of course, if others manipulate us, may not we practice a little manipulation too—purely for "defensive" purposes, of course? "And so it goes." But in order to practice politics as an art of collaboration, we must first have the ability to deal personally with other persons, and to inspire not just respect and fear, but trust. And basically and ultimately, the capacity to deal integrally with other whole persons on a basis of trust must be conferred on us by culture. Yet the culture cannot do this unless the integral and whole "person," rather than (as now) the atomized "individual," is the focus of the social order. If the social order is organized on a material principle that reduces the person merely to a physical object susceptible, for the system's purposes, to systemic regimentation, the integral wholeness of his personhood, which it is the basic purpose of his life to achieve, is instead directly attacked. It may be possible, and even for historical reasons desirable, to make one of the more material dimensions of social life (such as economics) society's organizing principle, as long as that principle or sphere remains subordinated to culture. In turn, the ability, which culture confers, to deal integrally with other whole persons is the most valuable of all political gifts, although not necessarily from the State's point of view. Nothing good can be accomplished without it, in any holistic sense, and the lack of this gift, or achieved quality, imposes severe limitations on one's policies and methods. The noblest rhetoric is not incompatible with manipulation—may be essential to it; but the rhetoric will never become any-thing more. Thus, the psychological capacities of the people in politics, even more than the structures in which they function (al-though these are a *sine qua non*), are crucial revelations of political life—*even* of political life, we might say.

But one of the most striking characteristics of many liberal heroes is their incapacity for friendship. The concern, which Liberal-ism values above all else, for "enlightened" social programs is basically an answer to the dangerous suggestion that liberal public life actually has no moral dynamism, no real vision, and no co-hesion, except as self-interest, understood in a material sense, pro-vides. This might suggest further that liberal society has no moral legitimacy, either. So even if they were wholly sincere, in order to vindicate their control of the "system," liberals would still have to concoct social programs (invariably described as "imaginative," "bold," "compassionate," etc.) that become themselves implicit social moralities, in that failure to support them or to recognize their "enlightened" nature becomes implicit immorality ("regres-sive," "unenlightened," etc.). Though liberals may remain enor-mously moral in person (and why not?—the system, as Charles Reich has written, gives them every reward if they do), in the group, crystallized around power, they become something else—their ideology forces them to it. Thus, their behavior on Vietnam should not really be so surprising.

And thus the rigors and stress of championing social programs become the excuse for their failure to make any friends. If the programs fail anyway, though, it is not because they or their ad-ministrators were lacking, it is because of the "unenlightened" re-sistance—a liberal always manages to smell (well, look) like a rose. Solitary John Lindsay of New York was only feebly pursued after corruption was discovered in so many of his appointees; the very impersonality of his relationships with them became his ex-culpation, and if no "evidence" pointed to his complicity in, say, the cover-up of police corruption, neither was there much of a search to find any. Not so in Republican Washington, though (thank God). But as the Russian novelist Solzhenitsyn wrote of the "hypocritical clamor" raised by liberal Democrats over Watergate: "What did they expect from a democracy that has no built-in ethical foundation, a democracy that constitutes a clash of interests and no more than interests, a clash regulated only by the Constitution, without any all-embracing ethical edifice?" Poor Solzhenitsyn! He had x-ray eyes for Russian society, but did not "understand" America!

What was Solzhenitsyn getting at? Simply this: American society, like Russian society, is economically "constituted," so economics is its crucial, its organizing, social sphere. But in order to banish "religious conflict," the liberals excluded the moral dimension from their economic total system, and turned the system entirely over to "enlightened" self-interest. As society's organizer, the total system then made moral questions socially irrelevant, "private" matters with which society as such had no direct concern. Of course, liberals have retained a vestigial moral code (becoming ever more vestigial), but it remains unanchored in the social order, and thus covertly manipulable to serve particular interests, since the exclusion of explicit public morality made those who could voice their own morality seem superior to the mass of men whose morality found no public expression. But mere codes of "personal" morality cannot affect or control the social order, so the established order must endorse ritual codes of public conduct and support them with moralizing. But the many who cannot respond to others as whole persons, and who therefore are most disposed to confirm society's designation of such mere conformity to ritual codes as "virtue," nevertheless have not much use for virtue itself, and seek, or yield to, ways to cut corners, so that the ritual codes, especially when defenseless against self-interest unleashed, gradually give. The mortar for any social order must be the capacity for personal friendship, yet at the same time this personal dimension (now ignored) must also find an explicit counterpart on the social level as such: The explicit arrival at and observance of common moral principles is what constitutes any society as basically human.

We could conclude that government bureaucracy is always somehow "bad" even on an empirical basis. No one in a government bureaucracy has any direct stake in its ostensible objectives; indeed, often the bureaucrat's interests lie in the eventual defeat of the objectives, achievement of which might cost him his job. The direct stake of the bureaucracy is in preserving its own position, for which the institutional objective becomes the excuse. Some bureaucrats, of course, do an excellent job, but their devotion as far as the institution is concerned is wholly adventitious and derives in all probability from a lingering cultural order. Those outside the bureaucracy who are somehow connected with its ostensible objectives are little more than grease for the institutional machine. Seldom do their real needs determine priorities; rather, the requirements of the bureaucracy subdue the target people. The good that a government bureaucracy does is done at the cost of a greater good. The all-important consideration for this bureaucracy is the nature of the ultimate interests, not objectives, it serves; if these actually are "cultural," the bureaucracy can be "creative," and serve some purpose greater than itself. But government bureaucracy has no built-in transcendental purpose, and the only power capable of controlling it happens to be the culture's main antagonist, the State. Government bureaucracy tends to serve above all the interests of established power, but must concoct its own meaning system in terms of which what it is doing can appear to be good, and this appearance is more important to the bureaucracy than the reality: The bureaucracy need not do good, but it must look good.

All this may seem to be unfair to the State, and certainly it suggests that, if we must rely on liberal-type social programs—which represent a compromise attempt to have "morality," but at an impersonal distance, with bureaucrats as intermediaries—the prospects are bleak. These intermediaries, because they must above all satisfy the bureaucracy, cannot afford to get personally involved, since the bureaucracy represents to them primarily the source of their *own* material security. For them, "professionally," the target people must be primarily the objects of an institutional program. Yet it is impossible to deal adequately with people on such a basis. It is not possible to deal "neutrally" with people for limited functional purposes because necessarily the lack of an explicit holistic human aim will cause the bureaucracy to bend the target people to its own administrative requirements: as its own judge, the bureaucracy will make itself absolute within its own sphere. Unless the bureaucracy serves a "cultural" purpose society recognizes, embodying also the bureaucrat's own most personal aspirations, and unless the bureaucracy is somehow directly answerable to the target people without the mediation of State power, the *basic* situation remains hopeless. (A State bureaucracy can be considered "creative" only if material problems can be considered more important than nonmaterial matters.) Even that the bureaucracy itself served a cultural purpose would not be sufficient if the bureaucrat had no truly cultural aim. The curve of his personal life must reflect not only a search for security and comfort—although these need not be rejected in principle—but a transcendental value acting as the dynamic principle of his social life, too.

Of course, a possible conflict seems to persist between the interests of the bureaucrats and the culture they ostensibly serve. But the conflict at least is amenable to resolution because it is not *institutionalized*. Not only is the cultural bureaucrat ostensibly devoted to the cultural objective his bureaucracy serves; the very bureaucracy's meaning system remains in principle identical with that of the culture, so that the bureaucracy is directly answerable for its legitimacy to the culture and the wider society, which can call it to account simply by pointing out its derelictions. If the bureaucrat allows his own interests to influence his institutional formulation of the objective, he is subject to exposure and correction from outside the bureaucracy much more easily than is the State bureaucrat, who is protected both by the "mediation" of State power and by the consequent autonomy of the bureaucracy's meaning system. The insistence on State programs as normative represents a deliberate attempt more to relieve the citizen of his rights and responsiblities than to "solve" social problems, which are thereby only postponed. As long as any culture remains, unless State programs are recognized as at best supportive, secondary, and negatively effective, the citizen's social life remains schizophrenically split. The enlightened liberal, whose programs (which do not spend *his* money) indeed may be "necessary" in the absence of any culture, may think himself altruistic, but he is just as concerned about where the power lies: Wanting to take away as much as possible from religious groups, he plunders the culture in doing so, but his only alternative is a monolithic State.

People who cannot respond to others see nothing very regrettable about a systematically impersonal system; after all, it puts them on the top. Yet they still require a way of making others willing instruments. And the only way left is raw power, to achieve which they need only ignore the unanchored moral standards with which they have little real sympathy anyway. They do not consciously seek to be evil, but do not know how, or even why, to be good, and after a while cannot tell one from the other, and proclaim as good whatever "society" says is good. Yet the tensions between an unanchored morality and the system grow worse, and since the system seems invincible, the morality will give. And if the average person derives his self-esteem largely from his success in dealing with the system, the morality becomes as unintelligible as it is inconvenient. Ferocious moralizing by the system's trustees may keep him docile a while longer, but eventually the system itself will sweep the morality away.

This suggestion that the capacity for friendship is the basic ingredient of all true achievement in politics (I do not say "political achievements," because these need not have any ultimate humanly beneficial value) may seem to conjure up specters of political machines and bosses, but bossism is bad not because it is personal but because it is manipulative (i.e., impersonal). Institutions supposedly running semiautomatically as protection for the "common man" from bosses can themselves throw out the baby with the bath, drain off more energies and become a further impediment to spontaneity and freedom. Besides, the farther removed from the basic personal levels of human interaction, the more do checks and balances in the system rely on the vitality and integrity of those who administer them, yet the farther away they get from easy scrutiny.

It is that solitary nature of the men who are often proposed to us as heroes that we will contemplate here for a moment—not in order to ridicule them but to understand the nature of *our* problem. Often hailed as leaders of epochal advances—which is often true, in a relative sense—they are still often very sick men.

Our first illustration—God save and protect us!—is Woodrow Wilson, whose notion of political "idealism," which Nixon greatly admires, has a now-familiar ring. Trying to demonstrate his noble dedication to principle, Wilson succeeded with his blind crusading in laying the foundations for another world war; his own phoniness irresistibly invited Clemenceau's vulpine subversions and led to a grossly unjust treaty. Oblivious of what it regarded as grubby political realities pursued by lesser men, Wilson's idealism reflected not a strong but a crippled spirit, which neither responded to nor shaped contingent realities. The "moral" activity of such a person, who is too "good" for politics and therefore has no business in it, is aimed primarily at reinforcing his own precarious sense of election and superior rectitude. But even as his personality delivers numberless indirect intimations of its true condition, it remains maddeningly opaque to him and forces him to rely for assurance on "moral" victories. His energies become absorbed by inner conflicts, and as he loses contact with reality, he seeks an intermediary to conduct his lonely and aloof relations with it. This intermediary, if he is to serve well, must have neither desire nor capacity to rise above his master, and should be equally neurotic, but in a complementary way. Barbara Tuchman writes: "Why the President (Wilson) listened to and depended upon this self-conceived, if naive, Machiavelli (Colonel House) for so long is an enigma."[1] To whom? If Wilson was not a clinically certifiable schizophrenic, as Freud and Bullock argued in their notorious study, he was at least schizoid, and the persisting unwillingness to see this is only another symptom of the disease. Instead, his inability even to get himself together is presented as a noble struggle between intellect and feeling, as if these are inevitably split in any politician.

Franklin Roosevelt (yes!) is another example. The perils awaiting anyone who intrudes on this sacred ground were demonstrated in the reception given FDR's son Elliott's book on how his parents appeared to him (the book was called "malicious" and "twisted"). But even Schlesinger's *The Crisis of the Old Order* circles the full diagnosis, although not actually arriving at it. Supposedly a master psychologist (and reputedly a first-rate temperament with a second-rate mind), Roosevelt proved oddly vulnerable to the all-time champion political criminal, Josef Stalin, and no less insensitive to the qualities of the key people—Chiang Kai-shek, Chennault and Stilwell—on whom the success of some of his most cherished policies depended. A President can choose his own lieutenants, but the sort of opaqueness others presented to Roosevelt and he presented to them and even to himself by no means was a consequence or requirement of his office, as some liberals would have us believe. As Burns says: "Those who knew Roosevelt best could agree fully on only one point—that he was a man infinitely complex and almost incomprehensible. . . . His character was not only complex, Robert Sherwood observed, it was contradictory to a bewildering degree."[2] (Burns then offers the explanation that Roosevelt lived between an old and a new world.) Unable to resolve his own inner conflicts by direct action, Roosevelt, like others of similar temperament, ignored them, and the impulses he failed to intergrate into his personality became subversive. He slowly came to resemble a compulsive robot, as the inner conflicts tied up his energies at the expense of the problems impinging from outside. Harry Hopkins, Roosevelt's own Colonel House, became indispensable because his mimicry of a type of "disinterested" objectivity, also more familiar to us in recent years, reassured Roosevelt, who sensed that Hopkins's own inner split left him unable to detect the real nature of Roosevelt's dependence. (Nixon was not the first to prefer incompetents as personal associates.) Hopkins substituted for Roosevelt's declining responsiveness the highly rationalized brain that in a personal family crisis concocted the tactic of simply dumping his family and turning to another, a resolute method that might work with objects, but still seems rather inadequate with real people. In his later years, Roosevelt probably never was a whole person, though he certainly was talented. Less than great, he was a robot who clung to power more out of sheer inner emptiness than out of any sense of devotion, which would have counseled him to give it up. His all but indecipherable "vision" of the future led him to stumble into the most tragic mistake of the whole war, its conclusion, and his miscalculations of Stalin's character and intentions, inexcusable after a personal meeting and deservedly fatal in a supreme politician, resulted in the domination of half of Europe by Russia, and prepared the fiasco in China. (Truman sniffed Stalin out at their first meeting.) Roosevelt routinely set others to fighting for control of overlapping domains, so as to "improve" their performance, thinking he could use people thus. He thought he could use Stalin too, but Stalin, like Chiang, turned out to be his equal, if not his superior, in this respect, and the losers in this spectacle of the expediencies of State power were the people.

What attracted Franklin to what was then a very inhibited wallflower, Eleanor? Sympathy, or the flattering attentions of a woman who had little dangerous appeal for other men? Young Franklin, with his inferiority complex, was superficially gregarious, but never with women (in this he was more like than unlike Nixon—one reason why liberals prefer not to go too scrupulously into *FDR's* inner life), and his marriage appears to have been a combination more of weaknesses than of strengths—an unpromising beginning for a marriage. Dwelling on the fact that Eleanor was a distant cousin and an unconscious analogue of Roosevelt's mother might seem ungallant, but the history of maternal domination on both sides is not uninteresting, although hardly well explored for clues. Roosevelt never confided in his wife, although he did depend on her, probably as an expiatory concession, in inessential things. He would have deserted her had his career not stood in the way (another instance of manipulation) and the interesting book by Joseph Lash suggests to at least one skeptical reader that after the shock of Franklin's abortive infidelity (in which he was probably still striving for wholeness) Eleanor became a sexless drudge, whose sadomasochistic resentment only imperfectly masqueraded as noble asceticism.[3] (This is not to say that Eleanor never developed any excellent virtues; but they were not those of a whole and fulfilled personality, except insofar as fame and adulation could approximate what personal fruition did not bring.)

Lincoln was a real mystery, Roosevelt only a puzzle. Lincoln's simplicity was part of a real greatness, while Roosevelt's complexity was only psychic dislocation, which generated the disconcerting vulgarity Schlesinger described in *The Coming of the New Deal.* With Roosevelt in the White House, having that deficiency, and able to tolerate around himself no one who could penetrate (like Farley, whom he sent away) too far into the personality of which even he was afraid (thus, his strange, loveless religiosity, which finally gravitated to Jeane Dixon's sortilege)—given all these things, Stimson's note in his diary probably was correct: "It is a godsend that [Hopkins] should be at the White House." But if Roosevelt was serene, if nothing ever bothered him, if he was "the least introspective man in the world," as Sherwood claimed, it was because he did not and could not really much care. A fatalist incapable of real love, he was, in spite of his exalted position, a man without a real inner destiny, who inspired in all who knew him an eerie sensation (with which also we have since become more familiar).[4]

An irresolvable inner conflict blocks off energies from the

frontiers of the victim's concerns and destroys the possibility of integrated action, so that the larger whole must be left to take care of itself. But still the personality's need for dynamic wholeness permits no middle ground or *modus vivendi* with its repressed elements, and an unhealthy condition that remains unacknowledged grows worse and puts the personality secretly on the defensive. If the matrix culture, though, suffers from a similar condition, the unhealthy subject sees himself as "normal," yet any remaining vitality in the culture forces upon him the suspicion that *something* inside is wrong, and he suspects some shameful secret flaw rather than a general malady invisible in its overwhelming universality. He develops a secret inferiority complex, which he might, if he is a man of action, try to hide from others by compensatory "overconfidence" discouraging real intimacy. Sherwood claims that Roosevelt was "spiritually the healthiest man I have ever known. He was gloriously and happily free of the various forms of psychic maladjustment which are called by such names as inhibition, complex, phobia." Then, echoing Burns, Sherwood says: "I could never really understand what was going on in Roosevelt's heavily frosted interior."[5] Sherwood could not put his two impressions together. Having little desire, and probably even less capacity, to understand Roosevelt's thinly veiled symptoms, he took Roosevelt at face value and practiced exactly the sort of worship of mere power that was "inexplicably" maintaining Hitler in Germany. (Sherwood's book on Roosevelt is a stupefyingly boring compilation of unsifted "facts.") Roosevelt's fascinated envy of Smith, and Nixon's of Kennedy, are not without similarities: Smith and Kennedy sprang out of rich Irish-American subcultures, while Roosevelt and Nixon were both basically WASPs. Here is American tragedy of the most authentic and terrible quality; how instructive that Sherwood, a "major American dramatist," could never see it. Nor can more recent writers. The liberal faith, in need of saints, turns to men of exceptional gifts like Wilson and Roosevelt. To recognize their alarming symptoms might raise doubts and bring on ideological paralysis.

The death of Roosevelt seemed to augur an end to this problem. Whatever else their failings, Truman, Eisenhower and Kennedy all seemed to be in possession of their own faculties (although not always using them) and able to call things by their names when the evidence became irresistible—e.g., Ike's military-industrial-complex speech. But in Johnson the problem resurfaced with a new virulence and a dialectical intensity reminiscent of Greek tragedy. The pressure of events slowly aggravated Johnson's weaknesses until a voracious inner need sucked everything else into its maw. Too unformed and incomplete, too unsure of his lovability, to be capable of confronting on their merits the moral issues on which whole personalities grow, he massively and immaturely subjectivized them as tests of his own personal appeal. Never having integrated moral values into the core of his own identity, he succumbed under pressure to a compensatory drive for power, and sinister forces independent of his more human impulses took over. But was this entirely his fault? The social order in which he lived had no use for explicit moral principles; what it really cared about was State power, and by that standard Johnson was a success. Afraid, though, he consulted polls like oracles, as Roosevelt had consulted the local soothsayer, and feared healthy people as much as (like his successor) he grudgingly admired them. The sycophants he did not drive off, and those who liked to be kicked around—the Rostows and Rusks, with no better morals but even "nobler" ideals (which remained ideals)—articulated their ideals in flat monotonous tones and applied them by way of secrecy and deception. Like these "best and brightest," Johnson wanted to do what was right, if only this could be deciphered in some way other than in the conflicting pressures of events that made moral decisions or indecisions self-revelations and self-judgments. Johnson never would have surrendered his power had not McCarthy been inspired to the single creative political act of the decade after Kennedy's Cuban Missile Crisis: challenging in the primaries a Johnson made invincible by all the other politicians who discovered their own scruples only after Johnson had come down. Johnson (like Nixon) needed release, and it was McCarthy who gave it to Johnson, by forcing a challenge to his tightly clutched illusions. Johnson knew that McCarthy alone had set him free; he never included McCarthy in his strictures against those he professed had ruined the party.

McCarthy's own liability was the intimation he conveyed of both arrogance and weird humility. Nothing antagonizes some like a more than rhetorical application of principle, while nothing so pleases others. Anyone who champions a principle in the face of prevailing wisdom inspires hate in others who prefer to assume that he is using his appeal to values largely or solely for personal gain. But for a reason known only to him (he said "there is something wrong with McCarthy, but no one knows what it is") McCarthy's emotional spontaneity was impaired. So he bore the double burden of seizing initiative while trying to compensate for his emotional debility. He appeared to be a calculator, and perhaps was, although he did not want to be, and did arrive at the complex truth far more swiftly than any of his critics. But his conflict pulled his efforts to offer leadership and to maintain his integrity into opposition. So though he had no rival in his comprehension of political principle, he could not overcome the distrust inspired by his personality, and eventually he too chose his career over his honesty—but characteristically *after* the convention, when he rejected his unfortunate wife Abigail, who had been too right in a losing cause by urging on her husband a more forceful campaign. Soon came portentous and hollow threats of withdrawal from politics, and then the gearing up for 1972 and promises of a more forceful campaign—four years, unfortunately, and one wife, too late.

It might be worth asking whether McCarthy, when proclaiming fidelity "no longer" a viable concept for marriage (if it once was, why is it no longer?), is cloaking a personal failure in a fashionable generalization, although it would not have been especially desirable to protract what perhaps never was a real marriage. Abigail was trying to make him see (perhaps partly in order to confront, as not infrequently happens in a crisis, a long-suppressed self-alienation that had poisoned the marriage) that his seclusion from others during the campaign, even from those most important to him, was not a sign of strength, but of weakness—much like his earlier improbable retreat to a farm. The bland, cold social "affect" of McCarthy's personality was a manifestation of inner conflict. If McCarthy was not going to face up at this climactic moment, he had to reject Abigail when she raised the challenge in that way. Still, by this time it might have done little good to face up.

It was another schizoid, Humphrey, who reaped the fruits of McCarthy's triumphs. As a freshman senator, Humphrey had tried to impose his doctrinaire will on the Senate, in a suicidal defiance mostly a compensation for his personal uncertainty. But at least his convictions made a difference. When Senator Byrd, however, humiliated him on the Senate floor, Humphrey not only recognized the futility of his tactics, but did what he had feared he would do: abruptly swung over, as if acknowledging the futility of his convictions, and joined the Establishment. He gradually became the natural satellite exposed in Chicago, who put "loyalty" before convictions, which he was no longer so sure about, and which, requiring a whole personality to apply them, no longer made much difference in the crunch. His sympathies were diluted in a mush of ritualized liberalism, and his inner life became a vacuum navigated with the aid of labels rather than perceptions, producing his corrosive compromises in Chicago. Humphrey too wanted to do what was right, but the labels had failed and he had no inner resources to discover it for himself. The political pragmatist no longer had any real vision to give direction to the expedient compromises. After Chicago, reporters noticed his odd psychological dependence on his physician, whose simplistic soothing bromides Humphrey hoped were some sort of bedrock folk wisdom that might give him access to the common man. The physician hated McCarthy.

So the voters were offered a choice between two schizoids. That neither could offer any notable qualities but ambition suited the power brokers fine, and in an agony of oscillating revulsion the voters finally settled on Nixon. This almost perfect expression of the nation's own inner condition thought his victory had finally demonstrated his competence as a man, and remained blissfully unaware of what it had really demonstrated. His fortress administration remained as out of touch with the real world as had been, and would be again, his campaign.

As Nixon's opponent in 1972, McGovern proved to be an effete version of Roosevelt. With his campaign growing ever more hopeless, in spite of the most potent arsenal of moral and political weapons any campaign ever enjoyed, he appeared to grow ever more serene. His supporters, naturally—even McGovern himself—saw this as evidence of moral superiority; unfortunately, it was the serenity of one who could not just then really care when it counted, because he too was split. The impending rout of all these urgent ideals seemed to call for something more persuasive than transfigured "serenity," which made even his concession speech another moralistic sermon. Affecting to despise mere vulgar "charisma" (translation: simple human wholeness), which Kennedy had desperately tried to inject into the campaign, McGovern relied basically on condescension and proved only his own emotional paralysis. Unlike Roosevelt, he disdained to cater to the mere crowd, since the bond between leader and follower, as he conceived it, was not humanity, but "moral intensity," as if this is not the biggest bore, and greatest danger, of all without emotional power. The resentment that McGovern and McCarthy felt for the Kennedys was probably sour grapes.

This recital of failures will appear ungrateful and carping to the noble-minded. It is not particularly gracious, but neither is our civic life. The object lesson here, though, is not personal weakness, but cultural weakness—the almost universal failure of the dynamic integration of personality. One last example in the interests of nonpartisan objectivity may suffice before we move on.

If Solitary-John Lindsay could not live up to the noble rhetoric out of which he forged a career, who could? Certainly he was a most attractive figure, and one feels compelled to acknowledge that perhaps he accomplished much during his tenure as mayor of New York, although exactly what might not be easy to say. But it would be a poor mayor indeed who accomplished nothing, and Lindsay did not accomplish what was most important—giving the city a sense of common purpose. For this, only a strong and integrated sense of his own self, not rhetoric, could have sufficed. Nixon knew how much liberal rhetoric without a convincing capacity to realize it enrages the public. But in person, with his glassy stare and olympian remoteness, Lindsay inspired only vague unease: Not unwisely did his palace guard depend on a media blitz when he grabbed for the brass ring. What troubled Lindsay about the bossism against which he built his career was not, apparently, its manipulations—he later began consorting with all the bosses he had bitterly condemned— but the need for dealing with others directly, which he could not do. He had even fewer friends than Nixon, and they found him to be as opaque as the press found the President. His solution for bossism was to centralize the city's administration in the palace guard of highly rationalized "whiz kids," whose enthusiasm for technique was exceeded only by their ignorance of the human heart and their stakes in Lindsay's career. (But what the media deplored in Washington they found entirely good in New York.) Hoping to circumvent, ignore or overpower any remaining organic structures in local politics, the innocents in City Hall, like those in the White House, harbored only contempt for the local sachems, hardly suspecting that their new "solutions" would only compound the problems they wanted to solve. And Lindsay was already doing what the bosses had done, but excused it as the price, in a naughty world, of staying in office: He made his deals with the real-estate interests ready with campaign contributions for being allowed to plunder the local communities. It seemed essential that someone with Lindsay's noble ideals remain in office, even though the ideals never found much concrete application. But liberalism, State power, and moral legitimacy have become identified in the liberal mind, because liberal programs have become themselves the touchstones of social morality, and the State is the necessary instrument for their implementation. A liberal in power, then, is regarded as a good in itself, and any compromises he makes are justified as the sacrifice thrown to the fascist masses for his own morally necessary advancement. If the masses fail to appreciate the nobility of his ideals, his maneuvers to preserve his career remain merely the price of his (necessary) advancement, not defections from principle or public trust: No liberal is ever expected to *sacrifice* his career to his "ideals," which conveniently depend on his advancement for their fulfillment. This points to the fundamental difference between a liberal and, say, a Christian: The liberal does not find any fundamental dislocation in existence; whatever social imperfection persists is attributable to ignorance and lack of imagination. The liberal thinks, as Irving Kristol has said, that all goods should be achievable simultaneously, and if they are not achieved, wicked people somewhere must be preventing their realization. These reactionary "forces" must be identified, exposed and ferreted out. All goods will be achieved when the liberal "enlightened," who alone see clearly, exercise benevolent power. There will be no conflict between power and virtue when the altruistic liberal wields the power; in his hands, the State will become a benevolent institution. Meanwhile, the ideals, at worst (for them), can look out for themselves when the liberal has to look to his own interests. When Lindsay's aides covered up evidence of police corruption, Lindsay took a light slap on the wrist from the media and appointed the Knapp Commission, but the aides who covered up stayed on till the end, with no protest from the media, much less any investigation. After all, liberal programs need liberal administrators, and not least in order to provide other "enlightened" with "rewarding" (and how) and "relevant" careers.

Basically, the liberal "coalition" since the New Deal has appealed to self-interest cloaked in "morality," rather than the other way around, and the coalition will fade when it becomes unable to increase gratifications for its enlistees. That it has in fact failed or al-most failed on the several occasions when it has taken its own rhetoric too seriously and actually, as in 1972, campaigned on "morality," suggests that liberals deceive themselves with their own rhetoric more than they do anyone else. Nixon's advantage over the liberals was that he preached (self-interest) what they practiced, while they preached what not only they did not practice, but no one could afford to practice in a "system" built merely on self-interest, however "enlightened." The difference between Nixon and the liberals was that, as Wills says, Nixon was a vestigial *Classical* liberal, and in two senses especially: He still had great confidence in self-interest, especially as a political force, but he also reserved a central role for religion, even in "public" life. So the people rallied to him in order to keep the liberals at bay. The trouble was that "traditional" religion, the kind Nixon liked, was both overly con-cerned with power, and (thus) highly conservative socially, and many with religious beliefs would exploit any opportunity (when a reasonable prosperity seemed for the moment assured) to retaliate upon the liberals for driving religion out in favor of an impersonal programmatic "morality," for which the people paid and the liberals took credit. Meanwhile, the liberals encouraged the exaggerated materialism (whose fruits Nixon instead reaped) simply that it might defuse the popular religiosity, to which, again, Nixon best appealed. It was a schizoid situation all around: The liberals were suicidally schizoid, the people were schizoid in an opposite sense, largely as a result of liberal provocations, and it took a schizoid per-sonality to exploit the schizoid situation—a machine man for whom his own interests and morality were identical. Yet, in the sense that he reflected the "system," Nixon was "normal": If a moral dimen-sion is denied to society as such, amorality becomes the epiphany of *public* life. And resenting fake liberal piety, and liberal attempts (shades of the old medieval Church!) to make people feel guilty for not meeting "moral" challenges that the very totalism of the liberal system made it impossible for anyone to deal with on any personal level anyway (thus liberals saw an opening for their pro-grammatic solutions that would justify their own power), and re-senting Liberalism's irreligion and contempt for what so many held dear, people turned to Nixon to defend not only their self-satisfac-tion, which they shared with the liberals, but also their "religious" ideals. But Nixon's virtual self-exposure as a crook seemed to be a judgment on these ideals as well, and people would now have to feel even guiltier for having preferred Nixon to the liberals. Thus, the old "ideals" Nixon had crowed about were discredited, and any lingering opposition to rationalist Liberalism seemed ripe for re-moval.

But liberal moralizing, as generously applied to Nixon, was as hypocritical as Nixon. Not that Nixon was innocent, but the liberals themselves were hardly much better, in fact had called him forth. Lucky for them that Nixon could become a scapegoat for Vietnam (after Watergate, who remembered Vietnam?). The liberals were putting it out that Vietnam had resulted merely from a deficiency in the structures. But as Wills says, the Vietnam War had not thwarted the people's will; if the system's purpose was to express the general will, the system was working quite well. Nixon's militarism had only reflected theirs; it was they who were reluctant to admit that America could ever be wrong about anything. After the war, liberals had second thoughts about their celebration of presidential power, but the presidency was still the indispensable dynamo for their social programs, so they confined their criticisms to presidential war-making power: Believing that all problems are structural, they start tinkering with the structures whenever anything goes wrong. But a better system might not have produced a better choice in 1972; at worst, the *people* had become debauched. By what? By the liberal total system. It was liberals who taught that self-interest holds society together, that all moralities are "private."

Of course, the people may not actually have chosen Nixon in 1972, but only rejected McGovern. The number that voted was small. Nor is it clear that they would not have accepted (!) peace had Nixon, who they thought knew best, wanted it. And were the earlier liberals any more moral in their conduct in Vietnam than was Nixon, by liberal standards? Yet no Democratic or liberal criminals went to jail; at the least, they now run foundations instead. Elliot Richardson was trumpeted as a hero after he resigned when at long last not to do so would have made him (worst crime of all) a public laughingstock, ending his carefully nurtured career, but the hero is one who sticks to a principle when it is unpopular, not he who at long last acts on "principle" when finally not to do so would expose him as a fool. Well, at least Richardson is no fool.

Liberals have been trying—almost desperately, it seems—to isolate Nixon as a monster of calculating evil. This is the classic scapegoat mechanism they deplore when they see it in others. As far as a comparison among Presidents goes, probably Nixon does stand alone. But Nixon is not necessarily an unrepresentative figure, in a general sense: As many pundits observed, Watergate was but an application to politics of the recent business way of life. Behind the question of Nixon's guilt is the question how he got in. What was it about the liberal alternative that made even Nixon seem preferable (if there *was* a liberal alternative)? To say that the voters only exhibited their natural "fascism" or reactionary prejudices is a rejection of democracy. The whole point of Nixon is that his development had never reached, because it had never *had* to reach, a moral level: Morality had been excluded from liberal society *a priori*. Thus, when liberals worked themselves into a lather because Nixon, upon resigning, failed to admit any guilt, they showed they had learned no more from Watergate than he had. If Nixon was a monster, he was a monster only of mediocrity. The difference between Nixon and a liberal arises mainly from the fact that the system itself is a liberal system, and will deliver every advantage to the liberal if he will simply go along with it and milk it, as the behavior of the Vietnam liberals showed they understood, and as the Washington law firms have long demonstrated. Political crimes like those Nixon thought necessary would be singularly gratuitous for the liberal. The whole ambiguity of the present situation is that no one can tell whether liberal moral "superiority" is in fact based on true morality or simply on this superfluousness of political crimes. That in liberal ideology morality and power are virtually indistinguishable means that either morality is automatically effected simply by adherence to prescribed procedures, or that in fact there is no morality. Certainly Nixon appeared to have few moral restraints, except one, which turned out to be at last no less his fatal flaw than the secret of his earlier success: mediocrity. He could still be President except for that. When his machinations were exposed, he had not the truly dangerous cynicism to destroy the only evidence that could convict him: his own tapes. He feared losing face (to himself) even more than he feared losing power. In the moment of decision he did not really trust in power but actually reverted to the pious "decencies" that until then had seemed no more than bromides for lulling the masses. It is to Nixon's morality that we owe his exposure more than to his immorality.

To have asked Nixon to be "sorry" at this late date, then, was not only unsporting—after all, we had confirmed him in his dwarfdom by calling him to office, and he never had to face it as long as he could still "win"—it was also completely beside the point. Enough that he was out. Similarly, it was not, as the *Times* brayed, the "American people" who in the Watergate trial condemned the conspirators, and Nixon; rather, the jury simply could not gainsay the clear and conclusive witness of Nixon's own tapes. All that the conviction proved was that American justice was not (yet?) wholly farcical or bankrupt. And apparently it would take liberals as long to acknowledge what they had done to society as it would take Nixon; thus the convenience of having him as a scapegoat. Like the liberals on Vietnam, Nixon had gone through his crimes like a somnambulist, not really knowing *what* he was doing, doing what came "naturally" just to be doing anything at all. He could not tell right from wrong because neither provoked any resonance in his own soul. He was no mystery, only a riddle. A mystery is transparent, invites penetration of its limpid but bottomless depths; a riddle only hints at meaning, but doesn't add up. Nixon posed the riddle of a splintered personality that reacts unpredictably to contradictory impulses; he is at their whim because he cannot get them to work together. Nixon was not a figure to be hated, but to be pitied for his inability to have any *human* experience at all. But there was the rub. There was no pity for him, only hatred, because he reflected the liberals' own emptiness back at them, and at all of us. Not only did he stand between the liberals and power; that one like him could so easily have acquired it suggested a certain cheapness in possessing power. But had Nixon been an advocate of "enlightened" social programs, he would not have been impeached, however much he might have deserved it. A crippled personality is no disqualification for liberal candidates, after all. Conversely, the liberals would not accept mere victory over Nixon; they would have nothing less than unconditional surrender: He also had to confess that they were right, so that "history" would, too. Apparently, they did not trust "history" to put the "right" interpretation on things. Presumably, though, historians would use their best judgment, and they would have plenty of evidence to go on. But what if they do not use it— what is that to us? Do we live for "history"? If "revisionist" historians are not interested in the truth, they will not find it no matter what we do, and if they are, they will not need us. Do liberals feel insecure about the rehabilitation of Hiss and the Rosenbergs? If "history" does not approve what we have done, that is "history's" problem: We must answer to ourselves. The liberals' need for vindication is almost Nixonian.

Claiming that Ford's pardon of Nixon made it impossible for teachers to proclaim the rule of equal justice, liberals say that national leaders who pursue immoral policies should not go unpunished. But as Russell Baker wrote, any teacher who ever taught that equal justice prevails here was either a fool or a liar: You get (witness the "Watergate Three") as much equality and justice as you can pay for. It would be time for Nixon to expiate and admit his crimes when liberals expiated theirs—on Vietnam, for example. We might settle for a full and frank confession of wrongdoing. Instead, liberals are preaching that Ford can serve the country best by reappointing "the best and the brightest" as his advisors. *Plus ça change, plus c'est la même chose.*

Johnson (whose "best friend" was Bobby Baker) could work (usually) within the system because he had a minimal ability to deal with people and to get what he wanted indirectly, even though what he wanted might have been "immoral." Not Nixon. He had no personal capacity for riding with the system and milking it; as Ehrlichman almost correctly (except for Nixon's own estate and tax chicanery) said, Nixon's may have been the "cleanest" administration in history, as far as ordinary peculation goes. No "high-caliber" Washington lawyers were pulling strings. When Nixon wanted something extralegal he had to use violently illegal means. And once Nixon was gone, liberals could discern great benefits in his impeachment. The mystical "solemn processes" (politics are enfolded in a nimbus of divine mystery) of impeachment had produced a magnificent catharsis: gone was their guilt, blotted out in Nixon's. Meanwhile, the problems requiring their unique ministrations had grown positively gargantuan. After the gross failures of Nixon's amateurs, liberals could say that only experts (themselves) are any longer fit to rule; the "common man" Nixon catered to had been discredited, not least because the common man had chosen Nixon over a liberal. There was something premonitory about the initial comments on Ford: "old-fashioned belief in honesty," "really believes," "simplistic views." The old ideals were as obsolete as Nixon; nothing could prevent a liberal takeover now, least of all a lightweight like Ford. To start, the "experts" would seek controls on prices, and rations on credit.

As Peter Drucker has pointed out, a purely rationalist ideology is culturally corrosive, with no intrinsic normative standards. It evaluates, or pretends to evaluate, everything from outside, as if it were itself "disinterestedly" outside what it is observing. The inner, personal dimension of social life gets shut out, and the rationalism becomes "structuralist," regarding all values but its own, which it does not acknowledge, as socially relative. Its opposition to injustices and tyrannies is only part of a larger irritation with any institutions whatever, which its leveling rationalist solvent reduces to a uniform, State-controlled monolithity. Although forever indignant, rationalist Liberalism cannot create true solutions or new institutions, but can only attack the ones that exist, and every discovered "problem" becomes a new excuse for attacking any structures that remain, which meanwhile, though, remain useful for justifying the indignation and the growth of liberal power. As Drucker said, the Western notion of freedom appears to be impossible before, and to become incomprehensible outside of, Christian culture, for only Christianity has held that no one is perfect (thus no man has any intrinsic right to rule) but everyone must seek perfection (thus every one must be free). Rationalist Liberalism acquired social hegemony here by means of a Keynesian theory that "saved" the economy as a going "system" by cannibalizing the culture. No doubt the devastation the "pragmatic" liberals inflicted in Vietnam is only a preview of what is in store here. Their attempted colonialization of Vietnam only extended their colonialization of society here. Liberals, talking much about morality, leave room only for interests. Nixon's rise was not accidental; when political power, seeking social power as well, reaches a sufficient arbitrariness, a Nixonian amorality becomes required to administer it with any consistency at all.

Nixon deserved impeachment. But we could be a little more sure his amorality was in a class by itself if the media had pursued liberal heroes as intently as they pursued Nixon. They positively loved to be manipulated by Kennedy, considering it a service to the national interest. Nixon is but the supreme example, and not necessarily in a class by himself, of a growing inability to trust other people as persons and to be open with them. He was repeatedly driven to the sorts of compromises and evasions that professionally interest the psychiatrist and the prosecutor. His fascination with foreign affairs may have merely reflected this personal incapacity: Domestic affairs would have required flesh-pressing.

Incidentally, the sociologist Alvin W. Gouldner can also help us to understand Nixon's methods.[6] The managers of a total system, he says, see their task as reducing the autonomy of the parts, forcing their submission to the systemic whole (much as liberals intend to do in economics). But, though speaking in the name of the system, the managers, like all the other parts, have a vested interest in their own functional autonomy. So their efforts at system-integration tend toward oligarchical centralization, because the integrating efforts are conceived and executed by only one part, which soon threatens the autonomy of the other parts and polarizes the system. Nixon's program (like the liberals' today) showed this centralizing impulse, but arose from no real strength. As Gouldner says, any person forms his own personality in two complementary ways: through self-esteem, which he derives from his conformity to group values, and through self-regard, which he derives from his potency in opposing others when this seems necessary to his own autonomy. Nixon fails on both counts. He referred to no group in order to support his self-esteem, but to an amorphous mass, the "silent majority," the least-common-denominator of all groups' weaknesses, now holding political preponderance in the nation because of the centrality of self-interest to the "system." And never, without the greatest reluctance, has Nixon ever confronted anyone, either. Challenged in person, he retreated and only when safely away would, if possible, overwhelm the challenger with power. To any opponent he expressed in person only complete sympathy, even when preparing in private to trample upon that person's rights. He had no sense of personal honor, but a lively sense of abstract honor that was almost equivalent to "face." In the greatest confrontation of his career he simply circumvented Eisenhower by discharging upon him the maudlin emotions of the masses. In his "kitchen debate" he was saved only by the cameras. Like Hitler in the Wolf's

Lair, Nixon could really "function" only in absolute isolation; to have made himself available to others would have been to expose his incapacity to deal with them. Working *on* it not *in* it, he isolated himself behind the system, making its structures a screen between himself and other participants. But reality's impingements reduced his real alternatives to two: either to get back into the political process in order to shape real solutions to problems, or to accelerate the consolidation of power in order to postpone the reckoning with reality until the centralized power could overwhelm all opposition and subvert the political process that raised challenges. He could not do the first, he had to do the second. To succeed he had to be aware to some degree of what he was really doing, so in order to square things again with his self-conception he proclaimed his real goal to be *decentralization* of power, the "liberation" of the atomized individual. But these efforts only became new expressions of inner conflicts he could not handle (Nixon was notoriously frightened that some psychiatrist who got into a room with him might actually read his mind). "Decentralization," in dismantling the federal bureaucracy (not a bad idea in itself) without relieving the citizens' basic atomization, would have left the citizen utterly helpless: Nixon's early-style liberalism could not have solved the problems of which it was a basic cause—the "individual" would only have lost the sole remaining channel by which his needs routinely became known to the decision-making centers and his voice was nationally amplified day by day. The bureaucracies, of course, had their own interests, which, though, unlike those of the President, had to coincide at least partly with the people's interests. The result of Nixon's policy would have been to bring the bureaucracies back with a vengeance, but responsive only to presidential, not public, interests. Then government would have had to compel Parsonian functional sociology, the present equivalent in sociology of early Classical economic theory, to combine with Keynesianism and become a social (or "sociological") Keynesianism. Nixon may have been checked by criticism and exposure, but as long as the cultural order is prevented from reviving time favors the Nixons of the world.

In order to consolidate, Nixon had to find others with whom he could deal in a spurious equality of machinehood, and it was morbidly fascinating to watch his serial attractions and repulsions. Congregated in the White House we found Mitchells, Ehrlichmans, Haldemans and Schultzes—martinets all, the blandness of their personalities amounting almost to malignance—creating mere imitations of life with a vacuous executive machine processing mostly its own fears and illusions. If Nixon had been forced to gather healthy people about him, as he almost was, not just consolidation but the government itself would have stopped—not a bad alternative under the circumstances. Focusing on procedural matters, on organization rather than the substantive questions with which it was supposed to deal (postponed), the power center had little interest even in the problems that provided its own excuse, except as pure influences on its political fortunes. But *Nixon* a problem? Nonsense. The real problem was a social order that could offer no resistance because it was secretly encouraging all this, and had to be saved in spite of itself by two tenacious reporters and a judge. Nixon was only carrying this social order's premises to their logical conclusions. Even the liberals, who conducted the war on the understanding that the "system" would set all right, thought that personal honor and integrity had no meaning when pitted *against* the "system," so that resigning would be "counter-productive" (especially for their careers). In this system, self-interest was expected to become somehow "enlightened" by a prudential respect for the common good, but where that lay never was very clear, while one's own material interests were always clear enough. Who by himself even knows *what* his enlightened self-interests are? The political means for conflict resolution are not in themselves sufficient to secure the common good; they merely assure that conflicts will not be ignored, suppressed or called by another name, but that they will be adjusted so that *the underlying cultural unity might be preserved.* And that unity consists in a moral order in the social order, acting as a standard to which self-interest must yield.

Was Nixon, in his dealings with the Communist powers, at last becoming a "statesman," or only once again ignoring the "moral" standards that could no longer advance his career? His actual motives might be as epochal as his policies: Rapprochement could express moral collapse, too. After the preliminaries proved inconclusive in Korea, and victory unaccountably failed to appear after another even more expensive invocation in Vietnam, confidence in the ultimate victory of Western ideology by the sheer weight of its inner rectitude perhaps was shaken, and the West discreetly prepared to abandon principles it had held for dubious purposes anyway. If the opposition to Communism was only a reaction to its demonstration of an alternative to our economic arrangements (as already stressed, American readiness to react at a cost of hundreds of billions to evils supposedly caused by Communists, but indifference to much greater sufferings with no apparent link to Communism elsewhere, suggest this might have been so), the new accommodations could have resulted simply from ideological exhaustion. Nixon may have been merely extending the dubious sort of pragmatism that marked his entire career: Material interests would now be pursued without hypocritical recourse to inconvenient principles or deference to spiritual beliefs inapplicable anyway by stunted men. If the status quo could be better served by rapprochement, principles could follow the old Cold War policies into oblivion, and become as superfluous in the new fellowship with the Russians as they were in Nixon's private life. Thus did the principles once convenient for justifying force used for the sake of material interests become as antiquated as force itself in the service of ideology, as Nixon again played three antagonists—China, Russia, and the American people —against each other by exploiting their common exaggerated materialism. His whole career was only a warm-up for this consummation.

American culture has had three major components, all three

highly individualistic in temperament. The first, and most under-valued, was its religious heritage. The enormous impact of the "Great Awakening" in the eighteenth century and of the Wesleyan revival in the next century are generally overlooked. Religion's *cultural* role is to form a community, but the Protestant religion, suspicious of communal structures after experiences with Rome, sought these structures in the secular order, which it tried to bind, as a sort of secular arm of religion, to religious objectives. Catholicism had a better-developed sense of community, but an authoritarian power structure not easily reconcilable with the main Western social tradition. So American religion on all sides—except for the Jews—remained highly conservative on social questions, because social change would have threatened "religious" community.

The second component was the old Liberal tradition, out of which the Constitution emerged. But rationalist Liberalism's highly individualistic idea of social order rendered it unsympathetic to the religious search for community. The rationalists substituted the atomized "system" for public values rooted in the social order as a cohesive bond, and this system became itself the third component of American "culture," and would begin organizing American society after the watershed American Civil War had finally deposed politics as the socially constitutive sphere. All attempts to remedy social problems by way of the economic "system" only aggravated the atomization.

So the critical factor in the political malaise is the need for community. Liberals continue to take community for granted, remaining at odds with religion insofar as religion contests the primacy of economics. But the cultural primacy of an atomized "system" should be unacceptable to any true Liberalism, and indeed Liberalism remains at odds with its own system over the contrast between its ideals and the atomization. The problem seems to be the lack of a social-meaning system that can perform religion's cultural function without recourse to secular power, even if only in "religious" matters. And since the "system" has subverted the culture, enthusiasm even for Liberalism's ideals wanes (and even among liberals) as everyone seeks security in the material status quo. Into this vacuum walked Nixon, exploiting the tensions between the three lobotomized components of the society he drove further to collapse. He exploited the resentment of liberal irreligion, and liberalism's own individualism, but he was neither whole himself, nor even really religious.[7]

A similar sort of crisis has matured in Russia. The Institute of Philosophy in the Soviet Academy of Arts and Sciences, the very inner sanctuary of Communist ideology, several years ago recognized the theoretical relevance of empirical sociology. Some astute observers, notably Talcott Parsons, saw this as a most significant paradox, for if Marxism has already deciphered the inner laws of history, where was the need for researches into facts? Yet if the old "principles" are becoming inconvenient, the Moscow power brokers too may be preparing to abandon them for a more pragmatic expediency. This course then might converge with the West's. But another current also has appeared within Communism, of which Georg Lukács, the recent theoretician of most consequence, might still remain the best spokesman. He saw the growing influence of power politics in dialectical materialism as a cul-de-sac, and urged a return to a dialectic in which the critical factor was not power but "consciousness." Much as Lukács considered American society bankrupt for reasons even many Americans might now endorse, he suspected that Marxism had been bankrupted too by its own descent into expediency. So Russian Communism and American Capitalism face the same choice: whether to dispense with moral rationality as well as economic ideology, and openly pursue mere power and material interests—in which case an accommodation between kissing cousins would not seem all that bad—or to search for a more adequate legitimating body of principles to which any accommodation would have to conform. The growing sense of ideological futility could precipitate final collapse, or lead to a rediscovery of spiritual values.

Whatever we see, it will certainly include a new global prominence for sociology. Economics has been the key to Western Capitalist and Communist social organization, as well as to their ideologies, and economics has been the key to their social conflict. But just as politics replaced religion after the Thirty Years' War, and economics replaced politics after the Napoleonic Wars, so the war in Vietnam may have started the displacement of economics, and sociology is the only possible remaining heir.

FOOTNOTES

[1] Barbara Tuchman, *The Zimmerman Telegram* (New York: Bantam Books, 1971).

[2] James MacGregor Burns, *The Lion and the Fox* (New York: Harcourt, Brace and Company, 1965), p. 422.

[3] Joseph Lash, *Eleanor and Franklin: The Story of Their Relationship* (New York: W. W. Norton & Company, 1971).

[4] Arthur Schlesinger, Jr., *The Coming of the New Deal* (Boston: Houghton Mifflin Co., 1959), pp. 585 and ff.

[5] Robert Sherwood, *Roosevelt and Hopkins* (New York: Harper, 1948).

[6] Alvin W. Gouldner, *The Coming Crisis of Western Sociology* (New York: Basic Books, 1970; also, New York: Equinox Books, 1971).

[7] Yes, Virginia, there really is a "they," the undefined and omnipresent oppressors of the "silent majority." Who are "they"? The managers and sponsors of the system-machine, which reduces men to atomized and mechanical functionaires.

Vietnam

A couple of years ago, many writers—for example, Garry Wills, reviewing Halberstam's book—were calling for an accounting on the responsibility for the war in Vietnam. Then came Watergate, and the accounting was postponed. Now that the independent government of South Vietnam (hereinafter, "SVN") has fallen, American liberals have been calling for a moratorium on "divisive" debate about who "lost" Vietnam, in view of the need for "national unity" to meet challenges ahead. The desire, so recently intense, to get on record for purposes of "history" this generation's judgment on Nixon, does not, for some reason, extend to Vietnam: The scholarly monographs of the future can decide on Vietnam all by themselves. Yet a certain modest difference between Vietnam and that dread precedent, China, seems to be overlooked: In Vietnam, we unjustly squandered not just a few liberal careers, but some $150 billion and 55,000 American lives. The desire to postpone an accounting seems to assume that, in spite of the staggering cost, nothing fundamental was at work in our Vietnam policy, and that therefore no fundamental or agonizing reappraisals need to be made now. Except for a little prophylactic tinkering, business can now proceed again as usual, with the "best and brightest" conducting it. But one might wonder whether the purposes best served by this are those of "unity" or those of whitewash. Against the possibility that the prevention now of the *reverse* of such mistakes might offset the offense to certain sensibilities, we might do well to attempt an accounting now, if, without pulling any necessary punches, we can still proceed without excessive or unbalanced recrimination.

There are also more immediate and personal reasons for making the attempt here. The reader may not yet be willing to admit that the foregoing considerations of the role of the State point to anything really deplorable in the State's present-day eminence, since any status quo seems to reflect the laws of both Nature and Nature's God. If, though, one could plausibly argue by way of illustration that something like Vietnam was almost unavoidable simply because our notions about our State led us to think that a reversal such as occurred there would be almost metaphysically impossible, perhaps our willingness to question the State might be somewhat increased. The liberals have already smoothed our way by raising the alarm when they saw that the State's growing power was beginning to engulf even them, and where once they saw nothing but opportunities for State "initiatives" they now see manifold possibilities of tyranny. This new caution still does not extend to their own control of the government, but it does suggest the possibility for a new and more realistic consensus.

We might best begin by reviewing some of the principles sketched with respect to the State in earlier chapters. The word "State" denotes no concrete thing; it is an abstraction. The State is not equivalent to the "government," which can serve either the State or the people or both. The State, if it "is" anything, is the nexus of pure power—including not just the physical apparatus of government, nor even the abstract relationships between government bureaucracies, but also, and most particularly, those accommodations to mere power that each citizen makes in the inner recesses of his own consciousness. In its concrete manifestations, the State is the sign of the human community's subjection to power instead of love. It arises from sources within the psyche, which it conditions to accept the State as normal and the ultimate law. The ambiguity surrounding the State arises from the people's need of the State—or, what might amount to almost the same thing, their belief that they need it—to protect their lives and their goods, even though the State, as an autonomous power, soon threatens the citizens almost as much as the evils it was called forth to prevent.

The citizen's main defense against this power is his culture—the common moral principles by which the State can be limited, and which the State must respect because even the State depends vitally on society's constituent meaning system. If the State violates the moral principles that constitute the foundations of its own subjective legitimacy in the minds of its subjects, it destroys this legitimacy and subverts its own authority. Every State needs to be endowed with legitimacy by some meaning system, even if it has to manufacture one for itself. Yet, though the State may observe the moral principles built into its charter, the State itself is not thereby "moral"; it is merely limited, for as the State's constituent principle is force, its basic aim is survival. The focus of the "pride and pomp of the world," the State does not aim to survive in order to protect its people (as a government may); it just aims to survive, even if the people must perish. Through their culture the people can keep their State in check, but the State itself is amoral. Its dealings with other States are limited by no moral imperatives, except out of mutual convenience. The successful State is not that which best observes moral rules, but that which survives most intact. Sometimes the observance of morality best serves, and sometimes it does not: It is all one to the State. Perhaps in the long run an immoral State cannot survive, yet Western experience teaches only that the culture has been strong enough to call especially malignant States to account, but provides no assurance for the future.

That people need their State to defend them from other States confers on the State a sort of negative legitimacy, but not moral integrity. The State, moreover, is never of itself "creative," but rather is more like an incubus: It can provide no real "solutions" to human problems, because its expedients are always based on force rather than on love and human concern, however much these may be included in the personalities of the people who administer State programs. The best the State can do is to shift the disposition of social "forces," to break earlier constellations of power and established interests, but it invariably substitutes new ones. At best, the State is only negatively effective as a "solution" for social problems, just as its legitimacy is only negative. In trying to force certain people to act charitably it sets up new power structures and creates new opportunities for abuse.

Having reviewed these principles, we can now ask how, with respect to them, liberals and conservatives line up. The conservatives would still tend to see American values (or virtue) and American power as linked, and would regard the status quo as basically acceptable, reflective of a "true" value system, one that reflects the truth. They would not be inclined to dwell excessively on the fact that the moral quality intrinsic to the old system might be gone, although they readily would own that problems persist, and especially, perhaps, those caused by liberal amorality. Conservatives would see the American State as the basic defender of Western values, the guardian of political liberties. They would hold as axiomatic that if American power does not defend these values nothing else can or will. The liberals in the 1950s generally shared this view. This is why foreign policy commanded a consensus then such as may be difficult to achieve in the future. But while the conservatives always placed more confidence in power, which they have always conceived to be especially crucial, the liberals were more concerned about what they were pleased to call "moral force," playing to the galleries, as it were, by making a display of moral rectitude and legality. Although even for liberals anti-

Communism still remained a no-holds-barred sort of commitment, they typically wanted to observe the legalities. The liberal vision has since changed, and now holds American power to be little short of malignant, but not because power *as such* is malignant, but because American power is being wielded in service of a "conservative" vision (Ford's and Kissinger's). Having become also largely alienated from the older Capitalist order, they still, however, look to the State to rectify its abuses—which is why they are more sympathetic to left-leaning States than to rightist States run by old elites. They tend to excuse the more obvious brutalities of Communist States by showing that rightist States are no better. They regard the worldwide drift toward leftist States as a sign of hope and progress and the tide of history.

Are the conservatives in any way "right" (no pun)? First, they are more realistic about power. They see that as the world is, or at least as it sees itself, power is the decisive factor. Without the support of power, almost nothing else is safe. So they are more skeptical of "noble" ideals and high-minded rhetoric aimed mostly at one's self in order to distinguish one from the "unenlightened" masses. They take with a ton of salt Communism's professed desire to improve mankind's lot; they see the Reds as intent rather mainly on power. What is wrong with the conservative vision? First, it does not sufficiently recognize power as only negatively effective. Power can destroy much but create nothing. It is two-edged: Power built to fight power destroys first those whom it is supposed to protect. Every increase in power brings a no less important loss elsewhere. Power is sterile. Second, it does not realize that its "ideals," when tied to the status quo, become hollow, too. The present system *is* exploitative. The values conservatives want to defend are not, as they think, actually promoted by the system.

Thus, the liberals also are right. First, they recognize that the system has become corrupted. (But they do not want to admit that liberals corrupted it, and they want to make the corruption an excuse for increasing liberal power, and for discrediting the old values. They see a need for new values, and think they know which.) Second, they seem to sense that power as such solves nothing, and want to make international life an expression of ideals. But, as they are unable to admit that they have corrupted the system, they are fatuous about power. If you are going to have a State, and rely primarily on it, as they clearly intend to do, then the main consideration has *got* to be power, and "ideals" can have at best only a marginal role. They think *their* power will be benevolent, but this very belief may be the greatest danger of all (as Graham Greene has written). They are also fatuous about ideals. They think that good intentions produce good effects, and that leftist governments will achieve more "good" than rightist governments. But governments of the left and of the right are equally bad. The conservatives at least want to preserve some culture; liberals don't even see the need for any.

All this will suggest why we got into Vietnam as we did. In the 1950s, almost the entire spectrum of American political opinion saw American society and "Western" civilization as virtually identical. Now, American society was the Capitalist society par excellence. The differences in emphasis within the basic consensus on foreign policy reflected the differences in emphasis with respect to the economic "system" that basically everybody accepted. The liberals advocated in economics—where our values were centered —a greater role for the State, the conservatives as small a role as would suffice. In foreign affairs this difference appeared in the strictly military concern of the conservative vis-à-vis the more activist, do-gooding notions of the liberal, who wanted to see American *government* fostering healthier and more democratic societies abroad—societies much like the American, which was the normative good society. The conservative saw the State as defensive, for protecting the American status quo; the liberal saw it as activist, for extending the status quo. All found common ground in the notion that America must (for the liberal, "at least"; for the conservative, "no more than") help other nations defend themselves against that ultimate evil for them as well as for us: Communism, which suggested an alternative to our economic arrangements. Note that given the basic premise—the identification of American society and Western civilization, and Western civilization with absolute good—the basic consensus followed quite reasonably. If America was not just a relative, but an absolute, good, an alternative proposed for it must be an absolute evil. So Kennedy talked about "bearing any burden, facing any foe" (meaning, of course, the Reds). It was consistent to make American foreign policy a war against Communism, and to favor governments with help according to their positions on this "theological" issue.

This was one influence that led us toward the quagmire, even after the evidence of danger had become quite obtrusive. The other element some have identified (with good reason) as the rigid and inflexible personalities of the Presidents who got us finally in and kept us there—Johnson and Nixon. (Eisenhower's and Kennedy's actions in Southeast Asia were simply part of the general strategy of "containment," not its focus. Their entanglement there was still *ad hoc* and reversible. They were never faced with an irreversible either-or that had to lead to either victory, defeat or disaster. It is conceivable that they would have gone all the way in, but improbable.) But we cannot ascribe the subjective flaws to only Johnson and Nixon, for not a single voice in the entire liberal Johnson Administration dissented, or none publicly. We are forced, then, to view this second element as the other face of the first: as the inner quality of the "system," as opposed to the foreign-policy face it presented to others.

The crucial element in the transformation of the liberal vision of the State was America's very entry into the Vietnam War, for this entry forced into the open the gap (actually required by liberal social theory, which sees material interests as society's unifying bond) between professed values and real practice, and showed how far the distance between them was. Whatever might be true about the intrinsic merits, it is also true that the bald exposition of a moral gap posed an enormous danger to the status quo. Thus, the liberals outside the government soon began to call for a retreat—any way out at all. When the government showed itself indisposed to go, the liberals were struck, for the first time, by the possibility, metaphysically inexplicable, that it might be somehow corrupt.

Note now the structure of the "problem." Liberal society is basically a society of competing interest groups, whose conflicts the State must arbitrate when the socially constitutive economic system itself cannot. The moral superiority of this society is seen to inhere not in its intrinsic content but in the procedures and structures that supposedly structure the content, toward which liberal society, though professing "neutrality," ostensibly allowing and encouraging everyone to profess his own values, is really hostile, regarding any values that aspire to become more than atomized and personal as a public threat. Actually, the content of public life is more like a vacuum of "moral"—or cultural—life because of the exclusive recognition granted to material interests in the public sphere, which has been drained of moral content by the attempt to make the economic "system" replace the culture (with its moral order) as society's integrator. Liberal society does not really pursue moral integrity—does not even regard morality as a public concern, except with regard to "procedures"—but only material gratification. (The "solution" would not be to inject someone's "morality" piecemeal into the economy but to subject economic life as a whole to a higher moral order—to give moral legitimacy as high a social priority as economic gratification.) This position can only be understood as a device for depriving religion, from which moral ideals usually derive, of public influence. It is a reaction against the power religion enjoyed in the old hierarchical order Liberalism has replaced. The trouble is, since it is not possible for liberal society actually to have any moral values beyond the procedures themselves, the State is not likely to pursue or even be limited by moral ideals. The liberal State has until now been

more or less limited only because liberal society has not yet succeeded in dispersing its culture. But it cannot really champion
"ideals" abroad while championing only procedures here, and,
since it recognizes only interests here, cannot be much concerned
about the "people" anywhere else. Since liberal society regarded
itself as the last word in social morality, it was compelled to regard
its defense of "procedures" abroad—of democracy and Capitalism
—as a defense of absolute good justifying any tactics. But since
the basic position was defective, the tactics soon appeared for
what they were—immoral. Unable to resolve the dilemma, the
liberals could only call for retreat, which, naturally, they presented
as a concern for procedures—in themselves, of course, quite important. The contradiction lay not so much in the violation of
procedures, though, which exposed the weakness of liberal theory,
but in the theory itself, which whenever concretely acted upon
would have led to similar violations.

How were the liberals to explain away the contradictions? Although liberals started the war, Nixon and Kissinger providentially
came along to finish it. The war could now be abandoned as a
"conservative" cause—abandoned for the wrong reasons in the
wrong way. The liberals, who envy the ability of leftist States to
deny any role to religion, like such States far more than they like
rightist States such as SVN became, and always felt uncomfortable
censuring Reds anyway.

Meanwhile, American youth, seeking something against which
to rebel, rejected American society, the entire war, and the U.S.
military as intrinsically evil. They also did not want to get shot.
Any real moral justification had evaporated, and self-preservation
naturally takes over when no real ideals are at stake. All that was
at stake in the war we prosecuted was the American status quo,
which, since it had replaced any "ideals," had removed any reason
to die. But though the radicals cheer Hanoi for having successfully
defied the U.S., Hanoi is no less corrupt. Like many liberals (e.g.,
Tom Wicker, who says we should look at the Cambodian death

march from the Communists' point of view), the radicals think of the Communists as latter-day agrarian-reforming nationalists. But Vietnamese Communism, centered wholly on power, makes few provisions for anything else, and any part of the world that succumbs to this sort of thing has suffered a great tragedy. This evil was brought upon Vietnam, and us, largely by the common liberal and conservative (for "conservative" read "Classical liberal") theory of the recent past, when little effort was made to help others for "humanitarian" reasons, until societies had deteriorated to a point where even Communism became attractive. We made little effort to ameliorate want and had to spend far more later to fight the Communism that appeared on the scene as an alternative.

Even the liberals seem sneakily to admire Hanoi, and think that it is far preferable to the right-wing Thieu. They think that Eisenhower's devious establishment of a separate South Vietnam was an interference in internal affairs, or a "civil war." They resent the old feudal Francophile Vietnamese elites who feared and opposed the "nationalist" Communist movement. But liberals had no right to judge them as "bad" and unrepresentative because of preferences to which they had a right. Whatever, the two Vietnams (which, now that the war is over, liberals seem more disposed to regard as reflecting ethnic realities) became a fact, just as Israel, which the U.S. and Britain carved out of Arab land, had become a fact. We support Israel now because Israel with all its people is a fact. And SVN's factuality was almost as good a reason for supporting SVN, which we did. The people of SVN had a human right, if not to live exactly how they chose, then to resist being made into Communists. SVN had become a State in being. But even granted that the division of Vietnam was to a degree an imposition of the American will, was the war in Vietnam only "civil"? We could interpret it so, were it not for one characteristic: that the "nationalist" side was being powerfuly abetted from Moscow and Peking. In this sense, Vietnam had become a cockpit of the international struggle between Red and Capitalist, not to mention Communism and democracy. There is little reason to think that Moscow or Peking regarded it as only a "civil" war, either.

Thus, from the first the Vietnamese conflict partook of a basic ambiguity. On the one hand, it was a civil war between the old French colonial society with its established interests, and a new nationalist movement. Rebuffed by the U.S., the "nationalist" movement had turned Communist. Yet, on the other, the "colonials" harbored many who, though nursing no desire to resurrect the old colonialism, had even less desire to go Communist, just as the nationalist side did not remain merely nationalist, but became one expression of what truly was and is an international movement —a movement with a common view of life and a common view of history. Now, liberals, who regard all societies as basically *political* units, cannot conceive that the convergence of Communist States on the level of meaning could have any great significance for international life. They think that Communist States will remain politically discrete and nationally oriented. But meaning systems not only cannot remain politically inert; they form the very context in which political life is conducted. It is a truism of social psychology that all societies are constituted by symbols. "Society" is an abstraction, little more than an *externalized* meaning system, a meaning system that concretely impacts on us. In this sense, the proliferation of Communist States would be ominous indeed. To view a Communist State as only a temporarily expedient solution for "social problems" is drastically short-sighted. The probability is, especially with the growing interdependence of all societies, that States with the same basic meaning system (especially a meaning system that gives the State as large a present role as Communism does) will eventually pursue a somewhat homogenous strategy, even though they squabble among themselves over immediate interests now. It is not precisely the military power of Red States that presents the great danger, although it is a danger, but their meaning system. The economic cast of the meaning system may eventually change, but its militant atheism probably never will, for, though this may not be immediately obvious, a militant atheism is a requirement for any totalist unitary social system. In fact, it is on this level that Communism and liberalism are converging, and for this reason that liberalism is inclined to view leftist States favorably. It is meaning that power must serve, and power needs a meaning system, or some surrogate, to support it.

The upshot is that the U.S. was in an especially ambiguous position in Vietnam. The non-Communist side sheltered many who above all did not want to become Communists (these included a large number of Catholics, whose liberties have never been a favorite object of liberal concern, and who, unsympathetic to the "nationalist" movement, probably deserve whatever they now get). To them the American people certainly had some obligation to provide whatever support they reasonably could. (The liberals had it, during the war, at least, that because the Communist side was "nationalist" it therefore appealed to most Vietnamese. The *Times* was comically studious in rhetorically searching for possible reasons why the refugees fled en masse before the Communist armies during the final rout. One reason it deciphered was that the refugees were afraid of violence from *both* sides. It saw no significance in the fact that their flight was *southward*. And whereas the peasants had stood their ground even during terrific violence previously, they fled when they knew the Communists were winning, even though hardly a shot was fired. But the refugees could not be admitted to have been fleeing the Communists; that would have tarnished the "liberator" image.) The South-Vietnamese State was a relic from the colonialist past, and the U.S. would only compromise itself by embracing that State too completely. But, nevertheless, the U.S. still had not only some sort of obligation, but also some sort of interest, in offsetting the outside support to the Vietnamese Communists that had made the conflict something more than an "internal" matter. The problem was, how was this obligation to SVN to be formulated?

Given that American society was conceived as an absolute good, the American State and the American people had to be regarded as identical. If this State, as States are wont to do, acted in its own interests, this still had to be regarded as a service not only to the American people, but also to the Vietnamese. And if even the American people, because of the earlier interventions by their government, had acquired a direct obligation to the Vietnamese, the conclusion could not be avoided that SVN had become entirely America's responsibility. No suspicion arose that the aims or interests of the American people might diverge from those of the American State, any more than that those of the Vietnamese might diverge from those of their State. The notion that Communism alone was the evil target exposed the American State as little better morally than a Communist State (a notion not entirely far-fetched, insofar as they were only States). It is in this sense that liberals now rightly resent our anti-Communist passion, a defense of our material status quo. Yet liberals should be no less willing to acknowledge their own responsibility for this confusion.

Diem's government was better by a long shot than any that replaced it. No American democrat, though, could relish supporting a mandarin who was also a Catholic. No accident that the man who unhorsed Diem—with the help of another do-gooding Washington idealist, Roger Hilsman, whom Johnson later fired for it—was that quintessential WASP, John Cabot Lodge (who, incidentally, now expiates his sins as ambassador to the Vatican!). But just because we did not like Diem's caste or his religion does not mean that we began to make correct distinctions. Rather, *our* "theology" provided the excuse for sweeping Diem away (if our society and our government were absolute goods, then they would be such for SVN, too, and getting rid of Diem would be a step on the way). So we put one foot into the quagmire. When the successive regimes proved to be wholly incompetent to prosecute the war, we went in to do it for them, and then had both feet in, and the Vietnamese on our backs. We could no longer get out simply by going back the way we had come.

It was wrong to take over the war, since this only complicated the political problems in SVN. We did it for ourselves: First, because this was the only direct clash with our enemy any longer possible since the atomic bomb had made total war, to say the least, inadvisable; and second, because our "prestige" seemed to be at stake (and it soon was). The move could be understood as correct because what was the absolute evil for us, the absolute good, also must be the absolute evil for the Vietnamese. So the South Vietnamese became our instruments as well as our protégés, and we became responsible for them, as Frances Fitz-Gerald wrote, as parents are for their children. We corrupted their political life and made the whole society lean directly upon the American State. We usurped whatever freedom the SVNese retained in order to ensure their "freedom" from Communism. We defined freedom as a negative, not as a positive, and not only failed to build up a society capable of sustaining freedom, but actually militated against it. This does not mean, though, that we had no obligation to the SVNese. But it was necessarily restricted to what the American people could do directly for them, or what the American State undertook to do for the SVN government, bad as we might think it to be. Perhaps the "nationalist" government can now "save" the Vietnamese from their material problems; no one can yet say. But it is a pure act of faith (one not readily supported by evidence from elsewhere) to hold that these material problems were worse than the problems of conscience a Communist State will provoke. Of course, in a certain type of mind, material problems are the only social problems conceived as "real." And the State would acquire the same role in Vietnam that it has had in recent liberal "vision": as the ultimate, absolute, and only cultural organ.

Since the emphasis on military power was for the liberals at first largely a concession to conservative "prejudice" in the interests of consensus, it was the liberals who first began to wake up to the contradictions America's usurpation of the war had made evident, but the American government did not. The liberals outside the Johnson Administration began to vocalize misgivings. They saw that the U.S. was acting too immorally. But meanwhile, now that American prestige had become wholly engaged, the conservatives got wholly behind the war. Since to them the State's role was almost wholly military, they thought that what was called for now was simply total military victory. They were right, in a way: If we were going to take over the war, it made no sense to settle for anything less. But the academic liberals observing the gap between power and values, saw American power as out of control and heading for self-annihilation in nuclear holocaust. Johnson's "conservative" side nevertheless prosecuted the war, while his liberal side tried to pursue the "Great Society" at home. Then conservative Nixon came in and just prosecuted the war. By the time it was all over, the gap between professed values and actual conduct had created a tremendous conflict at home as well.

Meanwhile, the war had become fixed in a highly specific framework that severely limited what might be done. The liberals took the easiest way. They summarily abandoned their old notion that virtue and the American liberal State were identical, and reverted to the simpler and safer notion that the State as such does not pursue "morality" but only interests. This revision became possible when they began to doubt that the State observed morality at all. So if the U.S. had no strategic interests in Vietnam, the U.S. had no business there, and should get out. But this completely ignored the even deeper basic obligation we had contracted to the Vietnamese by taking over the war. It was as if a parent, suddenly deciding it had been harmfully coddling its child, should abandon it in the woods. Once we had gone completely in, we could not simply walk out. The liberals, realizing this would be too dangerous and crass, demanded only gradual, but steady, disengagement.

But deeming no other provisions necessary, they only spread the blame over a longer period so that it could not create a domestic crisis. This course was just as immoral as our earlier usurpation of the conflict. For once we had taken over the war there really was no way back. The only real choice we had the liberals would not take, because they feared alienating the radicals, or confessing that they had been wrong all along. Besides, it would not have enough accommodated the Communist "nationalists." And neither would the conservatives have taken the only way, because it would have involved a repudiation of the old absolutist "theology." *No* one would have taken it because it would have meant dropping the mask of State "morality" that all the new moralists wanted to weld on.

Recall here what we said earlier: The State as such does not act for morality. It acts for survival. It presents a façade of legality to the world in order to dissimulate its amorality and to disarm criticism. The State chooses between moralities to observe. Any morality that gets in the way of what it perceives to be in its interests it ignores. The only power that can check the State is its own people. So it must somehow present a "moral" face to its people. The trouble is, though, that for their own selfish reasons the people like to indulge the State, milking it while it exacts its price, which they are indisposed to notice. Thus, the State can get away with a good deal of hypocrisy, and not always consciously, either. It would require a good deal of quite uncharacteristic honesty for the State, and a good deal more realism of its people than they generally are capable of, to admit that sometimes the façade of supposed legality must be abandoned in the interests of true morality. This does not imply that the State should be encouraged to abandon at will at least some semblance of legality, but that its citizens should be more aware that its observances are mostly a charade, and that when the State has blundered into some particularly egregious contradiction the citizens have a right to force it, in the interests of the people involved, to respond to the realities as well as the appearances. The basic obligation was on the part of the American people to those of SVN. The American government had already shattered the structures of legality. So what was now to be done?

It was clear that the Thieu government was too corrupt and incompetent (largely because of his direct dependence on us) to prosecute any war on its own. This was why Kissinger extracted assurances in Paris that the war would not return to a level with which Thieu could not cope. It is now claimed that the military provisions were obviously hollow from the start, and devised simply to save our face while we got out, because the Communists were bound to reinforce their military position as soon as we were gone. If so, liberals had no business tolerating these provisions, and must shoulder some blame for deceiving the SVNese people (as Kissinger and Nixon deceived Americans) who believed that America would see that the provisions were observed. But Thieu is condemned for ignoring the political provisions that would have produced "coalition" government. Insofar as Kissinger really hoped the Paris provisions would hold up, he was more "moral" than his liberal critics, whose measures to achieve their own objectives are now presented as "necessary" and "pragmatic." On the other hand, insofar as Kissinger and Nixon made secret promises to Thieu to the effect that he could disregard the political provisions of the Paris accords, they also deserve censure. This seems to be a case of the pot and the kettle calling each other black. Both the conservatives and the liberals simply wanted to save face, the former by staying in, the latter by getting out. (James Reston might have chosen a more fitting time, than the day Vietcong tanks rode into Saigon, to congratulate the media on accomplishing the liberal objective. And the very next day, incidentally, Anthony Lewis was asking for Kissinger's head; so much for a moratorium. Well, liberals would not have liked Metternich's conservative policies, either, but he produced the celebrated "peace" that lasted until 1914, the sort that Max Lerner says liberals should try for now.)

The crucial problem was the compounding corruption of the SVN government, which we had brought in. Since we had failed to support Ho Chi Minh when it would have done even us some good, and since now Thieu absolutely refused to negotiate (and why should he have negotiated? He represented no one but himself. And, besides, almost everyone agreed that "coalition" would have been tantamount to capitulation.), the only course we had was to take over the war completely in name as well as fact, meanwhile withdrawing all support from Thieu and abandoning our own hypocritical façade. But for us the convenient new recognition of the immorality of our façade became the desired excuse for renouncing any real responsibility for the Vietnamese, rather than for acknowledging the deeper moral obligation we had contracted by it. (Unlimited "humanitarian" aid today is no substitute for what would have been the correct policy then.) If the Thieu regime had insisted on hanging on, we should have either threatened to disengage or driven it out, and insisted on a political resolution (the first) of the internal political forces in SVN, until then bottled up by our neo-colonialist policies. This resolution might have included even the Vietcong, could their military power have been disarmed. When a new and more legitimate government had emerged we should have transferred the war into its keeping and disengaged. If that government could not have survived we could have done no more; at least we would have redeemed ourselves as far as we were able. Perhaps it would have survived, and rallied soldiers and people to it. American soldiers may have been more willing to sacrifice for this real honor than they were for the dishonor we pursued.

The objections will come thick and fast. Some will say that no government could have quickly enlisted the people. But since the only alternative was the Communists, it was worth a try. It will be said that we would have corrupted the internal politics of SVN even more. But they could not have been more corrupt. Besides, all legality had already been shattered. The choice was between observing hollow forms for *new* self-serving reasons, the desire to get out, or observing true morality—responding to what we knew were the real elements in the situation. It is true that if the new government had not "won" we would have been blamable for the defeat, in a purely formal sense. But we are just as blamable now. And it was always "perfectly clear" that the Thieu regime had no hope of winning, or even surviving. Few disasters, from SVN's point of view, could have exceeded the one that occurred. We cannot nobly decide for the Vietnamese that the "peace" of Communism is better than the killing of war; that should have been their responsibility. A last, and better, objection would be that the SVNese had never learned how to run a democracy, and could not have learned while fighting a war. Frances FitzGerald made some such point. She showed that Vietnamese tend to regard their (static) culture and their State as unitary, since their culture lacks the additional plastic dimension that gave rise to Western democracy and the notion of the social autonomy of the "in-dividual," a notion made socially potent by Western culture. But, willy-nilly, the Vietnamese must adapt to the modern age the West introduced, and if they were going to learn to be democrats rather than slaves this might have been the best chance.

In getting out, the liberals paraded themselves as virtuous, but to have taken the war over completely, then to have gotten out completely, would have required not only more honesty but also more courage and real disinterestedness than either the government or the liberals (trying to save their reputations) could summon. That for political reasons nobody could afford to support the only correct policy, and that the only policy with any chance of emerging was a mere compromise—all this only revealed again the mere expediency of State power and the moral disaster consequent on making it our primary concern. Reality would have required that we acknowledge truths that, had we acknowledged them earlier, would have prevented our going in, and, had we admitted them now, would have delayed our getting out. So it became ever less likely that we would acknowledge them. For just such occasions are the expediencies of State "morality" suited. Liberals think it may be better for SVN to live under a Communist regime than under Thieu: At least the new regime will be "nationalist," not militarist and bankrupt as he was. How quickly "nationalism," which liberals have blamed for so many disasters in the last few centuries, is being rehabilitated in praise of Communist regimes. In reality, "nationalism" has only a negative value, as an *anti-colonialist* strategy. But Communism does not become benign because it is directed from Hanoi rather than Moscow or Peking. It is somewhat presumptuous to decide on behalf of the Vietnamese, who, *pace* the *New York Times*, fled the Reds en masse, and who might have preferred Thieu to the Reds. In any case, because of America, they were never given any choice *but* Thieu or the Reds, but they might have been offered something better. Nor is it so obvious as some liberals imagine that a Communist regime in Saigon will present few problems for us.

Except for his colleagues Lewis and the inimitable Baker, the genus *Homo liberalis* may boast no higher representative than Tom Wicker, whose talents and qualities, lured from the cultivation of art, have adorned the pages of the *Times* and elevated the political discourse of our time. One would wish, then, to repay the general debt with something other than a savage attack, but unfortunately the views he has expressed with respect to the subject revolved here render nothing else adequate to the defense of the truth. This attack, it must be noted, is directed at what seem to be contradictions in his views rather than at his person.

Winging his way home over Cuba after a long (and Capitalist) Caribbean weekend, Wicker reflected bitterly on the knee-jerk opposition to "atheistic Communism." He seems to consider the "insurgent" forces seeking a leftist revolution in any State to be "indigenous," even though aided by Moscow or Peking, but rightest "forces" are not, even when wholly self-sufficient. Rightists are mere defenders of the status quo (which in liberal rhetoric is always bad). It's as if the rightists have less right than leftists to coerce others, because rightists don't have "history" on their side. Thus, for Wicker, it was heinous for the CIA to try to "destabilize" Allende's regime, but he could care less about Russia's arms for Peru, Portugal or the Arab States. Allende, whose ostensible objective certainly was good—to heal a deep social division—tried to force his own preferences upon a largely hostile population, but his ruinous policies resulted in a debacle far worse than the original ills. The liberals want to pin the blame on the CIA so that they need not admit how disastrous Allende was: Most Chileans originally welcomed the military coup. But Wicker thinks that Communism might be good for someone else. He never mentions, of course, that Communism is usually imposed on populations by force and is seldom spontaneously adopted. (Perhaps the people of Portugal would welcome a little destabilization there, too.) Liberals are more demanding of the U.S. than they are of the Russians. But what mere State ever observes all the legalities, or could indefinitely survive if it did? This is not to suggest that rightist regimes are not as bad as liberals say, but right and left alike give the primary role to the State. Liberals have a double standard. They like leftist States that not only envisage no role for religion but even sometimes successfully drive it out. That Allende was already a failure, and was causing greater problems with his reforms than they solved, is irrelevant compared to his noble atheism. Wicker, for whom a militantly atheistic regime elsewhere (perhaps even here too?) would be in itself no calamity, regards the appearance of leftist regimes as part of natural evolution, and probably the Russians and Chinese who foment a few as tuning in with "history." Thus, he proves Lenin correct, that Communism has "no enemies on the left."

After Attica, Wicker could "understand" why others become

revolutionaries, but he apparently has it too good here to become one himself. "No revolutionary," he. But some leftist revolution elsewhere might do some good. A liberal never sticks *his* neck out; he lets others do the dying. But why are Red atrocities ignored and those like Calley's endlessly bruited about? Not only because that is all you can expect of Reds, so it's not "news," and the media need something shocking, something that sells. Rather, Red atrocities are "exaggerated," because the left, compared to the right, is "good." Conservatives dislike liberals as much as liberals hate rightist governments. But liberals dislike conservative *policy* because conservatives as a bloc stand between liberals and power at home. A plague on both their houses; a pox on their States! If "destabilization" is futile, so is revolution. The problems these solve are only superficial. The answers do not lie with power but with reducing it as much as possible in the equation.

If we may no longer hold American society to be an absolute good, can we, must we, regard it as at best only a relative good, and only for ourselves, and other governments as mere internal matters? No! Such a relativism would be a death sentence on our own freedoms. Though we may have no right to impose our will (and we have no "vision" to impose) on others, it is mere hypocrisy or cant to claim that we cannot have preferences—as the liberals certainly have, in spite of their "philosophy." It may be more realistic to acknowledge American society as only a relative good, even if only for ourselves, but it would not be impermissible to view it also as still the best relative good around. For the liberals, the discovery that there may be something wrong in our democracy leads (because that something might be them?) to the conclusion that we are no better than others and have nothing to offer, whereas the correct conclusion is that we have never entirely succeeded in getting from the boat others are in into the one even they also desire for themselves. Instead, we decide that Communism is good enough for them. The correct conclusion might prompt us to search for those aspects of American society that keep it from becoming a greater good than it is. We would have to recognize ambiguity and look for its real causes. Yet, recognizing our relative good as still a standard of sorts, we would not have to abandon everyone else to his own devices. We could still support our values elsewhere, but we would have to go about it in a way fundamentally different from that we used before. The American people still have obligations to others, but the American State has, and must have, its own urgencies. We must be more clear about why we are doing what we do—whether for the good of others or for the good of our State. If we want to ease the grip the State has on our policies, let us not first weaken the State but give our culture primacy over it. In fact, the best way for the peoples of the world to get together may be by developing, each people out of its own culture, a common culture to which all States must submit. Oh, for a world religion—perhaps a synthesis of all religions—to bring all States back under control!

In the future, we must cease to rely on the State to hold back the "Red tide" all by itself, because this only allows the problems swelling the tide to grow. Our first priority should be to strengthen the U.S. from within, by renewing our culture and recasting our economic foundations. Our military should be at best a holding device, not the spearhead of our attack. More of our "defense" money should go to needy societies before they are tempted by Communism, and our "ideological" offensive should be rooted in the image of a better society here. If the meaning problem indeed is crucial, then the Communist "solution" would soon find itself at a greater disadvantage than it ever will be with respect to military power.

The bubble of illusion almost burst in Vietnam, the flooded constructions of our unreality proved permeable, and almost collapsed. Now the flood recedes through the interstices and old landmarks reappear. Except for the hole left by SVN, our lately unruly landscape seems basically familiar once again. Reassured, the liberals (who have often lectured us on our lack of a tragic sense of life) turn their optimistic faces to a rosy new day, for, though the Vietnamese prepare to read Lenin and Marx, only a slight readjustment is needed here. No one had called louder than liberals for an anti-Communist crusade, by putting themselves at the head of which they had hoped to deserve power. (Back then, "all good leftists were in the CIA," says William Sloan Coffin.) The failure of military power tumbled the liberals from political power, too, and yet they could not simply abandon the old crusade, because the problems it was supposed to resolve still persisted. Their solution was, if not original, quite ingenious: to say (again) that Communism is good (but still only for others), that Communism will solve the problems our military power did not. And so Uncle Dave Halberstam looks for a new "maturity" at home. Shades of the thirties! Liberals have just finished telling us that they were "duped" by Stalin back then. Do they intend to be duped again? Yet George Watson of Cambridge University, who has just completed a study on this point, says they were never "duped": ". . . poets and novelists were attracted to the most violent system on earth because it was just that. The Soviet dictatorship looked to them like a highly disciplined system that could, and should, conquer the world: The God that Failed was a savage god. Between 1933 and 1939 many (and perhaps most) British intellectuals under the age of fifty, and a good many in other Western lands, knowingly supported the greatest act of mass murder in human history. Even the accusing eye of the historian is bound to flicker in the bright light of that assertion. One could wish the evidence were not as overwhelming as it is." One also could hope that the liberal recommendation that we exchange our adolescent self-righteousness for a senile and morally relativist dotage, for a "tolerance" that reflects at last Yeats's lack of all conviction among the "best," will produce nothing more virulent than *déjà vu*. Still, present-day liberals not only are not original enough, they also are not courageous enough, to concoct such recommendations on their own: Just as their position in the fifties, which led to Vietnam, largely reflected popular prejudices, so may their new position. A liberal is better than a weatherman for finding out which way the wind is blowing. Before Vietnam, Americans believed that prosperity and what they considered "morality" (conveniently defined in the negative, as anti-Communism—which may be the only sort of "morality" achievable when pluralism becomes a cultural as well as political absolute) were easily compatible. But when it turned out that prosperity is not always certain, and "morality" can be expensive, our popular "morality" may not have become more "realistic" but only disappeared. Now, material interests must go unencumbered by inconvenient moral "ideals." The earlier untested "morality" may have been naive and self-regarding, but at least it brought a vital élan that made us rise to occasions. But now the devil take the hindmost, the Vietnamese be damned: Americans have no more stomach for a fight. Then Wicker might as well be right.

So bind up the nation's wounds, restore unity, regain our sense of pride—cultivate historical amnesia: Liberal abstraction lives! "Now, ye gods, stand up for liberals!" Yet liberals have no more "vision" now than they had in the fifties and thirties, maybe less. Indeed, whom the gods would destroy, they first make blind.

The End of the Road

Let God arise; let His enemies be scattered.
—ELIZABETH ANN SETON

Today this sentiment no doubt would be regarded as scandalous (an invocation of pogrom and purge?). Where in the "structuralist" liberal order could *God* (no less) even stir, much less "arise," and who, pray, are those "enemies" to be scattered by rank intolerance and dogmatism? Having recorded our ritual obeisance to what has turned out, apparently and surprisingly, to be some sort of "success" story—sainthood!—we extend to "Mother" Seton's words the ostracism and hostility she herself so abundantly endured while alive.

It might throw some uncustomary new light on this matter to ask whether the "humanitarian" good works for which even secularist liberals praise Elizabeth Seton would have been conceivable apart from her religious commitment: might some of the greatest social works performed by any single person in America have owed their origin to her belief in God? That is, would she have died an unremarked and unremarkable widow had she not believed? In a sense, the query is pointless—in her time a Mother

Seton would "always" have run the course that she did—but it does open a line of thought.

From whence arises the scandal in the "disturbing" and "divisive" quote above? The cause of the scandal, the embarrassment and unease, is the clear suggestion the words convey that real religion brings, not peace, but a sword! Mother Seton did not intend to do liberal-type "humanitarian" good works (in which, significantly, she nevertheless exceeded most others), but to serve God. She knew, of course, that one must serve men to serve God, but she would have understood just as well that to serve men in exactly the way she did—by personal sacrifice and in religious community with others—remains a perpetual rebuke to those who propose to serve men while ignoring God. Doubly offensive to some is the fact that she presumed to accomplish so much concrete good without any recourse to the State—this might suggest a challenge to them to do the same. To live in abject poverty, to start from the ground up—all this has become superfluous since the liberals' discovery of State power.

The liberal "philosophy" could be reduced to one proposition, that people should look out for each other, just as the "conservative" philosophy might be reduced to this: that people should take care of themselves. Both propositions, of course, are correct, and the liberal idea is even a little more adequate and comprehensive: You cannot really look out well for yourself if you look out for yourself alone. If we are talking about people, the liberals are surely most right. Yet if we are also including the State, they could not be more wrong. The liberal would make it easy for us, and, not incidentally, for himself: He would let the government do it "for" us. But the government—especially the government—looks out first of all for itself. This liberal nonsense, that if people will not look out for others, "compassionate" government can do it "for" them, is, though, singularly useful for getting liberals political power.

These reflections are inspired by certain striking thoughts the

sociologist Robert Nisbet has aired in the *Times*.[1] Only inches
from the editorial columns asserting the "inevitability" of increased
government interventions and "initiatives," Nisbet argued that
liberal social do-gooding has failed dismally. Epidemic disenchantment with the political sphere has generated a widely based movement toward voluntary associations for performing functions the
liberals would hand over to the State. The common basis of the
disenchantment with politics and the renewal of voluntary associations is the liberal Leviathan. The frightening growth of this
governmental monster, with its inquisitorial and repressive bureaucracy, reflected, says Nisbet, not a healthy development, but a
deterioration of liberal ideology since the time of Woodrow Wilson, and Nixon's evil and ineptitude were simply the logical results
of the Leviathan mentality. Nisbet thinks that a combination of
a "progressivism" oriented toward political power, and the trauma
of World War I, killed the spirit of social inventiveness that had
characterized American social life until 1914, and all this turned
Liberalism down the path it has followed to the end. Since 1914,
the political liberal's "vision" has extended no farther than the
government agency and bureau. The previous century, in contrast,
was, in spite of its reputed individualism, remarkably fertile in
voluntary associations—such as unions. In our time, says Nisbet,
the disenchantment with the political could either lead to militaris-
tic dictatorship, as it has in the past, or become the principle for
a whole new society of nonpolitical, autonomous, cooperative
alternatives to bureaucratic paternalism.

Actually, this revolt against politics only reflects the inevitable
consequences of making a civic religion out of the civic processes.
(To deny that politics can replace cult implies no contempt for
legitimate civic procedures.) What makes Nisbet's thesis most
interesting for our purposes is its total omission of any mention
of the one force that might be expected to provide the indispensable support for the voluntary-association movement. Don't even

mention its name—that social pariah; don't even think it—religion. Perhaps Nisbet hopes, almost unconsciously, to curry some favor with influential liberals by proving that he is more alienated than anyone else, and foresees no revival of a ridiculous anachronism. More probably, in spite of his own disenchantment with Liberalism (reflected earlier in his book *The Quest For Community*), the omission only reflects the ideological myopia typical of our time.

Yet this myopia makes his own analysis seem inadequate. Odd enough that Nisbet never explicitly suggests that what might have decisively enamored political liberals of government bureaucracy could have been the opportunity it offered to its liberal sponsors to seize and hold the political power they had just denied to the "Church." But even his characterization of the previous century seems somewhat inadequate, too. After all, if it was, in fact, an age of social individualism, what caused voluntary associations to proliferate so? Most probably, it was a general, background "consensus" that supported both the social individualism *and* the voluntary associations aiming at goals the underlying consensus prescribed as desirable but institutional society, with its bias toward individualism (itself a reaction against much earlier cultural tensions), was *not* achieving. The social duality expressed an unhealthy underlying cultural situation, a cultural "split." But this was still, compared to ours, a relatively healthy situation, because there still was a general consensus on social goals, and a culture still supporting at least the search for wholeness. But in the early part of this century, this culture, perhaps *partly* because of the shock of the war, apparently became unable to support any voluntary search for social integration. When the government bureaucracies took over, abetted by the liberals' new appreciation of power, the situation became decidedly unhealthy. Not only are the bureaucracies today not really giving effect to a general social consensus; *there is no longer any real consensus.* The major supplier of the earlier consensus had been religion. Religion had been driven out because of its attachment to power. Now liberals have acquired the social power they earlier succeeded in denying to the "Church."

Perhaps the voluntary associations of the nineteenth century were, because of the cultural schizophrenia, doomed in any case. There is an economy of social life. Every person has many needs and only a limited time in which to fill them. Many of these needs are precisely "social." It takes a common way of life to satisfy them all relatively well. Associating only for a particular and limited aim, however important, tends to take "too much" time. If the goal is overridingly important, the strains of achieving it will tend to break the association up. Most of the associations of that time seem to have been aimed at goals of bedrock importance, such as fair wages. Those of our day, though, do not (except for the communes) seem to be concerned with goals of bedrock importance, but with relatively limited utilitarian goals. There is nothing to object to in this, but it does encourage doubts that these present-day voluntary associations alone present as great a promise as Nisbet suggests.

People are associating today not only to achieve common goals that "society" is not achieving, but also to generate a consensus to support *any truly social goals at all* independent of the State. These associations are desperate measures, last-ditch stands. So atomized has liberal society become, so vulnerable to exploitation, that people are flocking to these associations simply to affirm, perhaps mainly to themselves, their very humanity. On such ambiguous foundations, the voluntary-associations "movement" may not even have a good chance of survival, much less of becoming itself the basis of a new social order. There is no inner cohesion to oppose to the integrated monolith, Leviathan, bearing down upon them. A "consensus" should be in place first, extending to a depth sufficient to absorb Leviathan's impact. From where else but religion this might come one could hardly guess.

If every mystique gives rise to a politique, every politique needs a mystique. The voluntary-associations "movement" is precisely a *negative* politique. To become anything more it must acquire a system of positive shared values embracing all aspects of social life. Religion (one does not say the "Church") could provide it. If this idea seems incomprehensible, let us recall another, almost archetypal, social movement (which almost exactly parallels Elizabeth Seton's achievement in the aspect of interest here): the Franciscan "movement" of the Middle Ages. Was the religious aspect of this movement a feature "local" to the times, something that might have been discarded, had Francis arrived at a later time? Again, the question is artificial: Any historical figure is a product of and for his times. What we mean to ask is whether equivalent "good" might have been accomplished without the religious "baggage." The question seems to answer itself: This "baggage" was itself the cause of whatever good Francis did, and even of his very desire to do good at all. His integrated poetic attitude toward even social life reflected his freedom to integrate even his religious life completely and explicitly into his social existence. It was this freedom that gave his "movement" its ability not only to cut through all social classes and ways of life, but also to effect reform without the State. (And there are no troubadors where there is no religion.)

As suggested above, there can be few reservations about voluntary associations, declared by de Tocqueville to be the most effective deterrents against totalitarian rule. Their recent revival at least proves that people are still functioning as human beings in spite of the efforts of "compassionate" bureaucracies. But if they are to support a new society, these associations must find some basis on which to unite in the struggle not just against particular deficiencies in society but also against the cultural sources of these deficiencies and, most emphatically, the Leviathan pretending itself to "solve" them. Something must give the associations the ability to evolve into a way of life. This is an opportunity for the "Church" perhaps even greater than that it surprisedly found on its doorstep in the early nineteenth century, and which, because of its own orientation to power, it botched by defending established interests instead.

The situation today is replete with ironies. Though "religion" gave liberals much of their power—urban Catholics, particularly, were the backbone of the Democratic strength in the East and Midwest—this could never be surmised from the patent derision and hostility in which the rationalist liberals have held their political base (it is written: "Anti-Catholicism is the anti-semitism of the intellectuals"). Religionists have tolerated the liberals in the past for several reasons. For one thing, they recognized the validity of the liberals' fear of religious power. For another, they knew that there would always be power and no lack of people fighting to wield it, and just to live in the world requires a certain indulgence of pontifical declarations of principle (such as "separation of Church and State") that secure power for the noble-minded. Besides, most of the religious people had little choice or say. And in return for their acquiescence, the liberals delivered a large measure of economic prosperity—no mean feat, even though the prosperity was purchased at a large cost in social freedom and social function. But do Christians and Catholics now need liberals more than liberals need them? Almost certainly liberals have delivered far more economic prosperity in the past than they will or could deliver again: The culture plundered for the sake of "prosperity" has now been bled white. At best, liberals can furnish only a State cocoon in which to hide from the real problems for another decade or two until their totalist system unmistakably reveals itself for the totalitarianism it is.

But there is a point where further passivity becomes craven, further concessions become suicidal as the knife slices past fat into cartilage and bone. We have come to that point; we are at the end of the road liberals have been taking us down. They have left only false assurances and deluded hopes. Their social nostrums have failed, but they cannot admit failure. Even Ford's timid reservations amount in their eyes to "pre-McKinley ideology." (Would that it were—we'd be better off.) What liberals really want now is absolute power, but they want it in the guise of "democratic" procedures.

The middle-class "ethnics" may be bigots, may be selfish, may be everything the liberals, in spite of their rhetoric, so obviously think them to be. (Yet no blacks are being bused into Harvard Yard. Like Elizabeth Seton, let liberals go bury themselves in Roxbury, then call on Charlestown for help.) If Christians have any real religion, and are not just using religion to justify the status quo or to achieve vicarious righteousness by getting on "God's side," then they have to ask themselves not only whether they really consider blacks to be brothers, but also whether they can any longer go along with the liberals. If poorer whites have to give up their communities, let liberals, as a token of good faith, give up their power. If liberals regard "religion" so lightly, let them get along without its political help, lest we have to get along without religion when the liberals' machine finally and completely takes over.

One problem is that many "Protestants" really don't know whether they are liberals or Christians; in certain sects, the two have been made a hybrid one, and there does not seem to be any basis (or reason) for choice. The best thing the other Christians could do (the "real" ones, one might say) is to join the voluntary-associations movement, where they belong. To do this they need only (1) fight against the liberal formula on separation (substituting a separation of sacral and secular *functions*) so that religious groups can perform certain functions now claimed by the secular State, and (2) become voluntary associations themselves. Most Protestant sects, liberal and otherwise, already are such. The Catholic Church would become a voluntary association simply if the "laity" wrested control of finances from the clergy. The power structure would collapse on the same night it lost control of the money. But clergy should administer sacraments, not budgets. The hierarchy has teaching authority to define what is and is not Catholic belief; it has no right to tell anyone what to do, or even what to believe.

If liberals, on the other hand, want to keep Christians in their coalition, let them: (1) abandon Leviathan; (2) put Kelso in their party plank; and (3) let the churches go about their proper business. If liberals will not, Christians will know their duty; even if it comes to that, they must be ready to spill their own blood. Religion is not religion that is not a preparation to die. Better to stand when everything hangs in the balance, than to sink later, when resistance would be too late.

Contrary to Nisbet's hopes, voluntary associations alone are not going to resist Leviathan. It is concerned with the whole, the associations (except for the communes—and if it is hard to run a commune on a religious basis, it is virtually impossible on any other) almost by definition with limited and specific goals. *Even in a society of voluntary associations, Leviathan could still be necessary to perform the social integrating function.* This is the basic role it is performing now. Leviathan is trying to integrate society on the level of function (when it tries to do so on the level of meaning, the game of freedom will have long since been up). It needs bureaucracies for this purpose—voluntary associations or no. The bureaucracies today are not only trying to "solve" social problems (and creating them instead) but to integrate the social order. Nisbet's apparent failure to realize this makes his vision like "a rage of dreaming sheep," and his predictions to rival in naïveté those of Charles Reich.

Voluntary groups need not, of course, all become "religious," and there may not be all that many religious people anyway. But something deeper than a series of utilitarian objectives has to suffuse the movement (which seems to have appeared because the integrating function has broken down: the market was not able to succeed alone and, when "helped" by the liberal bureaucracies, succeeded even less, and the bureaucracies alone will not succeed at all) if it is to become the principle of a new order. Though the voluntary groups need not become "religious" if their objectives impinge on no directly religious concerns, they should be aware that many of their self-appointed tasks result from the breakdown of integration, and are not really "solvable" without a "general solution" for the "social problem." They should at least not exclude religion, and should be receptive to it as a possible holistic remedy. Actually, we are talking about a new situation that would —except for the myth of hierarchical order—much resemble the Middle Ages, the age par excellence of voluntary associations (when society was integrated on the level of meaning).

Yet even an association for limited utilitarian aims very quickly raises questions about "ultimate values"—*how* the goal is to be pursued (what procedures would be "appropriate," and why) and *why* the goal is worthy to be pursued at all. Only with difficulty does a limited social goal embrace different "philosophies" for very long. But if religion rightly became a voluntary association, the overlapping with other such groups might well become natural and spontaneous, and lead at length to a new cultural integration such as now would seem "impossible."

Religion's "natural" allies are more among the "radicals" and communes than among liberals, who want to reduce religion to a household pet. At the same time, many allies could be found among conservatives who don't like a big State. "Religion" could become the link in a new coalition.

This suggestion of the possibility of a new *political* coalition virtually based on "belief" may seem an impractical, if not positively dangerous or nonsensical, idea. How realistic—nay, indispensable—it could be, might be demonstrated, though, by a reflection on the history of the rivalry between "Conservatism" and "Liberalism." For this purpose, no more valuable aid could be found than Clinton Rossiter's brilliant *Conservatism in America*, from which the following description of Conservatism is taken.[2] (Of course, the conclusions drawn from it are entirely my own.)

There are several levels of conservatism, says Rossiter, but that which deserves our greatest respect is philosophical Conservatism (dignified by Rossiter with the capital "C"), which is characterized by "awareness, reflection, traditionalism, and disinterestedness." This Conservatism is not a theory, but a mood, a faith, a sentiment, bias, or temper—a wonderful mosaic unifying a collection of principles. It prefers liberty over equality—conservatives, says Rossiter, desire a political elite—but not necessarily over justice. Conservatism regards society as a living organism with roots deep in the past, and as cellular (built on groups) rather than atomized (built on individuals). Institutions represent for it the accumulated wisdom of the race. Yet though society may be a structured unity, it is not static: Change is the rule of life. But society nevertheless must be stable. Conservatives try to discover the order inherent in things rather than to impose order upon them. The social order is the outward expression of an inner and uncoerced harmony, and social stability is constituted by unity, harmony, authority, security, and continuity.

In the political sphere, conservatism sees government as nature's answer to timeless human need. Thus, laws, like institutions, are the result of centuries of imperceptible growth. Government is a positive but not an unmixed blessing: Even human angels would need some political organization, but government serves only limited purposes, and even in its own area of operation its successes can only be limited. Government's greatest limitation is the imperfect nature of man. Government must, therefore, be constitutional and representative. Rulers must respect limits and power must be diffused and limited. A "reluctant democrat," the conservative seeks limitation and balance to restrain the potential tyranny of the majority.

But government not only defends the community against external assault; it is also the symbol of unity and the focus of patriotic fervor. It protects even the citizens against mutual violence, and acts as the major equilibrator in the balance of social forces. Government may even act sometimes as a humanitarian agency, although, as Burke said, "the laws reach but a very little way." (Or, in the words of Peter Viereck, there is "a line of diminishing returns for [government] humanitarianism. Beyond it, the increase in security is less than the loss in liberty.") Nevertheless, though the best government employs the least force, the reduction of force is a problem of reforming men, not of limiting the scope of government. The conservative tries to strike a workable compromise between the needs of the community and the rights of the individual. Whether the State be defined as the entire society or as that part of it known as government, no fundamental antithesis or conflict exists between it and man. Government serves man as the chief agent of society.

With respect to economics, conservatism defends the privacy of property as the chief bulwark against the State, and in recognition of man as he is, not as the left would have him be. The conservative distrusts both unqualified laissez-faire and unqualified socialism. But not only has he no precise "solution"; he holds that fine lines are "cruel and dangerous delusions." With respect to economics the conservative urges us to take note of the inadequacy of politics. He hates unjust coercion of any kind.

The mortar that holds the conservative mosaic together is religious feeling. Religion is the conservative's center of gravity, the "source of all good" (Burke). If the conservative is not a secularist, neither is he a clericalist, but he sees history as a teacher, and history reveals a "higher law," a moral law. The conservative places moral above material values, and hates all kinds of moral softness. He has, too, a healthy distrust of pure reason. He is an empiricist rather than a rationalist; in fact, political Conservatism first arose (with Burke) to do battle with men who used pure reason to tear down and rebuild whole systems. Since then, the conservative has sought to domesticate the reformers: In the century and a half between Burke and Churchill, Conservatism became more "liberal," just as Liberalism, under the American influence, became more "conservative." Conservatives and liberals here have established a détente, seeing their rivalry within a basic consensus as constructive. Both are devoted to liberty, but the conservative sees liberty as something to be preserved, while the liberal sees it as something to be enlarged.

For his part, the liberal has some basic criticisms to make of the conservative position. In short, he sees it as: mean in spirit— a psychology of fear and habit; materialistic—a defense of a way of life in which property is the indispensable element; selfish—an attitude of possession and fear of dispossession; smug—satisfied with things as they are; callous—ignoring suffering and injustice; negative—always on the defensive, never in the lead; self-contra-dictory—preaching both the inviolability of the person and the primacy of society; antihumanistic—defaming human nature; anti-democratic—having fought democracy savagely at every stage of its development; antiintellectual—distrusting reason and intelli-gence; and, finally, obstructionist.

A crucial clue to the real nature of this rivalry between liberals and conservatives might be found in what happened to it in the nineteenth century. Before the Civil War, the "progressives" had opposed the Hamiltonians, who wanted to use government to "bol-ster finance and encourage new industry" (Rossiter), while the progressives pushed for political and constitutional reforms to bring more little people into the seats of power. After the Civil War, though, the progressives "realized" that only government could man-age the challenge of change, so they suddenly became markedly sympathetic toward government authority. As a result, the conserva-tives, who were willing to use government to their own ends, but not to see it used against them, became opposed to reform. Thus, the agents of change became opposed to reform, while the progres-sive opponents of change (caused by Capitalist finance and in-dustrialism) became committed to reform!

But, as was argued earlier, the Civil War was most basically a *cultural* watershed in America—the moment when the United States

passed from the age of politics to the age of economics, when economics became the socially constitutive sphere. The progressives
had opposed early Capitalist industrialism because it was disruptive
but not visibly crucial; they were progressive only in the socially
constitutive political sphere. When economics became constitutive,
though, they became progressive in that sphere as well. In the ever-
lasting debate over man and the State, the liberals and conservatives
at this point changed sides. When the State was feudal, the liberals
wanted to drive it back. Now that the State was safely liberal,
Liberalism included a readiness to use State power, and the liberal
saw his aims as compatible with a very active policy of social
organization, involving a great enlargement of the functions of the
State. But while Conservatism had shunned both individualism and
collectivism, Liberalism had swung from one extreme to the other.
The explanation for all this seems to be twofold. First, the shift of
the social organizing function from politics to economics reflected
a further collapse of the culture, and therefore presented the State
with an opportunity the liberals could not resist (but perhaps if the
liberals had not, the conservatives would have had to seize it).
Second, the liberal-radical individualism necessarily required, as
social complement, the collectivism that the liberal total systems (increasingly functioning in place of culture) increasingly provided.
This paradoxical duality is the liberal analogue of the duality in
Conservatism that liberals see as self-contradictory, if not downright
hypocritical: that between the proclaimed inviolability of the person, and the simultaneous primacy of the social group. But while
the conservative duality *can* be wholly resolved on the level of culture, the liberal duality, which is a surrogate for culture, cannot be
resolved at all.

Since in the New Deal Liberalism became even more receptive to
Capitalist industrialism, the main constant in the antagonism
between liberals and conservatives was their respective attitudes
toward religion. *This is what the real conflict is all about.* The several parties may at different times have allowed their interests un-

duly to influence their "ideals," but they were always aware of what *essentially* divided them: religion, the stumbling block then, the stumbling block now. There is more truth than perhaps commonly suspected, even by those who quote it, in the observation about the necessary link between "politique" and "mystique." The battle between liberals and conservatives is a battle of faiths, not of reason; it is a process of finding "reasons" for what has already been decided to be the "nature" of human social life itself. At bottom, the real dispute is over religion, or even God. The conservatives say that the foundation of society is God, and even religion. The liberals do not (dare) directly controvert this, but hold that, as far as society is concerned, religion is a "private" matter. The most germane issue has not yet been joined, but, with conservatives holding that it is religion that integrates society, and liberals holding that the foundation of society is the State, the basic question presses ever closer toward consciousness: Does God exist, and, if so, is He adequately represented by "religion"—i.e., the churches—so that "religion" must be given some special leeway in the social order?

It is not just the liberals who are the heavies in this drama of misunderstanding. Since Liberalism's ideals are religion's own, all that is disputable by "religion" is whether the liberal policies can express these ideals or serve them. Nor have the liberals yet formally abjured religion; their attitude toward both it and the State is the result not so much of a conscious rejection of God as of a positive service to a prevailing myth that conservatives have espoused almost no less than liberals. The nostalgic ideal of the "real," historical Conservatism was the feudal hierarchical order, with its established church and aristocracy (with which conservatives, like the Middle Ages themselves, had identified religion). But if "modernity" had not been, their transformation into capitalists would have been, enough to make conservatives reject the feudal myth, and, like everyone else, trade it for the modern (liberal) myth of "autonomy." It was the influence of this new myth that made the conservative defense of (Puritan) religion take the ironical form of a defense, against the progressives when they went over to the State, of Classical-liberal laissez-faire, against which earlier conservatives had defended "Christian culture." With the new social constitutiveness of economics added to this myth, conservatives were able, overwhelmingly until 1930, to convince most Americans that the weird, but wholly explainable, combination of liberal democracy and laissez-faire were divinely ordained. In sum, modern conservatives—living contradictions because of their (self-serving?) fondness for myth mixed with their devotion to religion—are nothing more than Classical liberals with religion.

So here we finally get to the real heart of the matter. The healthy elements in both Liberalism (its ideals) and in Conservatism (its concrete and tragic respect for both human "reality" and religion) arose alike from the earlier Christian culture. The unhealthy aspects of both are largely attributable to the influence of myth, which has, though, a stronger hold on liberals, who appear to eschew religion, than it has on conservatives.

As we saw earlier, the political effect of a myth is to consecrate the State, and the State can be consecrated only by a myth. So if we are ever to resolve this impasse, it is essential to be more clear about what the "Christian" attitude toward the State "ought" to be. Is the State an absolute evil? No; the State may be an evil, but it is not an absolute evil—"worse" might be the chaos and injustice that the absence of a State might produce. But neither is the State an unqualified good; it is, at best, a *relative* good, compared to the evil it prevents. As the locus of legitimate power in human society, the State is the sign of the human community's subjection to power rather than love. In Hopkins's evocative phrase, it is "the blight man was born for." If the State is a "blessing," as conservatives hold, it is such only by virtue of what it (perhaps) prevents, not by virtue of what it *is*. Christians must face up to the fact that a way other than meeting power with power was suggested by the One they call "Lord." Certainly by the "world's" standards, meeting power with physical nonresistance has to be folly. But if Christians were what they claim or aspire to be, this strategy would be irresistibly successful: It is impossible to coerce one who fears nothing except the evil in himself. Those who can even welcome death as the gate to a better life have nothing to fear from power, but power has everything to fear from them: No power on earth could withstand them. The State is necessary because men do not have faith, not because they have it.

It is true that religionists must come to terms with the State. Especially at this late date it seems inconceivable, Marx's contrary contention notwithstanding, that the State will soon pass away. But any recognition of the State as a "normal" part of the nature of things is itself an act of faith, a statement not only of what is but of what ought to be. The conflict is, inescapably, between transcendental and nontranscendental visions of life. For the former, the State becomes, as a reflection of the world's pride and pomp, even more questionable than the world itself, but ultimately—and this perspective is available only to faith—a triviality. The State can be and often is a grave proximate danger, but the teeth of its ultimate threat, death, have long since been pulled.

It may be "unrealistic" to expect that many men will ever be real believers, much less saints, and the advice of nonresistance may have been more counsel than command. So we are left with an intrinsically ambiguous situation reflecting the ambiguity of human moral and social life itself. The State meets us as an objective and immovable fact. At once blessing and curse, it becomes the inescapable goad that drives us, willy-nilly, toward either virtue or corruption, and there is no hanging in between. A perpetual visible judgment on our moral lives, the State, God's harrow, is the price we unconsciously pay for our most cherished sins. In social life the State represents a "gray area," a zone of uncertainty, where the drama of moral growth and corruption (and redemption) is invisibly played out. The virtuous submit to the State, though it is evil, and become better men. The wicked embrace it, though it is a "good," and become more corrupt.

Now, anyone who entertains these refinements will realize at once that the conservative "tradition" appears in an ambiguous light. The conservative professes to see no fundamental antithesis or conflict between the State and man, but this position is itself probably a simple compromise between myth and culture. (Not for nothing does Conservatism resist strict formulation.) The reason why the compromise that the conservative tries to strike between the needs of the community and the needs of the individual cannot be clearly formulated is that the State is admitted into the "community," and the so-called "compromise" really tries to embrace what is a contradiction between culture and State power. (Yet this contradiction is still better than ignoring the needs of the community.) This would be clearly indicated by Rossiter's observation that conservatives seek a *political* elite to exercise power, rather than simply a *cultural* elite to help keep power in check. For conservatives, government not only defends the community against external assault, but also serves as the symbol of unity and as the major equilibrator (instead of culture?) in "the balance of social forces." (The Constitution as a sign of unity, yes; the State, no.) It is because Conservatism, in the very name of religion, has been oriented to power no less than Liberalism that Conservatism fought democracy every step of the way. (But, again, let us not too much blame conservatives: Even Teddy White unabashedly declares that "politics in America is the binding secular religion," of which the President is the "High Priest"!). But the State does not defend "values"—or, at least, not very enthusiastically.

The common ground that preserves domestic détente between liberals and conservatives is ostensibly their common ideals. But, actually, these have become largely fronts, as the liberals go off in search of power, and the conservatives defend their interests. The *real* common ground is the conservatives' acquiescence in the liberals' notion of the role of State power. For even the true conservative has normally believed that religion and morals must *necessarily* be "protected" by the State. The real common ground,

power itself, is what affords the opportunity to migrate opportun-
istically (like Connally) from one position to the other without
contradiction. And it is this very link that "justifies" the liberal
criticism of the conservative as selfish and timid: Because the order
to which he is committed is that already achieved by the State, the
conservative has no further "program" or suggestion for putting his
putative "ideals" into effect. The best Conservatism includes a
positive respect for culture; in contrast, modern Liberalism is a faith
in power. But the conservative appears undynamic because, while
the liberal has the initiative of power, the conservative ignores his
own source of secret and mysterious strength and falls back instead
on the status quo. The conservative pessimism may be accurate with
respect to the State, but the State hardly exhausts all possibilities
of social initiative. On the other hand, the liberal optimism may be
justified with respect to people—although the liberal does not seem
to realize how risky this faith is, how fraught with tragic possibilities, and how utterly dependent on the *personal* risk of love—but
it is not justified with respect to the State. If, though, even religion
is now the captive of largely its own power, the possibilities of creative reform outside the State would indeed seem to be very limited, as the failure of the radical revolt has already suggested. In
essence, the conservative position has always been a cultural holding operation in the face of ever more virulent power, both secular
and ecclesiastical. Religion has been unable to follow the maxim
that the best defense is a good offense (of course, we are not talking
here about power).

If Conservatism could give up its attachment to power, the only
remaining effective link with Liberalism would be snapped. The
conservative would become able to appropriate all the liberal ideals,
and try to put them into effect without the State by means of a
newly dynamic and truly *faith*-full religious community, and those
on the liberal side who "believed" in culture could come over to
the "conservatives." For if John Dunne's discovery of social myth—
an epochal discovery which, for all the modest unprepossession of

its elaboration, may be more fundamental and important than the discoveries of Einstein and Newton—removes the prevailing unhealthy link between Liberalism and Conservatism, it also removes the dividing line: Take away power, and the two "isms" become simply and solely matters of temperament, not philosophy, for the ideals of both, which neither any longer really holds, are almost identical. The real division now is a lingering reflection of the conflict between myth and religion. Liberalism wants to get rid of religion as a serious social force and Conservatism wants to preserve it, although Conservatism as much relies on power to preserve religion as Liberalism does to exclude it. Take away State power, and modern liberals, too, would have nothing left to lean on. They would perforce either have to turn back to religion or give up the game of ideals and become openly totalitarian. In effect, the political polarity reflects the basic cultural polarity of our time, between those who profess to believe in God, and those who believe only in power.

With these considerations, the opposition over "ideals" is resolved; the present link between liberals and conservatives (love of the State) is rejected.

Liberals will label this reformulation a threat to the old practical, pragmatic accommodationism within a context of "common values." But the point is, this putative context has become a rhetorical illusion. The common ground is a reliance not on values but on power. To the degree that the old "pragmatism" was really a cynical relativism relegating questions of Truth to social irrelevance, this reformulation is a threat to it. (However, it is really the liberals who, by insisting on *their* inflexible ideological cant about "separation," have violated the old accommodationism.) We can rightly admire the pragmatic attitude extravagantly: like the two-party system itself, it unites people and delays confrontations. We draw the line only at separation of "Church and State"—a formula aimed only at getting the churches out of the way. The new coalition we are proposing is more cultural than political—a union basically of all who believe in the value of culture. The political order is breaking down because of an abscess in what should be a culture but has become a desolation (T.S. Eliot's "wasteland"). The old consensus has broken down because Liberalism itself has already become as much a cultural strategy as a political philosophy or ideology. The new coalition would be based not so much on political philosophy as on an agreement as to the very place of politics in the social order. This is a response that, if nothing else, the rationalist liberals have made necessary. But the coalition holds the door open to liberals, in hopes of entering the new age united and in a position of real strength.

Since the modern Liberal political coalition has been based almost entirely on material interests, it might seem that a coalition based on "ideals" would be impracticable. But this objection would be misleading. If implemented "systematically" in the economic order, Kelso's plans could do for this coalition what Keynesianism did mostly for the liberals. On the other hand, Kelso's plans probably could not in the long term work without a renewed culture, because, to make them succeed, workers must have a sense of responsibility to others, and this comes only from a sense of social function, which in turn only a culture can provide.

The necessity for such a coalition reflects a sea change that, however, goes far beyond the physical borders of the United States. The crisis it reflects has incalculable proportions, and goes far deeper than questions of social organization. Coming to the fore now as questions of direct social import are matters of ultimate truth— such as the liberals pretended and hoped, with their compartmentalizing mechanisms, to exclude. Insofar as the old compartmentalization was philosophically superficial and disingenuous, the old "pragmatism" is obsolete. But our reformulation poses no danger to the healthy aspects of the American tradition; rather, it alone can save them. Yet the problem is also worldwide. An age is coming when the State may admit no limits. It is time for religion to take stock, time for it to realize that it will soon find itself, may already be, in a situation potentially more dangerous than any it has yet faced. It must be ready to produce new martyrs. To say "no" to the State may become the supreme act of courage and faith, the faith that confounds the wisdom of the wise. Not American-style Liberalism alone is the problem, but a world-historical epoch that may as much embody a hatred of God as the Middle Ages ostensibly embodied a love of Him. So if they are to have any concrete support in the struggle, and a sense of orientation and firm ground, Christians, and Jews, must become a real community. The problem of power in the Church is almost as large as it is in civil society.

Yet we may nevertheless tend to overestimate the perils of our own time. Every age is a crisis; life is a crisis. To be a real conservative you have to be a liberal; society, like the Church, is "semper reformanda"—always in need of renewal. And all our real American progressives (La Follette, Wilson, the Roosevelts) have been conservatives, changing in order to preserve, defending the old moral order against the new industrial disorder that the earlier "conservatives" had brought in. In the end, though, one must agree with Elizabeth Seton, one of our most accomplished doers: We put too much stock in our own efforts. God heals, not man. Our busybody activity only serves to distract us from our own vacuity. For us to realize this might be the beginning of wisdom.

FOOTNOTES

[1] Op-Ed page, *The New York Times,* September 23, 1975.
[2] New York: Vintage Books, 1961.

Why, we children of the Enlightenment will urgently inquire, must a cultural meaning system be super- (or sub-?) rational? It is not only because a person is both more and less than rational. It is also because of the primary challenge that each and every society, *as such*, must face or perish: the challenge of death. For the "individual's" personal mortality casts a pall of ultimate futility over his efforts to cooperate in maintaining a social order at all, and no society can survive that does not offer everyone sufficient reason to do so. It must offer him a "solution" for his own personal death. And the only "solution" that can be sufficient is the prospect of at least vicarious immortality. Yet there is no simply rational prospect of immortality. Thus, the solution must be, as John H. Dunne says in one of the most amazing (and neglected) books of this, or perhaps any, age, either mythic or religious in nature.[1] And, furthermore, the solution must be posed in an explicitly social way. But to say that the indispensable social solution for death is not primarily rational is not necessarily to suggest that the solution must be "false," only that it cannot be arrived at entirely by reason working alone. And though it might seem that, since society's survival depends above all on its ability to offer the "individual" a solution for his own death, this requirement is, as far as society is concerned, "merely" subjective, contributing nothing at all to the "objective" tasks society must perform once the solution to death has been achieved, this dismissal nevertheless would be artificial. For "society" itself is a mere abstraction, and the way the problem of death is "subjectively" resolved will decisively influence how society itself is "objectively" organized. The quality of the answer to the challenge of death is crucial to society as such even after it provides the answer. And this raises a further problem, for if even society's organization reflects merely a response to death, then death secretly gains a virtually unbreakable grip on life. Unless, that is, the answer to death is also more than merely an answer to death.

So now we must look more closely at those two possible responses to death: religion and myth. We will find (as John Dunne has suggested in other writings) that religion is the principle of culture, myth a principle only of civilization. And it is culture that brings *dynamic* integration and wholeness, culture that is a response to life, while civilization remains simply a defense against death. For, unlike myth, religion is not exclusively, not even primarily, concerned with death, at least in "objective" content, and apart from the "subjective" reasons why some may adopt religion. It is religion's ability to appeal to the whole man—body and soul, mind and spirit—that enables it to give rise to cultures. But if society cannot find its unity in religion, then it must find its basic unity in myth. In fact, even when society can find a basic unity in religion, it may choose nevertheless to look for its unity in myth.

As a practical matter, society usually relies for cohesion on both religion and myth. As we soon will see, this means that it relies on both culture and the State, two principles that are basically antagonistic, if not contradictory. This antagonism remains obscure to us because myth tends to adopt for its own purposes religious concepts that have wide currency—and religion may secretly be prized more for its support of myth than for itself alone. When it contributes to a myth, religion tends to become a good deal more popular than it might otherwise be. This has little, if anything, to do with the "rationality" or "irrationality" of belief or unbelief: in a "religious" age (one that is truly religious, or one that simply uses religious concepts in its myth) belief seems as "reasonable" and "natural" as unbelief in an "irreligious" age. Religion tends to become popular when it supplies the terms on which a myth is constructed. Yet myth is in a sense an evasion of religion, for it represents humanity's effort to satisfy its own desire for life. Religion ceases to be very popular when social myth ceases to rely on it. Real religion, though, is no more enhanced or expressed by the use than by the rejection of its metaphysical content by myth, for myth is almost an alternative to religion in that, having "faith" in a myth, one no longer "needs" any in God. (Nevertheless, since every myth in the

Part
THREE

The Witness of Art

When first shown to a competent editor, this essay was declared to be "scandalously inadequate." Of course, the writer had expected as much—I had had sufficient "grad school" experience to know what would and would not satisfy the scholars. Perhaps the editor had mostly them in mind. But a faint drumbeat in the back of my head eventually swelled to a question: "Inadequate for what?" After much experience, scholars rightly prefer to see an argument carefully built up, modest in its pretensions, and with every generalization buttressed with exhaustive support. An admirable standard, and difficult to meet. And this chapter does have by far the most footnotes of any chapter in this book, so at least the homework has been done. Of course, some churls think that many scholars of literature feel stuck with it and hate it, as one might begin to suspect after wading through a pile of literary journals without ever finding an article of the slightest discernible human interest even to scholars themselves. And what is suggested in this chapter would never please, much less satisfy, such scholars, no matter what form it was in.

But what is the purpose of literary scholarship? To refine our appreciation of literature, and ultimately of life. The scholarship industry, it is no secret, often accomplishes nothing of the sort. But in this essay we are not even trying to meet the legitimate standards of scholarship, or to refine anyone's grasp of literature—hard enough to refine our own. Here, we are simply trying to use what we already know or have learned from others so that we can better understand our *culture*.

What follows here is a brief survey of Western literature to see if it might confirm the earlier "thesis" about culture. Art is any culture's most accurate reflection, and a theory about culture not reflected in art must be suspect. This essay attempts, not to prove anything, but to suggest that Western art does not contradict our thesis about culture, and may be read as supporting it.

Because of, first, the identification of not so much the cause of the cultural problem, as the solution for it, and, second, the conclusions about what Western literature shows, the theme of this essay probably could not meet with the approval of many scholars. And to support what is claimed about even one of the writers discussed here might require several volumes and a lifetime's work. To do so for all of them, and then to make a comparative study, would seem to be impossible—except that Erich Auerbach has already done something very like that. But the conclusions are implicit in the writings of certain such universally admired scholars, and *implicit* there only because these scholars never undertook to think about the cultural problem in the wide context pursued here.

So, given sufficient time, one might perhaps be able to make this thesis as scholarly as anyone might require, yet again exactly the opposite tack from that scholars normally take has been adopted. Instead of arguments supported by endless scholarly citations, the reader will find an argument reduced almost to schematic form. Which, after all, is all that will humanly interest even the scholars. Whether the speculations reflect "reality" or not, anyone may decide for himself—as he would no matter how erudite the page might become. Everyone has been spared much tedium.

What gives someone confidence that he has adequately "understood" *any* of literature's towering figures? Partly, that he often finds his groping perceptions confirmed by the great critics. But most such critics simply better articulate what a reader who responds adequately to literature already "knows," and keep him from losing his balance under the weight of his own bumbling abstractions. Most of us, though, after reading even one major work by a great artist, already know more about him—him, not just his work or life—than we will ever learn by benefit of libraries full of biography and criticism. (Which are not, however, therefore dispensable; this is a compliment to art, not a slur on the critics.) We may not be able to articulate well what we "know," so we need the critic and are grateful for him. But we know that we know. Except, perhaps, some scholars.

Dante

Probably Dante's achievement could never be entirely comprehended, but the points important for us here are simple. The pellucid quality of his work makes it seem so inexhaustible at any point that no detail of *The Divine Comedy* does not contain the whole. "Every part, however self-contained, stands for the whole, calls the whole to mind, and mirrors it in an eminently Thomist sense, without in the least losing its own character. Wherever you may open the *Comedy* you have the whole of it."[1] The poem everywhere has the limpid transparency of crystal that becomes invisible as it acts as a lens. Yet—

> With all their transparent simplicity, Dante's poems have a powerful rhythm, an unbroken natural movement from within, that had not been witnessed since antiquity. The impression we are describing here, still more than other aspects . . . is purely sensuous, because its motivations were still wholly unconscious and involuntary.[2]

Dante was, aesthetically, both intensely pure and intensely erotic. T.S. Eliot noticed in Shakespeare's work, in contrast, a strange opaqueness. For example, the references to "the gods" in *King Lear* seem so contradictory that any resolution for them that can be found must arise from a painstaking analysis of patterns.

If every part of the *Comedy* contains the whole, any part must yield some insight into the whole. The most obvious single element is the love between Dante and Beatrice, which Dante views as the link between his own humanity and what he regards as his vocation as a Christian. Happily, an adequate understanding of the figure of Beatrice can be had if we simply meet her on her own terms, for her symbolic meaning grows to light in us only through her captivating and intense personality, and the physical sensuality which alone for Dante could suggest her spiritual significance. The real-life Beatrice was the ostensible reason for the poem's composition, for she was the most important event in Dante's life. As Hilaire Belloc wrote in his biography of Louis XIV, the experience of falling in love with the daughter of a minor noble so galvanized the young king's soul that no other woman could ever replace this first, and if few men ever have such an experience, for those who do it remains decisive. Dante's encounter with Beatrice in his ninth year made the *Comedy* possible, for to him she became the literal and visible possibility of Christian salvation and the means by which it was achieved. "If God can win him back it will be through her, and it is surely because Dante loves her still that God sends her to him."[3]

In the poem she represents more than herself. She symbolizes grace and theological wisdom, to whom Virgil, the exemplary poet and symbol of natural perfection, yields as Dante's guide. "The blessed Beatrice, identified with theological wisdom, is the necessary mediatrix between salvation and man in need of enlightenment."[4] In the conventions of the Italian *Dolce Stil Nuova* (sweet new style), woman represented the exalted Ideal, but Beatrice fills her symbolic function above all because she was for Dante the effective presence of the revelation that he thought theological wisdom to be for mankind as a whole. He may not have been suggesting that Christian salvation becomes a real rather than a theoretical possibility only through the mediation of a woman, but he was clear that that was his own experience. Milton later would insist on being saved only through the direct "spiritual" intervention of the Almighty, but the exact opposite is true of Dante: Since this "poet of the transcendent" was never well acquainted with Beatrice, whom he nevertheless considered the means of his salvation, we can only conclude that her effect on him was accomplished simply by her physical qualities. When he later "lost his way," as he put it, he could save himself from disintegration only by remembering what she had revealed. Perhaps only a poet could understand this. But it seems remarkable that Dante could try to suggest the intensity of his symbol of theological wisdom only by describing her physical qualities—carriage, lips, eyes—in concrete terms. She was an effective mediator, and effective symbol, only because of her concrete qualities as a woman. Sensually overwhelming, she was, and is, a "living synthesis of sensuous and natural perfection."[5]

The emotional power of *The Divine Comedy* is as intense as it is various, as terrific as it is subtly articulated. It never flags and never repeats, yet it still fits spontaneously into an explicit, structured and articulated rational system—the metaphysics of Thomas Aquinas. Yet the reinforcement and definition that each element receives from its inner relation with other elements do not result from the abstract (and therefore sensually denaturing) consistency of philosophy; to the contrary, in his "unflagging desire for a concrete embodiment of the truth," Dante chose to write not in the classical Latin prescribed for the epic, but in his own native Tuscan dialect, whose echoes could suggest an immediate but unfathomable mystery.[6] "No word is too crass or too plain for him, he summons all the senses to help him, the most common, everyday experience has its place if it helps to give his thought concreteness."[7] A perfect inner balance moves

Dante to sympathize passionately with sinners like Paolo and Fran-cesca without questioning the divine justice that condemns them to hell; but the emotional balance is not achieved at the expense of force, for the emotions are both perfectly spontaneous and over-whelming.

> The configured truth is exact and superhuman, it demands pre-cision and superhuman power of its poet; and similarly, it demands order of him because it is ordered. . . . The constraint does not hamper the poet's many-sided freedom; what is born of such constraint is not artifice nor mannerism, but a second nature, hard to come by but all the richer for that.[8]

The poem's pure translucence has never been matched. The poem moves simultaneously on several levels (literal, moral, allegorical, analogical) without apparent artificiality, yet on these different levels the carnal and the spiritual, man and woman, emotion and reason, clarity and mystery, all perfectly reinforce each other.

Critics who view a poem as independent of the poet may be hard put to explain why Dante could achieve this where all others failed. Personal talent is not the whole explanation. Perhaps Joyce's native talent almost matched Dante's. A poet cannot create what he does not already possess; poetic creation is self-discovery. As Auerbach writes:

> . . . For him beauty is not distinct from truth, and we have no ground for considering ourselves superior to such a view; it is far more reliable, more concrete and coherent than any other theories on the philosophy of art, and at most we may be justi-fied in regretting that so perfect a unity of reason and percep-tion can no longer (or perhaps not yet) have any validity for us.[9]

> . . . To Dante, whatever knowledge he can attain and impart is passionate personal experience.[10]

Nearly every line of the *Comedy* reveals enormous exertion, the language writhes and rebels in the hard letters of rhyme and meter; the forms of certain lines and sentences suggest a man frozen or petrified in a peculiarly unnatural position. They are monumentally clear and expressive, but strange, terrifying and superhuman.[11]

Yet Dante combined in his own life intense political activity, poetic genius and abstract philosophical activity of a high order. His public life, like his poetic skill, achieved impressive range, and his creative power grew without interruption. "When he entered upon the second period of his life (young manhood) . . . his vitality and inner sense of measure had so matured that, almost simultaneously it would seem, he turned to public life and philosophical doctrines, combining the two and beginning to shape them to his cast of mind."[12] Auerbach identified the ultimate cause of Dante's achievement:

Can a modern reader, even if he is supremely learned and endowed with the highest degree of historical empathy, penetrate to Dante if he is utterly unwilling to accept Dante's mode of thought? Of course the greatest creations of the human spirit are not tied inseparably to the particular forms of thought and faith from which they sprang; they change with every generation that admires them, showing to each generation a new face without losing their intrinsic character. But there is a limit to their power of transformation; where the form of admiration becomes too arbitrary, they refuse to go along. To put it very cautiously, it seems to me that with regard to *The Divine Comedy* such a limit has already been attained when philosophical commentators begin to praise its so-called poetic beauties as values in themselves and reject the system, the doctrine, and indeed the entire subject matter as irrelevancies which if anything call for a certain indulgence.

The subject and doctrine of the *Comedy* are not incidental;

they are the roots of the poetic beauty. They are the driving force behind the rich radiance of its poetic metaphors and the magical music of the poem's matter.[13]

Yet there is more to it. Dante must have owed some of his greatness as a poet to his religion's integration of the culture. Aquinas, Francis of Assisi, and Dante all appeared at roughly the same time. We can hardly ignore their intense individualities, but all stood at the end of a long and difficult cultural development that had made their individualities possible. The Christian faith had now fully suffused the culture, and was surfacing in tangible social and cultural forms. The dominant cultural leaders were Christian saints, and because of this cultural fusion what Auerbach describes now occurred:

> The historical world had to be rediscovered, and in a spiritualist culture, where earthly happening was either disregarded or looked upon as a mere metaphor of existence leading up to man's real and final destiny. Man's historical world could be discovered only by way of his final destiny, considered as the goal and meaning of earthly happening.
>
> But once the discovery was made in that way, earthly happening could no longer be looked upon with indifference. The perception of history and immanent reality arrived at in the *Comedy* through an eschatological vision, flowed back into real history, filling it with the blood of authentic truth.
>
> Later, even in very un-Christian artists, Dante's conception of individual destiny preserved the Christian force and tension which are Dante's gift to posterity . . . namely, the idea (whatever its basis might be) that individual destiny is necessarily tragic and significant, and that the whole world context is revealed in it.[14]

The process that Auerbach here describes continues, of course, to be ignored, pointing, as it does, so directly to the crucial importance of religion. Yet, since this book basically is about that very point, let us expand briefly on it here: It was only because the Christian religion thus filled history with the blood of authentic truth that time itself was discovered. The ancients were not interested in time, but in escaping it into an eternal harmony. For them, the perfection of form was a circle, and neither had they any use for perspective, by which we fix a scene not only in place but in a moment. It was religion that permitted us to discover, or acknowledge, history, and only religion can enable us to sustain its burdens, as we will now see.

Shakespeare

Henry IV (*Part I*) is the first play in which Shakespeare reveals his full emotional range and his ability to create character. The nobles are revolting against Prince Hal's father, who has gained his throne by devious plots. Unwilling either to alienate his father or to serve his methods, Hal has deserted the court. He passes his time in a tavern among clowns he permits to amuse him, and raises in the hard-pressed king suspicions of ingratitude and vagrancy. Hal's unwillingness to judge his father or even his own disreputable present companions—a capacity to live with apparent contradictions—clearly is an extension of the same capacity in Shakespeare himself. The play offers so many chances for dramatic moralizing that the temptation to impose some abstract pattern must have been strong. Shakespeare did have trouble organizing the refractory historical materials, but his characters do not fit any neat thesis. A seeming totally unrationalized spontaneity prevails. Hal's and Shakespeare's emotions can guide the intellect because they unfailingly sense the exact modulations and deficiencies of the human surroundings. While he waits for the right moment for action without knowing when it will arrive, Hal must avoid moralizing his position but still keep himself free from contamination by the obnoxious characters he good-naturedly allows to entertain him. He does not worry and relies completely on his instinctual and emotional integrity. Shake-

speare himself was more than occupied also with Falstaff and Hot-
spur and their complex interaction with minor characters, which
also seems completely spontaneous. Every character has a free rein
and the benefit of all possible "moral" doubt, for Shakespeare takes
no abstract or moralized position toward them. This early play suggests that Shakespeare reached maturity with no structural weaknesses in his own personality; if any irresolvable conflicts later
entered his drama, the cause was not entirely personal.

But by the time he wrote *Hamlet*, Shakespeare's own inner harmony seems to have been yielding to centripetal forces. Historical
science discredits Belloc's thesis that Elizabethan England was
crypto-Catholic but intimidated by the Cecils, who had acquired a
vested interest in the new Protestant order when Henry VIII wisely
distributed the wealth of the monasteries. Catholic Mary Tudor's
bloody repression had alienated the people, who in any case were
well accustomed to domination of the Church hierarchy by the
Crown. But whether the people were crypto-Catholic or not, the
religious turmoil, tension, and conflict had decimated, demoralized
and confused the lower clergy. Shakespeare grew up in the midst of
this trouble and confusion.

The reader should immediately recognize a contradiction in
Hamlet. The play turns on Christian concepts that advance or illuminate the action, but it also embodies a pagan ethic of blood-
vengeance patently opposed to Christian morals. If Hamlet seemed
aware of the contradiction it would be less puzzling. He professes
to be seeking an excuse for inaction, but this perfectly obvious possibility seems never to occur to him. But Shakespeare certainly must
have been aware of the anomaly. He must have concluded that the
play would appeal to the audience in spite of—yes, even because of
—the contradiction, for the audience may have received it not as a
logical contradiction, but as a strangely suggestive subjective reality
for themselves. Perhaps for our part we agree to overlook it not
because it is not very important, but because it is so fundamental
that to recognize it for what it is might threaten our enjoyment of

the play's many fascinations. Perhaps we are afraid that to notice might even make us appear naive. Yet this contradiction cannot be unimportant dramatically: Hamlet is a believing Christian, and the knowledge that retaliatory murder is sinful could absolve him from the ghost's commission. And if he so greatly respects the ghost's credentials, why does he determine to test whether it is a devil? Either way—whether Hamlet is a Christian or whether he is not— the play is an absurdity.

We overlook the contradiction because it seems a small price to pay for Shakespeare's enormous emotional power. But for Shakespeare it must have been an essential element of something that had seized his attention. By allowing the contradiction he could arrange a situation embodying a direct personal urgency for himself, and try to make it explicit with his emotional power. But he failed! Shakespeare never, as T.S. Eliot concluded, made it fully present to himself nor found an "objective correlative," because the emotion was intrinsically schizoid. The reality he was trying to body forth was the dramatic equivalent of a mathematical surd. Since all critics agree not only that this play was Shakespeare's most personal statement, but also that one of his primary concerns was to clarify the sources of human action, this contradiction may be the most significant aspect of the play. Yet few critics have made much of it.

Any "objective correlative" would have had to eliminate the contradiction and also the play, but having become fascinated by Hamlet, Shakespeare probably did not really want to solve the problem. The cause of both Hamlet's fascination for Shakespeare and Shakespeare's aesthetic failure was not in Shakespeare himself, and so he could not resolve the problem with purely personal resources. This may smack of heresy, but it was precisely because he so well reflected the cultural milieu that he could find no immediate and coherent purely personal solution for the problem. The maddening schizophrenic split in Hamlet was arising from Renaissance culture. It was not so much an intellectual as a cultural contradiction.

Compared to Dante's world, Shakespeare's is generally Christian in its values, but closed on itself. God and angels appear in *Hamlet*, at least by reference, but their effective presence is far weaker than the many references to them seem to suggest, and from our point of view they seem to be embellishments flowing from Shakespeare's inexhaustible emotional richness. By the time of *King Lear* they have been eliminated: The later Shakespeare's world no longer postulates transcendent powers; the "gods" become immanent pagan deities whose activities seem obscure and contradictory. But Shakespeare does not become non-Christian. Not only have the theological dimensions so prominent in Shakespeare's work no consistency; it is more true to say that as a whole they are inconsistent and confused. Some of our difficulties with all this might be due to our own limitations. But Eliot called attention to another puzzlement that seems related—the peculiar opaqueness in the personalities of Shakespeare's major tragic characters.[15] On the evidence of *Hamlet*, this opaqueness arises from Shakespeare's own incomplete presence to himself. Perhaps some early experience caused in him an inner imbalance never, unlike Dante's, fully overcome.[16] But in any case, the conspicuous vein of misogyny running through Shakespeare's work (with special prominence in *Hamlet*), together with the theological inconsistency and the opaqueness in the tragic characters, suggests an inchoate inner split in Shakespeare's own personality. The early plays gave no evidence of it, so we might be justified in speculating that it was the cumulative result of an incipient inner split in the culture inhibiting Shakespeare's own inner development. In the one major tragedy with a kind of crystal quality—*Othello*, which most critics consider aesthetically the most perfect—the action is removed from the cultural matrix to an island and elaborated as a polarization of flesh (blood) and spirit ending in the destruction of both.[17] Was this clarity achieved only by way of isolation? Did the action *have* to be removed from the cultural matrix because the *culture* had generated the contradiction in the character of the hero of Venice (Othello) which must have either risen into open opposition to that matrix or further corrupted it (yet the validity of the cultural matrix had to be granted dramatically because it had created all the qualities that had made Othello and the other characters interesting and even possible)? If the play's clarity was won at the price of isolating the action from the cultural matrix, and it then reveals an irresolvable division undermining the major heroic figure (and by implication also the culture in which his weakness matured yet remained undetected even by him because he accepted that culture's evaluation of him and of itself), then a new and corrosive skepticism has appeared.

Shakespeare later moved beyond these contradictions, but not by resolving them. Instead, he seemed aesthetically to rise above his own skepticism solely by developing a symbolic drama in which the contradictions appeared only as symbols and the action occurred on distant mythical shores. This solution was not necessarily an evasion, and showed that Shakespeare thought there was a solution, but it complicated other problems by pushing the drama back to a second remove from the spectator's immediate experience, there finding an allegorical frame in which the contradictions seemed to become at least compatible. But the experience itself no longer has the old immediacy and raw power, and the haunting music now has an indefinable sadness. The cultural material Shakespeare worked on simply refused a perfect integration.

The reason why, in this view, *Othello* is aesthetically perfect compared to the other major tragedies is that it isolates the inner antagonism poisoning Renaissance society and shows it in pure relief. Since the antagonism was produced in each character as much by society as by personal failings, the play's intimation of the artist's experience of society necessarily includes an irreducible, unintelligible opaqueness. The culture that produced him did not bestow on Shakespeare either the material or the inner harmony for a crystalline tragedy with the whole society and culture as its context and also containing Shakespeare's emotional power.

We conclude then that Shakespeare's work shows a wide range of spontaneous and powerful emotion, which he trusted at least as much as any capacity for thought to lead him unerringly to the truth, and which put him into intuitive touch with everything in his culture. But this very sensitivity to the culture uncovers in it an incipient and irresolvable flesh-spirit polarization and a muddying of the springs of personality. A corrosive skepticism begins to poison Shakespeare's spontaneous delight in creation. The cultural symbiosis of ideal and quotidian reality has begun to split. Shakespeare tries to maintain it almost singlehandedly (and only partly succeeds) by the power of his emotional resources.

Milton

Several years ago, Helen Gardner noted among critics an increasing exasperation with Milton. They more and more deplored his tedious self-righteousness and his pompous syntax.[18] For example:

> He turns in his poetry to the language of abstraction as not susceptible of limitation or confusion. The abstract and the general ought to be clearer and so more nearly true than the concrete and the particular. Because Milton has truth to communicate, he wishes passionately to be clear. His art, as it is in thrall to the rationalistic impulse, yearns to be delivered from poetry.[19]

> . . . a self-conscious and deliberate resort to a vocabulary that is generalized and abstract.[20]

> His hope is in generalizing his matter to make the particular occasion universally applicable.[21]

Miss Gardner answered that *Paradise Lost* requires first of all a generous willingness to concede, for Milton's greatness lies in his expression of certain personal convictions. This is a good point, and it is not impossible that the day will come when all of Western art will be forgotten because of a growing inability to understand it.

But the critics' objection is that although Milton may have used a cosmic, epic theme to express personal convictions, there now appears a striking disproportion between his ambition and his actual achievement, a gap that has been overlooked by readers who generally sympathized with his personal beliefs. It was Milton's greatness and good fortune that he was still able even to attempt to express personal beliefs in a cosmic, epic, poetic work, and even the partial success of the attempt now mocks our own incapacity ever to escape our narrow self-absorption. In this sense, Miss Gardner is perfectly right. But if Milton was aware of the logical contradictions in his treatment and faced them, as Miss Gardner claims, he faced them as abstractions; his imaginative treatment confirms them, for it did not measure up to his theology. As the critics point out, Milton's imaginative treatment suggests the very opposite of what Milton consciously intended; it suggests that the hero was Satan and the villain was God. Since the conscious intention was abstract and forced, the unconscious secretly took revenge. It might be significant that Milton could think he was achieving something it is obvious to us he was not; Dante or Shakespeare would more quickly than any of us know when they were not achieving something.

As a Calvinist, Milton believed he had a direct, "charismatic" relationship with God. Its quality is well suggested in *Samson Agonistes*, the ambitious play in which the blind Samson is unmistakably a figure of Milton himself. The question whether Milton was justified in his belief is complicated, as it was in Luther, by the elaborate recourse to theology, which is not exactly an empirically verifiable science. But in his personal life Milton certainly showed something less than the maturity expected of a prophet. When he was thirty-three and famous, he married an uneducated adolescent whom he soon concluded was the very devil, and he became that paradox, the first Puritan advocate of divorce. We might doubt that this position resulted from disinterested theological speculation. His violent recoil from his young wife clearly was not "objective." Why did he not marry, like Tolstoy, a woman who might more closely have complemented his own abilities? Because he was secretly fascinated by women but afraid of their personalities, he married a nubile girl whom he secretly hoped he could control, but even she turned out to be too strong. The severe Old Testament father-figure Jehovah, the God of the Calvinists, had few feminine qualities. Milton's own verse—rugged, vigorous, but often bombastic and inflated—perfectly expresses the aggressively masculine syndrome. A man who rejects the feminine elements of his own psychology and fails to integrate them into his personality destroys his intuitive sympathy with women. But the repressed elements continue to be active in the unconscious, and provoke defensive measures such as a moralistic rationalization of the difficulty and compensatory revulsion. Raging against women, Milton could not locate the cause of their power over him, which was the vacuum in himself. His pathetic predicament became comic only when he tried to justify it with theology. But if he could not have found a theological rationale for the anxiety, the religion he was using as a psychological prop would have been called fundamentally into question. That Milton's difficulties were more psychological than cosmic and theological seems to mock his aesthetic pretensions, until we realize that these pretensions were not really aesthetic at all. His insistence that women, whom he saw as incorrigibly immoral and unfathomable, be made abjectly submissive to men (as were his own daughters) came from fear. The special relationship with God that placed everyone else in the wrong was indispensable to explaining away his troubles; hence, his prophetic thunder. In *Samson Agonistes* the relationship seems at first not to work out: God forgets and provokes in Samson-Milton ever deeper self-preoccupation and moralistic preachiness. He finally pulls the house down on himself and his enemies after seeing a dubious sign. Prophetic act or death wish? Determined to justify himself, Milton never got himself together.

Milton's psychological formation was narrowed by his repressions, his psychological energies were channeled into narrow streams. He lost true spontaneous contact with much of reality and had to depend on the rationalized patterns of his great epic. The Genesis theme provided prefabricated mechanical structures and many occasions for organ and trumpet tones without requiring the creative fecundity of the unconscious—the feminine principle. But the rigid frame became a screen for the real action of the poem; for all the moralistic concern to "justify the ways of God to man," God and the good angels turn out to be villains while Satan achieves moral grandeur. The difference in quality, apart from intrinsic talent, between Milton and Dante is not insignificant. Each set out to write a great Christian epic. But Milton's epic, fabricated out of tortured "faith," mechanical cosmology, and defensive psychology, was the product of a personality with only a tenuous grasp of the spiritual who was revolted by his own carnality. Milton's work suggests a growing split between the male and female, the carnal and the spiritual, principles. Professor Empson's contention that the picture of Christian religion in Milton's epic is repulsive is accurate. (But he is unfair to conclude from this that Christianity is repulsive; let him first show that Dante's Christianity is repulsive.)

Barricading himself behind theology in all his difficulties, Milton caused the skeptical critic to seem either atheist or even more self-righteous and intolerant than Milton himself. The only way the critic can resolve the predicament is by recourse to psychology. But the critic must admit that Milton's natural powers were great, and that at his best he turned his troubles into aesthetic assets, as only genius can do. His verse often swells with real grandeur and pathos, and his introspection does at least issue in forceful action. All the more impressive must his achievement seem to an age that can offer nothing to compare with it. But Milton's moralizing tone never disappeared. He wrote hardly a half-century after Shakespeare's peak period, and in that short time the earlier emotional range and power had evaporated. In Milton, raw power thrashes in a near-vacuum. As Auerbach put it:

In Shakespeare's work the liberated forces show themselves as fully developed yet still permeated with the entire ethical wealth of the past. Not much later the restrictive counter-movements gained the upper hand. Protestantism and the Counter-Reformation, absolutistic ordering of society and intellectual life, academic and puristic imitation of antiquity, rationalism and scientific empiricism, all operated together to prevent Shakespeare's freedom in the tragic from continuing to develop after him.[22]

Racine

Chronically embattled antagonists acquire, as did the contending religions in the seventeenth century, a militant attitude that reduces life to convenient categories and victimizes cultural patterns not amenable to ideological regimentation. In France, where the Baroque south met the Protestant north, a compromise emerged—cultural secularism. The spiritual exhaustion caused by the religious wars left the Renaissance unable to sustain either its ego strength or the older religious preoccupations. And with religion now discredited as a creative cultural force, creative energy went instead into the unhealthy sublimations, but less refractory abstractions, of Idealist philosophy, while religion in France was reduced to State ideology. A systematic moralization of society began, conforming it to abstract categories. But the vaunted superclarity of intellect was only plastering over embarrassingly enervated instinctual responses. The earlier Christian cultural integration of "higher" and "lower"—of spiritual and carnal, even of upper class and lower class—disintegrated as the upper tyrannized over the lower, whose bile began accumulating for an explosive rebellion. Relentless systematization forced the older instinctual life into iron patterns, and narrow channels. The ancient pluralistic federative pattern of the medieval empire yielded to a political absolutism that reflected the intellectual absolutism of the age.[23] Again a poet turned the weaknesses into aesthetic assets. In Racine, the restricted emotions become a cataract of passion rushing toward death and disintegration. His precise, regular verse, crystal-like in its surface clarity, barely contains the suppressed, volcanic passions of his marblelike characters. These passions arise out of a hidden world of chaos and disorder.

This neoclassical France of the seventeenth century considered itself the most perfectly "natural" and "exemplary" civilization of all time, but it actually was a complex amalgam of almost contradictory forces acting on different levels, unified by, as it were, a basic intention. The period's luck, and ours, was to have Racine to combine the forces in an organic expression. But in him the split between spiritual and carnal appeared more complete than in any previous poet, just as, in the life of the nation, the upper classes cut themselves off from any functional or practical contact with the life of the people, and cultivated only an elegant dilettantism. To avoid contamination, aristocrats traveling in the country drew the curtains on their carriages. Ignored and exploited, the common people were left to the mercies of occasional saints like Vincent de Paul. "Polite" language became artificial and periphrastic, embarrassed by the existence of "common," ordinary objects. Racine, oscillating between the ascetic piety of Port Royal (home of Catholic Puritanism) and the anti-Christianism of his own drama, exhibits the split in his own life. Educated at Port Royal, he later migrated to the theaters of Paris; after a series of successes, he quit in disgust and retreated to Port Royal. Before long he was out again and producing plays of the same type. He flings himself, as it were, from the spiritual to the carnal and back without bringing them together. For all the intensity of his periodic efforts, his hold on spirituality remained precarious; his carnality could find expression only in cataracts of passion. He tapped the depths of personality not by integrating them into everyday life, as the culture once had done, but by unleashing them on it. They became monstrous and destructive. At the end of *Phaedra* a monster rises from the sea (classic symbol of the unconscious) and flings itself on the hero's horses, tearing them to pieces. But Racine wrote for aristocrats; the peasants continued in their immemorial ways, harassed by the Sun King's merciless exactions for his wars.

The growing complexity, not to say confusion, of the historical forces, as the arbitrary bloodless abstraction imposed on thought a growing irrelevance, made a real cultural integration impossible. Louis XIV instead resorted for intellectual and psychological assurance to an ideologized Catholicism, and pushed for a merely *practical* cultural compromise in an *externally* disciplined State. Imposing an iron regime on the nobles, who had never been bound by anyone and had always enjoyed whatever amenities life in France afforded, he confined them now within a tight physical and emotional compass. They in turn developed a "perfect self-discipline, an unerring appraisal of every situation, a subtly studied yet spontaneous demeanor in every word and gesture," such qualities as "have hardly ever been developed to such perfection as in the second half of the seventeenth century at the French Court."[24] The emotionally richer and more spontaneous society passed away. The new order was rational and dazzlingly orchestrated on the surface, but it was alienated from its secret roots. Public life became more rigid, more splendid, and more solitary. The new complexity of society may have made some systematization indispensable; but the exaggerated self-congratulations signaled the obliviousness to what had been sacrificed. The schizophrenic split in Racine's Catholic France was, if anything, even wider than in Milton's contemporary Protestant England.

Voltaire

The news coming from Lisbon of a catastrophic quake disturbed Voltaire so deeply that one need not apologize for thinking it was not the suffering of its victims that moved him: He had always been able to rise to philosophic resignation to others' concrete difficulties, except when they illustrated his ideological themes. For some time he had been off brooding alone, and what the earthquake in Lisbon brought up destroyed far more than a few lives. The news crystallized in Voltaire, with similar irrevocable finality, full conscious awareness of the absurdity of the Idealist pretensions, and like Augustine, Paul, Luther and Rousseau, he now experienced one of those conversions that periodically rock Western culture. The early Enlightenment had seen this world as of all possible worlds the best, and had appeased its insecurity with assurances that the evil forces of reaction were in headlong flight before inexorable Progress, represented, of course, by itself. But the rationalist-Enlightenment Idealist thought pattern had been savaging the unconscious, and the cumulative frustrations now exploded in Voltaire. The revelation from Lisbon galvanized him to creation, and within a month he had produced *Candide*.

But the path Voltaire was now taking did not bring the carnal and spiritual back together. *Candide* exhibits a paradoxical duality between the bright, intellectual and kinetic charm of its style, which Voltaire inherited from neoclassicism (adding to it his characteristic cheerfulness), and the savagely misanthropic message for which it serves as a vehicle. Voltaire now sees no reality in any kind of spiritual or "disinterested" human motivation; he "sees" that lust, greed, and self-interest universally prevail. "For Voltaire, it is a perfectly self-evident premise that no one in his senses can believe in an inner order of things or an inner justification of views. . . . Voltaire falsifies reality by an extreme simplification of the causes of events . . . from among the conditions which determine the course of human lives, none but the material and the natural are given serious consideration. Everything historical and spiritual he despises and neglects."[25]

The contrast between the style and the message was a fine instrument for irony, but has another significance. The carnal reality which Voltaire now "celebrated" had no higher purpose, while the intelligence which regarded it remained exterior to it and out of touch. Since the effect of the compensating reaction toward the carnal was to deny the reality of the spiritual, Voltaire's intellect now led a dry independent life of its own, nourished only by the residual juices of the neoclassical style. So the carnal became mechanical and automatic.

The superficiality of this attitude was just as destructive as the fortress Church Voltaire despised (frightened in its turn by the twin threats of Protestantism and radical secularism). Voltaire's solution merely compounded the problem. The absolutist instinct of the Idealists turned in him from its deluded intellectual and spiritual ambitions (which had prompted Leibniz to put himself in the place of God) to concrete temporal and material ambitions. But in its desire to re-create the social world, it had no regard for society's or the person's inner nature. This new attitude was no less doctrinaire than the old, and its concentration on material reality to the exclusion of all else, from outside and under the pressure of a covert absolutist intention, permitted no integration or dynamic harmony between the human spirit and human flesh. These merely coexisted in an armed truce. If Voltaire could never fathom the appeal of religion, it was because he never allowed the split within himself to become a matter of conscious concern. So when confronted in the Lisbon earthquake with unmistakable confirmation of the artificiality of the earlier position, he simply compounded the problem with his solution. His own absolutist *a priori* attitude had until now prompted him to ignore all evidence until it was forced upon him by the catastrophe and by unbearable inner pressures, for the inflexible emotional patterns he had inherited from the earlier period had removed from his experience the intimations that might have alerted him sooner to the artificiality of his position. Perhaps the rigors of combat with the Church had desensitized him even more. His emotional resources were still strong enough to keep him from any final personal catastrophe, but perhaps it is significant that he spent so much time in the unfashionable countryside among peasants he allowed himself to patronize. In this figure there was an almost total, but unacknowledged, schizoid split, which uncannily reflected the condition of the society around him—a condition that the Revolution would try to correct.

Goethe

Goethe concentrated the inexhaustible variety of his own work and life in his great poem *Faust*, which he began as a young man and completed in old age. The poem has an almost autobiographical quality, for its rhythms were those of his own life, and it never achieved complete self-containment as a work of art. Voltaire's artificial "objectivity" had yielded almost completely to the artist's subjectivity. Yet Faust's early quest for knowledge retains many of the qualities of the Enlightenment rationalism, for he seeks not so much wisdom as a magical key to experience—to that "experience" he should have been able to absorb as one benefit of a culture. He finally abandons what he recognizes as a futile ambition—to dominate life by means of intellect and abstractions—and at least in this moves beyond the limitations of the philosophes or Voltaire. But he then substitutes for abstractions the implacable drive of his own now absolutized will. Goethe acknowledges a schizophrenic split: Faust appears to represent Goethe's spiritual capacities while Mephistopheles represents the carnal, but Faust's new attack on Voltaire's old problem fails, for it simply dispenses with intelligence as so much baggage and merely transfers the absolutist drive into the will. The spiritual dimension of life, previously only isolated, is now crippled by the rejection of its intellectual component. There is much to admire in the Romantic poets' celebration of "Nature," especially for us who can find little that remains "natural" now. But to a large degree this celebration became a flight from culture, and a sign that the springs of culture had become hopelessly poisoned. Since culture defines "Nature" and appropriates it for human experience, the flight from culture transformed "Nature" itself into a mere abstraction.

Realizing that the consequence of the rationalist position is paralysis, Faust discovers an almost panicky desire for "experience," and tries to merge himself into the fluxes and rhythms of Nature. But his absolutized will also needs to dominate Nature and leaves him incapable of true response. Venturing out on Easter morning to mingle with his neighbors, who welcome him, he only feels, paradoxically, all the more alone. His absolutized will has succeeded in subjugating the feminine elements of his own personality. Thus, for Goethe, whatever issues are at stake in the poem (the reader is constantly aware of some vague menace) are focused in the relationship between Faust, a learned and famous doctor with colossal powers of mind and will, and Gretchen, an inconspicuous adolescent. Faust becomes almost another Milton. As a young man, Goethe himself twice fell in love and each time with a beautiful and extremely capable girl who ardently responded. The families of both girls were fully prepared for marriage, but in both cases Goethe stepped out, and only at the last moment. He surely was not indulging in cheap tricks: He thereafter visited both women periodically, but neither ever fully recovered (one never married, the other apparently married on the rebound but was shortly widowed). "One may think that the episode of a young man breaking off love relationships at the age of twenty-one and twenty-five is nothing so exceptional, and that one should not read things into it. But looking at it in the context of Goethe's entire life, particularly his experience with other women, there is no doubt: here lay his tragedy. It is, incidentally, most remarkable that just at the time of his break with Lili he made his first notes for the idea of *Faust* and *The Wandering Jew*."[26] Goethe's relationships with women began to exhibit curious stress and disorganization. "Actually, Goethe's entire life, when it comes to women, reads like a psychoanalytic case story."[27] For a time, he becomes a platonic soul-companion to a prudish, domineering woman who feels uneasy with any suggestion of physical sexuality; next, he goes to Italy and throws himself into an exclusively sexual, almost orgiastic, affair. Then he returns to Germany and adopts a factory girl as a concubine. He is genuinely fond of her, but also ashamed, and refuses to marry. He rushes her out of sight when friends visit, and finally lets her die sordidly, miserably and alone in the very house where he himself lies ill.

In the poem, Faust falls in love with Gretchen, but immediately begins to exploit her. Famished, in spite of all his natural powers, by his own inner poverty, he is increasingly fascinated by the girl's innocence and femininity—which call to the vacuum in himself. Ravenously hungry for human experience, he resorts to abuse and pushes the girl into a nightmare. The enormous cultural issues the poem revolves finally reduce to the question whether Faust can order his relations with an adolescent girl, for if the male and female principles must separate, if the carnal cannot be reconciled with the spiritual, the certain prospect is ruin. (The present-day "feminist" crisis is probably the usual delayed appearance in the social order of a problem that had been detected in the cultural order long before by artists.)

Actually, two male characters contribute to Gretchen's destruction. The other is Mephistopheles, who also destroys Faust. Faust and Mephistopheles are almost certainly two aspects of Goethe's own divided self. In conformity with the Romantic ethos (which Goethe himself did most to form), Faust admits no distinction between good and evil: His own subjectivity, his own ego, will abide no limitations. Defying the culture, the self sets itself up as an independent absolute. But then the unconscious exacts revenge by generating an alter ego—Mephistopheles, the carnal root, the ego-id complex—which acquires a mocking and subversive autonomy of the spiritual pretensions represented by Faust. By trying to establish a merely amoral *modus vivendi* instead of a proper integration, Faust jettisons all anchoring standards and gets swept up in a whirlwind. As Mephistopheles delivers on his loaded promises, Faust's troubles multiply and the devil becomes an increasingly necessary resort.

The relationship between Faust and Gretchen brings up the question of religion. Now, the modern liberal critic will find it rather unpleasant to be reminded of the religious elements in this poem. He prefers to think that a man as great as Goethe must have been like himself, and certainly would have been a secularist liberal had he been presented the opportunity. This critic finds the religious elements slightly embarrassing, and secretly assumes that Goethe, for some obscure reason, was trying to cater to the vulgar mob. (The same critic also thinks that *Antigone* is a modern liberal-type drama of "individual conscience" against the State or status quo. It is nothing of the sort—as Dunne shows, it is a drama of alternative allegiances to the gods of the living and the gods of the dead, a religious drama!) It would be almost inconceivable to this person that the work of someone as great as Goethe could actually *hinge* on its religious elements. Yet he is only projecting his own certainties upon poor Goethe, who in reality would probably not have been very satisfied with the liberal order. Any really faithful reading of this work can lead only to the conclusion that the religious elements constitute the very core of the drama.

To continue, then: Gretchen, sensing an unseen threat, insists on the importance of faith. Faust counters with calculated sophistries. Sophisticated readers today will smile, but Goethe knew that this duel represented the last barrier between civilization and most ominous consequences. The verses suggest the inner unrest behind the violent blows Napoleon even then was producing in Europe. Gretchen refuses to yield, and Faust must resort to deceit and suffers a moral defeat. Part One soon ends with the issue unresolved, and Goethe suspends composition for ten years.

Gretchen and all the important religious imagery in the poem are Catholic. Since Goethe was not, and often even displayed anti-Catholic feelings, the fact is worthy of notice.[28] Perhaps he thought that Catholicism put a higher value on women than did his own Lutheran religion, and the poem seems to turn on the significance of woman. It resembles *The Divine Comedy* in other ways—the earth-heaven-hell cosmology, and especially in the conclusion, when Paradise receives Faust as a result of Gretchen's intercession.

(Again, sophisticated readers would probably tend to write all this off as a concession to vulgar superstition.) If the mechanical structure is Catholic, however, the Christian content has been turned inside out. The systematic dualism relies on Christian concepts to structure and dynamize a profoundly un-Christian intention (first of all in Faust, but Goethe obviously has fixed his whole attention on it). For example, the figure of Satan, known only from revelation, dominates the poem's inner life with its power. Some may object that these images simply convey a "state of being," an experience. Yes, but it is also true that only these images can render the experience, and without them there could be no such experience. The Christianity, as in Dante, is not merely incidental to the experience. The contradictory dualism mirrors the schizophrenic cultural split, for society is torn between a Christianity with which it feels both saddled and liberated for new experiences, and a new kind of paganism. And this ambivalence, in turn, arises out of Christianity itself; Christendom's attachment to power indicates its own resentment of having to be Christian at all.

In Part One Goethe had attempted to solve his problem on the conscious level, and had ended with a qualified failure. In Part Two he attempts a solution through the unconscious. The intelligence is finally silenced, and the unconscious boils up in a broad and nearly formless stream. But Goethe relies on its patterns to integrate his experience. This new autonomy for the unconscious reflects the transfer in public life of the absolutist impulse from the aristocracy to the mob, which had just violently thrown off the aristocracy in France and set up an even more doctrinaire, but now democratic, dictatorship.[29] But Goethe gradually realizes that, whether the unconscious has any structure of its own or not, it endangers the defenseless ego. In the Philemon and Baucis episode, as Faust achieves his objective, amoral power, strange, alien and demonic forces invade the whole region and sabotage Faust's arbitrary "humanitarian" plans (a lesson for today for those who care to read it). In the end, Faust is saved, as by a *deus ex machina*, by the little Gretchen he had victimized long ago. Did Goethe secretly regret that he had been unable to recognize the solution himself (the feminine and spiritual principles), and did he wonder whether the inner dereliction of his later years had been worth the privilege of experimenting with dark powers? The forces Goethe discovered in the depths of his own soul and in his culture abscessed a century later with Hitler, who had the same absolutized masculine will to domination, the same schizophrenia, the same neurotic incapacity with women, and the same possession by destructive unconscious forces. Yet Goethe's civilization had so poorly applied the spiritual principle to its own affairs that his final greatness may appear in his persistent refusal to grasp at the facile solutions it piously recommended. He may not only have explored further than others; he may have sensed more clearly the nature of the "spiritual" problem.

Ibsen

Twain or Tolstoy might better represent their times than Ibsen, but several recent books have probed the split lives of Twain and Tolstoy, and Ibsen offers some contrast with the earlier dramatists already discussed.

Dr. Stockmann, the hero of Ibsen's play *An Enemy of the People*, asserts that although the vast majority of men are stupid, a few are fighting for "new truths." If the majority are as stupid and worthless as he represents them, why the few are so eager to instruct and save them remains unclear. Why have these "new truths" remained hidden until now? It is the author who is belaboring a catalogue of now well-worn clichés (in his day they seemed original) about "independence," "individuality," and so on, which, though, he fails to concretize in any genuinely dramatic emotion. Dr. Stockmann himself seems a mediocrity who rises only to new heights of self-righteousness as the plot stacks against him. His brother seems made mostly out of cardboard. In this play, characterization impinges on caricature just enough to hold attention, but the emotional quality, though strident, is weak. The hero appears to think that all truths have the same value, so that the issue on which the play focuses polarizes all the characters as good or bad according to their position on it. No real community could so easily shrug off all the outrageous things that happen in this virtually totalitarian nightmare. But the core of the play is ideological, and the characters hardly dare breathe. "Ibsen was surely an artist," says Walter Kerr, "but an artist who stumbled on a dialectical time and a dialectical form. He had an instinct for character," but also "a passionate determination to make points."[30] Ibsen's desire was to castigate society, a moralizing impulse. In several of his plays the characters seem to preserve their own vitality only against the constant pressure of their creator's moralizing. (How melancholy for us, who now get moralizing with no drama at all.)

The usual explanation for all this is that Ibsen was "alienated" from his society. Wandering in proud isolation from country to country, driven by "integrity," he refused to "compromise." That this isolation destroyed him, and that he lost his roots in a cultural order and became entangled in bloodless abstractions with no emotional content, only seem to confirm his noble autonomy. But more probably he was simply unable to cope, and was almost forced to rationalize and project his fears and inadequacies onto others. In a society such as the alienated describe everyone must be alone, and a better policy than suicide might be to stand and slug it out, recognizing the possibility of one's own contribution to the general malaise. But apparently Ibsen neither saw much hope for any general solution, nor felt the power by which to bring one about for himself, and moralizing in our turn about what he "should" have done is pointless. The psychological deficiencies in the artist as artist and the cultural deficiencies in his society are one and the same, and if society fails to nourish him the artist simply cannot function. Even with his genius, Ibsen never overcame the bloodless abstraction; it enveloped him as part of his culture. *An Enemy of the People* suggests that Ibsen's society was emotionally denatured. The continual return to Ibsen's drama for classical and paradigmatic models suggests that our society is even more denatured. Of course, to have any theater at all today is apparent cause for gratitude rather than carping, for certainly little better has appeared since Ibsen. But his talent, like Joyce's, was locked up in itself, and found very little to work with. This play suggests that the widening inner split in the culture is causing psychological paralysis.

The Present

It would be a task even more thankless than difficult to try to write with any finality about literature of our time. Yet sanguine claims by the "New Journalists" that they have replaced the novelists went pretty much unchallenged, and the very acquiescence in such claims may have been the best proof that they are right. Checking back over the last century, we find that the literary careers of eminent artists have dried up at an accelerating pace— perhaps because a real artist is exposed to society in a direct way from which the "average" person is protected by his particular or "professional" concerns. Flaubert and Baudelaire distintegrated, Henry James became artificial and hollow, Tolstoy and Twain succumbed to almost clinical schizophrenia, while Joyce, whose *Ulysses* is virtually a record of the human spirit locked in biological routine, became at last unintelligible. The inner division between spirit and flesh revealed in Yeats's great poems "Among School Children" and "Sailing to Byzantium" (written back to back) seems hopeless. T.S. Eliot's major theme was the paralysis and suffocation of the human spirit in its own flesh, and he finally leaped into an artificial mysticism.[31] "What we feel about all these men at times," says Frank Kermode, "is perhaps that they retreated into some paradigm, into a timeless and unreal vacuum from which all reality has been pumped."[32] (But why "retreated"? Rather, this is the reality they were trying, unsuccessfully, to *escape*.) Thomas Mann's whole *ouevre* is almost a clinical chart of disease, and his *Confessions of Felix Krull, Confidence Man* suggests the utter futility of hoping for any spiritual control of life. In short, in contrast to Dante and Shakespeare, and to most other earlier writers (how "naive" to notice) the careers of almost all recent writers (including Hemingway and Faulkner) have declined from initial successes, or abruptly ended. The problem is not talent, but development. Mailer has great talent, but has written every conceivable work but the novel that might have justified the hopes raised by his first. If *Portnoy's Complaint* is to be construed as some sort of literary advance, the picture of culture it presents is hardly reassuring.

What is meant here perhaps could be more clearly suggested by invoking an earlier figure who occupied a pivotal place in the cultural development we have illustrated above. William Wordsworth, too, completed most of his best work before his fortieth year, but he did not reach his "peak" early because he "could" not have achieved much more. Compare the curves of the lives of Wordsworth and Dante. This seemingly naive comparison is wholly relevant. Dante achieved a singular eminence not only as a poet, but also as a thinker and a politician of distinction, because he was able to integrate into his own personal life many aspects of social life that for Wordsworth had become inaccessible. It is not simply that Dante had greater talent, but that his culture encouraged an "organic" development in many directions at once. Even those, like Villon, who were not in practice very religious, were still so well nourished by the culture that they could become exceptional personalities in spite of very irreligious behavior. In Wordsworth's time, though, the culture had become too weak to make society truly reflect any "ideals," and the abstractions adopted by the French revolutionaries were no substitute for cultural vitality. So Wordsworth's superior and sensitive nature was rebuffed in its attempt to integrate itself in ideals, which remained abstract, and social life, which remained conflicted, so that Wordsworth's social development ceased, and his inner life became disrupted. In order to save some personal integration, therefore, he recoiled to "Nature," where he thought he saw reflected (but largely in retrospect) the integral wholeness he had last experienced as a dynamic possibility in childhood. The trouble was that this solution was implicitly schizoid in rejecting (although not without extreme provocation) the social world as unnatural. As several critics have written, Nature acquired its charm for Wordsworth only as a foil or contrast to society, and only insofar as it still resonated basically religious emotions from an earlier age. It was in the supreme effort to recover the childhood wholeness by way of a return to Nature— to a presocial existence—that Wordsworth created his greatest poetry. Yet in itself, as a strategy for realizing wholeness, this reversion was regressive: The only way to recover the childhood integration of potentials is to reproduce it on the social level in maturity, as Dante's society had in fact largely done. Eventually Wordsworth came to see that the secret of psychic survival was not "Nature" itself so much as the religion that had earlier secretly sustained his attitude toward Nature. But his earlier recoil from society toward "Nature" had ruined any prospect of uniting society and Nature in his personal life; the curve of his social and poetical life from now on was downward. Had Wordsworth been able to fuse society and Nature in his personal life, undoubtedly he would now be regarded as a far more talented and powerful poet than we acknowledge him to have been. Not that his Nature poetry is not true and great poetry; the tragedy, and most of all for him, is that he never went beyond Nature poetry later. But, for the cultural regression his poetry represented, he had no dynamic alternative, even though his strategy, taken in itself, is a strategy of despair. The same dilemma is reflected even more poignantly in the life and poetic career of John Keats.

But even the Wordsworthian recourse to Nature has become unavailable to us, for whom Nature not only has, in the continuing decline of religion, lost even what religious resonance it had for Wordsworth, but has been transformed finally into a helpless victim of intellectual and physical rape. We, for whom there is no recourse to Nature from the social machine, have only sex, drugs, the swamps of sterile introspection and, at last, psychiatric "adjustment."

Blessed are they who have faith, for they shall retain their humanity. But no longer—which is all for the good—can they save it by a conventional acquiescence. Faith must be repurchased, time and again, with the risk, full of tragic possibilities, of resistance to, and even defiance of, the established wisdom of the world and the benevolent social machine. Increasingly, to believe is to dare, and most of all in the secret recesses of one's own heart. This will distinguish true religion from the mere narcissistic cultivation of "inner life" in order to make one's life in the social machine more tolerable and "pleasant."

Wordsworth's failures as a poet reflect the inadequacies of his culture, just as his singular achievements are unconscious testimony to the culture's vestigial vitality (as perhaps is also his later return to faith, in the sense that Wordsworth still had the human qualities and experience to sense what the appeal of religion was). But Wordsworth's life, like that of Beethoven as reflected in his music, marks a turning point in Western culture; from this point, the person and the culture are split off from each other and thrown back on the defensive against the encroaching social machine.

The critic John Aldridge not long ago said that fiction and poetry were exhibiting only an unrelieved sterility.[33] Brooks Atkinson said that the theater had succumbed to the cynicism and banality of the sixties.[34] Alfred Kazin wrote that "none of the many gifted American writers today even gives the impression of believing that he will create a masterpiece."[35] A curiously suggestive passage from a book review perhaps sums the situation up best:

It seems to me that in the last decade or two there has been a great increase in the number of biographies and autobiographies being published, and I've been wondering why. . . . It may be that we've grown so doubtful about the meaning or the reality of our existence that we've developed a nostalgia, like a vitamin deficiency, for the merest evidence of it. "I'm a human being," is a cry one hears everywhere: from blacks, from "liberated" women, from everyone who feels slighted by life. It is conceivable that we are all beginning to feel this way. . . .

Perhaps, too, these biographies are filling a need that fiction once satisfied. There aren't many novelists today like Hardy, Trollope, Jane Austen or Tolstoy, writers who gave us characters almost redundant with humanity. Mary McCarthy remarked a few years ago that there hasn't been a really great woman in fiction since Madame Bovary. Our best writers' best characters often live on the edge of existence, in a blur of becoming. While 19th-Century characters existed in fact, were thick with quiddity and circumstance, ours so often seem to be in process, a thin fleshing out of a psychological or philosophical hypothesis.[36]

But that blur may be a blur, not of becoming, but of disintegration. The reader must judge for himself whether this suggestion is accurate, but if it is, art in any traditional sense of what art is, an expression of man's inner life, may soon fall entirely silent. And if the artist cannot function, who else can? Any great novel, for instance, requires, as the basis for a notion of the tragic, an accepted moral order within the society with whose "manners and morals" it deals; by failing this code a protagonist becomes subject to "tragic" reversal. But today, as Wilfrid Sheed writes, not only have we no accepted code of manners or morals; we fail even to be embarrassed by anything. Thus, Ron Ziegler can say "contrition is bull————," and the novel becomes superfluous, discarded with our morality. This necessary moral order is not concerned only with sex, but certainly includes it, for sex provides the energies that dynamize a culture. The problem is, though, that however much it may prattle about "imagination" and "bold vision" (whose?), a society that basically aspires only to be a machine does not need any excess of either psychic or physical energies— just enough of both to keep itself smoothly humming—and there- fore erotic energies must seek outlets other than the integrated activity of spirit and body in a culturally oriented social order. And all that is left is atomized (and temporary and unsatisfying) sexual indulgence among "individual" partners; thus, we find Bruce Jay Friedman descending from the initial tragic heights of *Stern* to his later odysseys of "getting laid."

Since the argument has now become (hopelessly or powerfully, as one likes) general, the reader may tolerate, for purposes of clarification, mention of the one major art form not discussed else- where in this book: visual art. For something quite similar appears to be happening there, too: specifically, the disappearance of the human figure. In his classic work on the Renaissance Bernard Berenson asserted that visual art is based on "tactile values," and that, consequently, its focal element is the human form. Now, we would not seek to defend that dead, academic nineteenth-century Classicism in which the human form last played its normative role in the accepted canons of art. Nor would we wish to deny a spectacular new beauty in the Impressionist works that supplanted it. Yet the Impressionists were the first to realize that in their art the human form had become dehumanized, and it is not too much to say that it later became subhuman. True, the human "spirit" is still very much "reflexively" present in the reconstruction of "re- ality" (or at least of our ways of perceiving and experiencing it) in Cubism and Expressionism. To some degree, this new intensity off- sets the disappearance of the specifically human reality from the "subject matter" of visual art. But the greatest heights of art, achieved in moments of supreme integration, also become foreclosed to visual art when the human form, "idealized" or not, disappears from it. What this demotion really reflects is exactly what literature and Western music also have been reflecting since about the time of Beethoven: the conquest of "man" by his circumstances, by "fate," if not, indeed, as the sterile works of Mondrian (who could no longer live with time and sought escape again in pure form) suggest, man's reduction to a machine. Just as recent philosophy, preoccupied with its "critical tools," has forgotten to construct anything with them, so modern art, preoccupied, as Kenneth Clark notes, with the "medium," has failed to deliver any message. (How vulgar to notice.) It would be truculent to deny a certain fitful stature in our literature today, but it largely reflects our cunning: Our affirmation of our *selves* seems ever more tenuous, and we do not prevail, but survive. At least as long as we still create any literature we still know we are *there*. But that cannot be sufficient for us, and how long can we thus go on?

The artist, in his act of creation, in which he transcends his personal limitations by whatever vibrant qualities he may possess, discovers reality for us by discovering the full significance of what he knows as "fact." Far from being a "screen" between us and the "real" world, his affectivity—that by which the whole reveals itself to him as more than the sum of its apparent ingredients—is the means by which his audience meets the real, and the integrating force by which his age achieves its own definitive self-revelation. But if an artist transcends his own personal limitations in his art, he never "transcends" his culture: The greater, aesthetically, his creations are, the more "typical" they become. So it is "natural" to seek in the works of great artists a reflection of the inner life of culture, and there to find it. And if at last it becomes, in this latter day, difficult to discover any "message," except in the very intensity of the anguish art transmits, the reason may simply be that society no longer permits, much less nourishes, any great artists on the old scale. So this brief survey may support the diagnosis of a continuing decline in the inner creative power of Western culture.

The growing cultural debility is reflected in literature as a widening schizoid split between carnal and spiritual latencies, a split that renders us unable to reconcile either the carnal and spiritual in our personal lives, or "object" and "subject" in society, now become a machine.

FOOTNOTES

[1] Erich Auerbach, *Dante, Poet of the Secular World*, trans. by Ralph Manheim (Chicago: University of Chicago Press, 1961), p. 170.

[2] *Ibid.*, p. 46.

[3] Etienne Gilson, *Dante the Philsopher* (New York: Sheed & Ward, 1941), p. 79.

[4] Auerbach, *op. cit.*, p. 62.

[5] *Ibid.*, p. 63.

[6] *Ibid.*, p. 62.

[7] *Ibid.*, p. 163.

[8] *Ibid.*, p. 169.

[9] *Ibid.*, p. 76.

[10] *Ibid.*, p. 79.

[11] *Ibid.*, p. 69.

[12] *Ibid.*, p. 69.

[13] *Ibid.*, pp. 158–59.

[14] *Ibid.*, pp. 177–78.

[15] Cf. T.S. Eliot on *Othello*.

[16] Cf. Ivor Brown, *Shakespeare* (Garden City, N.Y.: Doubleday, 1949), pp. 180–84.

[17] D.A. Traversi, *An Approach to Shakespeare* (Garden City, N.Y.: Doubleday, 1969).

[18] Helen Gardner, *A Reading of Paradise Lost* (Oxford, Clarendon Press, 1965).

[19] Russell Fraser, "On Milton's Poetry," *Yale Review* (Winter, 1967), p. 174.

[20] *Ibid.*, p. 175.

[21] *Ibid.*, p. 176.

[22] Erich Auerbach, *Mimesis* (Garden City, N.Y.: Doubleday Anchor, 1957), p. 285.

[23] Cf. Karl Barth, *Protestant Thought from Rousseau to Ritschl* (New York: Harper, 1959), Chapter 1; also, Lewis Mumford, *The Pentagon of Power* (New York, Harcourt, Brace, Jovanovich, 1970).

[24] Auerbach, *Mimesis*, Chapter 15.

[25] *Ibid.*, Chapter 16.

[26] Karl Stern, *The Flight from Woman* (New York: Farrar, Straus, and Giroux, 1965), pp. 241–42.

[27] *Ibid.*, p. 243.

[28] *Ibid.*, p. 267.

[29] Cf. Barth, *op. cit.*, Chapter 1.

[30] Walter Kerr, *How Not To Write a Play* (New York: Simon & Schuster, 1955).

[31] Cf. William Lynch, *Christ and Apollo* (New York: Mentor Omega Books, 1963), p. 178–9.

[32] Frank Kermode in *Partisan Review*, Summer, 1966. Cf. Anthony Burgess, *ReJoyce* (New York: Ballantine Books, 1966), pp. 57–70.

[33] John Aldridge, *In Search of Heresy* (New York: McGraw-Hill, 1956), p. 4; also, Aldridge, *Time to Murder and Create* (New York: David McKay Co., 1966).

[34] Brooks Atkinson, "No Time for American Drama," *The Critic*, December, 1966–January, 1967, pp. 19–23.

[35] Alfred Kazin, "The Literary Sixties, When the World Was Too Much With Us," the *New York Times Book Review*, December 21, 1969, p. 1.

[36] Anatole Broyard, "The Biographical Impulse," the *New York Times*, May 8, 1972, p. 35.

Sociology

It is thought by many today that the nation-State is a form of social organization too firmly entrenched to be in any danger of soon fading away. So projections into the future are dismissed as unrealistic that do not envisage almost an indefinite perpetuation of present forms of political organization, and, for example, the next age necessarily must feature a pentagonal world balance of power between, say, Russia, America, Japan, Europe, and perhaps India or the Arab States. Yet these projections might not adequately take into account a principle too easily overlooked: That a basic function of the State is to secure its citizens against fear for their lives. But between 100,000 and 1 million people even at this time have the knowledge to manufacture a nuclear bomb. Furthermore, there is, *outside* the five nuclear powers, enough nuclear material to fuel some 9000 bombs, and with new laser methods for generating plutonium almost anyone with the necessary knowledge can actually build such a bomb. The cumulative result is that the nation-State alone can no longer afford protection against certain death at the hands of anyone who threatens to inflict it, and just one scare of this sort might precipitate a sea change far more rapid than the present wisdom might think possible.

This is only the most dramatic example of mutual vulnerabilities that are invading all levels and units of international life, and especially the economic: From finance, to natural resources, to corporate organization, national societies are being subjected in their vital functions to "forces" that transcend mere national control. As a result, the nation-State more and more reflects only the atavistic interests of established elites, rather than, as it was "supposed" to, the autonomous "moral" life of its "people." Whatever "moral" function the nation-State was supposed to perform is slipping beyond its capacity to carry out. Certainly many nation-States will survive as nostalgic throwbacks to an earlier age, much as the separate states in the United States survive after the real power has passed to far more powerful corporations. But the days of the nation-State are numbered, and as the power elites begin groping for common ground, the race is on between the development of a world culture and the evolution of a world State, and the winner will take all.

It seems, then, that the nation-State may be destined to dry up from within, for if its population seeks to offset the diffusing, centripetal "forces" by restoring the balancing function in society to culture, the nation-State will be demoted, but the only other alternative for controlling these "forces" is a world authority with real power to perform the vital integrating and protective functions itself. Just as, a century or two ago, the physical and social environment retained no rights vis-à-vis the absolute autonomy of the individual it was conceived to be the State's function to protect, increasingly in coming years the individual will retain no abstract rights vis-à-vis the general functions over which it will be the main duty of the State or some common culture to preside. It will seem just as self-evident then that human social life is a unitary, if complex, whole, as it once did that social life was a mere foil for the "individual's" atomized self-realization. In the coming age it may be (as the record of political resignations for conscience already suggests) the rare "individual" indeed who will stand up against what "society" deems to be "self-evident," if only because it will become increasingly difficult for the "individual" to define himself in a way divergent from "society's" definition of his role. If the "individual" is to retain any potency at all in the face of the State, it will not be by virtue of his abstract "rights" (such as Russians now enjoy) that will be concretely abridgeable in the urgencies of collective survival, but rather by his membership in a true cultural group for whose own inner life his tragic stature and social autonomy are basic principles. It will become all too easy for the benevolent State to organize social life in such a way (and with such a meaning system) that both an autonomous culture and an autonomous "individual" will become all but inconceivable (and, when conceivable, doubly obnoxious).

To the question, by what means the world-State could be concretely ushered in, the answer seems to be clear: by means of sociology. All other levels of social organization have already been compromised by internecine conflicts that have made them unsuitable as rallying points. On the other hand, the cultural process itself has become so compromised and discredited that few people now would be receptive to any solution for social tensions explicitly proposed in terms of meaning. Rather, the only generally acceptable "solution" now would have to abjure the quest for meaning altogether, even though this renunciation, because of society's very nature, could be only temporarily effective. Still, it would cause no offense to the new world-State sponsoring a sociological order should present-day nation-States remain attached to their present economic ideologies, as long as these were not allowed to contradict the basic organizational provisions the world-State promulgated. Nor would this world-State, and its organizing function, be in themselves immoral, if they remained willing to subordinate themselves in principle to culture—that is, willing to forswear in principle the quest for a total system. Sociology could very easily prove to be an indispensable aid to cultural life, by radically easing the material problems that cause so much tension.

Rather than becoming impositions on local life, a supportive sociology (requiring a surrender of only some material autonomy in the interests of increased social autonomy) and even a world-State limiting nation-States already too powerful could help to restore to social life a dimension that has too long been missing from it. But as itself an autonomous *power*, sociology could become the sponsor of a tyranny that would make a weak prophet out of even Kafka. Sociology need not usurp economic life, but, for better or worse, could (as politics and religion once did in their own ways) organize it from outside—from a level "highest" with respect to material flexibility, and "lowest" with respect to specifically *human* values.

Thus, the nature of sociology and of its social functions would seem to be matters of some growing importance, but the "layman" might be surprised that, in spite of the wide currency of sociological jargon and of so-called sociological "explanations" for everything, and frequent adversions to something called "sociology" in the press, sociologists admit to having little idea what kind of science they are practicing. The most competent sociologists are the quickest to confess that the theoretical and philosophical foundations of the science are a mess, and neither are they slow to admit that the danger in this is growing as fast as the science's visibility and acceptance, although such considerations (rightly) no more prevent sociologists from going about whatever their business is than ignorance of the principles of gastronomic physiology prevents the rest of us from finishing our meals. And thus, however the "experts" may judge the ultimate accuracy of this short exploration, the "average" reader would probably welcome some discussion of this subject from the widest possible perspectives— widest, at least, in the formal sense, if not as to "vision"—and simply as preparation of the ground. Now, the widest possible perspectives on sociology itself are the philosophic and the cultural, so we will take these briefly one at a time.

One need not be an expert to know that philosophy is where

ultimately the basic problems concerning sociology as a science will have to be resolved. Sociologists must develop theory, but what they are shaping and what distinguishes their point of view from others is not of concern only to them, especially since sociology is going to have an increasingly important impact and influence on others. The best indication of the extremity to which we have come may be that the claim that philosophy could be, not even the controlling factor, but simply the corrective for absurd extremes of systematization from which the experts seem unable to extricate us, could be met with contempt, hilarity or resentment.

At one time, of course, all of the speculative sciences were considered philosophical; Samuel Johnson referred even to physics as "natural philosophy." Though there is every reason to distinguish between empirical science and philosophy (witness Galileo), it is no more correct to pretend that modern science has no philosophical or metaphysical foundations than to judge scientific theories by philosophical criteria. Modern science might be forgiven its myopia if medieval philosophy could be forgiven as well: too absorbed in the necessary first task of understanding itself as well as the rest of reality from its own point of view, medieval philosophy was unable to give adequate attention to the proper autonomy of the sciences, a possibility which had hardly been so much as suspected. Science could not spring full-grown like Minerva from Jupiter's brain; in fact, only with sociology has the catalogue of empirical sciences appeared to reach relative completion. In any case, we are not interested here in attempting to establish any primacy of philosophy *in* empirical science, but in trying to break social science out of a disastrous encapsulation that would cause the end of human culture if sociology went on to imitate economics' old ways of systematizing. If the only way to prevent this is to establish an adequate methodological framework, this is not to resurrect philosophy's old claims on science, a role that, as we said, was easily misconceived when the empirical sciences (whose growth medieval philosophy was encouraging through its high respect for reason)

were still inchoate. Just as the subject matter of the sciences now
overlap, so also are sciences united by the philosophical foundations of their methodologies. To say that sciences cannot establish
these is not new. And conflict between philosophy and science was
not primarily intellectual, but cultural, in nature; it was the result
of the spurious reinforcement secular power (exercised to please
the Church) gave to philosophic doctrine.

The deepest root of this cultural problem lies, like so much else
in our culture, in the tenth century, when the barbarian invasions
ceased and the populations of the feudal domains began to expand.
(The following description is taken from the writings of the psychologist Adrian van Kaam.) Surplus laborers driven from the
domains had three alternatives: to become vagrants, to cultivate as
independent tenant-owners the wastelands outside the domains, or
to engage in primitive trade between widely separated regions. The
new cultivators formed villages, while the new traders became
burghers and founded cities. These new groups soon broke into the
self-sufficiency of the domains, which then began to turn to the
merchants for relief in disasters. But this help carried the usual
interest charge, which appeared to the shocked serfs as self-
enrichment at their own expense. The laws established against interest and other commercial practices dangerously undermined the
merchants' self-esteem, for the merchants had never found a place
in the medieval ideology constructed before they had even appeared on the scene. And the new secular sciences the merchants
were incubating seemed to oppose them further to the dominant
socioreligious ideology.

Meanwhile, in order to conduct trade, the merchant class needed
a better administration of justice and better security than the feudal
order had yet provided, and had to purchase them from the kings
and higher nobles, who used the money to hire mercenary soldiers
and to become independent of the knights (laying the foundation
for the royal power's later subjugation of the aristocracy). Agri-
culture and commerce were considered unfit occupations for the

knights and minor nobles, who became superfluous, so they went into the Church, where they concentrated on secular power as bishops and abbots rather than as knights. Since the merchants still regarded the clergy as equivalent to the Church, they saw themselves as incarnations of all that was "bad," even though they themselves were more and more accomplishing the creative intellectual activity, developing the secular sciences and suggesting political and legal ways to curb the influence of the clerical and aristocratic powers—suggestions that only deepened their feelings of guilt (which the Church exploited by means of interdicts and excommunications). By the thirteenth century the burgher had become the prevailing social type, much as the businessman is today, but he was in guilt-ridden conflict with the also rapidly expanding, but ideologically dominant, clerical group. This tension in the culture exploded just after the Thomist intellectual synthesis appeared, and prevented the latter from taking cultural root.

Instead, secular learning and sacred learning split, and the growing unreality of theological learning inspired such feelings of inadequacy in the clergy that they desperately opposed any new advances in secular learning. The cumulative guilt found release in the fourteenth-century witch-hunts. Antiintellectualism appeared in the Church, and the shock of the Reformation made Catholic theology anxious and defensive. So intellectual life in the West began to display an inner schizophrenia, for secular learning erected its own defensive walls and repressed its awareness of religious needs. All that could lead to religious questions had to be excluded from consciousness; all risky issues—especially metaphysics, the psychology of values and of the self, even theoretical speculation itself—became tabu. Superficial scientism and a cheap materialism became final defenses against a mounting inner anxiety. This widening cultural schizophrenia perhaps accounts for the two most important factors influencing empirical sociology today: its growing cultural primacy, and its persisting isolation from the philosophic perspective.

Since the Middle Ages, one new empirical science after another has thrown off the apparently suffocating embrace of philosophy and proceeded on its own according to the methods first generally formulated by Bacon, *et al*. But the focus on pure materiality soon invaded subjects that even today should be considered internally oriented to the philosophic perspective—the sciences of man. It was the replacement of philosophy by the statistical method as the focus of social science that eventually gave empirical sociology its special primacy among social sciences (of which sociology is the most "naturally" oriented toward statistics), even though, paradoxically, it was sociology's initial openness to philosophy that had made it the academic and social pariah it remained long after Comte had coined its name. But this rejection eventually drove sociologists to emulate the prestigious economists, by trying to replicate "value-free" Classical physics in sociology and renouncing any further "subjectivism." Thus was elevated to sociological orthodoxy a model for sociological research that (because sociology is really as dependent on philosophy as on statistics) has remained in fact as irrelevant to sociology as it would have been to economics. According to this model, research begins with "nominal" definitions of terms in a hypothesis to be tested. In order to be testable, these must be converted into "operational" definitions referring to descriptions of measurements (i.e., to concrete events). The operational definitions, become working hypotheses, are then tested, and the results converted back into terms of the original nominal definitions.[1] At least, this is how research was "supposed" to look.

But aside from the fact that this model breezes somewhat casually past the question how the researcher can be sure that his operational definition of a term really has any intrinsic relevance at all to the concepts in the nominal definition, sociologists have never paid any attention to this model in theorizing. As Gouldner notes, what actually happens is just the opposite: Some would-be theorist, like Talcott Parsons, sits down in his study and begins constructing a theory almost out of whole cloth; if it appears to have some explanatory value it is promptly adopted by disciples, but, in Parsons's notable case anyway, no attempt is made to verify it, and, like Parsons, the theorist may even insist that not the smallest part of his theory could be challenged without bringing the whole structure down. It seems that the theoretical model of research was something of a fiction, by which sociologists could convince themselves of their scientific orthodoxy and attract the prestige of the natural sciences to their own efforts. The so-called middle-level theories that supposedly were to arise from research to provide the empirical basis for general theorizing never developed, and at least one reason was that the presence of the sociologist's own personality in sociological thought in an intensity not matched in physics was implicitly regarded as an embarrassment rather than an opening for even greater creativity. This special presence (the sociologist experiences society from within as well as from without) is one of sociology's distinguishing characteristics, and the self-abasing efforts to conform to an irrelevant model encouraged both hypocrisy and confusion.

The search for a scientific model had at least one healthy result: a growing, indeed at length exaggerated, respect for measurement. And this had another curious consequence. For other social sciences, with extended and distinguished traditions reaching back as far as Plato, were losing their own humanistic concerns in the general corruption of philosophy, and were reaching more and more themselves for hopefully self-justifying statistical measurements. So sociology eventually was surprised to discover itself, as *their* philosophical preoccupations evaporated, and *its* own natural orientation toward statistics became more evident, a *primus inter pares*, at the very time when it was becoming increasingly troubled by its continuing incapacity to understand itself. By now, sociology had a whole leg in the academy's door, and was making powerful friends, but the almost frenzied persisting resistance in many quarters also made it increasingly sensitive about a certain indefinable nonhuman quality in its own composition. This new self-doubt emerged just as the whole world seemed at last ready to capitulate to sociology's most extravagant claims, and in the very moment of triumph many sociologists began repudiating the old ideals of disinterested scholarship and scientific detachment and began claiming that sociology instead must serve "moral concern." That the putative presence of this motive as a driving force in scientific systematization could very obviously serve the crudest drives to power made the task of coming to some understanding about what sociology is seem even more urgent.

To this day sociologists have never explained what sort of science sociology is. The reason why they cannot explain it is that the explanation must be philosophical in nature. The amusement this idea will cause will remain somewhat hollow until someone succeeds in providing a persuasive alternative. Meanwhile, as the experts work on it, they might consider the thoughts of those who will have to live with what they decide on. And if what follows here is accurate, the professional skills of the experts would not be entirely relevant either, for the problem about the nature of sociology would be rooted in an area where the usual skills of sociology do not apply. If no self-respecting sociologist will risk his reputation in this direction, anyone else is entitled to try.

As the philosopher Bernard Lonergan sees them, the empirical sciences constitute a series of viewpoints each of which "makes systematic what otherwise would be merely coincidental on the preceding viewpoint," as "one proceeds from the subatomic to the chemical, from the chemical to the biological, from the biological to the sensitive, from the sensitive to the intelligent." "The higher genus is a higher systematization of manifolds that would be coincidental on the lower level, and a higher systematization is limited by the manifolds which it systematizes."[2] The modern physical sciences, which Lonergan calls "classical," proceed by means of "enriching abstractions"; that is, the mind, in globally apprehending an object in its relationship to other objects, discovers through "insight" a formula that describes this relationship and all like it. "Classical" sciences describe relations *between* objects, and an object's scientific intelligibility in Classical science derives from its place in increasingly comprehensive mathematical formulas. But this, note, does not mean that matter itself has become intelligible, for Classical science actually ignores matter as such; it deals only with the relationships *between* objects, whatever these objects are conceived to be. Such abstract system does not apply to individual objects taken individually; another method is needed for that. This other method, that investigates "coincidental aggregates" of *concrete* events, is statistics.[3] Thus, there is one method that investigates relationships *between* objects (Classical science) and another that discovers a further intelligibility in the "pure" materiality of discrete objects taken as such (statistical science). The hierarchy or "manifolds" of empirical sciences, therefore, begins with Classical physics, climbs through chemistry, biology and psychology, and ends finally with sociology, a terminal systematization of matter.

Does this mean sociology is just another material science? Not exactly. Biology, psychology, and sociology are empirical sciences, but not of the Classical type. The structures they study are not mathematically predetermined, so prediction of behavior in each individual case is not possible. Let us pass by biology and psychology here. Empirical *social* sciences seek only *general* predictability, for their statistical tools can deal only with concrete events —the purely material aspect of the subject. Empirical sociology is the quintessential statistical social science that studies human activity precisely as this is influenced by matter. Whether it is influenced by anything but matter is another question, but all human relationships do have a material component, so sociology's scope is as wide in its way as philosophy's and includes all human activity. Because sociology is not necessarily specified by any particular point of view within this orientation to matter, it is the most basic and comprehensive of all the statistical social sciences, of which it is the "queen" in the same sense that philosophy is the queen of the speculative, and physics the queen of the Classical empirical, sciences.

But it does not therefore follow that sociology is a self-contained science. Statistical laws deal with events, and are "of no greater scientific significance than the definitions of the events whose frequencies they determine; unless these definitions are determined scientifically, statistical thought lapses into prescientific insignificance."[4] The only assurance of precision in the definitions of events to be measured is a prior *philosophical* analysis of the events, for where Classical science "abstracts from the relations of things to us to determine the relations of things to one another," statistical theory deals "only with observable events and so must include the relations of things to our senses."[5]

It is as true as it seems odd that modern (Classical) physics has no idea what matter "is"; physics seeks mathematical formulas that describe the relationships between elementary particles, whatever these might "be." There is an old philosophical doctrine that matter itself is basically unintelligible, and modern physics seems to bear this out: Heisenberg's "uncertainty principle" holds that we can never know matter absolutely because we change it by observing it. The best definition that metaphysics gives for matter is a negative one: Matter is the pure potentiality for form (or as Karl Rahner, the German Jesuit, calls it, "the radical otherness of the spirit," meaning, apparently, that matter is that by which spirit comes to knowledge of itself). All this may seem rather strange and alien to our ways of thinking, for modern science would seem to have a quite solid knowledge of matter, but what it has knowledge of is not matter, but relationships between particles of it. (Einstein's theory, of course, states that whatever matter "is," it is also a form of energy.) In any case, "pure" materiality is unintelligible and, since unspecified, lacking in any specifying form, infinitely divisible. The consequence is that a science based on the statistical method will relentlessly break its subject down into a virtual infinity of components unless the specific aim of each study is clearly determined from the start. Sociology studies the social consequences of man's materiality as such, and seeks to uncover an additional intelligibility in it. But sociological studies that are assumed to be entirely quantifiable, and not to require strict prior definitions, produce only partial and tentative results. Researchers obtain useful results from such studies by making assumptions (perhaps quite reasonable ones) about the subject studied. But even reasonably clear definitions do not always dispel the potential for infinite reductionism of components, and dissatisfaction with the merely partial intelligibility offered by haphazard studies leads toward endless subdivision and a chaotic and ultimately unstructured mass of statistics. Empirical sociology approaches the material aspect of human relationships from the outside, focusing on their material dimension as such, rather than, like art or philosophy, on the formal, so unassimilable relationships and "subdivisions" will appear in the results of any study whose conceptual framework and definitions are not clearly constructed. Thus, "it is clear that as yet we have not verified any hypothesis in sociology which can claim universal validity."[6] Studies lead to "trivial conclusions with efforts toward maximum precision."[7] "The professional literature contains hundreds of sociological research papers in which the conclusion calls for further research, but only a handful in which the conclusion calls for practical action."[8] Yet sociological research is so exacting that there is little time for exhaustive validation and support studies, even serving a coherent design, and meanwhile empirical study still must be tied together in order to be useful. What this means is that if not philosophy, then inevitably ideology, will be used to hold sociology together, as it was used to hold economics together. Without a prior overt integrating scheme, studies remain more or less accurate guesses unified by unarticulated suppositions and tied to each other by at best wishful thinking. The resistance of social textures and structures to empirical study can be overcome only by the integrating effect of pure theory, and the integrating theories need not be derived from research, although they should be subject to it. An insistence that sociology be "purely" empirical overlooks the persisting dearth of those "interrelated propositions" that were supposed to lead to theories from the "purely empirical" direction.[9] Merely descriptive studies do not furnish explanations, and there is bound to be "lack of agreement about the precise language and formulation of laws."[10]

(A good example of the intrinsic unspecificity of statistics is the Bureau of Labor Statistics' Consumer-Price Index, which is used to measure inflation. Although indispensable for many calculations, it still is itself at best approximate. For it depends on multitudinous judgmental decisions—like those on the adequation of nominal with operational definitions—as to what are truly "representative" indicators. On the other hand, there is also an almost arbitrary exclusion of indicators judged to be unrepresentative of the "general" experience the CPI is supposed to gauge. The CPI measures no one's experience accurately, but presumably somehow more or less approximates the "average" experience of all. But experience of what? This raises two questions that statistics alone cannot answer: What exactly is it that is being measured, and how accurately is it being measured? To make the final statistic perfectly accurate [this would require more, not fewer, judgmental decisions] not only would be to make it impossibly unwieldy, but would also require perfect judgment as well as perfect analysis. We find here a sort of uncertainty principle of statistics: The more "precise" the measurement, the less definable what it measures. Whatever it is here, presumably it is some approximation of a significant common experience. It may be a mistake to suppose that much more is possible with social statistics than the optimum to which the Bureau may already have approached with its CPI. Statistics of even the utmost completeness still demand *a priori* patterning judgments if any coherence is to be revealed in them. It may become possible someday to make our economy almost unlimitedly flexible, but if we do not know for what ends, even greater chaos may prevail than mercifully does now. Statistics have no intrinsic intelligibility, but only measure what we already "know." Good statistics, like good sex, are in the head—as, for that matter, is good technology, as Robert Pirsig has eloquently argued. Statistics cannot lead us out of the quandary of theory, but, by themselves, can only plunge us more deeply into it.)

If, in short, sociology is to be a useful and practical science during the hopefully ongoing construction of sociological syntheses, integrating *philosophical* schemes may be indispensable. Philosophy, history and the arts are relevant to sociology from "above," through the mediation of a social philosophy. Empirical sociology and sociological theory, social philosophy and metaphysics, and the pair of pairs, perpetually strain to pull apart but flourish only through their polar tensions. No one can expect any sociologist to be a metaphysician, nor to justify every assumption formally, but it is when a sociologist is most creative that he illustrates in his own activity the dynamisms investigated by metaphysicians, which should not be regarded as intrinsic limits on the sociologist's creativity, but as its ground. Nor need sociology establish or conform to any particular philosophy, but it should be receptive to any insights that would make sociological research truly coherent and relevant—in other words, socially useful. Such insights might help to develop those cross-references between the social sciences now conspicuously lacking; indeed, philosophy may be the only way by which such cross-references, for so long now expected at any moment, can be achieved, and if philosophy itself seemed in a less parlous condition this suggestion would not seem so utopian or absurd. Any refusal to let philosophy in through the front door will simply drive it around to the back, because it is indispensable. Even Durkheim, to whom for lack of much alternative modern sociologists have turned for an example of "pure" scientific sociology, based his theory of "social fact" on a philosophically crude conversion of scholastic epistemological categories into so-called material, concrete things. (He corresponded frequently with the editor of a scholastic journal, and his methodology practically duplicates the scholastic proofs.)

A coherent research project requires, then, a philosophical theory of reality, implicit or explicit, and a practical objective determined in light of this theory. A sociologist proceeding without any larger conceptual scheme must draw his conclusions only in terms of his study itself, whose relevance must then remain unclear. A project without a theory of reality will come up with more proposals for further research than meaningful conclusions, since acquisition of knowledge is, as Lonergan shows, a dynamism that reflects the structure of the mind itself. The theory need not be wholly explicit, since the mind does operate spontaneously and reliably within the limited range of common sense, but the inner coherence of a project demands a basic pulse to hold the various calculations and choices together. Without this pulse, basically philosophical, research remains trivial and unfruitful. Significant conclusions drawn from basically promiscuous data lack the dynamic self-correcting quality a clearly guided project can bring, and research will otherwise endlessly call for further exploration of the same problems. On the other hand, the fluid relationship between empirical sociology and philosophy would counteract the mind-boggling proliferation of arbitrary and *ad hoc* empirical categories that is a major shortcoming in recent sociology, and would provide some of the power and integration that so far have eluded the area. Although "the vocabulary of theory changes radically from decade to decade . . . actual knowledge remains about the same."[11]

The growing visibility and functional prominence of the social sciences have inspired prophecies that they will replace the deteriorating arts.[12] But *effective* social sciences are themselves largely derivative. Social sciences can, drawing little criticism, far more easily pass off the spurious and dress up the obvious and silly in fancy clothes. Sociology could displace art only because it works in a single dimension, while art thrives on rich social textures. If these grow weak, superficial or merely abstract, art can no longer function, but sociology is no substitute for them. Indeed, it then becomes the more easily a servant of the absolutist urge to regiment life without passing through the inner experience and risk that alone reveal what life really is. This drive to squeeze the spontaneous life out of society would have no regard for the inner realities of personal life, which demand the inconvenient personal responsiveness of which doctrinaire types are usually incapable. All this would turn sociology into a mere whitewash of nosiness and spiritual violence, and in fact sociology is already displaying these symptoms.[13] The absolutist drive in sociology would easily take the form of a search for a universal and comprehensive theory that could reduce all social phenomena to systematization. But empirical sociology can never develop an absolutely comprehensive theory reducible to, say, a few differential equations. The deeper it moves into its subject, the greater is the resistance it experiences, and until it totally penetrates this material base (probably even a metaphysical impossibility) residues beyond completed schemes will always be found that overflow into potential new patterns. Unlike metaphysics (which Maritain described as the persistent grasp of fundamentals through insight penetrating ever more deeply into the same truths), empirical sociology cannot develop a totally comprehensive and "airtight" theory. Insofar as it approaches some relative universality, it must do so, in practice, either as the beneficiary of a dynamic inner unity in a well-integrated culture, or as the result of the denaturing of society into a human hive with a mathematical pseudo-unity. But the quality that makes an all-encompassing universal field theory impossible also makes sociology indispensable, for sociology provides a scientific insight into the very variety of human material interaction, and a way of organizing an open range of material factors and situations. Sociology could be humanly liberating if it keeps social planners aware of real conditions, and could actually protect personality and self-definition in an infinitely complicated social order. It will always call for that choice of goals and objectives, and of the means to attain them, that characterizes art, yet because the methods it uses must be scientific, it is also a science. Sociology is at once art and science, the limit on the material plane for Western thought and practice, and as the terminal science in a long chain that began with the philosophical sciences, continued through the Classical sciences and finally arrived at statistical science, it probably is the last formal stage in the rationalization of the material order.

If a cultural vacuum has in fact appeared, yet rational planning of the material order is increasing and must increase, the world seems headed for a cultural squeeze, a period of compression that will project sociology into practical ascendancy. What are now acutely sensed for the first time as limited geographical resources must support an expanding population subsisting on other material resources that also will be effectively limited for some time, yet human personality, at least for the immediate future, unless this grows dangerously traumatic, will probably retain its value orientation. This situation will raise pressures for a planned, even homogenous, social order coordinating material variables by some philosophical or ideological value system that, whether explicit or, as now, implicit, will be decidedly public in nature. The protection of personal freedom, its reconciliation with general planning, will be the overriding social problem of the coming period, and the only certainty about the result is that the winner will take all.

Sociology's practical ascendancy will become tragically monolithic if the culture weakens any further. The highly formalized "official" (and characteristically business) relationships of our time have already dangerously regimented spontaneous responses in favor of calculating, depersonalized modes of thought. The figures typical of our time, the technocrat, the bureaucrat, and the commissar, are practically nonhuman. But no technocrats will solve the cultural problem; nor does the rationalization of life dispense with spontaneity; earlier systematizations depended on it in structuring a crystallizing cultural core. Rational patterns become tyrannical when they move into vacuums left by receding, more vital cultural activity. Yet if the development of the social sciences does not proceed, great and preventable suffering may result. Medieval society was organized around the most "spiritual" of all organizers, religion and metaphysics, but in the coming period the most material and mathematical of all possible organizers will hold sway, for society will have to control and coordinate its material factors more efficiently, and no culture is left to help. But if the next age imitates the medieval (and modern) mistake of forcing upon society a mere ideology in the organizer, the values in which our fathers died—perhaps all values—will disappear from the face of the earth. The choice is between culture and system. The one will save us, the other will destroy us as effectively as nuclear war.

FOOTNOTES

[1] Hans Zetterberg, *On Theory and Verification in Sociology* (Totowa, New Jersey: The Bedminster Press, 1965).

[2] Bernard Lonergan, *Insight* (New York: Longmans, Green & Co., 1957), pp. 268, 442.

[3] *Ibid.*, pp. 56–57, 65, 87, 112.

[4] *Ibid.*, pp. 100, 112.

[5] *Ibid.*, p. 78.

[6] Zetterberg, *op. cit.*, p. 55.

[7] *Ibid.*, p. viii.

[8] Zetterberg, *Social Theory and Social Practice* (New York: The Bedminster Press, 1962), pp. 15–16.

[9] Zetterberg, *Theory and Verification*, p. 28.

[10] *Ibid.*, p. 26.

[11] Zetterberg, *Social Theory and Social Practice*, p. 16.

[12] John Aldridge, *In Search of Heresy* (New York: McGraw-Hill, 1956), pp. 110–122; and "Interview with George F. Kennan," *Encounter*, March 1960.

[13] Robert Nisbet, "Project Camelot: An Autopsy," *The Public Interest* (Fall, 1966), pp. 45–69.